Economics
and Mental Health

Economics
and Mental Health

Edited by

Richard G. Frank

Professor, Department of Health Policy and Management
The Johns Hopkins University School of Hygiene and Public Health
Baltimore, Maryland

and

Willard G. Manning, Jr.

Professor, Division of Health Services Research and Policy
University of Minnesota School of Public Health
Minneapolis, Minnesota

The Johns Hopkins University Press
Baltimore and London

The Johns Hopkins University Press
701 West 40th Street
Baltimore, Maryland 21211-2190
The Johns Hopkins Press Ltd., London

Library of Congress Cataloging-in-Publication Data

Economics and mental health / edited by Richard G. Frank and Willard
   G. Manning, Jr.
     p.   cm.
   Includes bibliographical references and index.
   ISBN 0-8018-4429-0 (alk. paper) ISBN 0-8018-4546-7 (pbk.)
     1. Mental health services—Economic aspects—United States—
Congress.   2. Mental illness—Economic aspects—United States—
Congress.   3. Insurance, Mental health—United States—
Congress.   I. Frank, Richard G.   II. Manning, Willard G.
   [DNLM: 1. Mental Disorders—economics—United States.   2. Mental
Health Services—economics—United States.]
RA790.6.E26   1992
338.4'33622'0973—dc20
DNLM/DLC
for Library of Congress   92-11603

Contents

Preface

The chapters in this volume were assembled in honor of Carl A.
Taube, in recognition of his leadership and substantive contributions to the economics of mental health. Beginning in the
mid-1970s, Carl was drawn to the methods of economic analysis as a
means of developing policy solutions for some of the most pressing
policy problems facing the delivery of mental health services in the
United States. He was concerned with the structure of private insurance for mental health care at a time when markets for mental
health care were emerging. Carl viewed cost-effectiveness analysis
of new treatment technologies as an important tool for making decisions regarding the public financing of mental health treatments.
Being a practical man, he understood that one needed to understand
fully the economic consequences of mental illness in order to offer a
convincing case for congressional support of mental health services
and research.

Based on this set of practical policy issues, Carl set out to develop
a program of research in the economics of mental health. He conducted research on the demand for mental health services, payment
system issues, and the design of insurance. At the same time, from
his base at the National Institute of Mental Health (NIMH) he ag-
gressively set out to build a community of researchers committed to
all aspects of the economics of mental health. Carl was able to com-
municate a sense of excitement, importance, and fun about research
on economic issues in mental health. Because of this ability, the
research community developed a consensus regarding the demand
response to cost sharing for ambulatory mental health services and
the supply response to prospective payment for inpatient services.
These are perhaps the most important policy research findings to
emerge from the field during its first ten years of existence.

The majority of chapters in this volume were presented at the
Fifth Biennial Conference on the Economics of Mental Health, held
in honor of Carl Taube in June 1990. All of the work presented in this
book bears Carl's mark. Virtually every chapter was affected by previous studies done by Carl or was directly influenced by his advice
and guidance. The phenomenon that would probably please Carl the

most is the increased attention being given to economic issues related to the public sector of the mental health system and to the treatment of individuals with severe mental illness. Carl had a long-standing scholarly interest in public mental health systems. He also had a deep personal concern for the amount and quality of care received by individuals with the most disabling mental disorders. It is therefore a fitting reflection of his leadership that contributions in this volume illustrate the increased focus by economists on the public sector and the care of individuals with severe mental illness.

Because Carl was so successful in creating a community of researchers, his untimely death has been a personal blow to those involved in the economics of mental health as well as a monumental loss to the field. It is our hope that Carl's example will continue to set a standard for all those working in the field. He perhaps best exemplifies what Professor Alan Blinder termed "a hard head and a soft heart." Carl's intellectual rigor, personal kindness, and desire to better serve populations who are among society's most vulnerable is a standard to which we can all aspire.

The development of this book required important contributions from a variety of parties, to whom we are grateful. Paul Widem and Agnes Rupp, of the NIMH, served on the program committee of the Fifth Biennial Conference and were instrumental in selecting many of the contributions in this volume. They gave willingly of their time and were steadfast in their efforts to make the conference a fitting tribute to Carl Taube. Jay Burke, then director of the Division of Applied and Services Research at the NIMH, actively participated in developing the intellectual agenda for the conference and was instrumental in arranging financial support for the conference. Thomas G. McGuire provided us with a great deal of good advice throughout the preparation of this book and prepared the excellent introductory chapter to the volume. Dorothy Pumphrey and Jane Raasch provided secretarial and logistical support that was crucial to the project. Finally, we express our warmest appreciation to Wendy Harris, of the Johns Hopkins University Press, who guided us through the publication process with good humor, good judgment, and a firm hand.

Contributors

Haroutun M. Babigian, M.D., Professor and Chairman, Department of Psychiatry, University of Rochester, Rochester, New York

Jon B. Christianson, Ph.D., Professor, Division of Health Services Research and Policy, School of Public Health, University of Minnesota, Minneapolis, Minnesota

Jerry Cromwell, Ph.D., President, Health Economics Research, Boston, Massachusetts

Partha Deb, Ph.D., Assistant Professor, Department of Economics, Indiana University—Purdue University at Indianapolis, Indiana

Randall P. Ellis, Ph.D., Associate Professor, Department of Economics, Boston University, Boston, Massachusetts

Michael Finch, Ph.D., Assistant Professor, Division of Health Services Research and Policy, School of Public Health, University of Minnesota, Minneapolis, Minnesota

Ellen Frank, Ph.D., Associate Professor, Department of Psychiatry and Psychology, University of Pittsburgh, Pittsburgh, Pennsylvania

Brooke S. Harrow, Ph.D., Associate, Mikalix & Company, Waltham, Massachusetts

Mark S. Kamlet, Ph.D., Professor of Economics and Public Policy, Department of Social and Decision Sciences, Carnegie Mellon University, Pittsburgh, Pennsylvania

Sander Kelman, Ph.D., Research Economist, State of New Jersey Division of Medical Assistance and Health Services, Trenton, New Jersey

David J. Kupfer, M.D., Professor, Department of Psychiatry, Carnegie Mellon University, Pittsburgh, Pennsylvania

Nicole Lurie, M.D., M.S.P.H., Associate Professor, Division of Health Services Research and Policy School of Public Health, University of Minnesota, Minneapolis, Minnesota

Phyllis E. Marshall, M.S.W., Executive Director, Integrated Mental Health, Inc., Rochester, New York

Thomas G. McGuire, Ph.D., Professor, Department of Economics, Boston University, Boston, Massachusetts

Leonard S. Miller, Ph.D., Professor, School of Social Work, University of California, Berkeley, California

Jean M. Mitchell, Ph.D., Associate Professor, Department of Economics, Florida State University, Tallahassee, Florida

Olivia S. Mitchell, Ph.D., Professor, Department of Labor Economics, Cornell University, Ithaca, New York

Ira S. Moscovice, Professor, Division of Health Services Research and Policy, School of Public Health, University of Minnesota, Minneapolis, Minnesota

Sylvia K. Reed, Ph.D., Department of Psychiatry, University of Rochester, Rochester, New York

Jeffrey Rubin, Ph.D., Professor, Institute for Health, Health Care Policy, and Aging Research, Rutgers—The State University of New Jersey, New Brunswick, New Jersey

Christopher J. Ruhm, Ph.D., Associate Professor, Department of Economics, University of North Carolina, Greensboro, North Carolina

David S. Salkever, Ph.D., Professor, Department of Health Policy and Management, The Johns Hopkins University, Baltimore, Maryland

Elizabeth Savoca, Ph.D., Associate Professor, Department of Economics, Smith College, Northampton, Massachusetts

Robert J. Schmitz, Ph.D., Senior Economist, Abt Associates, Inc., Cambridge, Massachusetts

Martcia Wade, Ph.D., Assistant Professor, School of Urban and Public Affairs, Carnegie Mellon University, Pittsburgh, Pennsylvania

Virginia Wilcox-Gök, Ph.D., Assistant Professor, Institute for Health, Health Care Policy, and Aging Research, Rutgers—The State University of New Jersey, New Brunswick, New Jersey

Economics
and Mental Health

1

Research on Economics and Mental Health: The Past and Future Prospects

Thomas G. McGuire, Ph.D.

The Growth of the Field of Economics and Mental Health

Rashi Fein's *Economics of Mental Illness,* published in 1959, is the natural starting point for a discussion of the field of economics and mental health. The broader field of health economics, in its modern form emphasizing physician behavior, information, and payment systems, also had its beginnings at about the same time with the publication of Kessel's "Price Discrimination in Medicine" in the first issue of the *Journal of Law and Economics* (1958) and Arrow's "Uncertainty and the Welfare Economics of Medical Care" in the *American Economic Review* (1963). Borrowing the terminology that Straus (1957) had used to describe medical sociology, Arrow and Kessel can be said to have studied the economics *of* health care, whereas Fein was concerned with economics *in* mental health. To preview a distinction I will make later, the economics *of* mental health deals with how economic variables, such as insurance, affect behavior. Economics *in* mental health is concerned with the consequences of mental disorder and its treatment for economic measures, such as cost.

For twenty years after the publication of Fein's book, the field of economics and mental health made little progress. Some new cost work had been done in Washington, D.C., with study of treatment cost and improvement on some of Fein's cost measures. There was no work at all on the economics of mental health. In the mid-1970s, no academically based economist was working on any variety of economics and mental health. My brief comments about the "past" will therefore begin with the research world at about 1978, before the sponsorship of economics research by the National Institute of Mental

Health (NIMH) and at the time of the President's Commission on Mental Health.

On 17 February 1977, in one of his first acts as president, Jimmy Carter signed Executive Order No. 11973 creating the President's Commission on Mental Health. The purpose of the new commission was "to review the mental health needs of the Nation and to make recommendations to the President as to how the Nation might best meet these needs." The President's Commission on Mental Health issued its report late in 1978 based on the work of thirty-five task panels, only one of which, the Cost and Financing of Mental Health Panel, relied on economic analysis.

There were two economists on the fourteen-person cost and financing panel, Rashi Fein from Harvard and Selma Mushkin from the Public Services Laboratory in Washington. Both were senior public policy/health economists, but neither was actively researching mental health economics at the time. The references used by the task panel show four entries specifically focused on the economics of mental health, only one of which was published. Daniel Levine coauthored two reports for the Department of Health Education and Welfare on the cost of mental illness (Levine and Levine 1975; Levine and Willner 1976). Lewin and Associates (1978) prepared a background paper for the task panel, "The Cost and Financing of Mental Illness." The final and only published study was a summary of the work of Louis Reed (1975), primarily on the utilization of mental health services by federal employees insured under two government-sponsored plans, which was done for and published by the American Psychiatric Association.

It can easily be seen that the panel could not carry the analysis of cost and financing very far. As they admitted in the executive summary, "The panel realistically limited the scope of its report to identifying the areas where public policy on mental health financing warranted immediate attention, and where the panel's expertise would be most beneficial." This turned out to be a very limited area of policy. The panel confined its recommendations to presenting a set of options for reforming Medicare and Medicaid financing of mental health care. The recommendations were quite general and amounted to a call for "parity" in fiscal treatment for mental conditions within these two government programs.

In 1978 economists had studied "cost." Beyond this, economic research made little contribution to identifying mental health needs or identifying ways to meet those needs. Today, if a new president's commission were formed, it would find the field of the economics of mental health to be a much greater resource. Research in economics and mental health has contributed to an understanding of the effect of insurance design on the use of mental health care (Wells et al. 1982; Manning et al. 1987; Keeler, Manning, and Wells 1988; Ellis and McGuire 1986), the economic effects of state regulation on mental health insurance (Frank 1989; Mitchell 1984; Lambert 1985), the competition and substitutability between mental health professionals (Fairbank 1989), the determinants of professionals' supply of services (Haas-Wilson 1989; Frisman 1990), the comparative costs of treatment alternatives (Dickey et al. 1986; Weisbrod 1983), the effect of mental illness on labor supply (Frank and Gertler 1989; Mullahy and Sindelar 1989), and the effect of prospective payment on the supply of care (Christiansen 1989; Frank and Lave 1986; Freiman, Ellis, and McGuire 1989), among other issues. The empirical and conceptual research on payment systems has recently been integrated in research sponsored by NIMH to produce recommendations for a "Model Mental Health Benefit" in private insurance (Frank, Goldman, and McGuire 1991).

This literature on economics and mental health is by now very large. Good sources for representative research are the publications from the four previous conferences sponsored by the NIMH. Papers from the first conference were published in McGuire and Weisbrod (1981). Four papers from the second conference appeared in a special issue of the *Journal of Human Resources* in 1986. Papers from the third conference were published in McGuire and Scheffler (1987). A special issue of *Inquiry* in 1989 contains papers from the fourth conference.

An Explanation of the Relations between Economics and Mental Health

The causality between economics and mental health services (or mental health itself) can run in both directions. Looking at the causality from economics to services, the economics *of* mental health studies how economic factors affect services use. The economics *of* mental health is concerned with the behavior of buyers, sellers, or other economic actors and how they respond to economic incentives in markets (or other settings where choice is possible) related to mental health and mental health care. Economics *in* mental health is concerned with causality in the other direction: the consequences of mental illness and mental health services for economic measures.

Most research on economics *in* mental health has been cost studies, but a recent and innovative area of work is the role of mental disorder and treatment in labor supply.

Economics *in* mental health has been the smaller field of late (at least as practiced by economists). It is an older literature dominated by issues of measurement. There is a regular need to "count up" costs across the whole economy, a simple-sounding task complicated by the many ways in which mental illness affects services (Rice et al. 1990). The relationship between costs of treatment for mental illness and treatment for other disorders is complex. Direct treatment costs can be summed by examining billing data. Mental illness can also increase costs within an episode of care through its presence as a co-morbid condition (Rice and Kelman 1989). Some "offset effects" of mental health treatment on other medical treatment costs for the same person have been identified (Goodman 1989). The next step in empirical research is to examine the cost of illness outside the individual patient altogether and most directly the cost to family members. Some work in this area has begun, but the "family burden" literature, where costs are understood in terms of both treatment costs and other care costs, is thus far undeveloped. The major innovation by Rice et al. (1990) was the inclusion of family costs based on the work of Franks (1990). Much more needs to be done to understand this important issue.

Cost studies play a large role in the evaluation of treatment or system innovations. It is increasingly being recognized that treatment has two classes of "outcomes": clinical outcomes defined in terms of the level of functioning, symptoms, etc., and economic outcomes defined in terms of resource use. Providing the information to balance the positive clinical gains against costs is the role of cost-effectiveness analysis. Clinical effects have many dimensions. Resources are usually measured in dollars, but often even this metric is hard to apply, as in the case of many family resources devoted to the care of a mentally ill adult child. In Franks' (1990) study of family costs, many parents answered the question of "how much time do you spend caring for your child?" at "24 hours a day." There is both error and truth in the response. How can the value of that time be captured by a dollar measure?

The search for common denominators in the cost-effectiveness field is probably the most active area of methodological work. The psychotherapy research field is familiar with the common measure of "effect size" used in meta-analyses of psychotherapy outcome studies. Although this allows studies to be compared, the effect size is a pure number, a unitless thing of little help in comparing the value of one improvement with another or in comparing the value of improvements with cost. Quality-adjusted life years are one candidate for a way to measure ultimate effect, but perhaps new work in mental health, where subjective valuation of users is closer to the surface in treatment outcomes, will be able to point the way to improved approaches (see chapter 12).

Although the practical importance of the cost of mental health services is great, this component of the field will likely remain a small part of the work on economics and mental health led by economists. In most cost-effectiveness studies the economist serves in a consultative role to research motivated by a desire to study a particular intervention.

A new area of research in economics *in* mental health is labor market behavior, where health and mental health influence employment, income, and wages. (See chapters 6–8 in this volume.) The study of labor market behavior is one of the most highly developed fields of economics, rich in theoretical ideas and empirical research. Indeed, the "human capital" approach pioneered by Grossman (1972) is one of the main underpinnings of the demand for health services. Work in mental health and labor supply may seem foreign to readers mainly familiar with mental health services research because of the application of refined econometric techniques. This body of work falls outside health services research but forms a new bridge to economic research that promises to add much insight to the connection between mental illness and economic behavior.

The economics of mental health, where economic factors are the independent variables, covers a large and diverse set of topics. The first behavior studied in mental health was the effect of insurance on "demand" for services. (This was the first subject of empirical study of behavior in health economics generally as well.) The economist's paradigm of insurance and demand set the agenda: empirical interest centered on the demand response to price because of the implications of demand response for coverage in private and public insurance plans (McGuire and Weisbrod 1981). In the late 1970s when interest in National Health Insurance was keen and any third-party payer had only insurance design to rely upon as a cost-control measure, measuring demand response was the main area of work in economics and mental health. Findings from empirical research are ready to be applied to policy issues (see chapter 11). Current empirical research, such as chapter 10 by Rubin, Wilcox-Gök, and Deb, tends to concentrate on the behavior of special populations.

In addition to coming to the conclusion that the demand for mental health care (at least outpatient care, the literature on inpatient demand being much thinner) was more responsive than the demand for physical health care, research on demand and mental health made some important methodological contributions. The mother of the invention in this case was the nonlinear price feature common to mental health benefit plans. Major conceptual advances, dealing with both benefit limits (Ellis 1986) and stoplosses (Keeler, Manning, and Wells 1988), set the stage for consistent empirical findings and stimulated the "episode" approach to mental health and health care demand (Goldman, Scheffler, and Cheadle 1987). In chapter 9, Manning and Frank review the approaches to estimating demand response in the presence of nonlinear price schedules, emphasizing the problems that remain unsolved.

More recently the economics of supply of mental health care has received more attention, as emphasis has shifted from the demand-side policies of third-party payers to the supply-side policies. In chapter 2 Harrow and Ellis review this emerging literature. Ignited by the indefinite grace period Medicare granted psychiatric facilities before bringing them under the diagnosis-related group (DRG)-based prospective payment system (PPS), research on prospective payment for mental health care flared in 1984. NIMH conducted some of this research (e.g., Taube, Lee, and Forthofer 1984), financed some of the rest, and masterfully managed the whole. Carl Taube of NIMH, leading a PPS and psychiatric care working group, directed timely and constructive exchange of thinking and results to produce research outputs that could be used for policy.

Three themes emerged and set the course for policy: (1) DRGs or feasible alternatives were weak measures of expected costs, and a prospective payment system based on such classifications would create large gains and losses, with losses hitting specialized psychiatric facilities; (2) supply-side cost sharing caused a large supply response; and (3) payment system modifications could weaken incentives for supply response and create fewer gains and losses. The recommendations contained in chapter 3 by Cromwell et al. are based on this important work conducted by researchers in and outside of government. Chapter 3 describes the design of a reimbursement system for psychiatric discharges for Medicare that forgoes case-level classification altogether and addresses goals of fairness and appropriate incentives by modifying the averaging and supply-side cost sharing in the reimbursement system.

Capitation-financed systems represent a form of prospective payment system where the unit of payment is the person per year (or per month) instead of the hospital episode as in Medicare's PPS. The issues raised for mental health services are similar, however, in this form of prospective payment. Will a capitation system pay fairly? Will capitated providers be willing to accept patients with severe mental illness? Once accepted, how are mentally ill persons served? Capitation systems promise to make costs predictable and controllable. The study of the performance of capitation, as in chapters 13 and 14, will be an increasingly important component of the study of supply response in mental health.

Roughly one-half of all mental health services are directly funded by public budgets to organizations, such as state hospitals or community-based agencies. In my view, the most mischievous force in the public supply of mental health services is the confusing and overlapping pattern of federal and state categorical funding programs and the way they distort what can be done for public clients. There are many Medicaid-related examples where the magnet of federal matching funds pulls clients to Medicaid-eligible programs. The most profound effect of Medicaid on mental health care was Medicaid's coverage of nursing homes and the opportunity this presented to states to move patients out of long-stay hospitals. Integration of funding to improve the services for patients is the rationale for the Robert Wood Johnson nine-cities demonstration (Goldman et al. 1990) and the Monroe-Livingston experiment described by Babigian et al. in chapter 14 (this volume).

The economics of mental health has been of little help to this part of the service sector. Public finance methods would seem to apply to such situations and, where they have been tried, have met with success. (See chapter 4 by Frank and Salkever for an example.) More has not been done, I believe, because the relevant institutional details of the fifty state mental health systems are a daunting barrier. Time will tell whether NIMH's commitment to centers studying the financing and organization of public services will provide the stable vehicle to support good public finance-based economics by experienced researchers on the public supply of mental health services.

Some Directions and Challenges

It can probably be said that the most significant contribution of research in the field of economics and mental health has been to demonstrate the large influence of both the demand and supply-side features of the payment system on access, care provided, and costs. These findings have forced attention to special features of mental health care and to careful payment system design. Improved distribution of mental health care depends upon the quality of information guiding the design of payment systems and the organization of supply. We have seen what can happen in the absence of research specific to mental health. Without justification for a special policy for mental health, the answer to a policy question falls to one of two default values: "do nothing because mental health is a problem" or "do what has been done for other health services." Medicare's DRG-based prospective payment system is an important recent example. Long-term care is a currently important one. In the debate over long-term care financing—the single largest category of health care costs paid directly by users but still consuming up to one-half of states' Medicaid budgets—little attention is being devoted by policy makers to a distinction between health and mental health issues. Radical reform of long-term care financing is certainly needed and may become politically feasible in the near future. Research on economics and mental health helped on the PPS front and could certainly help with long-term care, too.

The field of economics and mental health is developing rapidly on several fronts. The infusion of talent from labor economics, the closer integration with mainstream health economics, the maturation of researchers, and the pull from NIMH to turn attention to the public side of the care system are all having an effect. Two broad areas of work are concerned with public sector financing and payment system design.

Public finance is becoming more a part of overall health policy. In a tax-phobic world, the financing of a public initiative is tied to the policy itself, for which the repeal of Medicare's catastrophic coverage provides a most recent tragic example. In mental health the need to integrate a public finance perspective is particularly great because of the large direct services role played by public agencies. Public mental hospitals, for all their failings, had the great advantage that, when the hospital was viewed as the site of care for an indefinite period, there was one authority with a known budget that was responsible for the care of a set of patients. Now, the hospital and, in fact, every part of the mental health care system is just one element among the many groups of people, institutions, and funding sources that are jointly responsible for caring for patients. Complex and highly problematic federal-state, state-agency, and interagency relations are at the heart of the public care system. The piecemeal, haphazard growth of eligibilities, coverages, and other rules lays no claim to rationality. The states' major taps for federal funds—Medicaid and SSI payments—were not originally intended to support states' costs of treating mentally ill persons, and a cost-shifting game is played by federal regulators and state mental health and Medicaid administrators. Starting from scratch, presumably all parties would do things differently.

What knots should be cut to move from here to where we might want to go? The economics of intergovernmental and government-contractor relations is beginning to emerge to give some help. Traditional public finance theory is based on the idea of externalities. The role of a "higher" level of government is to undertake a system of subsidies and taxes to give lower-level actors (sometimes governments and sometimes firms, agencies, or individuals) the correct set of incentives. Researchers are now applying these public finance methods to public mental health care. As usual, however, the real world is ahead of the theory. Contractual relationships in mental health are much more complex than the tax/subsidy framework can easily accommodate and will require more sophisticated tools for conceptual and empirical analysis. Mental health researchers are doing a better job describing actual relations and broadening public finance to include ideas from contracting theory.

The problem remains that this is a very "messy" empirical area. A partially offsetting advantage is that regulatory practices in different states generate experience that in principle could be used to test theories. One hopes that the importance of progress in financing care for the seriously mentally ill and the many inefficiencies introduced by the fragmented responsibility for care will outweigh the difficulties and stimulate useful work.

In the area of payment systems, some of the most interesting work will come in what could be called "integrated payment system research." The central problem in health economics from the advent of third-party payment has been to design a payment system that protects patients against the financial risk of illness without inducing excessive demands for services. This dilemma was once viewed as fundamentally unsolvable. Historically, deductibles, copayments, and limits on benefits to patients carried the full burden of cost control. The only way to introduce incentives for efficiency was to impose a burden of cost and risk on patients. "Discriminatory" coverage for mental health became the norm. Providers were insulated from making hard choices about quality versus cost by a fee or cost-based payment system.

Design of payment systems to fulfill the multiple social goals of financial protection of patients, encouragement of cost-effective care, and fair payment to providers is now a much more complicated affair, involving both demand and supply-side payment design and the use of nonfinancial regulations by payers. Research on integrated payment systems deals with how these systems work and how they should be designed.

Combining demand and supply-side payment models, putting aside for the moment the regulatory practices of third-party payers, calls for some fundamental rethinking about how utilization is determined. The patient, based on the financial incentives in his or her insurance plan, may desire more (or different) care than the providers, based on the incentives in the reimbursement system, would like to supply. When providers are paid under a system resembling cost-based reimbursement, there is no financial incentive for providers to resist patients' demand for treatment. Under forms of prospective payment, however, incentives are created to supply less than the patient demands. When both the demand and the supply sides of the payment system are used to affect decisions about treatment, there will in general be disagreement between desired demand and desired supply. Social observers of health care have noted a change in the physician-patient relationship in the context of new payment systems, but models of health care decision making, including economic models of demand and supply, have not as yet incorporated payment system–created conflict and its resolution into their view of how utilization is determined. One interesting and important implication of integrating demand and supply-side thinking is that, if providers bear more (and possibly all) of the burden of cost control, parity in insurance coverage becomes a realistic goal.

A program of research in integrated payment systems must also contend with the role of clinical norms in the sense of both norms that the provider brings to the health care encounter and those that may be imposed by an outsider as a condition of payment. This topic will put in sharp relief some dubious assumptions underlying much of economic analysis of health care utilization determination, specifically the use of demand and supply models, with all they entail about the clarity of vision and motivations of the agents being described.

The idea that providers work according to behavioral norms is not completely foreign to thinking in health economics. The "target income" theory is a behavioral theory based on the derogatory view that physicians prescribe treatments not according to clinical norms but according to the economic norm that they should make a certain amount of money. This primitive behavioral theory has many adherents, but I speculate that it is attractive mainly because there is such skepticism about the more conventional profit- or utility-maximizing models. If a better behavioral theory was articulated based on clinical standards guiding behavior, the "target income" model would quickly lose favor.

Arnold Relman has called this use of clinical information the "next health care revolution." For purposes of research, norms represent a very challenging (threatening?) topic. The norm idea could at once substitute for satisfaction of consumer demand as the normative standard in economics and could also substitute for the positive models of demand and supply. We should recognize that our cherished demand and supply models, in both their normative and positive forms, are very vulnerable in health care and do not command wide acceptance even within the health economics field, let alone outside of economics. It will be fascinating to see how the new synthesis on norms and behavior emerges over the next several years.

At a practical level, norms have revolutionary potential as well. Clearly, if third-party clinical judgment can intervene effectively to determine services worthy of payment, there may be a reduced role for demand or supply-side cost sharing. Adding norm-based policies to demand and supply-side payment policies has the potential to revise our ideas about health payment systems fundamentally, much in the same way that they were revised after prospective payment. Do they make demand and supply-side payment policies obsolete? If not, what shape should these new policies take in relation to more familiar demand and supply-side cost sharing?

Acknowledgments

I am grateful to Randy Ellis, Richard Frank, and Chris Ruhm for comments on an earlier draft. Opinions in the paper are my own. Support for the preparation of this paper was provided by National Institute of Mental Health grant K05-MH00832-01.

References

Arrow, Kenneth. 1963. "Uncertainty and the Welfare Economics of Medical Care." *American Economic Review* 53:941–73.

Christiansen, J. 1989. "Capitation of Mental Health Care in Public Programs." In R. Scheffler and L. Rossiter (eds.): *Health Economics and Health Services Research,* Vol. 10, pp. 281–311. Greenwich, Conn.: JAI Press.

Dickey, Barbara, Nancy L. Cannon, Thomas G. McGuire, and Jon E. Gudeman. 1986. "The Quarterway House: A Two-Year Cost Study of an Experimental Residential Program." *Hospital and Community Psychiatry* 37:1136–43.

Ellis, Randall P. 1986. "Rational Behavior in the Presence of Coverage Ceilings and Deductibles." *Rand Journal of Economics* 17, no. 2; 158–75.

Ellis, R., and T. McGuire. 1986. "Cost Sharing and Patterns of Mental Health Care Utilization." *Journal of Human Resources* 21:359–80.

Fairbank, Alan. 1989. "Expanding Insurance Coverage to Alternative Types of Psychotherapists: Demand and Substitution Effects of Direct Reimbursement to Social Workers." *Inquiry* 26:170–81.

Fein, Rashi. 1959. *Economics of Mental Illness.* New York: Basic Books.

Frank, Richard G. 1989. "Regulatory Policy and Information Deficiencies in the Market for Mental Health Services." *Journal of Health Politics, Policy and Law* 14:477–503.

Frank, Richard G., and Paul J. Gertler. 1989. "The Effect of Medicaid Policy on Mental Health and Poverty," *Inquiry* 26:283–91.

Frank, Richard G., Howard H. Goldman, and Thomas G. McGuire. In press. "A Model Mental Health Benefit." *Health Affairs.*

Frank, Richard G., and Judy R. Lave. 1986. "The Effect of Benefit Design on the Length of Stay of Psychiatric Patients." *Journal of Human Resources* 21:321–37.

Franks, Deborah D. 1990. "The Economic Contribution of Families Caring for Persons with Severe and Persistent Mental Illness." *Administration and Policy in Mental Health* 18, no. 1:9–18.

Freiman, Marc P., Randall P. Ellis, and Thomas G. McGuire. 1989. "Provider Response to Medicare's PPS: Reductions in Length of Stay for Psychiatric Patients Treated in Scatter Beds." *Inquiry* 26:192–201.

Frisman, Linda K. 1990. "Social Workers and Private Practice Opportunities." *Administration and Policy in Mental Health* 18, no. 1:65–78.

Goldman, Howard H., Richard M. Scheffler, and Allen Cheadle. 1987. "Demand for Psychiatric Services: A Clinical Episode Model for Specifying 'the Product.'" In T. G. McGuire and R. M. Scheffler (eds.): *The Economics of Mental Health Services,* pp. 255–74. Vol. 8 of *Advances in Health Economics and Health Services Research.* Greenwich, Conn.: JAI Press.

Goldman, Howard H., Anthony F. Lehman, Joseph P. Morrissey, Sandra J. Newman, Richard G. Frank, and Donald M. Steinwachs. 1990. "Design for the National Evaluation of the Robert Wood Johnson Foundation Program on Chronic Mental Illness." *Hospital and Community Psychiatry* 41:1217–21.

Goodman, Allen C. 1989. "Estimation of Offset and Income Effects on the Demand for Mental Health Treatment." *Inquiry* 26:235–48.

Grossman, Michael. 1972. "On the Concept of Health Capital and the Demand for Health." *Journal of Political Economy* 80:223–55.

Haas-Wilson, Deborah. 1989. "Employment Choices and Earning of Social Workers: Comparing Private Practice and Salaried Employment." *Inquiry* 26:181–92.

Keeler, E. B., W. G. Manning, and K. B. Wells. 1988. "The Demand for Episodes of Mental Health Services." *Journal of Health Economics* 7:369–92.

Kessel, Rubin. 1958. "Price Discrimination in Medicine." *Journal of Law and Economics* 1:20–53.

Lambert, D. 1985. "Political and Economic Determinants of Mental Health Regulations." Ph.D. diss., Brandeis University.

Levine, Daniel S., and Dianne R. Levine. 1975. "The Cost of Mental Illness—1971." DHEW Publication (ADM 76-265). Washington, D.C.: U.S. Government Printing Office.

Levine, Daniel S., and Shirley G. Willner. 1976. "The Cost of Mental Illness, 1974." Mental Health Statistical Note No. 125, National Institute of Mental Health. Washington, D.C.: U.S. Government Printing Office.

Lewin and Associates, Inc. 1978. "The Cost and Financing of Mental Illness." Prepared for the President's Commission on Mental Health, January.

Manning, W. G., J. P. Newhouse, N. Duan, E. B. Keeler, A. Leibowitz, and S. Marquis. 1987. "Health Insurance and the Demand for Medical Care." *American Economic Review* 77:251–77.

McGuire, Thomas G., and Richard M. Scheffler. 1987. *The Economics of Mental Health Services.* Greenwich, Conn.: JAI Press.

McGuire, Thomas G., and Burton A. Weisbrod (eds.). 1981. *Economics and Mental Health.* National Institute of Mental Health, Series EN No. 1, DHHS Publication No. (ADM) 81-114. Washington, D.C.: U.S. Government Printing Office.

Mitchell, J. 1984. "Psychiatrists' Behavior under Mental Health Insurance Regulation." National Institute of Mental Health (Contract 278-84-0012). Needham, Mass.: Health Economics Research.

Mullahy, John, and Jody Sindelar. 1989. "Life-Cycle Effects of Alcoholism on Education, Earnings, and Occupation." *Inquiry* 26:272–83.

President's Commission on Mental Health. 1978. *Report.* Washington, D.C.: U.S. Government Printing Office.

Reed, Louis S. 1975. *Coverage and Utilization of Care for Mental Conditions under Health Insurance—Various Studies 1973–74.* Washington, D.C.: American Psychiatric Association.

Rice, Dorothy P., and Sander Kelman. 1989. "Measuring Comorbidity and Overlap in the Hospitalization Cost for Alcohol and Drug Abuse and Mental Illness. *Inquiry* 26:249–61.

Rice, Dorothy P., Sander Kelman, Leonard S. Miller, and Sarah Dunmeyer. 1990. "The Economic Costs of Alcohol and Drug Abuse and Mental Illness: 1985." Report submitted to the Office of Financing and Coverage Policy of the Alcohol, Drug Abuse, and Mental Health Administration, U.S. Department of Health and Human Services. San Francisco: Institute for Health & Aging, University of California.

Straus, R. 1957. "The Nature and Status of Medical Sociology." *American Sociological Review* 22:200–204.

Taube, Carl A., E. S. Lee, and R. N. Forthofer. 1984. "DRGs in Psychiatry: An Empirical Evaluation." *Medical Care* 22:597–610.

Weisbrod, Burton A. 1983. "A Guide to Benefit-Cost Analysis as Seen through a Controlled Experiment in Treating the Mentally Ill." *Journal of Health Politics, Policy and Law* 7:808–45.

Wells, Kenneth B., Willard G. Manning, Jr., Naihua Duan, John Ware, Jr., and Joseph P. Newhouse. 1982. *Cost Sharing and the Demand for Ambulatory Mental Health Services*, R-2960-HHS. Santa Monica, Calif.: Rand Corporation, September.

PART I

The Supply of
Mental Health Care

M ental health services are provided by a complex delivery system, by a wide range of organizations, and in a variety of settings. These span the offices of psychiatrists, mental hospitals, free-standing clinics, and specialized residential treatment facilities. The mental health sector is also what economists term a *three-sector economy;* that is, for-profit, nonprofit, and publicly owned providers of care play important roles in supplying care for the treatment of mental disorders. The organizational complexity of the mental health services system creates important challenges for public policy. Public policy makers must not only understand the direct effects of their actions on the organizations they intend to affect, but also anticipate how their policies will indirectly influence other providers of mental health services.

The role of public policy is particularly large in the mental health sector. Roughly 57 percent of all expenditures in the specialty mental health sector involve public dollars. State governments assume the role of the provider of services through a large system of publicly owned hospitals and clinics. Government also is a major source of insurance coverage via the Medicare and Medicaid programs. Finally, state governments regulate insurance and may exert important influences over the structure of private insurance coverage. The tools available for influencing the supply of mental health services vary considerably with the role that governments assume in this sector of the economy. Reimbursement policy is important when government is an insurer. Budgeting and intergovernmental transfer policy are important when government serves as a direct provider. Mandated insurance legislation is the primary vehicle for making policy to affect the private insurance market. This strategy primarily affects the demand side of the market and is addressed in a subsequent section of this volume.

The chapters in this section focus on policies that affect the efficiency and distribution of the services supplied. Chapter 2, by Brooke Harrow and Randall Ellis, reviews the research on supply response to reimbursement. The authors examine what is known about various forms of prospective payment and its influence on inpatient psychiatric care. They also focus on the use of supply-side payment policy in the ambulatory care sector. Supply-side policy for ambulatory mental health care is receiving renewed attention during the 1990s. The Medicare program is moving toward the implementation of a physician fee schedule, and a great deal of concern focuses on the expected supply behavior of physicians. Harrow and Ellis provide a complete assessment of research up to 1990.

The work on payment policy sets the stage for a subsequent

round of research on the design of an optimal payment system. Chapter 3, by Jerry Cromwell, Randall Ellis, Brooke Harrow, and Thomas McGuire, provides an alternative approach to per case prospective payment for inpatient psychiatric care. The research shows that by modifying the existing TEFRA system, used to reimburse psychiatric hospitals under Medicare, one could achieve a system that provides incentives to be economical while at the same time paying providers "fairly." This research builds directly on the body of research reviewed by Harrow and Ellis. The empirical results show the practical significance of the current research program in the field of economics and mental health.

Government decisions regarding the management and size of public mental hospital systems involve the allocation of approximately $6 billion annually. Decisions regarding resource allocation in the public hospital system also have a great influence on privately owned providers of inpatient psychiatric care. Medical indigency is a particularly large problem among mentally ill people. Nonprofit general hospitals play a significant role in providing care for medically indigent persons in the United States. Moreover, new proposals are emerging to shrink public mental hospital systems. To evaluate the merits of such proposals, we must understand the influence of the public mental hospital system on private nonprofit providers of inpatient psychiatric care. Chapter 4, by Richard Frank and David Salkever, explores the effect of the public mental hospital system on the supply of psychiatric care for indigent patients by nonprofit general hospitals. This analysis points to the importance of understanding the interrelationships among the components of the three-sector economy when evaluating specific policy proposals.

Research on supply-side policy has evolved tremendously over the past several years. The chapters in this section offer an evaluation of where we stand today and some fertile directions for policy research in the immediate future.

2

Mental Health Providers' Response to the Reimbursement System

Brooke S. Harrow, Ph.D.,
and Randall P. Ellis, Ph.D.

This chapter examines the literature on the supply response of mental health providers to the manner in which they are reimbursed, a topic that has recently been the subject of considerable policy and research interest. The chapter stands in useful contrast to chapter 9 in this volume, which reviews the evidence on consumer response to demand-side cost sharing on mental health services. With demand-side cost sharing (i.e., copayments, deductibles, and coverage ceilings), the consumer is made to bear some of the financial cost of mental health services. With supply-side cost sharing, providers are placed at risk for some or all of the cost of mental health services. As highlighted in this chapter, supply-side cost sharing can take on a variety of forms and result in a variety of different outcomes. Some of these effects are beginning to be well understood, while others have thus far received very little attention. After reviewing the literature, one of the objectives of this chapter is to identify areas deserving further research.

Demand-side cost sharing has a long tradition as an instrument for reducing the "moral hazard problem," whereby a heavily insured consumer will tend to overconsume services relative to the socially appropriate level. Yet demand-side cost sharing suffers from two well-known limitations: it can impose unacceptably large financial risks on consumers, and it can limit access: high-need, low-income consumers are most likely to have access difficulties.

Over the past decade supply-side cost sharing has increasingly been adopted to correct the overconsumption problem. Medicare's prospective payment system, implemented in late 1983, is the most notable form of supply-side cost sharing. Other payers, including many state Medicaid programs, some health maintenance organizations (HMOs), public hospitals, and some private insurers have also implemented various forms of provider reimbursement which rely to varying degrees upon supply-side cost sharing. In response to the growth of supply-side cost sharing, a large literature, including both theoretical and empirical investigations, has examined the supply response to these changes in the reimbursement system.

Ellis and McGuire (1986, 1990) argued that the use of supply-side cost sharing to create incentives to contain costs can be superior to the use of demand-side cost sharing. Supply-side cost sharing places the financial risk on providers rather than consumers; because of their large number of patients, providers are better able to bear this risk than are individual consumers. In addition, providers often have more control over the costs of treatment than does the patient; in many cases financial incentives placed on the supply side can be more effective than those placed on the demand side.

The main objective of supply-side cost sharing is to use financial incentives to promote more efficient provision of services. Other important objectives are to be fair to both the patients and the facilities, to reduce financial risk, and to promote access to facilities. The study of provider response to supply-side cost sharing can help us to determine whether these objectives are being met by existing reimbursement systems. In addition, we can learn how better to design future reimbursement systems to achieve the objectives of supply-side cost sharing.

Understanding provider response in the area of mental health is particularly important for several reasons. One reason is the concern that the supply response may be stronger for mental health than for regular medical care (English et al. 1986; Grazier and McGuire 1987; Lave and Frank 1990). If mental health providers respond more strongly to supply-side cost sharing than do other health providers, this may justify not using the same reimbursement system for mental health providers as for others.

A second reason for studying mental health provider response to the reimbursement system separately from that of other health providers is that, as discussed by Frank and McGuire (1986), mental health services show more demand response than do most other services. Partly in response to this, insurance plans have traditionally given less generous coverage to mental health than to other services. If supply-side cost sharing is relatively effective at improving incentives for mental health services, this may provide an opportunity to reduce demand-side cost sharing, thereby reducing both the financial risk and the access barriers facing consumers. Finally, a third reason for focusing on mental health supply response is the disproportionately large role played by the public sector in the provision of mental health services. This large role of the public sector would justify a more complete understanding of supply response even if it turned out to be no different from other health services.

Analytic Models

Providers can respond to supply-side cost sharing in many ways. Ideally, provider response will take the form of increased efficiency with little or no loss of quality of care or reduction in access to appropriate care for patients. Implicit in this provider response is the likelihood that increases in efficiency will lead to decreases in costs.

On the inpatient side, predicted supply responses include the following: selective admissions, discrimination against certain classes of patients, undertreatment and premature discharge or transfer, strategies to increase payments with minimal changes in services rendered, increased admissions, "dumping" of undesirable patients, and inpatient/outpatient substitution and unbundling of services (Jencks, Horgan, and Taube 1987; Enthoven and Noll 1984). On the outpatient side, provider responses to supply-side cost sharing might include reducing the number or quality (e.g., time) of outpatient visits, inappropriately recommending inpatient treatment when that results in more generous reimbursement, cost shifting onto other payers, and recoding diagnoses so as to increase payments.

Most of the analytical models that describe provider response have focused on inpatient treatment and addressed the issue of undertreatment and premature discharge or transfer. Some inpatient provider response models examine the effect of reimbursement limits on length of stay and transfer decisions. Other models study provider response to physician fee limits. Researchers have also studied the effect of the incentives created within HMOs with respect to the level of mental health services.

Attempts to explain supply response to the reimbursement system were given great impetus by the introduction of Medicare's PPS, which was implemented precisely because of its expected supply response: the increased efficiency and reduced cost of inpatient care. Two seminal analytical models developed shortly after the introduction of PPS are those of Ellis and McGuire (1986) and Seidman and Frank (1985). Ellis and McGuire developed a model of provider response to cost sharing imposed by prospective payment to suggest a standard by which to judge the desirable degree of supply response.

In the Ellis and McGuire model, the physician is the key decision maker who acts as the agent for both the patient and the hospital. The physician values both benefits to the patient and hospital profits, both of which enter as arguments into the physician's utility function. Patient benefits are a function of the quantity of hospital services consumed. The physician's agency is characterized by her marginal rate of substitution between profits and quantity of patient treatment. Ellis and McGuire consider the physician to be a "perfect agent" if she attaches equal weight to both patient benefits and hospital profits.

In their model, the degree of supply-side cost sharing is related to physician agency. Under cost-based reimbursement, revenue is assumed to be identical to costs, so that profit is always zero and the physician will always choose that quantity of services that maximizes the benefit to the patient, regardless of degree of agency. Under prospective payment reimbursement, if the physician is an imperfect agent, valuing the financial interests of the hospital too much relative to patient benefits, there is a possibility of undersupply of care.

Ellis and McGuire (1986) showed that in their model optimal cost sharing on the supply side is equal to the index of agency. When the physician is a perfect agent, marginal benefit to the patient is set equal to marginal cost. As agency for the patient falls, some decrease in cost sharing to bring about an increase in marginal revenue is necessary to counter the tendency of the imperfect agent to undersupply. Ellis and McGuire suggested that a desirable response to prospective payment should be equal to the demand response of a perfectly informed consumer to the elimination of insurance coverage.

The Ellis and McGuire model examines provider behavior on the margin, for a given fully insured patient. It fails to adequately address three issues. First, competition for patients is not modeled. Second, since behavior is examined only on the margin, the income effects of the overall financial solvency of the provider are not explored. Finally, the model assumes a fully insured patient and does not examine the simultaneous effects of demand and supply-side cost sharing.

The Seidman and Frank (1985) model extends the model of Ellis and McGuire (1986) by explicitly modeling quality of care. Hospitals have both net revenue and quality of care in their objective function. Quality is a function of length of stay and a vector of intermediate hospital services provided in each day of a given hospital stay. Seidman and Frank examined possible combinations of net revenue and quality of care under three payment methods: retrospective cost-based reimbursement, prospective payment per case, and prospective per diem reimbursement.

Seidman and Frank suggested that, regardless of preferences between net revenue and quality, the maximum level of quality possible will be provided under cost-based reimbursement. However, the length of stay provided under either prospective payment method depends upon the preferences of hospitals and medical staffs for net revenue as compared to quality of care.

Frank and Lave (1986), in an empirical report, used an analytic framework similar to that of Ellis and McGuire (1986) and Seidman and Frank (1985). In this analysis, physicians are again the key decision makers for hospitals. Profits and quality are in the hospital's objective function, and quality is a function of the quantity or days of care. Frank and Lave modeled hospital behavior with respect to three different reimbursement schemes: cost-based reimbursement, prospective per diem rate setting, and limits on reimbursable days. Their model demonstrates that rate setting with no limits on days of care leads to the longest hospital stays, followed by cost-based reimbursement and limits on reimbursable days.

In two later papers, McGuire (1989) and Ellis and McGuire (1990) looked at the simultaneous effects of demand and supply-side cost sharing. They extended the Ellis and McGuire (1986) supply-side cost-sharing framework to incorporate the effects of both demand and supply-side cost sharing. Both papers used a game-theoretic Nash bargaining approach to determine a solution to the patient-provider conflict over desired health care utilization. Their joint paper developed the formal model as it applies to all health services, whereas McGuire (1989) elaborated on its implications for inpatient mental health.

For the consumer in this model, the desired demand for health services is determined by the patient's degree of cost sharing. For the provider, or physician/decision maker, the desired supply of services depends upon the percentage of costs borne by the supplier at the margin, that is, the provider's degree of cost sharing. In general, the patient's desired demand is not equal to the provider's desired supply, and bargaining is necessary to reach agreement about treatment decisions. Both papers concluded that supply-side cost sharing can be used to restrain costs while insurance on the demand side can be used to protect patients against financial risk. Prospective payment should be associated with improvements in insurance coverage.

The preceding discussion focused on models of the length-of-stay decision. Ellis and Ruhm (1988) developed a model that also reflects another key decision: the decision of whether to transfer a patient to another facility. Although their model does not focus on psychiatric hospitals, it does have particular relevance to them because transfers do play a key role for many psychiatric patients.

Ellis and Ruhm identified three objectives that should be of concern when designing the reimbursement policies directed toward transferred patients: the efficient frequency and timing of transfers, the equity of payments for transfers, and the efficient length of stay at the receiving facility. In general, there is a tradeoff when attempting to achieve these three objectives, and no single payment system will achieve the social optimum.

Ellis and Ruhm examined Medicare's existing PPS reimbursement system for transfers, under which the sending hospital receives a per diem payment up to the limit of the DRG payment and the receiving hospital also receives a full DRG payment. They showed that this system will in general lead to too many transfers. This occurs both because total payments are increased when a transfer takes place and because the sending hospital may systematically undervalue the costs imposed on the receiving hospital.

Efficient transfer decisions generally require that the sending hospital bear some of the burden of the receiving hospital's costs. Ellis and Ruhm (1988) did not consider the specific implications for psychiatric hospitals. Of special interest are public hospitals, which play an important role. This area deserves further attention.

The above discussion has focused on the effects of reimbursement policy on the provision of inpatient mental health services. In the mental health area, relatively little analytical modeling has been done on the effect of the reimbursement system on outpatient mental health services. Rather, analytical work has generally been done in a context of supply response by all types of providers to physician fees.

The most relevant literature relating to physician response to fees is the literature on "supply-induced demand." This theory is intended to explain the empirical observation that areas with high ratios of physicians per capita also tend to have high rates of services provided. This empirical observation is seen even after controlling for demand-side factors, which could also introduce such an empirical relationship. McGuire and Pauly (forthcoming) review the literature on supply-induced demand and point out that surprisingly little analytical work has been done on the topic. Most of what has been done relies upon a very simple "target income" model, whereby physicians seeing a reduction in allowed fees try to maintain their current incomes by increasing the quantity of services. This increased quantity is then labeled "supply-induced demand." As McGuire and Pauly point out, this model does not provide any rationale for why physicians did not increase quantities even before fees were reduced. Also, the model is far too simplistic in that it neglects the presence of multiple payers and multiple services, not all of which will face the same reduction in fees.

McGuire and Pauly (forthcoming) provide a new paradigm for examining physician-induced demand in the context of multiple services and multiple payers. They show that the notion of supply-induced demand is closely related to strong income effects and that the target income model corresponds to a perfectly inelastic marginal utility of income function at the income target. Even if the target income model holds, so that physicians try to maintain their incomes fully when fees are reduced, this will in general not necessarily result in an increase in expenditures by one payer on those physicians. Because of the substitution effect, physicians may plausibly increase the quantity of services paid for by other insurers. They will be most likely to increase the services to payers with relatively high fees.

The McGuire and Pauly model has important implications for mental health providers, since many mental health providers do provide services paid for by more than one insurer. It suggests that, when one payer's fees are changed, one should expect to find differences in behavior based on the market share and the initial fees of the payer. Consider Medicaid as a fee-for-service payer for outpatient services. In response to a decline in Medicaid fees, the McGuire and Pauly model would predict that, since their market share is small and fees are already low, the major effects will be to substitute away from Medicaid patients and possibly increase the number of services paid for by other payers. In contrast, a private insurer such as Blue Cross/Blue Shield, which has more generous fees and accounts for a larger market share in many states, is more likely to see an increase in total quantity of services when it attempts to limit its fees.

Empirical Literature

The majority of the empirical work studying mental health supply response has focused on response to inpatient reimbursement. In particular, most of the work has examined the effect of supply-side cost sharing on length of stay for psychiatric patients.

Evidence from the Medicaid Program

In a series of papers (Frank and Lave 1986; Lave and Frank 1988; Frank and Lave 1989; Lave and Frank 1990), Frank and Lave examined how various reimbursement schemes influence provider behavior under the Medicaid program. A key feature of Medicaid is that provider reimbursement varies across the fifty states. In contrast, demand-side incentives are very similar across states: patients are fully insured. This provides an opportunity to look across the states and examine provider response without cost sharing on the demand side.

Using ordinary least squares regression analysis (Frank and Lave 1986; Lave and Frank 1988), the authors estimated the factors influencing length of stay using a national probability sample of about one thousand Medicaid discharges from general hospital psychiatric units. The independent variables included patient characteristics, hospital characteristics, and state-level Medicaid program benefit structure.

Frank and Lave (1986) found that providers respond to limitations in both coverage and reimbursement. Their results showed that the length of stay is lower for Medicaid patients hospitalized in states that limit the number of covered days than for those hospitalized in states with no limits. In addition, the average length of stay is 39 percent shorter in states with a length-of-stay review program than in states with no review program. States that have a per diem rate regulation have between 18 and 21 percent longer lengths of stay. Overall, as a class, the benefit structure variables explain nearly as much of the variation in length of stay as do the diagnosis variables. The authors concluded that the treatment of psychiatric patients responds strongly to financial incentives.

The average length of stay of psychiatric patients covered by reimbursable limits is about 32 percent shorter than that of patients who are not (Lave and Frank 1988). The authors also found that the existence of outpatient departments had a significant and positive association with length of stay. The length of stay of patients in units affiliated with community mental health centers is significantly shorter than that of patients treated in unaffiliated units.

The authors also examined the question of supply response using nonparametric and semiparametric estimation techniques (Lave and Frank 1988; Frank and Lave 1989). In their 1988 study they used a single year of data and performed survival analysis to compare the survival distributions for Medicaid psychiatric patients in states with and without limits on reimbursable days. Their nonparametric analyses confirmed the finding that reimbursement limits affect the overall length-of-stay distribution and that limits affect the distribution unevenly.

The other study (Frank and Lave 1989) used a semiparametric duration estimation model applied to a national sample of 5,200 hospital Medicaid discharges for the years 1981–84. Separate hazard models were estimated for each of four Medicaid payment systems: per diem, per case, limits, and cost based. Comparisons were then made across the four models. The authors found that, relative to cost-based reimbursement, per case payment results in a smaller percentage of patients leaving after short durations of one to ten days, as well as a reduction in the percentage of longer-stay patients (over thirty days), resulting in a lower mean length of stay.

Prospective per diem rates were found to reduce both short stays and long stays relative to those of cost-based reimbursement. Hospital duration was affected most by limits on reimbursable days. The percentage of patients being discharged at all durations was greater in states where Medicaid set limits on reimbursable days, resulting in a 16 percent reduction in the mean length of stay.

Lave and Frank (1990) further examined the effect of different payment methods on the length of stay of Medicaid patients, this time comparing supply response by type of patient (medical, surgical, and psychiatric) and by hospital ownership. The authors used a subset of Medicaid discharges from the 1,670 hospitals that subscribe to the Professional Activity Study of the Commission on Professional and Hospital Activities.

From their ordinary least squares regression analyses, Lave and Frank found that per case payment systems and negotiated contracts lead to significant decreases in the length of stay. For example, for psychiatric cases, per case payment was associated with an 8 percent decrease in the length of stay in nonpublic hospitals and an 18 percent decrease in public hospitals.

They also found that the supply response is stronger for psychiatric patients than for medical and surgical patients and that publicly owned hospitals are more responsive to payment system incentives than are nonpublic hospitals. In nonpublic hospitals the supply response for psychiatric patients was roughly four times that for medical patients for three payment systems: prospective per case payment; negotiated contract; and preadmission screening.

This series of papers provided evidence of provider response to Medicaid reimbursement systems. However, this work raised at least three important issues. First, Frank and Lave did not control for state characteristics other than the Medicaid program benefit structures. Differences in the states' mental health systems, availability of alternatives to general hospital psychiatric units, and practice patterns could all be contributing factors in accounting for the differences in average lengths of stay across states and are plausibly correlated with the included explanatory variables.

Second, with the exception of the last paper (Lave and Frank 1990), there is no control for hospital characteristics that can affect the degree to which facilities respond to financial incentives. In particular, none of the papers examined possible income effects on supply response. More specifically, both the facility's dependency on Medicaid patients and the general financial solvency of an institution may affect the level of supply response. Facilities that are either doing poorly financially or have a large proportion of Medicaid patients may respond more strongly than other facilities for which the Medicaid reimbursement rate is less important overall.

Finally, as the authors pointed out, the evidence of shortening lengths of stay as a provider response leads to questions about whether this is only bringing about greater efficiencies or is producing adverse patient outcomes.

Evidence from the Medicare Program

The majority of Medicare's psychiatric discharges are reimbursed under the TEFRA system: those discharges that come from distinct psychiatric units of general hospitals and those patients treated in psychiatric hospitals. However, over 20 percent of Medicare psychiatric discharges are from nonspecialized scatter beds in general hospitals and are reimbursed by Medicare's DRG-based PPS system. A series of articles examined the provider response to PPS reimbursement for psychiatric patients.

In three separate papers, the same group of authors used psychiatric discharges from Medicare's 1984 PATBILL file to examine the effect of the PPS during the first year of the program (Frank et al. 1987; Lave et al. 1988; Taube et al. 1988). Psychiatric discharges from Medicare's 1984 PATBILL file were divided into two groups according to whether they occurred before or after the hospitals came under PPS (Lave et al. 1988; Taube et al. 1988). For all general hospitals, the average length of stay for psychiatric patients was 13.8 percent lower during the PPS period than during the pre-PPS period. For just those general hospitals without a psychiatric unit, the average length of stay fell 23.2 percent post-PPS.

In their multivariate work, the authors used regression analysis to explain length of stay as a function of patient characteristics, environmental characteristics, a dummy variable indicating whether the discharge took place during the PPS period, hospital characteristics, and two variables indicating the number of days the discharge occurred either before or after the implementation of PPS (Frank et al. 1987; Lave et al. 1988). Overall, this model accounted for 12 percent of the variation in length of stay. The authors concluded that the full effect of PPS was to reduce the length of stay per discharge in hospitals without a psychiatric unit by about 17 percent.

The authors also tried to determine if there were obvious shifts in types of patients admitted to hospitals without exempt units by examining admission patterns and lengths of stay for hospitals with and without units. They found no significant shift in resource-intensive patients between the two types of hospitals. However, the authors examined only one year of data, at the introduction of PPS. In addition, the measures of "resource intensity" used were very crude, with long-stay patients and disabled patients considered more resource intensive.

Freiman, Ellis, and McGuire (1989) performed a multivariate regression analysis on Medicare discharge data for the years 1984 and 1985 to examine reductions in length of stay for psychiatric patients treated in general hospitals without specialized psychiatric units. Using the discharge as the unit of observation, the authors controlled for a number of patient and hospital characteristics. In addition, a PPS gain variable was included to measure the degree to which a hospital gains from a shift to DRG-based payment. The primary focus was the effect of the proximity to the date of a facility's going onto PPS (PPS time) on the length of stay for individual discharges.

Separate regressions were performed for not-for-profit and for-profit hospitals. The PPS gain variable (PPSGAIN) had a significant influence on length of stay. The authors found that discharges from hospitals with a higher level of PPSGAIN will have shorter lengths of stay at the start of PPS but that lengths of stay will decline at a slower rate than will the lengths of stay for discharges from hospitals with lower levels of PPSGAIN. This PPSGAIN variable, however, measures the difference between PPS and cost-based reimbursement rather than the difference between PPS and TEFRA.

Provider response was greater for for-profit hospitals than for not-for-profits. The estimated change in length of stay was −21.5 to −25.7 percent for not-for-profit hospitals and −26.4 to −31.5 for for-profit hospitals. The authors also found a strong anticipation effect in their regression results. The greatest declines in lengths of stay occurred before or right at the time when the hospital began to be paid under PPS. Lengths of stay continued to decline but at a more gradual rate during the two years after PPS. As the authors pointed out, it is hard to separate the anticipatory effect from the effect of TEFRA's supply-side cost sharing.

Grazier and McGuire (1987) examined the effects of both demand and supply-side cost sharing on resource use for psychiatric, medical, and obstetric services in a large acute care hospital. This study included the analysis of both Medicaid and Medicare reimbursement limits. The authors found that, for psychiatric services, supply-side cost sharing has at least as large an effect on utilization as does demand-side cost sharing. The supply-side cost sharing effect is weakest in the medical service and strongest in the psychiatric and obstetric units.

The articles reviewed in this section showed evidence of provider response to Medicare's PPS reimbursement system. The authors controlled for hospital characteristics and found varying degrees of response with respect to both hospital ownership and the level of gain achieved by switching from cost-based reimbursement to PPS. Overall, there was about a 20 percent reduction in length of stay due to PPS, with a larger response in for-profit hospitals. Not all of this response took place immediately, and it is difficult to separate out the PPS effect from the TEFRA reimbursement limits in place before the PPS began. Only nonexcluded facilities were examined in these papers. This leaves open to further study the response of PPS-excluded facilities to TEFRA reimbursement limits.

Other Forms of Supply Response

The preceding discussion focused primarily on the effect of reimbursements on length of stay. There is also a limited amount of evidence of other influences of the payment system. Jencks, Horgan, and Taube (1987) noted the possibility of efforts to maximize payments either by manipulating diagnostic coding or encouraging readmissions. Unclear diagnostic boundaries and the relatively high prevalence of readmissions which characterize psychiatric admissions make these admissions particularly vulnerable to such strategic behavior. Evidence from New Jersey indicates that there was an increased frequency in coding of psychosis after the introduction of DRGs, but this tendency was short lived (Kamis-Gould and DeLucia 1986). Rupp, Steinwachs, and Salkever (1984) reported that hospitals paid prospectively in Maryland were characterized by slightly higher rates of admissions for their psychiatric patients than were hospitals paid on the basis of costs. Further research on readmissions and recoding which would pay particular attention to mental health would be desirable to establish the empirical importance of these payment maximization strategies.

Another strategy for altering behavior in response to the payment system is to alter the rate of transfers and readmissions. Freiman et al. (1988) examined transfer and readmission patterns for psychiatric Medicare patients. They found relatively low rates of transfers (3.5 percent of all psychiatric cases). Although the most common type of transfer was from a nonexempt facility to an exempt one, which tends to increase total reimbursements by Medicare, there was no evidence that this was being done inappropriately or excessively by certain hospitals. The analysis of readmission data did not provide strong evidence of hospitals providing inadequate courses of treatment in response to PPS incentives. However, the ability to detect inappropriate reliance on inpatient rather than outpatient care in their sample of discharges is probably poor.

Evidence of Nonpsychiatric Supply Response

Much of the inpatient supply response literature has focused on mental health services. However, other work has been done on provider response to inpatient reimbursement limits for all patients. This section summarizes some of the empirical supply response work that is not restricted to analysis of reimbursement for psychiatric patients.

Sloan, Morrisey, and Valvona (1988) performed regression analysis of hospitals' responses to Medicare's PPS. They found that PPS had statistically significant effects on length of stay, labor cost per adjusted admission, nonlabor cost per adjusted admission, and total margin for the voluntary and community hospitals they studied. They concluded that, although they found significant cost-reducing effects of Medicare's PPS, the savings appeared to have been generated almost entirely as a result of reduced admissions.

Rosko and Broyles (1986) used multivariate regression analysis to examine the effects of two different prospective payment programs in New Jersey. The first system, SHARE, used prospectively determined per diem rates to regulate Blue Cross Plan and Medicaid revenues. The other system was the all-payer New Jersey DRG program. The authors found that the DRG program restrained costs more effectively than did the per diem–based SHARE program. The DRG system resulted in an average reduction in the cost per admission of 4.4 percent and an average reduction in length of stay of 3.4 percent.

Salkever, Steinwachs, and Rupp (1986) studied the influence of Maryland's per case payment system on hospital total inpatient costs and average cost per case. The authors found that the cost per case was significantly affected only for those hospitals in which the per case payment level was set below their historical experience.

Hadley and Swartz (1989) analyzed hospital costs for 1,293 hospitals in forty-three standardized metropolitan statistical areas (SMSAs) during a five-year period (1980–84). The authors estimated the possible influences of hospital rate regulation, health insurance coverage, and competition on the slowdown in the growth of hospital costs during this period. They found that both TEFRA and PPS have statistically significant and large effects on total hospital costs. PPS hospitals have expenses that are 12.5 percent lower than those of nonregulated hospitals. Hospitals reimbursed under TEFRA were estimated to have total expenses 7.4 percent below hospitals in non-regulated states.

Outpatient Treatment Supply Response

In contrast with the relatively extensive literature on the effects of reimbursement policy on inpatient treatment patterns, there is a much smaller literature on the influences of reimbursement policy on outpatient treatment. This section discusses evidence from two lines of analysis: research that examines outpatient mental health services offered by health maintenance organizations, which may differ in the method of reimbursing providers, and research that examines the consequences of changes in fee limits permitted for providers reimbursed on a fee-for-service basis.

Although variations in the reimbursement structures for providers in HMOs provide an important opportunity to examine differences in behavior, such comparisons also suffer from two key weaknesses. The first weakness is that comparisons involving HMOs invariably involve different organizational structures and delivery systems as well as different reimbursement systems. Hence, observed patterns will tend to reflect both of these effects. The second difficulty is that all of the results on provider response are contaminated by selectivity effects. This selectivity is of two forms: the characteristics of people enrolled in HMOs can be systematically different from those of people enrolled in fee-for-service plans, and the mental health providers who work for the HMOs may also differ from those in the fee-for-service sector.

Bearing in mind the likelihood that differences may, in part, be due to both selectivity effects and the confounding of reimbursement and delivery system effects, available evidence suggests that patterns of mental health service use in HMOs are quite different from those in traditional fee-for-service insurance plans. In HMOs, inpatient psychiatric services are used less frequently and outpatient services can be used either more or less often than in traditional fee-for-service plans.

Analysis based on data from the Rand Health Insurance Experiment (HIE) provides perhaps the most useful picture of the magnitude and form of the possible supply response of mental health providers. One of the plans to which participants in the HIE were assigned was the Group Health Cooperative (GHC) of Puget Sound, a well-established HMO in Seattle, Washington. By contrasting GHC enrollees with other HIE participants, Wells, Manning, and Benjamin (1986) were able to compare patterns of outpatient use in the GHC with patterns in conventional insurance plans. Since benefits for participants in the GHC were essentially the same as those for participants in the "free care" HIE plan, from the point of view of the patient the demand-side incentives were the same. The two plans differ, however, in the incentives created for suppliers to provide care. At the margin in the fee-for-service sector, providers are reimbursed at 100 percent of their cost (or fee); in the GHC, however, the marginal payment is zero because the provider is on salary and the GHC absorbs the full cost of any treatment. With the above caveats about contamination of selection effects and alternative structures, the comparison of the free care plan and the HMO can be interpreted as a comparison of supply-side cost sharing.

Wells, Manning, and Benjamin (1986) used a two-part regression model of the probability and level of use of outpatient care. For the Seattle participants, the probability of use was virtually identical in the GHC and the free care plan. The decision to seek at least some outpatient treatment seems to be driven by demand-side incentives and not influenced by the reimbursement system. In contrast, the decision of how much treatment the patient receives seems to be dominated by supply-side incentives. For enrollees in the GHC, both expenditures and visits per patient were about one-third the level of those in the "free care" fee-for-service plan.

Another aspect of the effect of HMO reimbursements on mental health provider behavior is found in Jennison and Ellis (1987). They contrasted the number of outpatient visits per month provided by a group of mental health professionals before and after a change in the way that the providers were reimbursed. In their study the population served and the demand for services were unaffected by the reimbursement change, so the subsequent change in reimbursement was interpreted clearly as a pure supply-side response. Their finding was that psychotherapists provided 18 percent more visits per month when they were paid on a fee-for-service basis than when they were paid on a salary basis. Hence, individual providers are sensitive to the form of their own individual reimbursement, even while incentives within the HMO remain the same.

Further information on the supply response to the reimbursement system can be found in physicians' responses to fee limits imposed by various Medicaid programs, private insurers, and the Canadian health system. A number of studies have examined the effects of fee limits on a broad set of procedures to see the change in quantity of services resulting. A relatively complete review of physician response to fees (not focusing on mental health) is provided in Gabel and Rice (1985). Here we summarize the findings of two recent articles that explicitly contrast mental health with nonmental health providers.

Mitchell, Wedig, and Cromwell (1989) examined the influence of Medicare's 1984 physician fee freeze, which affected all types of physician services. Despite the physician fee freeze, total spending continued to increase, and 1986 spending on physician services (as indicated by total allowed charges) was 29.5 percent above 1983 levels. Spending on psychiatrists grew 43.0 percent during this same period, increasing from $4.21 per beneficiary to $6.02 per beneficiary. As the authors pointed out, numerous other policies were changed over the sample period (notably the introduction of the PPS and the participating physician program); however, their study does suggest that the fee limit had less effect on psychiatrists than on other physician specialties.

Hurley, Labelle, and Rice (1990) examined provider response to fee limits and included contrasts among twenty-eight medical, surgical, and psychiatric procedures. Their study was conducted using data from Ontario, Canada, covering the period 1975–87, during which relative fees for many services were changed substantially. Because Canada has universal health coverage, fee levels chosen by the provincial governments apply to essentially all patients; hence, this study avoids the complications of multiple payers and different demand-side coverages that exist in the United States. Hurley, Labelle, and Rice did not find any statistically significant effect of fee changes on the four psychiatric procedures considered. Among procedures that showed statistically significant patterns, they did not find any consistent pattern with regard to medical versus surgical. Procedures were split about evenly into those with positive and those with negative coefficients. The procedures were not selected randomly but instead were chosen deliberately to be those with large fee changes that were most likely to show a supply response; for example, trauma and nondiscretionary procedures were deliberately excluded. Hence, the failure to find significant patterns is stronger than a result from a random sample of procedures.

Summary and Conclusions

The literature reviewed in this chapter provides evidence of supply response to the reimbursement system by mental health providers.

Most of the empirical literature has focused on inpatient length-of-stay supply response. Comparisons of inpatient lengths of stay across states under the Medicaid program reveal that inpatient psychiatric stays in states with reimbursable limits can be over 30 percent shorter than stays in states without these limits. Examination of the effect of Medicare's PPS on psychiatric length of stay showed 22 to 32 percent reductions in length of stay. Providers are responding to reimbursement incentives on the outpatient side as well. Psychotherapists reimbursed on a fee-for-service basis provide 15 to 20 percent more visits than do their salaried colleagues.

Although numerous studies support the view that providers do respond to reimbursement limits, they leave open normative questions about whether or not this supply response leads to adverse outcomes with respect to access to care and patients' benefit from treatment. The ideal supply response promotes greater efficiency without adverse outcomes for the patients. Further research is necessary to examine the effect of supply response on patient outcomes. The study of patient outcomes could include examination of patients' clinical status at the end of their hospital stay, readmissions, and transfers to the state mental health system. Studies of the response of providers to inpatient reimbursement limits should be coupled with an analysis of the community and social support systems available for the patient outside of the hospital.

Newhouse (1989) addressed the issue of whether unprofitable patients faced access problems. He tested whether patients in DRGs that had negative profits were more likely than other patients to be transferred from hospitals other than those of last resort and whether they were more likely to be cared for in hospitals of last resort. Newhouse defined hospitals of last resort as county, city, city-county, and hospital district or authority facilities as defined by the American Hospital Association. Newhouse's results were ambiguous, and he concluded that, although he did not find strong evidence of access problems for unprofitable patients under Medicare's PPS, the access issue should continue to be examined in future work.

Several other areas of research with respect to supply response are still left to be addressed. The theoretical literature has begun to look at the simultaneous effects of demand and supply-side cost sharing (McGuire 1989; Ellis and McGuire 1990); however, the empirical work has only looked at both types of cost sharing separately. This work would be particularly important for private insurers, which often use both types of reimbursement limits. Further research that models demand and supply-side incentives simultaneously and examines the empirical behavior of providers in such settings is needed.

The supply response literature generally has examined the effects of one payer's (i.e., Medicare or Medicaid) reimbursement limits on the quantity of care provided. However, most providers are reimbursed by a mix of payers. The provider response to a particular reimbursement scheme might vary according to how dependent the provider is on that payer. For example, a provider with 10 percent of its patients reimbursed under Medicare might respond very differently to changes in Medicare reimbursement than would another provider that is dependent upon Medicare payment for one-half of its patients. McGuire and Pauly (forthcoming) develop an analytical model describing physician behavior in the context of multiple payers and multiple services. Future empirical research is needed to test the implications of their model for both physician and hospital providers.

Supply response literature has generally focused on the provider's response to marginal incentives under a particular reimbursement scheme. There is room for future study that examines not just the marginal incentives under a given reimbursement scheme, but also the income effects. Some early evidence suggests that facilities with different degrees of financial solvency might respond differently to supply-side cost sharing. Salkever, Steinwachs, and Rupp (1986) and Feder, Hadley, and Zuckerman (1987) found that supply response is likely to be stronger in hospitals experiencing severe financial pressure. Freiman, Ellis, and McGuire (1989) found that patients discharged from hospitals with a higher level of PPSGAIN (measure of hospital's gain from shifting to PPS) had lower lengths of stay at the start of PPS but had slower declines in lengths of stay than had patients discharged from hospitals with lower levels of PPSGAIN. A study currently in progress by Harrow is examining both the marginal incentives and the income effects on provider response for PPS-excluded psychiatric facilities that are under Medicare's TEFRA reimbursement system.

A final issue that has received little attention is the role of market forces on provider response to the reimbursement system. Most of the theoretical research has used a stylized model of provider behavior, without embedding the provider in a market setting. Such models cannot predict whether provider response will change according to the changes in demand or according to changes in nonreimbursement supply-side features, such as the number and type of mental health providers. Similarly, empirical studies of provider response have always included supply-side variables in addition to reimbursement variables. Some of these supply-side variables should probably be interacted with the reimbursement variables. Theoretical research is needed to identify whether some of these supply-side variables might not only directly affect the dependent variable (e.g., length of stay or costs), but also alter the nature of the supply response to reimbursements.

The above discussion has identified several aspects of provider response to the reimbursement system which are deserving of further research, some of which are currently being investigated. Although a great deal of progress in understanding mental health provider response has been made over the past decade, much remains to be examined. The next decade of health services research on provider response to the reimbursement system promises to be informative.

References

Ellis, Randall P., and Thomas G. McGuire. 1986. "Provider Response to Prospective Payment: Cost Sharing and Supply." *Journal of Health Economics* 5:129–51.

———. 1990. "Optimal Payment Systems for Health Services." *Journal of Health Economics* 9:375–98.

Ellis, Randall P., and Christopher J. Ruhm. 1988. "Incentives to Transfer Patients under Alternative Reimbursement Mechanisms." *Journal of Public Economics* 37:381–94.

English, Joseph T., Steven S. Sharfstein, Donald J. Scherl, Boris Astrachan, and Irvin L. Muszynski. 1986. "Diagnosis-related Groups and General Hospital Psychiatry: The APA Study." *American Journal of Psychiatry* 143:131–39.

Enthoven, A., and R. Noll. 1984. "Prospective Payment: Will It Solve Medicare's Financial Problem?" *Issues in Science and Technology* 1 (Fall): 101–16.

Feder, J., J. Hadley, and S. Zuckerman. 1987. "How Did Medicare's Prospective Payment System Affect Hospitals?" *New England Journal of Medicine* 317:126–29.

Frank, Richard G., and Judith R. Lave. 1986. "The Effect of Benefit Design on the Length of Stay of Medicaid Psychiatric Patients." *Journal of Human Resources* 21:321–37.

———. 1989. "A Comparison of Hospital Responses to Reimbursement Policies for Medicaid Psychiatric Patients." *Rand Journal of Economics* 24:588–600.

Frank, Richard G., and Thomas G. McGuire. 1986. "A Review of Studies of the Impact of Insurance on the Demand and Utilization of Specialty Mental Health Services." *Health Services Research* 21:241–66.

Frank, Richard G., Judith R. Lave, Carl A. Taube, Agnes Rupp, and Howard Goldman. 1987. "The Impact of Medicare's Prospective Payment System on Psychiatric Patients Treated in Scatterbeds." In Thomas G. McGuire and Richard Scheffler (eds.): *Advances in Health Economics and Health Services Research: The Economics of Mental Health Services*, Vol. 8, pp. 1–22. Greenwich, Conn.: JAI Press.

Freiman, Marc P., Randall P. Ellis, and Thomas G. McGuire. 1989. "Provider Response to Medicare's PPS: Reductions in Length of Stay for Psychiatric Patients Treated in Scatter Beds." *Inquiry* 26:192–201.

Freiman, M. P., T. G. McGuire, R. P. Ellis, A. M. Hendricks, J. B. Mitchell, C. Carter, B. S. Harrow, and A. G. Stone. 1988. *An Analysis of Options for Including Psychiatric Inpatient Settings in a Prospective Payment System.* Final Report submitted under Contract No. NIMH-278-86-0002, Health Economics Research, June.

Gabel, J., and T. Rice. 1985. "Reducing Public Expenditures for Physician Services: The Price of Paying Less." *Journal of Health Politics, Policy and Law* 9:595–609.

Grazier, Kyle L., and Thomas G. McGuire. 1987. "Payment Systems and Hospital Resource Use: A Comparative Analysis of Psychiatric, Medical and Obstetric Services." In Thomas G. McGuire and Richard Scheffler (eds.): *Advances in Health Economics and Health Services Research: The Economics of Mental Health Services*, Vol. 8, pp. 75–96. Greenwich, Conn.: JAI Press.

Hadley, Jack, and Katherine Swartz. 1989. "The Impacts on Hospital Costs between 1980 and 1984 of Hospital Rate Regulation, Competition, and Changes in Health Insurance Coverage." *Inquiry* 26:35–47.

Hurley, Jeremiah, Roberta Labelle, and Thomas Rice. 1990. "The Relationship between Physician Fees and the Utilization of Medical Services in Ontario." *Advances in Health Services Research* 11:49–78.

Jencks, S. F., C. Horgan, and C. Taube. 1987. "Evidence on Provider Response to Prospective Payment." *Medical Care* 25 (Suppl.):s37–s41.

Jennison, Kathleen, and Randall P. Ellis. 1987. "A Comparison of Psychiatric Service Utilization in a Single Group Practice under Multiple Insurance Systems." In Thomas G. McGuire and Richard Scheffler (eds.): *Advances in Health Economics and Health Services Research: Research Issues in Economics and Mental Health*, Vol. 8, pp. 175–94. Greenwich, Conn.: JAI Press.

Kamis-Gould, E., and N. DeLucia. 1986. *The New Jersey DRG Prospective Payment System.* Part I of final draft. NIMH Contract 86M047489701D. Rockville, Md.: National Institute of Mental Health.

Lave, Judith R., and Richard G. Frank. 1988. "Factors Affecting Medicaid Patients' Length of Stay in Psychiatric Units." *Health Care Financing Review* 10, no. 2:57–66.

———. 1990. "Effect of the Structure of Hospital Payment on Length of Stay." *Health Services Research* 25:327–47.

Lave, Judith R., Richard G. Frank, Carl A. Taube, Howard Goldman, and Agnes Rupp. 1988. "The Early Effects of Medicare's Prospective Payment System on Psychiatry." *Inquiry* 25:354–63.

McGuire, Thomas. 1989. "Combining Demand and Supply-Side Cost Sharing: The Case of Inpatient Mental Health Care." *Inquiry* 26:292–303.

McGuire, Thomas G., and Mark V. Pauly. Forthcoming. "Physician Response to Fee Changes with Multiple Payers." *Journal of Health Economics.*

Mitchell, Janet B., Gerald Wedig, and Jerry Cromwell. 1989. "The Medicare Physician Fee Freeze: What Really Happened?" *Health Affairs* 8, no. 1:21–31.

Newhouse, Joseph P. 1989. "Do Unprofitable Patients Face Access Problems?" *Health Care Financing Review* 11, no. 2:33–42.

Rosko, M. D., and R. W. Broyles. 1986. "The Impact of the New Jersey DRGs System." *Inquiry* 23, no. 1.

Rupp, Agnes, Donald Steinwachs, and David Salkever. 1984. "The Effect of Hospital Payment Methods on the Pattern and Cost of Mental Health Care." *Hospital and Community Psychiatry* 34:456–59.

Salkever, D. S., D. M. Steinwachs, and A. Rupp. 1986. "Hospital Cost and Efficiency under per Service and per Case Payment in Maryland: A Tale of the Carrot and the Stick." *Inquiry* 23:56–66.

Seidman, R. L., and R. G. Frank. 1985. "Hospital Responses to Incentives in Alternative Reimbursement Systems." *Journal of Behavioral Economics* 14 (Winter): 155–80.

Sloan, F. A., M. A. Morrisey, and J. Valvona. 1988. "Case Shifting and the Medicare Prospective Payment System." *American Journal of Public Health* 78:553–56.

Taube, C. A., Judith R. Lave, Howard H. Goldman, Richard G. Frank, and Agnes Rupp. 1988. "Psychiatry under Prospective Payment: Experience in the First Year." *American Journal of Psychiatry* 145:210–13.

Wells, Kenneth G., Willard G. Manning, and Bernadette Benjamin. 1986. "Use of Mental Health Services in an HMO and Fee-for-Service Plans: Results of a Randomized Controlled Trial." *Health Services Research* 21:453–74.

3

A Modified TEFRA System
for Psychiatric Facilities

Jerry Cromwell, Ph.D.,
Randall P. Ellis, Ph.D.,
Brooke S. Harrow, Ph.D., and
Thomas G. McGuire, Ph.D.

I n fiscal year 1983, the Medicare TEFRA Payment System was implemented for all hospitals. TEFRA, named after the Tax Equity and Fiscal Responsibility Act of 1982, established a per discharge target amount, placing reimbursement limits on total operating costs and extending the so-called "section 223 limits" to constrain both routine and ancillary costs. Hospital costs were reimbursable up to a limit that was the lesser of a hospital-specific cost target and a peer group target. There were seven peer group categories based on bed size and urban or rural location and no case mix adjustments. When Medicare's Prospective Payment System was introduced in fiscal year 1984 for general acute care hospitals, certain specialized facilities including psychiatric hospitals and units of general hospitals remained under TEFRA.

Like the PPS, the purpose of the TEFRA payment system was to create incentives for efficiency in the context of a fair payment system. The major problem with TEFRA is that the current target amounts, or payment caps, are based on outdated 1982 average costs trended forward by PPS annual update factors. TEFRA is predicated on the hospital's own target amount being a reasonable "target" for each facility (peer groups were dropped after TEFRA's first year). In the eight years since the targets were first calculated, actual average costs have diverged widely from the 1982 figures, making TEFRA a very unfair payment system to many institutions.[1] Large gains and losses are generated using outdated target amounts. Furthermore, TEFRA (as we will explain later) is asymmetric in its treatment of gains and losses, aggravating the fairness problem.

In spite of its limitations, TEFRA, with significant modifications, can be an equitable and efficient basis of Medicare payment for psychiatric facilities. Our recommendations include a more symmetric sharing of losses and peer groupings to instill more cost competition.

PPS Payment Biases and TEFRA Incentives

PPS Biases

A unified Medicare payment system with all facilities under PPS was not adopted in fiscal year 1983 because of anticipated problems of paying the excluded facilities on the basis of DRGs. The major concern at the time was the "fairness" of DRGs (Jencks et al. 1984). If patients at specialized facilities were more costly in ways not accounted for by psychiatric DRGs, the facilities would be underpaid on the basis of a national average payment. Subsequent research corroborated this concern (Freiman, Mitchell, and Rosenbach 1987; Taube, Lee, and Forthofer 1984; McGuire et al. 1987; English et al. 1986).[2]

A second concern with extending the PPS to psychiatric facilities was a fear of an excessive supply response to incentives in the payment system. When payment per discharge is fixed by the DRG amount (with the exception of the small amount paid for outlier cases), facilities have strong incentives to reduce the supply of care per discharge. Studies of Medicare costs (Guterman et al. 1988; Prospective Payment Assessment Commission 1989) and of psychiatric discharges covered by the PPS (Frank et al. 1987; Freiman, Ellis, and McGuire 1989) found a gradual decrease in length of stay before the PPS and a continuing, slower decline after a facility came onto the PPS. TEFRA also has incentives to reduce care per discharge, but these are not as strong as under the PPS. Using data on Medicaid discharges from psychiatric units of general hospitals in 1981, Lave and Frank (1988) concluded that the presence of limits reduces the average length of stay (LOS) by 32 percent in comparisons to states with no limit.[3]

TEFRA Payment Incentives

Facilities remaining under TEFRA as the PPS was phased in were allowed to keep 50 percent of the amount by which their average costs fell below the target amount, up to a maximum of 5 percent of the target. If costs exceeded the target amount, however, the facility was responsible for all of the overrun. The target amount for the first year of TEFRA was equal to the operating costs of the previous year plus an inflation adjustment. Annual TEFRA adjustments were set equal to the same update factor for PPS facilities, which fell well below the PPS market basket inflation rate.

If a TEFRA facility's average costs exceed its target amount at year's end, the facility, in effect, bears the full marginal costs of each discharge as under the PPS. Facilities well below their allowed targets enjoy incentive payments from Medicare and operate under incentives similar to cost-based reimbursement. If a facility accurately forecasts that it will end up within 90–100 percent of the target amount, it shares financial risk with Medicare 50-50. A one dollar increase in average cost raises net revenue by fifty cents.

The very asymmetric treatment of facility gains and losses, coupled with the use of low PPS update factors, argues for modifying the current TEFRA system. PPS allows the facility to keep all of the gains from constrained costs but requires that it bear almost all of the losses for costs above the DRG payment, modified only by the per case outlier provisions. TEFRA, like the PPS, has no risk sharing by Medicare on the loss side but, unlike the PPS, requires extensive profit sharing on the gain side. Facilities face the risk of gaining little but losing much under TEFRA; under the PPS, however, large gains in one year can be used to offset losses in the next.

Another argument for modifying TEFRA is the lack of cost competition that is so prevalent under the PPS, where each hospital is paid a fixed rate. Elsewhere (Cromwell, Harrow, and McGuire 1990), we have shown the positive correlation between TEFRA base year costs and subsequent profitability. Hospitals with higher base year costs did better later on—possibly because they had more slack to begin with. Equity and improved efficiency are two reasons for introducing peer group payment rates that adjust for base period inequities.

The Data

The primary sources of data for our simulation of TEFRA modifications are Medicare cost reports for psychiatric hospitals and distinct-part units with cost-reporting periods on or after October 1, 1984, and before October 1, 1988. These facilities are all reimbursed by Medicare under the TEFRA payment system.

The Medicare cost reports contain information on costs and utilization that enable the program to determine reasonable costs and TEFRA payment amounts for these PPS-excluded facilities. The utilization data include the number of bed days and discharges both for Medicare and for total utilization. Inpatient operating cost data include routine and special care service costs as well as breakdowns of a hospital's or unit's costs and charges by ancillary cost center. Annual target amounts are also reported.

Providers often begin their fiscal years at different dates. For the purposes of our analysis, we classified each cost report according to its fiscal year end date. Within-year inflation effects were accounted for by using a quarterly adjustment based on the market-basket inflation update. Records with cost-reporting periods of less than six months were dropped. Provider records with fiscal years that were shorter than twelve months but at least six months were prorated upward so that the cost and utilization data could be compared with twelve-month reports.

So that peer groups could be constructed, additional hospital-level variables were merged onto the 1986 cost reports from the 1985 NIMH Medicare Hospital Aggregate file. The variables were originally taken from several sources including the Medicare 1985 MEDPAR file, the Health Care Financing Administration (HCFA) FY1987 Impact Analysis Public Use File, the 1985 Provider of Service File, and the 1983 and 1984 American Hospital Association Surveys of Hospitals. The following variables are available to be used as a basis of peer groups: urban/rural designation, SMSA size, region, ownership, bed size, HCFA area wage index, and residents per bed.

We trimmed the data before analysis to eliminate large outliers and possible reporting errors. Since we had no specific information about the accuracy of the cost reports, we assumed that the top ($14,102 threshold) and bottom ($940) 1 percent values for average cost were erroneous. Applying these thresholds to data for both 1986 and 1987 eliminated 35 facilities from the 1986 data and 13 facilities from the 1987 file, leaving a sample size of 942 and 992, respectively, including roughly 300 psychiatric hospitals.

Constructing Exempt Psychiatric Unit Peer Groups

This section presents alternative peer groupings for reimbursing exempt *psychiatric units* under a modified TEFRA prospective payment system. Psychiatric hospitals are treated separately later in this chapter. Previous research (Freiman et al. 1988) and expert opinion provided a set of potential cost explainers, or stratifiers, which were used in various combinations to form peer groups. Group means and cell sizes were then compared to evaluate the feasibility and appropriateness of each peer grouping for reimbursement.

Choice of Peer Group Stratifiers

In developing peer group classifications, the primary goal is to avoid systematic payment bias arising from factors outside the hospital's control (e.g., higher local wage rates, a more complicated case mix). Several of these variables are continuous, including the local PPS area wage index, bed size, size of residency programs, proportion of discharges that are Medicare patients, and disproportionate share percentage. Discrete groupings were created for all but the wage index, which was used to deflate the actual labor and other costs for geographic differences.

Categorical stratifiers included the following. Geographical region (REG9) included the standard nine census divisions. Two different measures were used to describe the urban or rural location of the facility. The variable URBAN is the PPS variable that indicates whether the facility is located in a county that is part of a metropolitan area (MSA). Because deflated costs of facilities in smaller urban areas are more similar to those in rural areas than they are to large urban areas, MSA3 further divides exempt units into three groups: (1) those located in an MSA of over 500,000 population; (2) facilities in smaller MSAs with a population under 500,000; (3) and rural or non-MSA areas.

Several measures of teaching status were considered. The usual (PPS) measure of teaching status is the total number of physician residents per bed. RESB4 categorizes hospitals into four groups: (1) nonteaching; (2) 0–0.15 residents per bed; (3) >0.15–0.25 residents per bed; and (4) >0.25 residents per bed. In major teaching hospitals, the average cost per case was over 40 percent higher than in nonteaching institutions. The variable, MDPHDBED3, groups hospitals into three categories according to the relative number of psychiatrist and psychologist residents per bed: (1) no psychiatric residents; (2) 0–0.173 residents per bed; and (3) >0.173 psychiatric residents per bed. A third measure of teaching status, ALMHRES3, includes all mental health residents, social workers, and psychiatric nurses as well as psychiatrists and psychologists.

The variable, BEDS8, categorizes hospitals into eight bed-size groups. Standardized costs per case rise fairly consistently as the number of hospital beds increases, with the largest difference (=$1,000) between hospitals with more or less than 700 beds. PSYBED4 categorizes the hospitals into four groups according to the size of their psychiatric units, rather than across all bed units. DISCH4 also divides hospitals into four groups depending upon their total number of discharges rather than reported bed size.

Medicare dependency, measured as the proportion of total hospital discharges covered by Medicare, has been categorized into three groups (MEDDEP3): (1) 0–17 percent Medicare patients; (2) >17–29.8 percent; and (3) >29.8 percent. Average cost per case declines slightly as dependency increases and then rises again for the one-quarter of hospitals that are heavily dependent on Medicare.

The proportion of Medicaid and Medicare crossover eligibles in total hospital discharges, or PPS disproportionate share, has been divided into four groups (DSHP4): (1) less than 9 percent; (2) 9–14 percent; (3) >14–22 percent; and (4) >22 percent. Across the four DSHP4 groups, the pattern of average cost per case is once again U-shaped.

With so many potential stratifiers and individual groups, it was necessary to aggregate in order to generate a statistically meaningful number of peer groups. REG4 collapses the nine census divisions into four regions based on contiguous regions with similar costs. MSA2 combines facilities in small urban and rural areas, creating essentially a large-urban area dummy variable. RESB3 collapses the middle two RESB4 categories and allows for only nonteaching, minor teaching, and major teaching categories. The variable RESB2 further collapses teaching status into two groups of <0.25 or ≥0.25 residents per bed. Bed size was recategorized into four, three, and two bed-size groups in addition to the original BEDS8. PSYBED3 collapses the original PSYBEDS4 variable into three groups. DISCH3 collapses the middle two discharge groups of DISCH4. DISCH2 simply distinguishes between hospitals with <16,399 or ≥16,399 discharges in 1986. Medicare dependency was recategorized into two groups (MEDEP30): <29.8 percent or ≥29.8 percent of their patients covered by Medicare.

Analysis of Variance

Analyses of variance were performed, first, for undeflated Medicare 1987 allowable inpatient operating costs per discharge in 732 exempt units and, second, for HCFA wage-deflated costs, using the seven uncollapsed categorical variables as main effects.

Deflating each unit's average cost by the HCFA wage index explained 26 percent of the nominal differences in exempt unit costs per case. Treating the seven classifying variables as main effects without interactions explained another 25 percent of the total sum of squares of deflated costs, or 45 percent altogether including the prior HCFA wage adjustment. This is relatively high considering that only categorical variables are being used (except for wages) and no interactions are included. On the other hand, it does mean that over one-half of the cost variation goes unexplained.

Table 3.1 presents the results of the interacted analyses of variance using standardized costs per discharge as the criterion variable. Our strategy focused, first, on the three most important variables identified in the main effects analyses: region, teaching status, and urban-rural location. The top third of the table presents results using nine census divisions interacted with alternative measures of teaching status and hospital size, as well as urban-rural location. Asterisks between variables indicate fully interacted groupings. Once we identified the most powerful definitions of teaching and size in the top panel using an R^2 statistic, we then interacted a third level of

Table 3.1   Analysis of Variance of 1987 Standardized[a] Medicare Operating Costs per Discharge in 732 Exempt Psychiatric Units

Grouping	Number of Groups	R^2	F-Value
1. REG9*RESB2	18	.20	10.2
2. REG9*RESB3	27	.21	7.1
3. REG9*ALMHRES3	27	.11	3.1
4. REG9*MDPHDRES3	27	.14	3.9
5. REG9*BEDS2	18	.12	5.7
6. REG9*PSYBEDS3	27	.09	2.8
7. REG9*DISCH2	18	.09	4.3
8. REG9*MSA2	18	.11	5.5
9. REG9*MSA3	27	.12	3.9
10. REG4*RESB2	8	.17	21.1
11. REG4*RESB2*MSA2	16	.21	12.9
12. REG4*RESB2*BEDS2	16	.22	13.2
13. REG4*RESB2*DISCH2	16	.19	11.5
14. REG4*RESB2*MDEP30	16	.20	11.7
15. MSA2*RESB2	4	.16	45.9
16. MSA3*RESB2	6	.16	28.2
17. MSA2*RESB2*BEDS2	8	.20	25.6
18. MSA3*RESB2*BEDS2	10	.20	20.3
19. MSA3*RESB2*DISCH2	12	.18	14.4
20. URBAN*RESB2	4	.14	40.7
21. URBAN*RESB2*BEDS2	6	.19	33.2
22. URBAN*RESB2*DISCH2	8	.16	19.9
23. URBAN*RESB2*MDEP30	7	.17	24.1

Note: See text for variable definitions.
[a]Standardized by dividing actual Medicare-covered costs per discharge by (.75*WAGEI + .25*COLI), where WAGEI = HCFA 1984 wage index and COLI = state cost-of-living index = 1.2 for Hawaii, = 1.0 elsewhere.

stratifiers to pick up some residual cost variation not reflected in the two-stage interactions. Because of the rapid increase in the number of cells, we used only the modified four census regions or urban-rural location in the tripartite interactions. It was also at this level that we considered the effects of Medicare dependency and disproportionate share.

The first two models in table 3.1 report the explanatory effects of groupings based on the usual HCFA definition of teaching status, residents per bed, interacted with the nine census divisions (REG9). The first, dichotomous classification of teaching into major versus all-other, RESB2, stratified by census division, produced eighteen cells in 1987 and an $R^2 = .20$. These eighteen peer groups together explained 20 percent of the variation in exempt unit deflated costs per discharge, or 41 percent altogether, counting the wage adjustment effect. Using the more common three-part grouping (RESB3) of non-teaching and minor and major teaching hospitals adds another nine groups yet raises the explanatory power only one point. The overall F-value is also much higher for model 1, indicating greater explanatory power per cell.

Apparently, the costliness of treating psychiatric cases in exempt units depends more on the overall teaching intensity of the institution than on the services of psychiatrically trained residents, as evidenced by the low R^2 values in models 3 and 4. Given that a large proportion of exempt unit costs are stepped down from overhead cost centers, which are more numerous and expensive in teaching hospitals, this result is not too surprising. It also implies that unit-specific measures of teaching status can be ignored in favor of broader, hospitalwide measures. Teaching status is a far more powerful cost explainer than either bed size or discharges. (Compare model 1 with models 5 and 7.) Nor is the size of the psychiatric unit as powerful as total beds in explaining costs in the psychiatric unit. A regional urban-rural stratification is also quite inferior to one using teaching status (compare models 8 and 9 with model 1).

The middle third of table 3.1 shows the effects of collapsing nine census divisions into four regions and then further stratifying. A major teaching breakout (RESB2) within each of four regions requires only eight cells yet explains nearly as much of the cost variation as one using all nine divisions. This implies a fair degree of cost homogeneity across divisions within a census region.

The loss in explanatory power from collapsing nine census divisions into four regions is more than regained by adding either a large urban or a bed size stratifier (compare models 11 and 12 with model

1). Using discharges rather than bed size as a third stratifier remains slightly less efficient but still quite adequate (model 13).

Model 14 shows the effects of a dichotomous measure of Medicare dependency as a third stratifier along with census region and major teaching status. This model is almost statistically identical to model 1 but is slightly inferior to models 10–12.

Dispensing with any regional stratifier in favor of an MSA variant (see the bottom third of table 3.1) produces many fewer groups, somewhat lower explanatory power overall, but very high cost discrimination among cells, as evidenced by the associated F-values. Even using a simple urban-rural stratifier in lieu of four or eight regions would seem to be a viable alternative. Model 21, for instance, involves just six groups but captures essentially the same cost variation as model 1 requiring eighteen cells.

Illustrative Peer Groupings for Psychiatric Units

The analysis of variance identified several peer groupings that are statistically superior to other options. Of these, three are selected for illustrative purposes based on the following criteria: relatively high explanatory power, reasonable number of units in each cell, simple peer grouping with logically consistent rates, and peer grouping similar to that of the PPS or the original 223 cost limits.

The first peer grouping, shown in table 3.2, is based on model 1 in table 3.1. There were eighteen groups in 1987: nine census divisions with a further distinction between major teaching and all other hospitals. The grouping performs well on most of the selection criteria. There are fewer than twenty groups, and costs are generally much higher for major teaching institutions. Many of the major teaching cell sizes are small, however, and the Mountain and West/South Central divisions present definite problems given the lack of major teaching hospitals in these areas.

A tripartite way of decomposing hospitals is shown in table 3.3, corresponding to model 13 in table 3.1. Minimum cell sizes are a little larger, and costs differ systematically in the expected direction except for large hospitals in the Northeast.

Table 3.4 replaces region with an MSA locational stratifier, further decomposed by a dichotomous major teaching and bed-size classification. The result is 10 groups with fair cost discrimination. The differences in average costs between large and small urban areas, in particular, suggest a slightly more disaggregated measure of urban-rural location than under the PPS, although it would be possible

Table 3.2   Model 1: Exempt Unit Peer Groups by Nine Census Divisions and Major Teaching Classes

Census Division	Teaching Status[a]	Number of Units	Standardized Cost per Case[b]
New England	0	58	$4,957
	25	11	6,608
Middle Atlantic	0	117	4,301
	25	20	6,144
South Atlantic	0	84	4,191
	25	14	6,172
East/North Central	0	137	4,227
	25	21	6,457
East/South Central	0	29	3,937
	25	1	5,345
West/North Central	0	73	3,932
	25	8	4,120
West/South Central	0	34	4,538
	25	4	6,259
Mountain	0	40	3,816
	25	3	5,114
Pacific	0	64	3,778
	25	14	4,483

[a]For teaching status: 0 = other than major teaching; 25 = major teaching = >25 residents per 100 beds.
[b]Standardized by dividing actual Medicare covered costs per discharge by (.75 + WAGEI + .25*COLI), where WAGEI = HCFA 1984 wage index and COLI = state cost-of-living index = 1.2 for Hawaii, = 1.0 elsewhere.

statistically to combine small urban with rural units because of their similarity of costs.

Simulation of Reimbursement System Options

It is clear that no single peer grouping is superior on all evaluation criteria. Those explaining a greater proportion of cost variance often generate groups that are too small for reimbursement purposes. They also tend to produce inconsistent cost trends with respect to analytic stratifiers such as bed size.

Our results indicate that region, urban-rural location, teaching, Medicare dependency, and hospital size all affect costs. As no one peer grouping can pay on all of these characteristics simultaneously,

Table 3.3   Model 13: Exempt Unit Peer Groups by Four Census Regions, Major Teaching Status, and Discharge Size Group

Census Division	Teaching Status[a]	Discharge Size Group[b]	Number of Units	Standardized Cost per Case[c]
Northeast	0	0	150	$4,527
	0	1	25	4,507
	1	0	13	6,316
	1	1	18	6,303
North Central	0	0	161	3,242
	0	1	60	4,137
	1	0	11	4,983
	1	1	24	6,967
South	0	0	144	3,965
	0	1	32	4,287
	1	0	10	4,536
	1	1	6	5,554
West	0	0	57	3,733
	0	1	7	4,145
	1	0	7	4,069
	1	1	7	4,897

[a]For teaching status: 0 = nonmajor teaching; 25 = major teaching.
[b]For discharge size group: 0 = <16,400 discharges; 1 = ≥16,400 discharges.
[c]Standardized by dividing actual Medicare covered costs per discharge by (.75 + WAGEI + .25*COLI), where WAGEI = HCFA 1984 wage index and COLI = state cost-of-living index = 1.2 for Hawaii, = 1.0 elsewhere.

some systematic payment bias may remain when only two or three stratifiers are used. Simulation methods are used to isolate remaining biases.

In this section we combine the peer groups with two other dimensions of payment system choice: blending and risk sharing. *Blending* refers to the calculation of the target payment amount using a blend of a facility's own historical average cost and the base period average cost of the facility's peer group. The blended rate would be updated using an acceptable inflation index. *Risk sharing* refers to the use of the facility's *current* average cost in any given rate year for purposes of determining the year's end final payment. The purpose of risk sharing is to provide protection to both Medicare and the facility against short-run random shocks.

A blended payment system can be completely prospective, whereas risk sharing by the government makes the payment system partly retrospective at year's end, much like the current TEFRA system. A prospective blended system with no risk sharing provides the

Table 3.4   Model 18: Exempt Unit Peer Groups by MSA Size, Major Teaching Status, and Two Bed-size Groups

MSA Group[a]	Teaching Status[b]	Bed-size Group[c]	Number of Units	Standardized Cost per Case[d]
Large urban	0	0	335	$4,409
	0	1	34	4,388
	25	0	55	5,454
	25	1	25	7,438
Small urban	0	0	154	3,966
	0	1	7	4,416
	25	0	10	4,823
	25	1	1	6,065
Rural	0	0	107	3,824
	25	0	5	3,756

[a]Large urban = 500,000 or more population; small urban = under 500,000 population; rural = non-MSA.
[b]For teaching status: 0 = nonmajor teaching; 25 = major teaching = >25 residents per 100 beds.
[c]For bed-size group, 0 = <700 beds; 1 = ≥700 beds.
[d]Standardized by dividing actual Medicare covered costs per discharge by (.75 + WAGEI + .25*COLI), where WAGEI = HCFA 1984 wage index and COLI = state cost-of-living index = 1.2 for Hawaii, = 1.0 elsewhere.

maximum possible incentives at the margin to limit care. Risk sharing mitigates these incentives by Medicare's sharing in losses if costs exceed the target.

Simulation Criteria

One important policy criterion for choice of a payment system is the level of predicted Medicare payments. In our "basic" simulation, we use the current TEFRA target amounts that are based on original 1982 cost data. For all other simulations, we *rebase* TEFRA using 1987 costs to determine a facility's own and peer group average costs. This "rebasing" changes Medicare's costs and outlays considerably in some cases.

The form of risk sharing can also affect Medicare costs and hospital gains and losses. To evaluate the distributional effects of more symmetric risk sharing, we report estimated Medicare payments in relation to actual costs under alternative risk-sharing scenarios, but always after rebasing.

The overall fit of the payment system—how well payments relate to average costs at the individual facility level—is measured by an R^2 statistic:

$$R^2 = 1 - [\Sigma_i\Sigma_j(P_{ij} - C_{ij})^2/\Sigma_i\Sigma_j(C_{ij} - C)^2]$$

where

P_{ij} = payment to the jth facility in the ith peer group,

C_{ij} = average costs per discharge of the same facility, and

C = (weighted) national average cost.

If the payment system paid all facilities the same amount (namely, the national average cost, C), the R^2 statistic would be zero. Even a simple peer grouping system would have some positive R^2 because (presumably) the peer group payment rates would more closely resemble hospital costs than a single national average cost (used in the denominator). The R^2 calculated in this way can apply to any form of payment system once the facility's payment is calculated, including simulation alternatives that use blending and risk sharing.[4]

A simulation payment alternative can provide a good fit overall but be unfair to particular subsets of facilities by creating large predicted differences between payments and average costs. For each simulation, we report the profit rate by region, MSA size, teaching status, bed size, unit size, Medicare dependency, and disproportionate share. The *TEFRA profit rate* is defined as payment less cost divided by payment. This is multiplied by 100 to convert the profit rate to a percentage amount.

Description of the Simulation Model

The simulation model uses as data the average cost for each facility, the number of discharges, the current target amount, and the facility characteristics needed for peer grouping and descriptive analysis. The model is confined to 1987 data, ignoring supply responses. This allows the simulations to be performed at the facility level rather than at the discharge level where marginal incentives can differ at the same facility. This greatly simplifies the programming and allows the analysis of many more payment system options. The simulation also takes no account of Medicare's exception policy designed to handle cases when the target amount falls far below actual average cost.

Simulations were performed using three peer groupings numbered according to model numbers taken from table 3.1. These peer groups were chosen to illustrate the effects of different approaches on provider equity (table 3.5).

Table 3.5   Peer Groups Used for Simulations

Peer Group Model Number	Stratifiers	Number of Groups	R^2
1	Nine regions, two teaching	18	.20
16	Three MSA, two teaching	6	.16
18	Three MSA, two teaching, two bed size	10	.20

We consider three blends for all simulations: a "no blend" option where the target amount for a hospital is simply the peer group average; a second option that weights the hospital's own costs by 25 percent and the peer group average cost by 75 percent; and a third option with 50-50 blending. In all three cases, the hospital is paid a fixed amount and keeps all profits and losses (i.e., no risk sharing).

Three risk-sharing formulas (depicted in fig. 3.1) are analyzed in the simulations.

Risk Sharing Description	Line Segment on Figure 3.1
Current TEFRA	DEBC
Enhanced TEFRA	DEBGH
Symmetric TEFRA	FEBI

A fourth possibility of no risk sharing is a purely prospective blended system (see flat line ABC in fig. 3.1). Under this alternative, the facility keeps all profits when costs are below the target amount and incurs all losses above the target.

The relation between facility average cost and payment under the asymmetric current TEFRA system is represented by line DEBC. For average costs above the target, payment equals the target. Below 90 percent of the target, payments equal costs plus a 5 percent incentive payment. Between 90 and 100 percent of the target, the incentive is only 50 percent of the difference between the target and the 45° average cost line. Under an enhanced TEFRA system (line DEBGH), Medicare would share 50 percent of any losses above a 10 percent corridor. For example, if a facility had average costs 25 percent over the target amount, their losses under this enhanced TEFRA payment system would be reduced to 17.5 percent (10 percent plus one-half of the amount by which costs exceeded their target). The last risk-sharing option (symmetric TEFRA) assumes equal sharing of all gains or losses by Medicare and the hospital and effectively eliminates "corridors and kinks" around the breakeven target amount (line FEBI). In the simulations performed below, *historical* average costs (used in blending) and this year's *actual* costs (used in risk

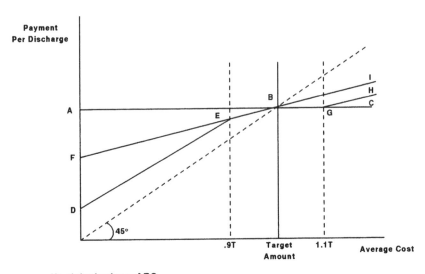

No risk sharing: ABC
Current TEFRA: DEBC
Enhanced TEFRA: DEBGH
Mixed System: FEBI

Figure 3.1   Risk-sharing options to TEFRA: *line ABC*, no risk sharing; *line DEBC*, current TEFRA; *line DEBGH*, enhanced TEFRA; *line FEBI*, mixed system (symmetric TEFRA).

sharing) are identical because we use just one year of data for simulations. Thus, the 50-50 blend is equivalent to a 50-50 symmetric system in our simulations and is not reported separately. This would not be true in an actual payment system where current costs differed from historical average costs.

For each of the three illustrative groupings, we also model a system using a 25 percent blend of own and peer group costs with enhanced TEFRA risk sharing (i.e., 50 percent loss sharing beyond the 10 percent corridor). Each simulation also compared to average TEFRA profit rates under the current system without any rebasing, blending, or risk sharing.

Simulation Results

Table 3.6 reports average profit rates for the 1987 TEFRA system using actual hospital-specific target amounts. (For all other simulations, target amounts are rebased as part of the modification of the payment system.) Under the 1987 target amounts, TEFRA payments produced an average facility Medicare TEFRA profit rate of −11.2

percent, a result of the asymmetry in the payment system and inadequate target updates. Average losses are similar across categories of facilities, with the largest discrepancies by region and teaching status. TEFRA overall in 1987 was paying 8.4 percent less than actual costs on average for these facilities. (TEFRA profit rates are even lower because payments rather than higher costs are used as a denominator.) The "fit" of TEFRA was still relatively high in 1987, as indicated by an R^2 value of .74, but was falling rapidly. In 1986, the R^2 was .84. This is a substantial one-year decline and may be a harbinger of very low correlations of costs and payments in the 1988–93 period.

The rest of table 3.6 contains the results of simulations using eighteen region-teaching peer group prospective rates based on 1987 rebased costs. The column titled "0%" blending shows the simulation results for a payment system using peer group averages, with no blending or risk sharing. Overall, the pure peer group system coincidently produces a profit rate of zero averaged across all exempt units. Each region and teaching group on which the peer grouping was based also shows a zero profit rate, which, of course, is not coincidental. This payment system produces systematic winners among small, rural hospitals. Large hospitals and those more dependent on Medicare would be big losers. Under a 1987 "rebased" system, this pure peer group system increases Medicare payments by 8.7 percent (see next to last line in table 3.6) to roughly hospital costs on average. The R^2 of .36 is much lower than the .74 in column 1 because eighteen peer group rates are much less accurate in predicting costs than rebased hospital-specific costs.

With greater blending of a hospital's own costs with its peer group rate (see columns 3–4), the fit of the payment system rises rapidly to 84 percent at the 50-50 level. The estimated losses and gains for subgroups of facilities have been moderated somewhat but remain substantial in a few cases. The overall unweighted average profit rate is no longer zero with blending. A given dollar profit produces a higher profit rate with blending because of the smaller payment denominator associated with low-cost facilities.

For the two simulations under the risk sharing heading, the target amount is based on one of eighteen rebased peer group rates with no blending of own costs. The "current TEFRA" risk-sharing approach (column 5) reintroduces asymmetry into the sharing of gains and losses, unlike column 2, which includes no such retrospective sharing. The average TEFRA margin for all exempt units falls from 0.0 to −8.2 percent because of risk-sharing asymmetry, even though rates have been "rebased." Simply rebasing and using the

Table 3.6 Average Exempt Unit Profit Rates by Nine Regions and Two Teaching Peer Groups, 1987

Simulations	Hospital's Own Cost Blend Percentage[a]				Risk-Sharing Method[b]		
	Current TEFRA	0%	25%	50%	Current TEFRA	Enhanced TEFRA	25% Blend, Enhanced TEFRA
Average profit rate (all units)	-11.2%	0.0	1.6	2.1	-8.2	-3.2	-2.2
Region							
New England	-18.9	0.0	1.5	1.9	-7.9	-2.2	-1.4
Middle Atlantic	-12.0	0.0	1.5	2.0	-8.1	-3.7	-2.6
South Atlantic	-12.5	0.0	1.8	2.4	-8.6	-2.9	-2.0
East North Central	-8.3	0.0	1.5	1.9	-8.5	-3.4	-2.3
East South Central	-11.3	0.0	1.4	1.8	-8.5	-4.2	-2.8
West North Central	-5.3	0.0	0.8	1.1	-5.9	-3.5	-2.4
West South Central	-13.4	0.0	1.3	1.7	-7.0	-2.8	-1.8
Mountain	-13.6	0.0	2.4	3.3	-11.8	-4.4	-3.0
Pacific	-15.3	0.0	2.2	2.9	-9.0	-2.5	-1.6
SMSA Size							
MSA ≥ 500,000 population	-10.3	-4.4	-1.8	-0.3	-10.4	-5.3	-4.0
MSA < 500,000 population	-12.9	7.5	7.3	6.1	-4.2	0.5	0.9
Rural	-13.2	11.8	10.9	8.8	-3.2	1.8	2.2
Teaching Involvement							
Nonteaching	-15.1	-0.1	1.5	2.0	-8.2	-3.1	-2.1
0–25 residents/100 beds	-8.0	0.0	1.5	2.0	-8.1	-3.4	-2.4
>25 residents/100 beds	-11.0	0.0	1.9	2.5	-8.5	-3.0	-2.1

Bed Size						
1–99 beds	−7.5	11.7	10.9	8.9	−3.1	2.2	2.4
100–399 beds	−12.7	1.4	2.8	3.1	−8.0	−2.4	−1.4
400–699 beds	−9.7	0.6	2.0	2.3	−7.6	−2.8	−1.9
≥700 beds	−10.3	−7.7	−4.9	−2.7	−11.1	−7.9	−6.1
Unit Size						
<30 psychiatric beds	−14.2	4.2	4.8	4.4	−6.3	−1.1	−0.5
≥30 psychiatric beds	−10.1	−1.6	0.3	1.2	−9.0	−4.0	−2.9
Medicare Dependency						
0–17 percent	−12.0	2.4	3.7	3.8	−7.1	−1.9	−1.1
>17–29 percent	−11.5	5.3	5.6	4.8	−5.3	−0.4	0.2
>29 percent	−10.5	−8.3	−4.8	−2.4	−12.8	−7.7	−6.0
Disproportionate Share						
<9 percent	−13.0	−6.0	−3.3	−1.5	−10.7	−6.5	−4.9
9–22 percent	−10.5	1.3	2.5	2.7	−7.5	−2.5	−1.6
>22 percent	−11.0	3.2	4.5	4.4	−7.4	−1.4	−0.8
Summary Statistics						
Payment relative to actual average cost	−8.4%	−0.5	−0.3	−0.2	−9.1	−5.2	−4.2
Payment relative to current TEFRA	0.0%	8.7	8.8	8.9	−0.7	3.6	4.6
R^2	.74	.36	.64	.84	.59	.78	.84

Note: The following definitions apply. *Blend percent*—Percentage of facility's own average cost that is blended with peer group average. *Current TEFRA*—Facilities keep 50 percent of profits below the target amount, up to a maximum of 5 percent of target. If costs exceed the target amount, the hospital is responsible for the entire loss. *Enhanced TEFRA*—Same risk sharing as current TEFRA when costs are below the target amount. Medicare program shares 50 percent of losses for costs 10 percent or more above target.
[a] Blending without risk sharing; 50 percent equivalent to 50–50 symmetric risk-sharing system.
[b] Risk sharing without peer group rates only as target ceilings.

eighteen peer group rates while maintaining TEFRA asymmetric profit sharing does little to ameliorate the losses shown in column 1. This is because winners cannot keep large gains to offset large losses of other facilities.

The enhanced TEFRA system, by contrast, moderates the downside risk for facilities, as many big losers are partially protected. The average loss improves from −8.2 percent to −3.2 percent, and the largest average percentage loss in any region rises from −11.8 percent to −4.4 percent using peer groups and the current TEFRA risk formula. Other big loser categories are helped by enhancing TEFRA risk sharing. This is to be expected, since the extra payments incurred by the "enhancement" are directed to the facilities with the largest losses. From the point of view of improving the fairness of the payment system, the extra 3.6 percent in rebased Medicare payments is put to the best use possible.[5]

The final column of table 3.6 uses a 25 percent blend to determine the target amount along with the more symmetric TEFRA risk sharing. The payment system retains some risk asymmetry and, even with rebasing, Medicare pays an average −4.2 percent less than average actual 1987 costs. Blending coupled with risk sharing produces the fewest deviations in average profits among subgroups of any simulation in the table. The largest winners and losers are only on the order of 6 percent, and no region loses more than 3.0 percent.

Table 3.7 shows the results using just six peer groups based on three MSA sizes and two teaching levels. Using MSA location instead of region as a basis for peer grouping reintroduces large regional winners and losers. Unless the blend rate is set very high, there would be major regional (and bed-size) redistributions. Blending and more symmetric risk sharing, however, narrow the profit differences considerably.

Table 3.8 adds a bed-size stratifier to the MSA and teaching peer groups, creating a total of twelve payment cells. A separate peer group for large hospitals (over 700 beds) corrects large losses incurred under earlier simulations but does not address the regional discrepancies in a significant way, although they are generally insignificant under the mixed system (see last column).

Simulation Results: Psychiatric Hospitals

All of the analyses thus far have been conducted on exempt psychiatric units of general acute hospitals. Psychiatric hospitals present special problems because of systematic differences in beneficiary coverage. Because of the 190-day coverage limitation and nonreporting of uncovered days and costs after coverage is exhausted, Medicare discharges from public facilities appear relatively inexpensive. For example, based on data from our 1986–87 HCFA Medicare file, average (covered) costs per discharge in private psychiatric hospitals are several hundred dollars greater than in public hospitals (e.g., $4,831 versus $3,923) (Cromwell, Harrow, and McGuire 1990). If one were to develop a set of peer groups that pooled public and private psychiatric hospitals with exempt units, the resulting payment rates would systematically underpay the latter two kinds of facilities and inadvertently reimburse public hospitals for uncovered services. Neither can peer groups based on per diems (as was suggested by Frank and Lave 1985) adequately address this problem because costs per covered day also differ systematically between the private and public hospitals (i.e., $294 versus $213, respectively, in 1987). However, per discharge peer grouping of psychiatric hospitals, combined with adequate blending and risk sharing, can produce an equitable payment system without setting distinct rates by ownership type.

Results in table 3.9 are based on eighteen region-teaching peer groups using rebased 1986 costs (1987 data were inadequate for the evaluation of psychiatric hospitals). Teaching and Medicare share categories have been adjusted to reflect more accurately the distribution of psychiatric hospitals. (Coincidentally, the revised Medicare dependency ranges for psychiatric hospitals are identical to those for disproportionate share for exempt units.) The first column, as in the previous simulation tables, assumes no blending or risk sharing, implying that hospitals incur all losses and enjoy all gains from being in one of the eighteen peer groups. The systematic payment bias by ownership type is reflected in the large positive profit rate for public hospitals, 13.4 percent on average, versus a loss averaging 8.6 percent in private institutions. Other groups exhibit some gains or losses as well (e.g., 400- to 700-bed hospitals), but no systematic relationship by stratifier is evident.

If current asymmetric TEFRA payment rules were applied to *rebased* 1986 costs without peer groups, the average loss would be 12.9 percent. This does not imply that hospitals as a group would do worse after rebasing. Their payments, in fact, would increase, but compared to actual 1986 costs they would still lose 12.9 percent on average because of asymmetric risk sharing. Under this system, no hospital group would gain on average. Both public and private hospitals would lose, and the average loss among private hospitals would be more than double that among public hospitals.

The third column of table 3.9 gives expected profit rates if a 25–75 percent blend of rebased hospital costs and the peer group target

Table 3.7 Average Exempt Unit Profit Rates by Three MSA Size and Two Teaching Peer Groups, 1987

Simulations	Hospital's Own Cost Blend Percentage[a]				Risk-Sharing Method[b]		
	Current TEFRA	0%	25%	50%	Current TEFRA	Enhanced TEFRA	25% Blend, Enhanced TEFRA
Average profit rate (all units)	−11.2%	0.0	1.6	2.1	−8.3	−3.1	−2.1
Region							
New England	−18.9	−15.0	−9.0	−4.9	−18.7	−10.2	−8.0
Middle Atlantic	−12.0	−2.3	−0.2	0.9	−9.7	−5.0	−3.5
South Atlantic	−12.5	−3.8	−1.1	0.3	−10.9	−5.0	−3.8
East North Central	−8.3	−2.6	−0.4	0.7	−10.0	−4.4	−3.2
East South Central	−11.3	0.6	1.8	2.1	−7.6	−3.3	−2.3
West North Central	−5.3	7.7	6.7	5.1	−1.2	1.6	1.7
West South Central	−13.4	−6.4	−3.3	−1.3	−11.5	−5.7	−4.3
Mountain	−13.6	12.0	11.1	9.2	−2.6	2.0	2.3
Pacific	−15.3	11.2	10.5	8.6	−2.7	2.6	2.7
SMSA Size							
MSA ≥ 500,000 population	−10.3	0.0	1.5	1.9	−7.9	−3.0	−2.1
MSA < 500,000 population	−12.9	0.0	1.9	2.5	−9.2	−3.2	−2.1
Rural	−13.2	0.0	1.8	2.4	−9.5	−3.3	−2.2
Teaching Involvement							
Nonteaching	−15.1	−1.0	0.9	1.7	−9.0	−3.2	−2.3
0–25 residents/100 beds	−8.0	0.9	2.0	2.3	−7.4	−2.8	−1.8
>25 residents/100 beds	−11.0	0.0	2.0	2.8	−9.8	−3.9	−2.7

	(1)	(2)	(3)	(4)	(5)	(6)
Bed Size						
1–99 beds	−7.5	7.0	7.4	6.5	−5.2	0.4
100–399 beds	−12.7	1.2	2.7	3.0	−8.3	−1.4
400–699 beds	−9.7	1.5	2.5	2.7	−7.0	−1.6
≥700 beds	−10.3	−8.0	−4.9	−2.6	−12.0	−6.0
Unit Size						
<30 psychiatric beds	−14.2	1.0	2.5	2.8	−8.2	−1.7
≥30 psychiatric beds	−10.1	−0.4	1.3	1.9	−8.4	−2.3
Medicare Dependency						
0–17 percent	−12.0	3.1	4.4	4.5	−7.7	−1.1
>17–29 percent	−11.5	3.2	4.0	3.8	−6.6	−0.6
>29 percent	−10.5	−5.7	−2.9	−1.1	−11.1	−4.7
Disproportionate Share						
<9 percent	−13.0	−4.4	−2.0	−0.6	−9.8	−3.9
9–22 percent	−10.5	0.3	1.8	2.2	−8.1	−1.8
>22 percent	−11.0	3.8	4.8	4.7	−7.4	−1.0
Summary Statistics						
Payment relative to actual average cost	−8.4%	0.1	0.1	0.0	−9.0	−4.0
Payment relative to current TEFRA	0.0%	9.3	9.3	9.2	−0.7	3.8
R^2	.74	.31	.61	.83	.59	.84

Note: For definitions, see note to Table 3.6.

[a] Blending without risk sharing; 50 percent equivalent to 50–50 symmetric risk-sharing system.

[b] Risk sharing without peer group rates only as target ceilings.

Table 3.8 Average Exempt Unit Profit Rates by Three MSA Size, Two Teaching, and Two Bed-Size Peer Groups, 1987

Simulations	Current TEFRA	Hospital's Own Cost Blend Percentage[a]			Current TEFRA	Risk-Sharing Method[b]	25% Blend, Enhanced TEFRA
		0%	25%	50%		Enhanced TEFRA	
Average profit rate (all units)	−11.2%	0.0	1.5	2.0	−8.1	−3.0	−2.0
Region							
New England	−18.9	−17.0	−10.5	−5.9	−20.2	−11.9	−9.3
Middle Atlantic	−12.0	−2.0	0.0	1.1	−9.7	−4.9	−3.5
South Atlantic	−12.5	−2.4	−0.2	0.9	−9.6	−3.9	−2.9
East North Central	−8.3	−2.5	−0.5	0.6	−9.6	−4.3	−3.1
East South Central	−11.3	2.5	2.9	2.7	−5.6	−2.5	−1.4
West North Central	−5.3	7.8	6.7	5.1	−1.1	1.9	1.9
West South Central	−13.4	−5.9	−3.0	−1.2	−10.7	−5.3	−4.0
Mountain	−13.6	9.6	9.3	7.8	−4.3	0.5	1.1
Pacific	−15.3	9.7	9.3	7.7	−3.4	2.3	2.5
SMSA Size							
MSA ≥ 500,000 population	−10.3	0.0	1.4	1.8	−7.6	−2.9	−2.0
MSA < 500,000 population	−12.9	0.0	1.9	2.4	−9.0	−3.0	−2.0
Rural	−13.2	0.0	1.8	2.4	−9.5	−3.3	−2.2
Teaching Involvement							
Nonteaching	−15.1	−0.9	1.0	1.7	−9.0	−3.1	−2.2
0–25 residents/100 beds	−8.0	0.8	2.0	2.2	−7.4	−2.9	−1.8
>25 residents/100 beds	−11.0	0.0	1.6	2.2	−8.2	−3.1	−2.1

Bed Size						
1–99 beds	−7.5	7.0	7.4	6.5	−5.1	0.0	0.4
100–399 beds	−12.7	0.1	1.9	2.4	−8.9	−2.7	−1.8
400–699 beds	−9.7	−0.6	1.0	1.6	−8.3	−3.5	−2.4
≥700 beds	−10.3	0.0	0.7	1.0	−5.5	−3.1	−2.2
Unit Size						
<30 psychiatric beds	−14.2	0.0	1.8	2.3	−8.9	−3.2	−2.2
≥30 psychiatric beds	−10.1	−0.0	1.5	1.9	−7.8	−2.9	−2.0
Medicare Dependency						
0–17 percent	−12.0	2.2	3.8	4.0	−8.3	−2.0	−1.2
>17–29 percent	−11.5	3.4	4.1	3.8	−6.1	−1.2	−0.5
>29 percent	−10.5	−5.7	−2.9	−1.1	−10.9	−5.9	−4.5
Disproportionate Share						
<9 percent	−13.0	−4.4	−2.1	−0.6	−9.7	−5.5	−4.0
9–22 percent	−10.5	0.5	1.9	2.2	−7.8	−2.5	−1.6
>22 percent	−11.0	3.4	4.4	4.3	−7.1	−1.7	−0.9
Summary Statistics						
Payment relative to actual average cost	−8.4%	0.1	0.1	0.0	−8.6	−4.6	−3.8
Payment relative to current TEFRA	0.0%	9.3	9.3	9.2	−0.2	4.1	5.1
R^2	.74	.37	.65	.84	.61	.78	.85

Note: For definitions, see note to Table 3.6.
[a]Blending without risk sharing; 50 percent equivalent to 50–50 symmetric risk-sharing system.
[b]Risk sharing without peer group rates only as target ceilings.

Table 3.9   Average Psychiatric Hospital Profit Rates
by Nine Region and Two Teaching Peer Groups, 1986

Simulations	No Blend, No Risk Sharing	Current TEFRA Risk Sharing	25% Blend and Enhanced TEFRA Risk Sharing
Average profit rate (all units)	0.0%	−12.9%	−2.4%
Region			
New England	0.0	−14.9	−1.8
Middle Atlantic	0.0	−10.7	−3.7
South Atlantic	0.0	−13.3	−2.2
East North Central	0.0	−21.9	−2.1
East South Central	0.0	−8.1	−3.1
West North Central	0.0	−11.8	−0.8
West South Central	0.0	−11.8	−2.5
Mountain	0.0	−13.0	−0.5
Pacific	0.0	−11.2	−3.1
SMSA Size			
MSA ≥ 500,000 population	1.0	−12.5	−2.3
MSA < 500,000 population	−0.9	−12.2	−2.9
Rural	−2.8	−15.8	−2.1
Teaching Involvement			
Nonteaching	0.5	−12.6	−2.4
0–8.5 residents/100 beds	−3.2	−16.0	−3.1
>8.5 residents/100 beds	0.0	−9.2	−1.1
Bed Size			
1–99 beds	8.8	−6.6	1.2
100–399 beds	−3.3	−14.3	−3.8
400–699 beds	−15.6	−29.3	−9.1
>700 beds	2.1	−15.5	−1.5
Facility Type			
Private psychiatric hospital	13.4	−7.5	2.7
Public psychiatric hospital	−8.6	−16.3	−5.7
Medicare Dependency			
<9 percent	−3.0	−19.5	−2.4
9–22 percent	4.8	−10.7	−0.5
>22 percent	−5.9	−14.1	−5.2
Summary Statistics			
Payment relative to actual average cost	0.2%	−14.2%	−6.5%
Payment relative to current TEFRA	9.4	−6.3	2.1
R^2	.30	.63	.87

Source: Data from 1985–87 TEFRA facility file.
Note: All statistics are based on payment rates rebased from 1982–83 to 1986.

was used, along with an enhanced TEFRA system that had the government sharing 50-50 in any losses that were 10 percent above the target amount (as well as sharing in any gains as currently designed). As with the exempt units, this arrangement drastically reduces losses (i.e., −2.4 percent on average). Its effects (relative to a pure

PPS system represented in column 1) are largest by facility owner-ship. Under a PPS-like system with eighteen peer groups, the 13.4 percent average for public hospitals would be reduced to a modest 2.7 percent under the revised system. Average losses in private hospitals, although still negative, would improve to −5.7 percent, or only one-third of the losses that could be expected after rebasing. Slight changes in the blending or risk sharing arrangements could elimi-nate nearly all of the systematic difference, if so desired.

Summary and Conclusions

The TEFRA system, with certain modifications, can become a more efficient and equitable payment system for psychiatric facilities. Ab-sent a way of directly measuring case-mix severity, we recommend that payment be based on a global per case rate. This rate would be a blend of each hospital's base period costs per case and its associated peer group's average costs. This prospective payment would be ad-justed at year's end for incurred gains or losses.

The current TEFRA risk-sharing formula should not be used with a simple blend of own costs and peer group rates for calculating the prospective payment. A highly asymmetric payment system re-quires a close fit between the target amount and the actual average costs of a facility. Use of peer group averages in place of a facility's own average costs trended forward can introduce very large losses because of the asymmetry.

Asymmetry in the risk-sharing formula can be maintained with an "enhanced" TEFRA system including some risk sharing on the loss side. Particularly when used in combination with a light (0.25) blend of a hospital's rebased costs in determining the prospective component of the payment, a 50-50 sharing of losses beyond a 10 percent corridor sharply improves the position of financially dis-tressed facilities.

A separate system of per case peer groupings, with blending and risk sharing, is feasible for public and private psychiatric hospitals as well, with only small expected redistributions from private to pub-lic facilities.

At a technical level, a regional and teaching stratifier should be part of any peer group scheme because of systematic cost differences. The HCFA area wage index is a powerful explainer of geographic cost differences and should be used first to adjust costs.

On the basis of 1987 data, rebasing TEFRA, along with other modifications to the payment system, is likely to increase Medicare payments by 4 to 8 percent, depending on the payment system chosen. Program outlays are predicted to rise 2–3 points per year because of the failure of PPS updates to cover cost inflation in psychiatric facilities.

Acknowledgments

This research was supported under contract no. HHS-100-0037 from the assistant secretary for planning and evaluation, Department of Health and Human Services (DHHS). The views and opinions in this chapter are the authors' and no endorsement of DHHS or HCFA is intended or should be inferred.

Notes

1. The impact of TEFRA on psychiatric facilities is described in detail by Cromwell, Harrow, and McGuire (1990).

2. The problem of fairness is not confined to patients with diagnoses treated at the specialized facilities. DRGs are an imperfect adjustor for per case differences in costs across the range of diagnoses. (See Prospective Payment Assessment Commission 1989, 136–37.)

3. Newhouse and Bryne (1988) recently pointed out that the overall LOS in Medicare has fallen less than the LOS for PPS-paid patients because of a shift of expensive patients to exempt facilities paid under cost-based TEFRA.

4. The R^2 statistic used in this section differs from the R^2 used in the earlier section in one important way. The sums of squares used here are based on unadjusted actual costs and payments, including differences due to area wages.

5. Ellis and McGuire (1988) and Keeler, Carter, and Trude (1988) argued on the basis of analogies to insurance design that targeting "outlier payments" to losing hospitals and losing cases is the best use of these dollars. The enhancement of TEFRA proposed here is analogous to the hospital-level outlier policy proposed in Ellis and McGuire (1988).

References

Cromwell, Jerry, Brooke Harrow, and Thomas McGuire. 1990. *TEFRA Psychiatric Hospital and Unit Peer Group and Case Outlier Analyses*. Report performed under Contract No. HHS 100-88-0037, DHHS/ASPE, January 19.

Ellis, Randall P., and Thomas G. McGuire. 1988. "Insurance Principles and the Design of Prospective Payment Systems." *Journal of Health Economics* 7:215–37.

English, Joseph T., Steven S. Sharfstein, Boris Astrachan, Donald J. Scherl, and Irvin L. Muszynsl. 1986. "Diagnosis-related Groups and General Hospital Psychiatry: The APA Study." *American Journal of Psychiatry* 143:131–39.

Frank, Richard G., and Judith R. Lave. 1986. "Per Case Prospective Payment for Psychiatric Inpatients: An Assessment and an Alternative." *Journal of Health Politics, Policy and Law* 11:83–96.

Frank, Richard G., Judith R. Lave, Carl A. Taube, Agnes Rupp, and Howard H. Goldman. 1987. "The Impact of Medicare's Prospective Payment System on Psychiatric Patients Treated in Scatter Beds." In Thomas G. McGuire and Richard Scheffler (eds.): *Reimbursement Issues in Economics and Mental Health*, pp. 1–21. Vol. 7 of *Advances in Health Economics and Health Services Research*. Greenwich, Conn.: JAI Press.

Freiman, Marc P., Randall Ellis, and Thomas McGuire. 1989. "Provider Response to Medicare's PPS: Reductions in Length of Stay for Psychiatric Patients Treated in Scatter Beds." *Inquiry* 26:192–201.

Freiman, Marc P., Thomas McGuire, Randall Ellis, Janet B. Mitchell, Brooke S. Harrow, Ashley C. Stone, Anne M. Hendricks, and Carol Carter. 1988. *An Analysis of Options for Including Psychiatric Inpatient Settings in a Prospective Payment System*. Report performed under Contract No. NIMH-278-86-002(BA), Health Economics Research.

Freiman, Marc P., Janet B. Mitchell, and Margo L. Rosenbach. 1987. "An Analysis of DRG-based Reimbursement for Psychiatric Admissions to General Hospitals." *American Journal of Psychiatry* 144:603–9.

Guterman, Stuart, Paul W. Eggers, Gerald Riley, Timothy Greene, and Sherry A. Terrell. 1988. "The First Three Years of Medicare Prospective Payment: An Overview." *Health Care Financing Review* 9, no. 3:67–82.

Jencks, Stephen, Alan Dobson, Patricia Willis, and Patrice Feinstein. 1984. "Evaluating and Improving the Measurement of Hospital Case Mix." *Health Care Financing Review, Annual Supplement*, pp. 1–12.

Keeler, Emmett B., Grace M. Carter, and Sally Trude. 1988. "Insurance Aspects of DRG Outlier Payments." *Journal of Health Economics* 7:193–214.

Lave, Judith R., and Richard G. Frank. 1988. "Factors Affecting Medicaid Patient's Length of Stay in Psychiatry Units." *Health Care Financing Review* 10, no. 2:57–66.

McGuire, Thomas G., B. Dickey, G. Shively, and I. Strumwasser. 1987. "Differences in Resource Use and Cost among Facilities Treating Alcohol, Drug Abuse and Mental Disorders: Implications for the Design of Prospective Payment Systems." *American Journal of Psychiatry* 144:616–20.

Newhouse, Joseph P., and Daniel Byrne. 1988. "Did Medicare's Prospective Payment System Cause Length of Stay to Fall?" *Journal of Health Economics* 7:413–16.

Prospective Payment Assessment Commission. 1989. *Medicare Prospective Payment and the American Health Care System: Report to the Congress*. Washington, D.C., June.

Taube, Carl A., Eun Sul Lee, and Ronald N. Forthofer. 1984. "DRGs in Psychiatry: An Empirical Evaluation." *Medical Care* 22:597–610.

4

Do Public Mental Health Hospitals Crowd Out Care for Indigent Psychiatric Patients in Nonprofit General Hospitals?

Richard G. Frank, Ph.D.,
and David S. Salkever, Ph.D.

The problem of medical indigency received a great deal of national attention during the latter part of the 1980s (Congressional Research Service 1988). The problem has been, and continues to be, especially acute for individuals with mental disorders. For example, in 1986, 9.5 percent of psychiatric patients discharged from short-stay U.S. hospitals had no insurance, compared with 7.6 percent of all patients (National Center for Health Statistics 1987). Psychiatric patients accounted for 5.8 percent of all uninsured discharges and 9.3 percent of uncollected charges from short-stay U.S. hospitals in 1983, while accounting for about 4.4 percent of all discharges from short-stay hospitals (Sloan, Valvona, and Mullner 1986).

The problem of medical indigency among those with mental illness has historically been addressed through the differentiation of the mental health service system. A large public mental health care system has served as the "provider of last resort," allowing other providers to assume rather modest responsibilities for indigent psychiatric patients (Goldman, Taube, and Jencks 1987). In spite of a 69 percent reduction in state mental hospital beds over the past twenty years, the public hospital continues to be a major source for indigent psychiatric care. In 1985, 49.6 percent of all specialty psychiatric beds were in public (nonfederal) psychiatric hospitals (NIMH 1987).[1] These hospitals provide the bulk of care to uninsured mentally ill persons. Patients with no insurance comprise roughly 61 percent of the approximately 370,000 patients admitted to state mental hospitals (NIMH 1985).

Public mental hospital systems have continued to shrink, as have the number of beds in public general hospitals, another provider of indigent psychiatric care. These trends have led to renewed debate regarding (1) the desirability of further reducing the size of public psychiatric hospital systems and (2) the appropriate role for the public mental hospital if it is to continue to exist (Mechanic and Rochefort 1990).

The literature offers two strong normative views of the differentiation of the mental health system. One view is that the differentiation of the system is undesirable because it creates a "two-class" system of care in which the poor and uninsured get minimal custodial care and the more economically advantaged get relatively intensive mental health treatment (see Brown 1985 for a review of these issues).[2] A second view of the differentiation of the mental health system is that it is based in part on a specialization of providers and may in fact result in greater access to a range of treatments than would a system where little or no differentiation was present (Goldman, Taube, and Jencks 1987).

In this chapter we seek to explore one aspect of the rationale for the differentiation of the mental health service system: the influence that the presence of a public mental hospital exerts on the supply of indigent psychiatric care by general hospitals. This parallels work of economists who study charitable donations and have estimated the extent to which public spending "crowds out" private charitable activity.[3] The results of our empirical analysis suggest that the degree of crowding out of indigent psychiatric care by public mental hospitals is modest. We explore the importance of specialization by the public sector in treating certain types of difficult patients as a reason for the weak crowding-out results.

A Model of Crowding Out

In this model based on "purely altruistic" motives,[4] the nonprofit general hospital is assumed to maximize the objective function,

$$U = U(R, N), \tag{4.1}$$

whose two arguments are net revenues (R) and the amount of need among the medically indigent psychiatric patients that is unmet (N), where $U_R > 0$ and $U_N < 0$. The disutility associated with N indicates that the nonprofit hospital is concerned with a "public bad," unmet need for inpatient psychiatric care. Unmet need might encompass some of the homeless mentally ill persons, incarcerated mentally ill persons, and some persons living in the community who are disruptive and potentially dangerous. This formulation of the objective function is referred to as "purely" altruistic in N because the hospital cares about only the level of unmet need in the community, regardless of which hospital gets "credit" for serving indigent psychiatric patients. Hospital net revenue is defined as the sum of the endowment income (E)[5] and revenues stemming from the sale of services, $PQ + rD$, where P is the fixed price of hospital care,[6] Q is the number of paying patients, r is the subsidy per indigent patient, and D is the number of indigent psychiatric cases treated. The hospital's cost function is $C = C(Q + D)$. The net revenue function is defined as

$$R = PQ + rD + E - C(Q + D). \tag{4.2}$$

The level of unmet need in the community (N) is equal to the total need (T) minus the amount of charity care provided by other types of hospitals. N is thus

$$N = T - D - H - G, \tag{4.3}$$

where H is the level of charity psychiatric care provided by other nonprofit hospitals, G is the level provided by public psychiatric hospitals, and D is the amount of charity psychiatric care provided by the hospital of interest. We adopt the Nash-Cournot assumption that each hospital chooses the optimal amount of charity psychiatric care given the charity care provided by other hospitals. The hospital is assumed to choose Q and D to maximize utility. Substituting equations (4.3) and (4.2) into equation (4.1) allows us to rewrite the objective function as

$$U = U[PQ + rD + E - C(Q + D), (T - D - H - G)]. \tag{4.1'}$$

The first-order conditions for a maximum with respect to Q and D are

$$U_D = U_R (r - C_D) - U_N = 0 \tag{4.4}$$

and

$$U_Q = U_Q (P - C_Q) = 0. \tag{4.5}$$

Equation (4.4) indicates that at the optimum the hospital will admit indigent psychiatric patients up to the point where the financial loss is just balanced, in utility terms, by the marginal reduction in unmet need. Equation (4.5) indicates that private admissions will be expanded until marginal cost equals price.

The second-order conditions for a maximum of U are $U_{QQ} < 0$, $U_{DD} < 0$, and $U_{QQ} U_{DD} - U_{DQ}^2 > 0$. These conditions are satisfied when

$$U_{NN} - 2(r - C_D) U_{NR} + (r - C_D)^2 U_{RR} < 0. \tag{4.6}$$

Inequality (4.6) follows from the convexity of the indifference curves of $U(R, N)$ and the first-order condition given in equation (4.4). Our main interest in this research is in the effects of changes in G on equilibrium values of D. An expression for this is derived by differentiation of the first-order conditions.

$$dD/dE = \{U_R C_{DD}[U_{RR} \cdot (r - P) - U_{NR}]\}/|J| \tag{4.7}$$

Equation (4.7) shows the pure income effect on D. That is, equation (4.7) represents the influence of an increase in exogenous endowment income on the supply of charity psychiatric care.

Equation (4.8) allows us to examine the conditions under which public mental hospital care crowds out the provision of charity psychiatric care at private nonprofit general hospitals.

$$dD/dG = \{U_R C_{DD}[U_{RN} \cdot (P - r) + U_{NN}]\}/|J| \tag{4.8}$$

We can make use of inequality (4.6) and equation (4.8) to derive a relationship between the crowding-out and the income effects:

$$dD/dG + (r - C_D) \, dD/dE = -1 \tag{4.9}$$

Note that if income effects are 0 ($dD/dE = 0$), then crowding out will be complete ($dD/dG = -1$). Equation (4.9) further states that dD/dG will be negative unless $dD/dE > [1/(C_D - r)]$.[7] Therefore, dD/dG will be negative unless an increase in the endowment income produces an equal or larger increase in the provision (in dollar terms) of indigent psychiatric care. Only large positive income effects are inconsistent with crowding out.[8,9]

An Empirical Test of the Basic Model

Our empirical strategy for testing the crowding-out hypothesis under purely altruistic preferences is to examine both direct measures of crowding out (variables representing dD/dG and dD/dH) and an indirect indicator, a variable representing dD/dE.

Data

To test for the presence of a crowding-out effect, we analyzed data for fifty voluntary general hospitals in the state of Maryland during the years 1980–84. Table 4.1 presents definitions and descriptive statistics for the variables used in this study. The dependent variable in the purely altruistic crowding-out model is the number of major diagnostic category (MDC) 19 discharges that were classified as either self-

Table 4.1   Variable Names, Definitions, and Means

Variable	Definition	Mean
Dependent *Variable*		
$\sqrt{\text{IPSYCS}}$	Square root of annual number of MDC19 self-pay and charity inpatient	3.69
IPSYCS	Annual number of MDC19 self-pay and charity inpatient discharges	24.53
LNIPSYCS	Logarithm of 1 + annual number of MDC19 self-pay and charity inpatient discharges	2.221
Explanatory *Variable*		
PUBADMAL	Estimated state mental hospital uncompensated inpatient admissions of county residents	657.4
PRVIPCS	Equivalent admissions from private psychiatric hospitals within the county	2.514
GHIPCS	Annual number of MDC19 self-pay and charity inpatient discharges from other general hospitals within the county	163.5
AFDC	Monthly number (for February) of AFDC recipients within the county	
AGE65	Number of persons with age $\geq$ 65 in the county	48,323
REVCASE	Gross patient revenue per equivalent admission	2,840
NNINC	Nonoperating income of the hospitals	655,477
OWNBEDSP	Psychiatric unit beds within the hospital	11.70
OWNNPBED	All nonpsychiatric beds within the hospital	278.66
TEACH	1 if hospital has certified residency program, 0 otherwise	.144
SSI	Number of nonaged SSI recipients in county	5,652
INCOME	Median household income in county	21,968
RNCOST	General duty RN wage plus benefits per hour	9.15
TXX	Dummy variable for year 19xx (1981–84)	

pay or charity cases.[10] We report three specifications of the dependent variable: (1) the number of MDC19 charity cases, (2) the logarithm plus one of the number of MDC19 charity cases, and (3) the square root of the number of charity cases. These measures will serve to underestimate the amount of psychiatric charity care supplied by general hospitals, since the measure pertains to only inpatient cases. Unfortunately, it is not possible to separate outpatient uncompensated psychiatric care from either hospital financial records or discharge abstract data.

Separate crowding-out regressors are included for (1) other general hospitals in the same county (GHIPCS), (2) private psychiatric specialty hospitals in the same county (PRVIPCS), and (3) state psychiatric hospitals (PUBADMAL). The first of these is measured as the number of psychiatric (MDC19) discharges with no insurance from other general hospitals in the same county. Uncompensated care provided by private psychiatric hospitals in the county is measured by their reported dollar volume of uncompensated care divided by their average gross patient revenue per case.[11] To obtain a measure of public uncompensated psychiatric care, we first computed 65 percent of the annual admissions to each of the state psychiatric hospitals. (The 65 percent figure for uncompensated care was based on national survey estimates.) We then allocated each of these figures among the counties within each state hospital's catchment area on the basis of the estimated number of persons with no insurance in each county.

Four variables were used to proxy for the level of need (T) in each county: the number of nonaged individuals receiving Supplemental Security Income (SSI), the number of individuals over age 65 (AGE65), the number of recipients of Aid to Families with Dependent Children (AFDC), and the median household income (INCOME). The rationale for including the SSI population is that those with severe and persistent mental disabilities who are poor become eligible for SSI. SSI enrollees are categorically eligible for Medicaid. Thus, where SSI enrollments are high, *ceteris paribus,* the need for charity psychiatric care should be lower. Elderly people are very low users of any psychiatric care and are covered by Medicare for hospital treatment. Larger percentages of elderly residents in a county might be expected to reduce the need for charity psychiatric care. The number of AFDC recipients measures the poor population that has access to Medicaid coverage. This variable is posited to be negatively related to the number of uninsured, holding other factors constant. Median household income is intended to proxy for the level of need in a community. Household income has been shown to be strongly related to insurance coverage.

The net nonoperating income (NNINC) of each hospital was obtained from hospital financial statements filed with the HSCRC. The price paid by paying customers (P) was measured by gross patient revenue per equivalent admissions (REVCASE). This measure will slightly overestimate the average price figure, since some patients (e.g., Blue Cross enrollees) receive modest discounts (on the order of 9 percent). The subsidy (r) is assumed to be 0 for all hospitals.[12]

Several variables were included in the regression models to control for variations in cost conditions among hospitals. The wage plus fringe benefits per hour of general duty nurses (RNCOST) is the indicator of labor costs. We also include the number of designated psychiatric beds and the number of nonpsychiatric beds in each general hospital. One reason for these inclusions is that the size of the hospital and its psychiatric unit is likely to affect the marginal cost of uncompensated cases. Moreover, the commitment to the care of psychiatric cases as measured by the number of psychiatric beds may reflect the preferences of the hospital. For example, general hospitals with large psychiatric units are more visible and therefore may assume a more central role in the community mental health system than hospitals with lesser commitments to mental health care. To allow for the differences in preferences between teaching and non-teaching facilities, we include a dummy variable to denote the presence of a residency program approved by the American Medical Association.

Estimation

In this model, the strategy for estimating the supply of charity care consisted of several steps. In view of the possibility of hospital-specific, temporally stable omitted factors in the pooled data, we estimated fixed effects and variance components models (Fuller and Battese 1974). We tested the variance components formulation against the fixed effects model using a Hausman (1978) test. We rejected the consistency of the variance components estimates. The χ^2 statistic for the Hausman test was 43.3. Table 4.2, therefore, includes only fixed effects estimates.

We were also concerned with the possibility that our measures of H and G (general hospital, private psychiatric hospital, and public mental hospital indigent cases) were endogenous because, in part, of the presence of unmeasured factors representing the demand for charity psychiatric care. We tested the degree to which our measures of H and G were exogenous using a Wu (1973) test. Using this test, we failed to reject exogeneity of the measures of H and G (F test = 0.15). Thus, the H and G measures are treated as exogenous in all specifications.[13]

Results

Table 4.2 presents five fixed effects specifications of the charity care supply functions. The estimates for our measures of H and G are virtually all significantly different from 0 at the 0.01 level. The significant negative coefficient for the measure of G (PUBADMAL) indicates a crowding out of general hospital indigent psychiatric care by public mental hospitals. The effect of an additional public hospital indigent admission is to reduce the general hospital supply by between 0.04 and 0.05 cases.

One measure of H, the number of indigent psychiatric dis-

Table 4.2   Regression Results, Crowding-out Model

Variable	LNIPSYCS	LNIPSYCS	LNIPSYS	$\sqrt{\text{IPSYCS}}$	IPSYCS
PUBADMAL	−0.0017	−0.0017	−0.0015	−0.0035	−0.054
	(3.62)	(3.41)	(3.57)	(2.99)	(2.95)
PRIVPCS	0.045	0.045	0.030	0.125	2.477
	(2.44)	(2.48)	(1.92)	(2.89)	(3.73)
GHIPCS	−0.004	−0.004	−0.004	−0.012	−0.179
	(4.11)	(4.14)	(4.10)	(5.38)	(4.89)
REVCASE	−0.0003	−0.0003	−0.0002	−0.0006	−0.009
	(1.17)	(1.17)	(0.98)	(1.14)	(1.04)
AGE65	−0.0001	−0.0001	—	−0.0001	—
	(1.49)	(1.58)	—	(0.18)	—
AFDC	−0.0001	−0.0001	—	−0.0001	—
	(1.07)	(0.95)	—	(1.96)	—
NNINC	5.92×10^{-8}	5.77×10^{-8}	4.13×10^{-8}	1.41×10^{-7}	3.30×10^{-7}
	(0.83)	(0.80)	(0.58)	(0.81)	(0.10)
OWNBEDSP	0.006	0.006	0.006	0.027	0.773
	(0.91)	(0.89)	(0.93)	(1.79)	(2.96)
OWNNPBED	−0.0001	−0.0001	−0.0001	−0.0049	−0.115
	(0.09)	(0.09)	(0.05)	(1.34)	(1.79)
TEACH	0.365	0.371	0.401	1.143	13.280
	(1.83)	(1.86)	(2.26)	(2.36)	(1.75)
SSI	−0.0005	−0.0005	−0.0011	−0.0012	−0.040
	(0.86)	(0.86)	(2.77)	(0.93)	(2.34)
INCOME	−0.001	−0.0001	−0.0001	−0.0002	−0.006
	(1.78)	(1.84)	(2.39)	(2.35)	(3.38)
RNCOST	—	0.216	—	—	—
	—	(0.57)	—	—	—
T1	0.361	0.214	0.369	1.116	16.65
	(2.18)	(0.70)	(2.26)	(2.77)	(2.40)
T2	0.641	0.312	0.687	1.752	34.19
	(2.26)	(0.49)	(2.44)	(2.54)	(2.86)
T3	1.193	0.746	1.190	3.294	64.61
	(0.40)	(0.85)	(2.97)	(3.35)	(3.80)
T4	1.445	0.916	1.579	3.857	77.04
	(0.479)	(0.88)	(3.38)	(3.31)	(3.88)
Intercept	5.255	4.094	5.26	10.77	172.92
	(4.87)	(1.78)	(5.19)	(4.10)	(4.01)
N			250		
R^2	0.89	0.89	0.89	0.87	0.78
F	23.51	23.07	24.04	19.42	10.40

Note: The t statistics are in parentheses, and forty-nine hospital dummy variables are included.

charges from other general hospitals (GHIPCS), also had a negative coefficient and was significant. An increase in indigent supply by all other general hospitals reduces the supply from any given general hospital by roughly 0.18 cases.

The coefficient for the measure of indigent care supplied by private psychiatric hospitals is positive and significant. This indicates that an increase in the supply of indigent care by private psychiatric hospitals leads to increased numbers of indigent cases treated by general hospitals. One explanation for this is a referral or so-called dumping phenomenon. Another possibility is that there remain some unmeasured demand factors, even after the fixed effects have been taken into account. This latter explanation seems somewhat less plausible when considered in conjunction with the Wu test result.

The coefficient estimates for dD/dE (hospital nonoperating income) were positive, small, and not significantly different from 0. This indicates an income effect that is essentially 0. Since the crowding-out effects reported above are also small, our results are inconsistent with the conditions set out in equation (4.9). As we pointed out above, this result argues against the pure altruism formulation of hospital preferences.

The proxies for T are generally significant and in the expected direction. The coefficient estimate for the median income variable is especially strong. The significance of the SSI variable suggests that this entitlement program serves to reduce medical indigency among the mentally ill.

The number of psychiatric beds in a hospital was estimated to have a positive but not significant effect on the supply of charity psychiatric care in the semilog specifications. Where the square root and linear specifications were used, the coefficient was positive and quite precisely measured. The number of nonpsychiatric beds was negatively related to the volume of charity psychiatric care, although these coefficients were very imprecisely estimated for the most part. Teaching status was estimated to have a positive and significant influence on the supply of charity psychiatric care. We interpret this as reflecting hospital preferences for providing community services. The magnitude of the coefficient reveals that teaching hospitals provide 36–60 percent more indigent psychiatric care than otherwise similar hospitals. The price variable had estimated coefficients that were negative, although not significant. This offers some evidence of a dominant substitution effect.

Altruism with Heterogeneous Patients

Theory

The lack of support for crowding out argues against the position that there is no functional differentiation in the mental health system. As a means of explaining our results, we propose an extension to the pure altruism model that relies strongly on a functional differentiation of the mental health service system. This is accomplished by relaxing the assumption that indigent psychiatric patients are homogeneous. We assume, for reasons of simplicity, that there are two types of patients differing in the cost of treatment.[14] We define the population of indigent psychiatric patients as

$$T = T_1 + T_2, \tag{4.10}$$

where T_1 are the more desirable (less costly) indigent patients and T_2 are the less desirable (more costly) indigent patients. It is further assumed that public hospitals serve only the least desirable indigent patients but that not all such patients are served in the public sector (i.e., $G < T$). A variety of institutional mechanisms support this type of role for the public hospital. For example, many emergency medical systems take indigent patients directly to public hospitals. Also, in the mental health sector, indigent patients involved in the legal system (arrests and involuntary commitment) are commonly referred to mental public hospitals (Lamb 1982). We therefore define the probability that an indigent psychiatric patient seeking care from a non-profit general hospital will be from the undesirable group (T_2) as

$$d = (T_2 - G)/(T_1 + T_2 - G). \tag{4.11}$$

This probability depends on the volume of care provided by the public mental hospitals.

This formulation requires a sort of differentiation of function between the various providers of inpatient mental health care. That is, the most difficult (and presumably most costly) indigent psychiatric patients are treated in the public system, while the remainder receive care in the private sector. This suggests that one way in which public hospitals affect the willingness of nonprofit hospitals to provide indigent psychiatric care is by reducing the number of difficult patients with whom nonprofit hospitals have to contend, thereby reducing the costs of serving indigent psychiatric patients. This is represented by rewriting the cost function as

$$C = C[Q, D, d(G)]. \tag{4.12}$$

Using this cost function to obtain C_D and C_Q in first-order conditions given by equations (4.4) and (4.5), we derive the following expression for the crowding-out effect for a purely altruistic hospital facing a heterogeneous population of indigent psychiatric patients:

$$dD^*/dG = \frac{U_R C_{QQ} U_{RN}(C_D - r) + U_R C_{QQ} U_{NN}}{|J|}$$

$$- \frac{U_R C_{QQ} C_G [U_{RR}(r - C_D) - U_{RR}]}{|J|}$$

$$+ \frac{U_R{}^2 (C_{QG} C_{QD} - C_{QQ} C_{DG})}{|J|} \tag{4.13}$$

To examine the effect of adding patient heterogeneity to the basic model, we rewrite equation (4.13) as

$$dD^*/dG = [dD/dG - C_G(dD/dE) + U_R{}^2(C_{QG}C_{QD} - C_{QQ}C_{DG})]/|J|. \tag{4.13'}$$

Equation (4.13′) suggests that dD^*/dG consists of the original crowding-out effect (dD/dG) from equation (4.8) minus the product of C_G and the income effect (dD/dE) plus the expression $U_R{}^2(C_{QG}C_{QD} - C_{QQ}C_{DG})$. The first term of equation (4.13′), dD/dG, will be negative, as shown above, except in the case of a very large positive income effect. C_G will be negative according to equations (4.11) and (4.12). If dD/dE is positive, the second term of equation (4.13′) will be positive. The third term will be positive if the following condition holds:

$$(C_{QG}/C_{DG}) < (C_{QQ}/C_{DG}). \tag{4.14}$$

This states that the effect of a change in G on the ratio of the marginal costs of Q and D has to be greater than that resulting from a change in Q. This is plausible, since an increase in G is assumed to have a direct and negative influence on the costliness of indigent patients, which should increase C_Q relative to C_D. If inequality (4.14) holds and dD/dE is positive or 0, we can unambiguously state that introducing patient heterogeneity attenuates the crowding-out effect.

Toward a Test of Heterogeneity

A key aspect of the model of heterogeneity relates to the degree to which there is functional differentiation between the public and private nonprofit sectors of the mental health system. This is represented in the theoretical characterization by the proposition that $dd/dG < 0$. The implication for empirical work is that one must find a measure that allows one to differentiate between T_1 and T_2 patients. A further practical requirement for conducting a test of the heterogeneity hypothesis in the context of the research presented thus far is that the measure be developed on the basis of information collected in discharge abstract data sets. This seriously constrains the options available. However, there is one measure that we believe is consistent with a body of recent research that identifies an unusually difficult-to-treat patient population, the so-called dually diagnosed. These are psychiatric patients who also are diagnosed substance abusers.

The co-occurrence of substance abuse with severe mental illness creates special problems for the diagnosis and treatment of patients. The co-occurrence of these conditions makes identifying the primary clinical problem difficult and may make choosing the most appropriate treatment difficult (Tsuang et al. 1982). Substance abuse also seems to contribute substantially to the dysfunction of severely mentally ill persons, especially the so-called young chronic patients (Ridgely, Goldman, and Talbott 1986). These effects have been particularly noticeable in studies of homeless people. These studies show that the combination of major mental disorders with substance abuse increases the duration of periods "on the streets," increases the likelihood that an individual has spent time in jail, and makes establishing residences significantly more difficult than for similar individuals without both sets of conditions (Ridgely, Goldman, and Talbott 1986).

Dual diagnoses also seem to be linked to more disruptive behavior among severely mentally ill clients of community support programs for mentally ill people (McCarrick et al. 1985). This type of behavior complicates treatment and reduces the probability of successful management of severely mentally ill patients. For these reasons, we constructed an indicator of "less desirable" patients based on the presence of a primary diagnosis of psychosis (DRG430) accompanied by a secondary diagnosis of substance abuse (an MDC20 DRG).

Issues of Estimation

We make use of two measures of the amount of care provided to indigent dually diagnosed persons. The first is the percentage of a hospital's indigent psychiatric cases that are dually diagnosed (measured from 0 to 100). The second is the count of dually diagnosed patients where the total number of cases is taken into account in specification of the right side of the model. Estimation of this model must take account of three key characteristics of the data: (1) there is a large mass of observations with a value of 0 (about 60 percent); (2) the data are skewed to the right; and (3) our data consist of pooled time series and cross-section observations. Our estimation strategy consists of taking two main approaches: (1) the use of a square root transformation of the percentage measure as suggested by McCullagh and Nelder (1989) and (2) the estimation of a negative binomial regression (see Cameron and Trivedi [1986] for a review of this class of models) of the count of dually diagnosed persons.[15] In the first instance, we can take account of the pooling of the data by using either fixed effects or variance components, since the square root transformation is designed to transform the dependent variable to approximate normality. With the negative binomial model[16] the non-normality of the left side variable leads us to adopt a quasi-likelihood estimator proposed by Zeger and Liang (1986).[17]

Results

The specification of the right side of the model of heterogeneity consists of most of the same variables that were included in the crowding-out model. The variables used in the analysis along with the relevant parameter estimates appear in table 4.3. Columns 1 and 2 of table 4.3 present the least squares dummy variables and variance components estimates of the transformed percentage of the dually diagnosed, respectively. Note that the test statistic for the Haus-

Table 4.3   Heterogeneity Model Estimates

Variable	LSDV	Var Comp	Neg Bin
PUBADMAL	−0.0020	−0.0005	−0.0003
	(0.00120)	(0.0007)	(0.001)
PRIVPCS	0.1150	0.012	0.014
	(2.57)	(0.013)	(0.010)
GHIPCS	0.0004	−0.0020	−0.0037
	(0.002)	(0.0012)	(0.001)
REVCASE	-8.10×10^{-5}	0.00040	-5.60×10^{-5}
	(0.0005)	(0.00024)	(2.00×10^{-4})
AGE65	-7.68×10^{-5}	-1.5×10^{-6}	-1.9×10^{-5}
	(0.0001)	(1.3×10^{-6})	(0.9×10^{-5})
AFDC	-1.2×10^{-6}	3.5×10^{-7}	-4.7×10^{-6}
	0.9×10^{-6}	(4.9×10^{-7})	(3.5×10^{-6})
NNINC	3.08×10^{-8}	0.00	0.00
	(1.71×10^{-7})	(0.00)	(0.00)
OWNBEDSP	0.012	0.021	0.0029
	(0.015)	(0.008)	(0.005)
OWNNPBED	0.0008	1.0×10^{-6}	−0.0020
	(0.0035)	(0.0008)	(0.0005)
TEACH	0.712	0.422	0.668
	(0.45)	(0.375)	(0.330)
SSI	0.0015	0.00012	0.00018
	(0.0012)	(0.00009)	(0.00008)
INCOME	-1.5×10^{-6}	-1.5×10^{-6}	-5.7×10^{-6}
	(0.0001)	(0.0004)	(2.2×10^{-5})
RNCOST	0.345	0.269	0.520
	(0.96)	(0.585)	(0.147)
INTERCEPT	−2.111	−2.085	−7.022
	(6.07)	(3.59)	(0.876)
Mean sq. error	1.34	1.81	1.31
Hausman χ^2		5.40 (16 df)	
N	250	250	250
Scale parameter			1,089

Note: Robust standard errors in parentheses.

man test is 5.41 with 16 degrees of freedom, which implies that we cannot reject the hypothesis that the vectors of coefficients in columns 1 and 2 are equal. For this reason, we focus our attention on the more efficient variance components estimates. Column 3 reports estimates obtained from the quasi-likelihood estimation of the negative binomial model. The results across all model specifications display a similar pattern.

The estimates for the heterogeneity effect (dd/dG) show a consistent negative relationship between the amount of care supplied to the T_2 (less desirable) segment of indigent psychiatric patients and the supply of public psychiatric care. Since we have strong a priori expectations concerning the direction of dd/dG, we use a one-tailed significance test. For the variance components and negative binomial models, the standard errors are larger than the estimated coefficients. In the fixed effects specification, the PUBADMAL coefficient has a t statistic of 1.65, which is significant at the 0.05 level. These results are very weakly supportive of the heterogeneity hypothesis.

A second notable set of results concerns the effect of the number of other private psychiatric beds on the supply of care to dually diagnosed indigent psychiatric patients. This amounts to testing the effect dd/dH. The estimates are consistently positive, yet only the negative binomial model attains standard errors that are smaller than the coefficient. The presence of psychiatric beds in other general hospitals is estimated to reduce the share of dually diagnosed patients in any given general hospital. The estimates are quite precise in the variance component and negative binomial specifications. This suggests avoidance behavior on the part of general hospitals.

Finally, the more psychiatric beds in a general hospital, the higher the rate of dually diagnosed psychiatric patients treated. This result was consistently obtained and is statistically significant in the variance component and negative binomial specifications. This result is consistent with the result from the model of the supply of indigent psychiatric care. That is, hospitals with more psychiatric beds seem to have a preference to play a more central role in the community mental health system. This is reflected by a greater commitment to treating indigent cases and to treating more difficult psychiatric patients.

Summary and Conclusions

The aim of this chapter was to study the supply of charity psychiatric care by nonprofit general hospitals. Of particular interest was understanding the influence of the public mental hospital system on the supply of charity psychiatric care. The consideration of this topic raises some fundamental questions regarding the role of the public sector within the broader mental health services system. In particular, is the care provided by the public mental hospital a perfect substitute for private charity care, or does the public hospital system serve a more specialized function? A strong substitutability between public mental hospital care and private charity psychiatric care implies strong crowding out.

Our theoretical model identified specific conditions under which crowding out will occur. These involve purely altruistic preferences, a homogeneous patient population, and weak positive or negative income effects. The empirical analysis of the supply of charity psychiatric care by general hospitals in Maryland offered little evidence of any significant crowding out of private charity care by public psychiatric hospitals. The results were not consistent with the notion of homogeneous functions by differing ownership arrangements in the mental health system.

The basic theoretical model of the supply of charity psychiatric care was extended to allow for functional differentiation. The specific form of functional differentiation posited was specialization by public hospitals in more difficult and probably more costly patient populations. The theoretical analysis shows that under reasonable conditions heterogeneity in the patient population accompanied by functional differentiation in the mental health system would lead to a substantial weakening of the crowding-out effect.

The heterogeneity hypothesis was examined by specification and estimation of a model of the rate of treatment of dually diagnosed indigent psychiatric patients. We made use of econometric models that took account of a number of special features of the data using techniques that minimize the effect of distributional assumptions. The results were at most weakly supportive of the heterogeneity hypothesis.

The equivocal results may occur, in part, because dually diagnosed patients may serve as a rather crude proxy for our T_2 population. The precision of the estimates might also be enhanced by a finer measurement of the dually diagnosed persons. For example, there have been important differences in the clinical status of severely mentally ill patients according to the types of substance abused. For this reason, we believe that extending this line of analysis would be fruitful.

A second related area of research that may prove useful would be to characterize more carefully the mechanism by which indigent mentally ill persons are sorted to various hospitals. The mechanism proposed above relies on processes that are in large part exogenous to the hospital. Although these forces are certainly important, they probably do not fully characterize the sorting process.[18]

Finally, our results suggest that the presence of public psychiatric hospitals in a system consisting of a mix of ownership and organizational forms increases the total amount of care to mentally ill persons who are indigent. Thus, at a time when further reductions in mental hospital systems are being considered, policy makers need to assess how the need for inpatient psychiatric care will be met. This may be especially problematic for the subgroup of psychiatric patients who are most difficult to treat and therefore most needy.

Acknowledgments

Support for this research comes from grant MH44407 from the NIMH. We are grateful to Diane Ferro for expert research assistance, to Alison Jones for statistical assistance, and to Will Manning, Marty Gaynor, Tom McGuire, and Barbara Wolfe for comments on earlier drafts. We also benefited from discussions with seminar participants at Yale University, the University of Illinois at Chicago, and the Johns Hopkins University Department of Psychiatry and Behavioral Sciences.

Notes

1. A *specialty psychiatric bed* is one that is within a psychiatric hospital, a distinct-part psychiatric unit of a general hospital, or another provider of residential mental health care. A large number of psychiatric patients are also treated in medical/surgical beds within general hospitals. These are often referred to as scatter beds.

2. The general hospital has been put forth as a central provider for mental health care in a restructured system. General hospitals offer relatively easy access, serve the mainstream of society, and avoid inefficiency associated with publicly owned providers of mental health care.

3. A precise definition of crowd-out is provided below. In general, *crowding out* refers to a reduction in private charitable activity that occurs in response to increased governmental spending on a public service (Abrams and Schmitz 1986).

4. This model of the hospital was first proposed by Frank and Salkever (1991). We present a condensed version here. Extensions of the model and more detailed developments can be obtained from the earlier paper.

5. Endowment income can be viewed as consisting of two components: (1) that which is tied to indigent care and (2) general purpose endowment. That which is linked to indigent care can be included as part of r. E represents general purpose endowment.

6. The price of hospital services may be fixed for several reasons: (1) because the state has hospital rate regulation, as in our empirical study of Maryland; (2) because the market is competitive (profits can be non-0 due to donated capital); or (3) because an insurer is dominant in the local market.

7. Assuming strong separability of $U(R, N)$ and $U_{NN} < 0$ will also guarantee crowding out. In our 1989 paper we demonstrated that the left side of equation (4.9) is negative. We are indebted to Thomas Bradley of the Rand Corporation for extending this proof to obtain equation (4.9).

8. Note that, under a purely altruistic specification of preferences, the dD/dH and dD/dG effects are the same.

9. These results are not sensitive to alternative specifications of the objective function (quantity maximization with a break-even constraint) or the demand constraint.

10. This variable is constructed from hospital discharge abstract data reported by hospitals to the Health Services Cost Review Commission (HSCRC), which sets rates for hospitals that apply to all payers. These data are periodically audited for reliability by outside reviewers under contract to the HSCRC. MDC19 contains the psychiatric DRGs. MDC20 cases, which involve substance abuse, are often considered in conjunction with MDC19 cases. We do not follow that practice here because there is considerable divergence in policy making for the two classes of disorder.

11. There were six private psychiatric hospitals in Maryland during the study period, including both for-profit and nonprofit facilities. Note that PRVIPCS will also include some substance abuse (MDC20) services.

12. The HSCRC adopted an explicit subsidy scheme for uncompensated care in the mid-1980s. No subsidies were available in the state during the period studied, so hospitals can reasonably be assumed to bear the full cost of charity care.

13. The instrument used for identification was the number of beds in each type of hospital.

14. The same results can be generated by assuming that the hospital's marginal utility of treatment differs for the two types of patient. However, the algebra is far more involved and the point remains the same.

15. The negative binomial model is preferred to the simple Poisson, since the condition in the Poisson model that the mean equal the variance is seldom met. This assumption is not met in our data. The overdispersion of the dependent variable makes the negative binomial attractive.

16. In the specification of the negative binomial model, we assume that individual hospitals may have differing rates of dual-diagnosis patients that are drawn from a gamma distribution. The model is specified to assume that the logit of the rate of dually diagnosed patients is a linear function of hospital and market characteristics. This allows us to take into account the total number of indigent psychiatric patients treated.

17. The quasi-likelihood approach is attractive because variance esti-

mates are consistent even if the covariance matrix is misspecified (Mc-Cullagh and Nelder 1989, 332–36).

18. We are grateful to Emmett Keeler for discussion of this point.

References

Abrams, B., and M. D. Schmitz. 1986. "The Crowding-Out Effect of Governmental Transfers on Private Charitable Contributions." In S. Rose-Ackerman (ed.): *The Economics of Nonprofit Institutions,* pp. 303–12. Oxford: Oxford University Press.

Brown, P. 1985. *The Transfer of Care.* New York: Routledge.

Cameron, A. C., and P. K. Trivedi. 1986. "Econometric Models Based on Count Data: Comparisons and Applications of Some Estimators and Tests." *Journal of Applied Econometrics* 1:29–53.

Congressional Research Service. 1988. *Health Insurance and the Uninsured: Background Data and Analysis.* Washington, D.C.: U.S. Government Printing Office.

Frank, R. G., and D. S. Salkever. 1991. "The Supply of Charity Services by Nonprofit Hospitals: Motives and Market Structure." *Rand Journal of Economics* 22:430–45.

Fuller, W. A., and G. E. Battese. 1974. "Estimation of Linear Models with Crossed-Error Structure." *Journal of Econometrics* 2:67–78.

Goldman, H. H., C. A. Taube, and S. F. Jencks. 1987. "The Organization of the Psychiatric Inpatient Services System." *Medical Care* 25:S6–S27.

Hausman, J. A. 1978. "Specification Tests in Econometrics." *Econometrica* 46:1251–71.

Lamb, H. R. 1982. "Young Adult Chronic Patients: The New Differs." *Hospital and Community Psychiatry* 33:465–68.

McCarrick, A. K., et al. 1985. "Correlates of Acting-Out Behaviors among Young Adult Chronic Patients." *Hospital and Community Psychiatry* 36:848–53.

McCullagh, P., and J. A. Nelder. 1989. *Generalized Linear Models.* London: Chapman and Hall.

Mechanic, D., and D. A. Rochefort. 1990. "Deinstitutionalization: An Appraisal of Reform." Working Paper, Rutgers University.

National Center for Health Statistics. 1987. *Data from the National Hospital Discharge Survey 1986.* Hyattsville, Md.

National Institute of Mental Health. 1985. *Mental Health U.S., 1985.* Washington, D.C.: U.S. Government Printing Office.

———. 1987. *Mental Health U.S., 1987.* Washington, D.C.: U.S. Government Printing Office.

Ridgely, M. S., H. H. Goldman, and J. A. Talbott. 1986. *Chronic Mentally Ill Young Adults with Substance Abuse Problems: A Review of Relevant Literature and Creation of a Research Agenda.* Mental Health Policy Program, University of Maryland.

Sloan, F. A., J. Valvona, and R. Mullner. 1986. "Identifying the Issues: A Statistical Profile." In F. A. Sloan, J. F. Blumstein, and J. M. Perrin (eds.): *Uncompensated Hospital Care: Rights and Responsibilities.* Baltimore: Johns Hopkins University Press.

Tsuang, M. T., et al. 1982. "Subtypes of Drug Abuse with Psychosis: Demographic Characteristics, Clinical Features and Family History." *Archives of General Psychiatry* 39:141–47.

Wu, D. 1973. "Alternative Tests of Independence between Stochastic Regressors and Disturbances." *Econometrica* 41:733–50.

Zeger, S. L., and K. Y. Liang. 1986. "Longitudinal Data Analysis for Discrete and Continuous Outcomes." *Biometrics* 42:121–30.

PART II

The Economic Cost
of Mental Illness

R ecent estimates of the costs that are incurred as a consequence of mental illness (indirect costs) put the total loss to society at $56.6 billion in 1985. The estimates of social costs of illness used by the federal government focus primarily on the effects on the labor market. Studies of the consequences of mental illness on the labor market are important for a couple of reasons: (1) to gauge the potential benefits to society from improved techniques aimed at preventing and treating mental illness and (2) to contribute to our understanding of policy issues related to labor markets generally. For example, to what extent does successful treatment of serious mental disorders allow affected individuals to earn income at levels comparable to those of individuals of similar age and educational attainment? Addressing such questions may have important implications for treatment and disability policy.

Research on this aspect of economics *in* mental health is relatively recent. Establishing precise empirical links between mental disorders and labor market behavior remains a high priority for research. Examining the different types of effect that mental illness has on various segments of the potential working population will allow for a far more refined view of the social cost of mental illness than has existed previously. Developing estimates of the labor market response to mental illness in specific subpopulations will allow targeting of investments in treatment and prevention.

The chapters in this section reflect the application of sophisticated empirical analyses developed primarily in the area of labor economics. Each of the studies in this section makes use of data collected by large epidemiological investigations of health and mental health status. As a group, the chapters demonstrate the strong payoffs of including measures of labor market outcomes in epidemiological studies.

Chapter 5, by Leonard Miller and Sander Kelman, is a broadly based analysis of the effect of mental health problems and substance abuse on income. The authors make use of a dynamic model of earnings to estimate the productivity loss due to these disorders. This approach seeks to use more information regarding the timing of disorders than has previously been possible. As in previous studies, rather strong consequences of impairments due to alcohol and drug abuse and mental illness were found in the empirical analysis.

Chapter 6, by Elizabeth Savoca, is methodological in character and reveals that mismeasurement of mental health status can cause misleading inferences regarding the influence of race on labor market outcomes. In Chapter 7, Christopher Ruhm estimates the effect of health and mental health status on the labor force participation of females. The analysis focuses on women between the ages of 45 and 57. Ruhm shows strong effects of depression on female labor force participation.

Jean Mitchell is also concerned with dynamic aspects of mental illness. In chapter 8, she empirically examines links between the emergence of mental health problems in adolescence and antisocial personality disorder in adulthood and subsequent labor market behavior. This is one of the first analyses to begin to tie the life cycle of mental disorders with their economic consequences. This initial study finds a clear connection, although the empirical estimates suggest that the magnitude of the labor market effects are modest. Work on the dynamic consequences of mental illness is clearly at the frontier of research, and these chapters serve as a first generation of research on that topic.

Taken as a group, these chapters advance the precision of our characterization of mental illness and its specific effects on various segments of the population. They challenge the field explicitly to take account of the persistent nature of many mental disorders and to use dynamic models to trace the consequences of these illnesses. Such efforts will produce a clearer understanding of mental illness and its disabling effects over the life course.

5

Estimates of the Loss of Individual Productivity from Alcohol and Drug Abuse and from Mental Illness

Leonard S. Miller, Ph.D., and Sander Kelman, Ph.D.

T he productivity loss that follows from alcohol and drug abuse and from mental illness (ADM) results in a cost to society. A central, unsolved problem in estimating this cost is the achievement of estimates of productivity loss which are unambiguously attributable to these ADM diagnoses. The purpose of this chapter is to present a solution to this problem, the one used to provide the most current estimates of the cost to society from ADM (Rice et al. 1990).

An economic analysis of the effect of ADM on society was probably initiated with Ohlin's analysis of the loss induced by alcohol (Osterberg 1983). Harwood et al. (1984) cited eleven studies of alcohol-induced losses, six of which preceded the important Berry and Boland (1977) estimates. Cruze et al. (1981) presented the first estimates of the effect of drugs on productivity. Hu and Sandifer (1981) noted that Malzberg (1950) and Fein (1958) presented the first productivity loss estimates associated with mental illness.

The underlying theoretical basis of these studies (and others to be described below) is the human capital paradigm. People have personal characteristics, assets, and skills for hire. The productivity of these characteristics and assets is impaired by ADM disorders. Competitive forces cause the value of the impaired productivity to be reflected (imperfectly) as reductions in personal earnings. The value of output not produced is approximated by the value of income lost. The effects of reduced work, labor skill, and motivation on the return to capital and/or the rate of profit are ignored.

Since productivity is approximated by earned income, estimating productivity loss requires a model of income loss. In the simplest cases, the income loss model is the difference between the average income of a group sharing a common disorder and the average income of a group absent the disorder. More generally, averages are controlled for demographic and educational factors, and sometimes consideration is given to regional factors, the existence of other health problems, and the extent of disabilities (Luft 1975; Bartel and Taubman 1979; Hartunian, Smart, and Thompson 1981; Salkever 1988).

Before Rice et al. (1990), the estimates of ADM-induced productivity loss by the Research Triangle Institute (RTI) were the extant national estimates (Harwood et al. 1984; Cruze et al. 1981). For alcohol and drug use separately, the RTI specified a relation between the natural logarithm of (household) income (not earnings), on the left-hand side (LHS) of an equation, and measures of presumed income-influencing and substance use characteristics (including education level and occupation), on the right-hand side (RHS). In their alcohol loss equation they incorporated quantity of alcohol consumed and indicators of a problem drinking condition (but they used only problem drinking in their national cost estimate). In their drug loss equation they identified the group of individuals who had an episode in their life of daily marijuana use for a month or more. Because the LHS is expressed as the logarithm of income, an unknown coefficient on the RHS multiplying an indicator of impaired group membership is said to represent the average percentage difference in income between the group indicated/not indicated, controlling for personal characteristics. Population-based, household surveys provide their data (Clark and Midanik 1982; NIDA 1982); regression analysis was used to estimate the unknown coefficients. Thus, for alcohol and drug use taken separately, RTI employed the average-comparison-by-group-membership method, controlling for other factors. Their estimated differences were assumed to be caused by each of the problems indicated.

Two issues about estimates of income loss are central to an accurate estimate of the cost to society from ADM disorders. First, there is the issue of association versus causation. The objective of the exercise is to estimate the cost to society caused by ADM disorders. Thus, estimated income differences are assumed to be caused by membership/nonmembership status. Second, there are issues about obtaining unbiased estimates of the income differences between the groups (Heien and Pittman 1989). We begin with a discussion of association versus causation.

When the link between a specific disorder and physical or cognitive capacities is direct and clear, as with spinal cord injuries (Berkowitz 1985), multiple sclerosis (Inman 1984), stroke, blindness, paralysis, brain injury, or spina bifida (Mitchell and Butler 1986), the causal nature of the comparison is obvious. In contrast to the sudden loss of income caused by certain diseases or injuries, ADM disorders are more likely to lead to the gradual depletion of an individual's skill level and work effort. The process includes declines in punctuality, consistency, reliability, and on-the-job safety; in peer, hierarchical, and customer relations; in judgments rendered; and in quantity and quality of performance. In response, firms pay less, reduce responsibility, make fewer human capital investments in the individuals, and dismiss faster (Becker 1967).

When the link is less immediate or less clear, as in the relation between income loss and poor or deteriorating health or between income loss and ADM disorders, greater elaboration is needed to improve the underlying formulation so that it reflects losses caused by the impairment that follows from these conditions.

Efforts to move from an earnings model, where loss is associated only with group membership (e.g., individuals who had an episode in their life of daily marijuana use for a month or more), to a model where loss is caused by the condition defining group membership usually involve incorporating a temporal dimension of the problem. For example, Bartel and Taubman (1979) incorporated respondents' age group at the onset of a major disease into their earnings model. This allowed them to estimate how time since onset affects income. Using health status indicators, Chirikos and Nestel (1985) described four different ten-year longitudinal profiles: continuous health, health gains over the period, gradual diminutions over the period, and continuous poor health. Parnes and Meyer (1971) analyzed longitudinal data and concluded that "the [longitudinal] data permit [them] to be more confident than [they] otherwise could be that poor health is actually a cause of, rather than a mere rationalization for, withdrawal from the labor force."

Our efforts to allocate estimated income differences unambiguously to the productivity losses from ADM disorders move in this direction of incorporating temporal consideration. We hypothesize and specify processes that could represent the relation between impairment and income loss for periods of impairment. These models translate information about the time and duration of group membership into explicit models of the impairment process. They are a translation of a group membership indicator into a temporal history of a person's ADM impairment. Most generously, the models can be interpreted as causal models of the impairment process.

We turn now to an examination of the bias issue. When membership in an impaired group is indicated in an income model and the RHS omits factors that correlate with both income levels and group membership, biased estimates of the income differences between the groups are obtained. For example, if blue-collar life-styles lead to greater alcohol abuse and dependency rates and blue-collar jobs pay less on the average than white-collar jobs, when occupational classification is omitted the coefficient on the problem drinking indicator reflects both the loss in income due to alcohol impairment and the correlation between blue-collar income levels and alcohol abuse or dependency. In this example, the estimated associative relationship among alcohol use, group status, and income loss would show a larger loss than the loss actually caused by an alcohol-related impairment to productivity.

Occupation, however, is jointly determined with income. Consequently, it should not be directly placed into the income equation; a system of simultaneous equations is in order. Moreover, as the example illustrated, alcohol and drug use are associated with cultural practices, which are partially determined by occupational group. The omission problem has become a problem of simultaneity, which leads to biases in the estimated coefficients. Modeling always requires making judgments about what is to be predetermined and what is to be jointly determined.

Our approach to the simultaneity problem was less inventive. ADM disorders are taken as predetermined. The public-use Epidemiologic Catchment Area (ECA) data tapes, which are discussed in greater detail below, did not appear to afford sufficient detail to enable a properly identified simultaneous equation system. Recognizing that education is affected by the early onset of ADM disorders and that occupation is jointly determined by education and income, an unconstrained reduced form equation is estimated with omitted education and occupation variables.

Causal Models of Impairment

Model 1: The Effect on Income of a Constant Rate of Impairment That Is Noncumulative and Nonpersistent

The rate at which an individual engages in a disordered behavior or thought process, hereafter referred to as a rate of disorder, is denoted by δ. For example, δ might represent the quantity of alcohol an individual consumes per unit of time, or it might represent the intensity or frequency of occurrence of a psychologically dysfunctional process per unit of time. If the disorder process occurs over the interval between τ and $\tau + \Delta$, then the level of the impairment from the disorder process is a function of $\delta \, \Delta$.

In model 1, we assume that engaging in a disorder at time t (with a disorder rate δ) instantaneously affects an individual's productivity, causing an instantaneous reduction in income. Denoting income at time t by $Y(t)$ and the instantaneous income change by $dY(t)$, the instantaneous percentage of change in income experienced at t is given by $dY(t)/Y(t)$.

Ψ represents a scalar translating the effect of an instantaneous disorder rate on productivity into an instantaneous percentage income loss at t. Because a disorder causes an impairment to productivity, Ψ is less than zero ($\Psi < 0$). In this first model, the instantaneous income loss is assumed equal to the market translation of the rate of disorder. Equation (5.1) expresses this relation:

$$dY(t)/Y(t) = \Psi \, \delta \, dt. \tag{5.1}$$

Equation (5.1) describes an instantaneous causal process that translates the existence of a disorder rate into an impairment to productivity, which is measured as an expected income reduction. The full loss from the disorder at time t is experienced at time t. Models 2 and 3 (to follow) have increasingly complex descriptions about the effect of a disorder on the temporal distribution of impairment.

The hypothesized impairment yields a total income loss for an individual that depends on the length of time during which the individual experiences the disorder. Let tb denote the time of onset of a disorder, A denote the time of a respondent's interview, and te denote the time at which an individual's disorder ends. T is the minimum of te and A [$T = \text{MIN}(te,A)$]. Losses occur over the tb to T period.

An expression for the annual income loss experienced at the time of an interview follows from integrating equation (5.1) over the impaired period. Equation (5.2) expresses this relation:

$$\ln Y(A) - \ln Y(tb) = \int_{tb}^{T} [dY(t)]/[Y(t) \, dt]. \tag{5.2}$$

Equation (5.3) evaluates equation (5.2) under the instantaneous loss conditions described by equation (5.1). Since $\ln Y(tb)$ is the logarithm of the income of an individual at the onset of the impairment process and impairments are the only reason for income losses in this model, the LHS of equation (5.3) describes the difference between the logarithm of an individual's actual income at an interview and the logarithm of the income that person would have had if ADM disorders had not been experienced. The RHS of equation (5.3) shows that the percentage loss occurring at the time of interview is simply the product of the constants representing the market translation of the rate of disorder, Ψ, the rate of disorder, δ, and the length of time during which the individual experienced the impairment process.

$$\ln Y(A) - \ln Y(tb) = \Psi \, \delta \, (T - tb). \tag{5.3}$$

This description is a stationary process in the sense that income loss is independent of when the process occurred. Income loss depends only on the length of time over which the process occurred. No distinctions are made between individuals who had an impairment process but no longer experience it (those for whom $T = te$) and individuals who experienced the process and continue to do so (those for whom $T = A$). The dependence only on duration of an impairment, with independence from when that impairment occurred, is true for model 2 but not true for model 3.

Model 2: The Effect on Income of a Constant Rate of Impairment That Is Cumulative and Nonpersistent

In model 2, an instantaneously experienced disorder at time τ causes both immediate and future productivity losses. The further into the future, the less effect a particular disorder is expected to have on income. Past disorders can affect future income by influencing the human relations surrounding production. For example, if a disorder stigmatizes an individual, future assigned responsibility and human capital investments paid by employers might be reduced.

In model 2, future effects from an instantaneous disorder are experienced only so long as the individual experiences the disorder. In model 3, future effects continue after a person no longer experiences an ADM disability.

Much of the notation and assumptions used in model 1 hold here as well. The rate at which an individual engages in an impairment process is assumed to be constant and is denoted by δ; the effect experienced at time t causes an instantaneous percentage income loss at t, denoted again by $[dY(t)]/[Y(t)]$; the constant Ψ denotes the market translation of the disorder experienced at t into the instantaneous percentage income loss that occurs at t; the situation where a respondent's disorder has ended before the interview is distinguished from the situation where the respondent's disorder still exists at the time of the interview; and T is again the minimum of te and A.

Some additional notation must be introduced to understand how impairment accumulates over time. Let τ measure a moment in time when a particular disorder occurs and t measure a future moment. The effect on an individual's productivity at time t from the disorder that occurred at τ, $(\tau < t)$, at the disorder rate δ, is assumed to be described by equation (5.4):

$$\delta \exp [-\nu(t - \tau)]. \tag{5.4}$$

In equation (5.4), the rate at which a disorder's effect diminishes over time is represented by ν, which can be thought of as the exponential recovery rate from the damage caused by the disorder at τ. As an example, if this model describes human relations surrounding production, ν is the rate at which co-workers forget or forgive a particular disordered behavior.

The disorder experienced at t arises from the stream of impairing behavior between onset, tb, and t. Equation (5.5) describes the relationship between the instantaneous income loss and the magnitude of the impairment to productivity experienced at t.

$$dY(t)/Y(t) = \Psi \int_{tb}^{t} \delta \exp[-v(t - \tau)] \, d\tau. \tag{5.5}$$

The total income loss up to the time of interview, A, is the sum of the instantaneous percentage income losses from onset to the time when the individual's disorder ends or the interview is taken, T. An expression for the total income loss experienced by the respondent at time A follows from integrating equation (5.5) over the period of the impairment. Equation (5.6) expresses this relationship, and equation (5.7) evaluates the relationship under the assumptions described by the model.

$$\ln Y(A) - \ln Y(tb) = \Psi \int_{tb}^{T} \left\{ \int_{tb}^{t} \delta \exp[-v(t - \tau)] d\epsilon \right\} dt \tag{5.6}$$

and

$$= (\Psi \, \delta/v)((T - tb) + (1/v)\{\exp[-v(T - tb)] - 1\}). \tag{5.7}$$

Given the state of software development when this study was undertaken, it was necessary to transform equation (5.7) into an estimable form. Power series methods are used. The well-known and converging power series expansion of order 3 of the exponential expression $\exp[-\nu z]$ is given by equation (5.8) (Sherwood and Taylor 1954):

$$\exp(-\nu z) = 1 - \nu z + (\nu^2 z^2)/2 + O(z)^3. \tag{5.8}$$

Substituting $(T - tb)$ for z, equation (5.7) is simplified to the linear form represented by equation (5.9):

$$\ln Y(A) - \ln Y(tb) = (\Psi \, \delta/2)(T - tb)^2 + O(T - tb)^3. \qquad (5.9)$$

Ignoring the third and higher-order terms, note that equation (5.9) shows that the percentage of income loss causally induced by the impairment process is a linear function of the square of the length of time the respondent experienced the impairment process.

Model 3: The Effect on Income of a Constant Rate of Impairment That Is Cumulative and Persistent

Model 3 describes a respondent's income loss when the effect of the impairment process on productivity and income functions like model 2 but continues to reduce productivity beyond the time when the respondent's disorder ends. Model 3 is more likely to apply where employment or promotion is based on a thorough consideration of past performance. Perhaps managerial and professional jobs are more appropriately described by this model. Perhaps certain disorders are never perceived by the market as overcome, even though personal or medical perceptions of the disorders have ended.

Model 3 describes respondents who are in remission. The model is adapted from Chiang and Conforti (1989). The notation and most of the assumptions used for model 2 are used here as well.

In model 3, one portion of an individual's total productivity/income loss arises while the person is incurring a disorder. This part is analogous to the condition where $T = te$, that is, $A > te$ in equation (5.9). Another portion arises as a continuing consequence of having had a disorder, the period between te and A. Equation 5.10) describes the sum of these two portions, and equation (5.11) evaluates the relationship under the assumptions described by the model.

$$\ln Y(t) - \ln Y(tb) = \Psi \left(\int_{tb}^{te} \left\{ \int_{tb}^{t} \delta \, \exp[-v(t - \tau)]d\tau \right\} dt \right)$$

$$+ \left(\int_{te}^{A} \left\{ \int_{tb}^{te} \delta \, \exp[-v(t - \tau)]d\tau \right\} dt \right) \qquad (5.10)$$

$$= \Psi \, \delta/v^2 \{ \exp[-v(A - tb)]$$
$$- \exp[-v(A - te)] + v(te - tb) \} \qquad (5.11)$$

As illustrated for equation (5.8), order 3 power series expressions are used to approximate the two exponential expressions on the RHS of equation (5.11). The result simplifies to equation (5.12):

$$\ln Y(A) - \ln Y(tb) = \Psi \, \delta/2 \, [(A - tb)^2 - (A - te)^2$$
$$+ O(A - tb)^3 + O(A - te)^3] \tag{5.12}$$

where $(A - tb) \geq 0$ and $(A - te) \geq 0$.

Ignoring the third and higher-order terms, note that in Model 3 income loss is approximated by a constant multiplying the difference between the square of the time since onset and the square of the time since discontinuance of a disorder. Note also that, when the interview is conducted while the respondent is still impaired (i.e., when model 2 applies rather than model 3, $A = te$), equation (5.12) reduces to equation (5.9). In the discussion below, reference to model 3 implies that the respondent was in remission at the time of the interview and reference to model 2 means that the respondent's disorder continued to exist at the time of the interview.

Data and Estimation

In the ECA survey (Regier et al. 1984; Eaton et al. 1984; Robins et al. 1984; Myers et al. 1984; NIMH 1988), information about personal income ranges, demographic characteristics, and disorders was collected with the diagnostic interview schedule (DIS) (Robins et al. 1981; Robins 1985). The income information included earned and unearned income. Algorithmic processing of responses about disordered feelings and behavior yielded DSM-III diagnoses (from the *Diagnostic and Statistical Manual of Mental Disorders,* 3d edition [American Psychiatric Association 1980]) for alcohol abuse and dependence; for drug abuse and dependence for each of six substances (barbiturates, opiates [heroin], cocaine, amphetamines, hallucinogens, and cannabis [marijuana]), as well as a summary measure of the six; and for mental illness disorders for each of twelve psychiatric diagnoses. For the drug and psychiatric disorders there are also severity criteria.

The ECA survey also provided data for a simple temporal history about substance use and/or mental disorders. In this study, time of onset is taken to be the age when a person first had alcohol- or drug-related problems or had the first mental illness symptoms; it is denoted tb in the models above. The interviewee's age when experiencing the most recent symptom is taken as the time of discontinuance and is denoted te in the models above. The interviewee's age at the time of the interview is denoted A in the models above. Since life-history information about the relative intensities of disorders is not part of the database (quantity-frequency consumption of alcohol, e.g., at different periods in the interviewee's life), the δ parameter is actually suppressed in the estimation, and the product of the market transformation of a loss and the rate of disorder is estimated, $\Psi \, \delta$.

Because of limitations in the data, the models were developed under the assumption that disorders exist over the entire period ($T - tb$). To the degree that the history of an individual disorder has many stops and starts, the actual (unobserved) timing measures are less than their measured values. This may introduce a bias into the estimate of loss. We believe, however, that this bias will be minimized by a compensating diminished bias in our regression coefficients.

The hypothesized models describe an impairment process that results in income loss. They yield a specification of the relationship between income loss and model-specific measures of time of disorder. Although these "timing measures" differ by model, in all cases they are functions of an interviewee's present age, age at time of onset, and age at time of discontinuance (A, tb, and te, respectively). In the discussion to follow, the model-specific functions of these timing variables are referred to as "timing measures." For model 1, the units of the timing measure are years. For models 2 and 3, the units are years-squared. As we stated above, a properly identified system of simultaneous equations was not possible with the ECA data tapes. The use of these timing measures in such a system of equations would integrate the structure of simultaneous equation systems, necessary to address the simultaneity bias problem, with the description of the impairment process leading to income loss, a method closer to *cause* than *association*.

A slight change of notation facilitates incorporating the effects of overlapping disorders and leads to estimable forms for the three models. Suppose I_j is an indicator (1/0) of a lifetime DSM-III diagnosis of disorder j. Time of onset (tb) and time of discontinuance (te) are measured in years of a person's life. A is the age of a respondent at the time of the ECA interview. Given that I_j is 1, tb_j is the respondent's age at the onset of disorder j and te_j is respondent's age at the last symptom of disorder type j.

In the absence of ADM disorders, all δ_j values are zero (and so too are the durations of impairment). The RHSs of the final equations for each model [(5.3), (5.9), and (5.12)] equal $\ln Y(tb)$, implying no loss from ADM impairments. The expression $\ln Y(tb)$ is to be interpreted as the income of an individual who has never had DSM-III disorders. Note also that, in these models, losses in productivity and income occur only when respondents have met the DSM-III criteria for disorder.

Let the income of an individual who has not experienced disorders, $\ln Y(tb)$ be modeled as a stochastic linear function of individual characteristics. Equation (5.13) describes the specification. Since early manifestations of the disorders also reduce the level of education and since education affects occupation, education and occupation are jointly dependent with income on ADM disorders. Consequently, these variables are not included in the X matrix of equation (5.13). Equation (5.13) is therefore an unconstrained reduced form specification.

$$\ln Y(tb) = \beta X + v, \qquad v \text{ distributed } N(0, \sigma_{v^2}). \tag{5.13}$$

Let ϵ be an error term, one for each model [equations (5.3), (5.9), and (5.12)], that includes (1) all of the omitted third and higher-order terms; (2) deviations from expected income values when disorders have been experienced; and (3) the error term in the reduced form description of income without disorders, v in equation (5.13). Assume that ϵ is distributed $N(0, \sigma_{\epsilon^2})$.

Substituting equation (5.13) and ϵ into the final equation for each model yields a stochastic linear expression for each of the three models developed above. The stochastic linear expressions for models 1, 2, and 3 and for disorders j are given by equations (5.14), (5.15), and (5.16), respectively:

$$\ln Y(A) = \beta X + \Sigma_j \, \beta_j l_j (T - tb_j) + \epsilon, \tag{5.14}$$

where $\beta_j = (\Psi \, \delta_j)$;

$$\ln Y(A) = \beta X + \Sigma_j \, \beta_j l_j (T - tb_j)^2 + \epsilon, \tag{5.15}$$

where $\beta_j = (\Psi \, \delta_j/2)$; and

$$\ln Y(A) = \beta X + \Sigma_j \, \beta_j l_j [(A - tb_j)^2 - (A - te_j)^2] + \epsilon, \tag{5.16}$$

where $\beta_j = (\Psi \, \delta_j/2)$.

Recall that personal income is reported in ranges. For example, an income reported in range g lies between the questionnaire boundary values B_{g-1} and B_g. The probability of observing an income in this range, when income is described by model 1 [equation (5.14)], is given by

$$\text{Prob}[B_{g-1} < Y(A) \leq B_g] = \text{Prob}\{\ln B_g - [\beta X + \Sigma_j \, \beta_j \, l_j(T - tb_j)]$$
$$\leq \epsilon \leq \ln B_{g-1} - [\beta X + \Sigma_j \, \beta_j \, l_j(T - tb_j)]\} \tag{5.17}$$

Equation (5.17) is evaluated by equation (5.18), where $f()$ denotes the standard normal density function:

$$\text{Prob}[B_{g-1} < Y(A) \leq B_g] = \int f(\epsilon/\sigma_\epsilon) \, d\epsilon \quad \genfrac{}{}{0pt}{}{\{\ln B_g - [\beta X + \Sigma_j \beta_j I_j(T - tb_j)]\}/\sigma_\epsilon}{\{\ln B_{g-1} - [\beta X + \Sigma_j \beta_j I_j(T - tb_j)]\}/\sigma_\epsilon} \tag{5.18}$$

Similar probability expressions are calculated when income loss is described by models 2 and 3 [equations (5.15) and (5.16), respectively]. They differ only in the timing measures in the integral boundaries. The likelihood function for each model is formed with the model-specific probability expressions for the sample of observations. The Grouped Data option in LIMDEP was used to calculate maximum likelihood estimates of the coefficients on the timing measures, the models' parameters (Greene 1986, 1990).

Descriptive Statistics

The control variables include AGE, intercept adjustments by age group (AGEGROUP_), and slope adjustments by age group (AGE*GROUP_); an indicator of being married (MAR); an indicator of having children under 12 (KIDS); indicators of race/ethnic groups (HRACE for Hispanic, BRACE for black, and ORACE for other, not white); an indicator of whether the interviewees considered themselves sick most of their lives (SICK); and six time-location adjustment indicators—TLY0 and TLY1 indicating that the interview took place in New Haven, Connecticut (conducted by Yale) in 1980 and 1981, respectively; TLH1 indicating that the interview took place in Baltimore, Maryland (conducted by Johns Hopkins) in 1981; TLD2 and TLD3 indicating that the interview took place in the vicinity of Durham, North Carolina (conducted by Duke), in 1982 and 1983, respectively; and TLL3 indicating that the interview took place in Los Angeles (conducted by UCLA) in 1983. Los Angeles 1984 is the excluded time-location variable.

Discussion will focus on the coefficients associated with each ADM disorder. ALCTIME denotes the alcohol abuse or dependency timing measure; DRGSTIME denotes the timing measure associated with drug abuse or dependency and the severity condition indicating recognition by the interviewees that drug use has had a serious effect on their lives or that they have sought help. The psychiatric diagnoses and timing measures are aggregated into four groups. SCHTIME is the timing measure associated with schizophrenia or schizophreniform disorders. AFFTIME is the timing measure associated with affective disorders—mania, depression, and/or dysthymia. ANXTIME is the timing measure associated with anxiety disorders—obsessive-compulsive disorder, phobias, and/or panic disorders. ASPTIME is the timing measure associated with the antisocial personality disorder. The prevalence rates for two diagnostic categories, somatization and severe cognitive mental disorders, are low, and these conditions were combined into a single indicator (dummy variable) measure, rather than a timing measure; this is indicated by SOMCOGA.

Tables 5.1A through 5.1D and 5.2A through 5.2D present conditional descriptive statistics of the timing measures for the three mod-

Table 5.1A   Weighted Descriptive Statistics of Timing Measures
for ECA Men Eighteen to Twenty-four Years Old

	Given Timing Measure > 0		
Variable	Model 1	Model 2	Model 3
ALCTIME			
Mean	3.56	18.10	21.66
SD	2.34	22.33	23.72
Number[a]	127.00	127.00	127.00
Minimum	0.25	0.63E-01	0.44
Maximum	10.70	114.50	120.90
DRGSTIME			
Mean	4.59	27.67	32.48
SD	2.62	24.60	29.96
Number[a]	33.00	33.00	33.00
Minimum	0.25	0.63E-01	0.44
Maximum	9.98	99.60	128.00
SCHTIME			
Mean	9.59	128.90	133.20
SD	6.34	133.90	133.40
Number[a]	12.00	12.00	12.00
Minimum	1.20	1.44	2.16
Maximum	19.98	399.20	400.00
AFFTIME			
Mean	4.69	41.04	44.85
SD	4.46	74.74	78.88
Number[a]	25.00	25.00	25.00
Minimum	0.25	0.63E-01	0.44
Maximum	16.25	264.10	288.40
ANXTIME			
Mean	11.41	166.30	182.60
SD	6.04	143.60	144.70
Number[a]	81.00	81.00	81.00
Minimum	0.98	0.96	1.00
Maximum	22.98	528.10	529.00
ASPTIME			
Mean	11.82	149.30	169.20
SD	3.12	74.45	80.02
Number[a]	60.00	60.00	60.00
Minimum	4.98	24.80	25.00
Maximum	19.70	388.10	399.90

[a]Number of observations.

els for males and females, respectively. These statistics are based on all sampled individuals who had lifetime DSM-III diagnoses of one or more of the relevant disorders. The tables present descriptive statistics about timing measures for four age groups. Tables 5.1A and 5.2A describe interviewees who are eighteen to twenty-four years old, tables 5.1B and 5.2B describe those twenty-five to thirty-four years old,

Table 5.1B   Weighted Descriptive Statistics of Timing Measures for ECA Men Twenty-five to Thirty-four Years Old

	Given Timing Measure > 0		
Variable	Model 1	Model 2	Model 3
ALCTIME			
Mean	7.56	77.69	95.98
SD	4.55	85.06	88.12
Number[a]	300.00	300.00	300.00
Minimum	0.25	0.63E-01	0.44
Maximum	24.98	624.00	625.00
DRGSTIME			
Mean	5.97	51.79	77.63
SD	4.04	58.33	61.35
Number[a]	67.00	67.00	67.00
Minimum	0.25	0.63E-01	0.44
Maximum	15.98	255.40	256.00
SCHTIME			
Mean	10.37	149.00	155.70
SD	6.6	139.80	139.30
Number[a]	18.00	18.00	18.00
Minimum	0.98	0.96	1.00
Maximum	23.98	575.00	576.00
AFFTIME			
Mean	6.37	62.79	77.62
SD	4.75	75.28	82.24
Number[a]	67.00	67.00	67.00
Minimum	0.25	0.63E-01	0.44
Maximum	17.25	297.60	323.40
ANXTIME			
Mean	16.69	349.30	380.90
SD	8.43	273.10	269.40
Number[a]	176.00	176.00	176.00
Minimum	0.70	0.49	0.91
Maximum	31.98	1,023.00	1,024.00
ASPTIME			
Mean	17.95	341.50	400.80
SD	4.41	159.30	159.50
Number[a]	178.00	178.00	178.00
Minimum	7.00	49.00	119.00
Maximum	29.98	898.80	900.00

[a]Number of observations.

tables 5.1C and 5.2C describe those thirty-five to fifty-four years old, and tables 5.1D and 5.2D describe those fifty-five to sixty-four years old. Each cell in each table contains a vector of five statistics that are presented as a stacking of mean, upon standard deviation, upon number of observations, upon minimum, upon maximum.

The general feature of these tables is that the average time a

Table 5.1C   Weighted Descriptive Statistics of Timing Measures for ECA Men Thirty-five to Fifty-four Years Old

	Given Timing Measure > 0		
Variable	Model 1	Model 2	Model 3
ALCTIME			
Mean	13.88	272.50	369.30
SD	8.96	296.70	326.30
Number[a]	298.00	298.00	298.00
Minimum	0.14	0.20E-01	0.44
Maximum	37.00	1,369.00	1,443.00
DRGSTIME			
Mean	12.28	194.10	257.50
SD	6.71	201.50	218.60
Number[a]	24.00	24.00	24.00
Minimum	1.00	1.00	23.00
Maximum	32.25	1,040.00	1,088.00
SCHTIME			
Mean	17.47	613.90	631.70
SD	18.35	916.60	908.60
Number[a]	12.00	12.00	12.00
Minimum	2.00	4.00	16.00
Maximum	52.98	2,807.00	2,809.00
AFFTIME			
Mean	13.13	274.80	324.60
SD	10.22	322.40	360.30
Number[a]	47.00	47.00	47.00
Minimum	0.25	0.63E-01	0.44
Maximum	34.70	1,204.00	1,225.00
ANXTIME			
Mean	26.92	933.40	976.90
SD	14.49	762.30	764.40
Number[a]	160.00	160.00	160.00
Minimum	0.25	0.63E-01	0.44
Maximum	51.98	2,702.00	2,704.00
ASPTIME			
Mean	27.09	818.60	1,113.00
SD	9.26	480.30	414.00
Number[a]	113.00	113.00	113.00
Minimum	8.00	64.00	369.00
Maximum	48.00	2,304.00	2,304.00

[a]Number of observations.

disability has been experienced by a group rises as a group's age rises. For example, ALCTIME is the value of the average timing measures for the alcohol abuse or dependence disorder. The mean ALCTIME for the model 2 timing measure, thirty-five- to fifty-four-year-old women (table 5.2C), is 204.5 years-squared. This value is the average of the square of the time individuals experienced the alcohol disorder. The

Table 5.1D   Weighted Descriptive Statistics of Timing Measures for ECA Men Fifty-five to Sixty-four Years Old

		Given Timing Measure > 0	
Variable	Model 1	Model 2	Model 3
ALCTIME			
Mean	24.03	758.80	951.70
SD	13.51	632.90	622.10
Number[a]	150.00	150.00	150.00
Minimum	0.70E-01	0.49E-02	4.62
Maximum	55.98	3,134.00	3,136.00
DRGSTIME	No observation of prevalent individuals		
SCHTIME			
Mean	51.49	2,655.00	2,657.00
SD	2.73	278.70	278.80
Number[a]	2.00	2.00	2.00
Minimum	48.98	2,399.00	2,401.00
Maximum	52.98	2,807.00	2,809.00
AFFTIME			
Mean	25.46	957.30	978.80
SD	17.95	907.40	928.50
Number[a]	25.00	25.00	25.00
Minimum	0.98	0.96	1.00
Maximum	48.70	2,372.00	2,401.00
ANXTIME			
Mean	31.79	1,371.00	1,478.00
SD	19.10	1,226.00	1,199.00
Number[a]	83.00	83.00	83.00
Minimum	0.25	0.63E-01	0.44
Maximum	62.90	3,956.00	3,969.00
ASPTIME			
Mean	40.69	1,790.00	2,269.00
SD	11.85	836.00	397.80
Number[a]	25.00	25.00	25.00
Minimum	14.00	196.00	1,260.00
Maximum	56.00	3,136.00	3,136.00

[a]Number of observations.

standard deviation of these squared times is 259.4. There were ninety-four observations in this group in the ECA sample. The minimum of the squared time was almost one-half year-squared (0.49); the maximum was 1,225 years-squared (35 years).

Results

Model Estimates

Tables 5.3A and 5.3B present the empirical estimates of the three models for males. Tables 5.4A and 5.4B present similar results for

Table 5.2A   Weighted Descriptive Statistics of Timing Measures for ECA Women Eighteen to Twenty-four Years Old

	Given Timing Measure > 0		
Variable	Model 1	Model 2	Model 3
ALCTIME			
Mean	2.91	13.54	16.87
SD	2.28	22.24	24.14
Number[a]	63.00	63.00	63.00
Minimum	0.25	0.63E-01	0.44
Maximum	10.90	118.80	140.00
DRGSTIME			
Mean	2.66	10.59	18.55
SD	1.90	16.52	20.42
Number[a]	38.00	38.00	38.00
Minimum	1.00	1.00	1.00
Maximum	10.00	100.00	140.00
SCHTIME			
Mean	5.82	46.66	65.62
SD	3.66	53.27	61.68
Number[a]	21.00	21.00	21.00
Minimum	0.98	0.96	1.00
Maximum	16.00	256.00	256.00
AFFTIME			
Mean	4.61	33.62	40.96
SD	3.55	46.60	56.03
Number[a]	61.00	61.00	61.00
Minimum	0.25	0.63E-01	0.44
Maximum	14.70	216.10	273.00
ANXTIME			
Mean	11.17	158.60	165.40
SD	5.83	136.40	136.50
Number[a]	191.00	191.00	191.00
Minimum	0.25	0.63E-01	0.44
Maximum	22.70	515.30	528.90
ASPTIME			
Mean	11.36	140.90	155.60
SD	3.48	82.42	82.98
Number[a]	41.00	41.00	41.00
Minimum	5.00	25.00	36.00
Maximum	19.00	361.00	361.00

[a]Number of observations.

females. Tables 5.3A and 5.4A contain estimates of the coefficients multiplying the control variables. Tables 5.3B and 5.4B present estimates of the coefficients multiplying the timing measures associated with each disorder. Estimates of the parameters of four models are presented—the three timing models and a model where all disorders are represented by indicator variables for comparative purposes.

Table 5.2B   Weighted Descriptive Statistics of Timing Measures for ECA Women Twenty-five to Thirty-four Years Old

	Given Timing Measure > 0		
Variable	Model 1	Model 2	Model 3
ALCTIME			
Mean	5.49	44.92	61.41
SD	3.86	55.14	61.69
Number[a]	87.00	87.00	87.00
Minimum	0.70	0.49	0.91
Maximum	14.98	224.40	247.00
DRGSTIME			
Mean	5.85	52.89	83.25
SD	4.36	63.83	72.63
Number[a]	50.00	50.00	50.00
Minimum	1.00	1.00	3.99
Maximum	16.98	288.30	289.00
SCHTIME			
Mean	11.77	198.80	211.50
SD	7.85	232.00	231.70
Number[a]	45.00	45.00	45.00
Minimum	0.70	0.49	0.91
Maximum	31.98	1,023.00	1,024.00
AFFTIME			
Mean	7.60	90.56	107.00
SD	5.74	121.70	127.20
Number[a]	159.00	159.00	159.00
Minimum	0.25	0.63E-01	0.44
Maximum	26.70	712.90	728.90
ANXTIME			
Mean	16.66	353.50	372.70
SD	8.73	290.80	291.00
Number[a]	413.00	413.00	413.00
Minimum	0.25	0.63E-01	0.44
Maximum	32.00	1,024.00	1,024.00
ASPTIME			
Mean	17.34	329.00	399.50
SD	5.37	192.20	195.70
Number[a]	62.00	62.00	62.00
Minimum	8.00	64.00	144.00
Maximum	28.00	784.00	784.00

[a]Number of observations.

Each cell in each table contains a vector of statistics: a stacking of coefficient estimate, upon its standard error, upon a two-tail significance level for tables 5.3A and 5.4A or a one-tail significance level for tables 5.3B and 5.4B. The appropriate tests for tables 5.3A and 5.4A are one- or two-tailed, depending on the variable, but the tests appli-

Table 5.2C   Weighted Descriptive Statistics of Timing Measures for ECA Women Thirty-five to Fifty-four Years Old

	Given Timing Measure > 0		
Variable	Model 1	Model 2	Model 3
ALCTIME			
Mean	11.39	204.50	261.60
SD	8.70	259.40	280.30
Number[a]	94.00	94.00	94.00
Minimum	0.70	0.49	0.91
Maximum	35.00	1,225.00	1,505.00
DRGSTIME			
Mean	7.26	80.41	129.10
SD	5.35	116.20	122.90
Number[a]	29.00	29.00	29.00
Minimum	0.98	0.96	1.00
Maximum	22.98	528.10	529.00
SCHTIME			
Mean	16.97	438.20	491.40
SD	12.43	484.00	502.10
Number[a]	36.00	36.00	36.00
Minimum	2.00	4.00	9.00
Maximum	38.25	1,463.00	1,520.00
AFFTIME			
Mean	12.42	233.30	268.20
SD	8.92	269.10	287.80
Number[a]	175.00	175.00	175.00
Minimum	0.25	0.63E-01	0.44
Maximum	34.70	1,204.00	1,428.00
ANXTIME			
Mean	26.23	875.80	942.10
SD	13.72	707.50	705.30
Number[a]	441.00	441.00	441.00
Minimum	0.25	0.63E-01	0.44
Maximum	52.98	2,807.00	2,809.00
ASPTIME			
Mean	30.72	1,000.00	1,098.00
SD	7.62	494.20	474.30
Number[a]	37.00	37.00	37.00
Minimum	11.00	121.00	473.00
Maximum	47.25	2,233.00	2,303.00

[a]Number of observations.

cable to the timing measures of the disorders (tables 5.3B and 5.4B) are always one-tail tests—a null hypothesis of zero tested against the alternative of a loss resulting from a disorder.

A cautionary note—except where disorders are represented by an indicator, as in a comparative model where all disorders are repre-

Table 5.2D   Weighted Descriptive Statistics of Timing Measures for ECA Women Fifty-five to Sixty-four Years Old

	Given Timing Measure > 0		
Variable	Model 1	Model 2	Model 3
ALCTIME			
Mean	14.15	332.40	499.80
SD	11.69	423.10	548.80
Number[a]	30.00	30.00	30.00
Minimum	0.25	0.63E-01	0.44
Maximum	39.00	1,521.00	1,833.00
DRGSTIME			
Mean	11.58	360.70	526.90
SD	21.29	723.90	1,018.00
Number[a]	2.00	2.00	2.00
Minimum	1.00	1.00	21.00
Maximum	33.00	1,089.00	1,551.00
SCHTIME			
Mean	27.47	963.90	1,135.00
SD	15.47	864.60	755.00
Number[a]	8.00	8.00	8.00
Minimum	5.00	25.00	115.00
Maximum	44.98	2,023.00	2,025.00
AFFTIME			
Mean	20.65	670.90	780.20
SD	15.81	783.50	778.60
Number[a]	46.00	46.00	46.00
Minimum	0.25	0.63E-01	0.44
Maximum	51.98	2,702.00	2,704.00
ANXTIME			
Mean	40.39	1,948.00	2,040.00
SD	17.83	1,216.00	1,190.00
Number[a]	238.00	238.00	238.00
Minimum	0.98	0.96	1.00
Maximum	62.98	3,966.00	3,969.00
ASPTIME			
Mean	44.76	2,062.00	2,422.00
SD	8.27	705.10	342.90
Number[a]	7.00	7.00	7.00
Minimum	32.00	1,024.00	1,984.00
Maximum	53.25	2,836.00	2,915.00

[a]Number of observations.

sented by indicators and by the SOMCOGA indicator (in every timing model), the results presented in tables 5.3B and 5.4B are not estimates of the percentage of loss per prevalent individual. The loss per prevalent individual is estimated as the product of the average timing measures (from tables 5.1A to 5.2D) and the estimates of their model coefficients, which appear in tables 5.3B and 5.4B.

Table 5.3A Estimates of Coefficients on Control Variables for Alternative Timing Models of Income Loss for Men

Variable	Indicators of Disorder	Model 1	Model 2	Model 3
ONE				
Coefficient estimate	3.888	3.796	3.804	3.805
SE	(0.327)	(0.334)	(0.335)	(0.335)
Significance	0.000	0.000	0.000	0.000
AGE				
Coefficient estimate	0.239	0.245	0.244	0.244
SE	(0.0154)	(0.0157)	(0.0157)	(0.0157)
Significance	0.00.0	0.000	0.000	0.000
AGEGROUP2				
Coefficient estimate	4.598	4.660	4.643	4.639
SE	(0.422)	(0.430)	(0.430)	(0.430)
Significance	0.000	0.000	0.000	0.000
AGEGROUP3				
Coefficient estimate	6.501	6.719	6.672	6.669
SE	(0.369)	(0.377)	(0.377)	(0.377)
Significance	0.000	0.000	0.000	0.000
AGEGROUP4				
Coefficient estimate	8.132	8.341	8.289	8.272
SE	(0.798)	(0.809)	(0.812)	(0.812)
Significance	0.000	0.000	0.000	0.000
AGE*GROUP2				
Coefficient estimate	−0.196	−0.199	−0.198	−0.198
SE	(0.0179)	(0.0183)	(0.0183)	(0.0183)
Significance	0.000	0.000	0.000	0.000
AGE*GROUP3				
Coefficient estimate	−0.249	−0.256	−0.255	−0.255
SE	(0.0158)	(0.0162)	(0.0162)	(0.0162)
Significance	0.000	0.000	0.000	0.000
AGE*GROUP4				
Coefficient estimate	−0.277	−0.284	−0.283	−0.282
SE	(0.0196)	(0.0200)	(0.0201)	(0.0201)
Significance	0.000	0.000	0.000	0.000
MAR				
Coefficient estimate	0.379	0.383	0.388	0.388
SE	(0.0324)	(0.0328)	(0.0327)	(0.0327)
Significance	0.000	0.000	0.000	0.000
KIDS				
Coefficient estimate	0.768E-02	0.811E-02	0.767E-02	0.756E-02
SE	(0.991E-02)	(0.995E-02)	(0.999E-02)	(0.996E-02)
Significance	0.438	0.415	0.442	0.448
HRACE				
Coefficient estimate	−0.467	−0.511	−0.509	−0.510
SE	(0.0521)	(0.0521)	(0.0521)	(0.0520)
Significance	0.000	0.000	0.000	0.000
BRACE				
Coefficient estimate	−0.144	−0.450	−0.447	−0.447
SE	(0.0385)	(0.0386)	(0.0386)	(0.0386)
Significance	0.000	0.000	0.000	0.000

(*continued*)

Table 5.3A *(Continued)*

Variable	Indicators of Disorder	Model 1	Model 2	Model 3
CRACE				
Coefficient estimate	−0.473	−0.478	−0.471	−0.473
SE	(0.0647)	(0.0661)	(0.0662)	(0.0661)
Significance	0.000	0.000	0.000	0.000
SICK				
Coefficient estimate	−0.637	−0.613	−0.648	−0.637
SE	(0.0818)	(0.0860)	(0.0864)	(0.0865)
Significance	0.000	0.000	0.000	0.000
TLY0				
Coefficient estimate	−0.488	−0.509	−0.510	−0.509
SE	(0.0566)	(0.0507)	(0.0573)	(0.0570)
Significance	0.000	0.000	0.000	0.000
TLY1				
Coefficient estimate	−0.514	−0.518	−0.522	−0.522
SE	(0.0725)	(0.0728)	(0.0733)	(0.0730)
Significance	0.000	0.000	0.000	0.000
TLH1				
Coefficient estimate	−0.463	−0.528	−0.528	−0.527
SE	(0.0612)	(0.0618)	(0.0617)	(0.0616)
Significance	0.000	0.000	0.000	0.000
TLD2				
Coefficient estimate	−0.532	−0.570	−0.566	−0.566
SE	(0.0596)	(0.0600)	(0.0601)	(0.0599)
Significance	0.000	0.000	0.000	0.000
TLD3				
Coefficient estimate	−0.476	−0.517	−0.512	−0.510
SE	(0.0849)	(0.0857)	(0.0857)	(0.0855)
Significance	0.000	0.000	0.000	0.000
TLL3				
Coefficient estimate	−0.146	−0.164	−0.170	−0.169
SE	(0.0571)	(0.0577)	(0.0576)	(0.0577)
Significance	0.010	0.005	0.003	0.003
SIGMA				
Coefficient estimate	0.842	0.854	0.854	0.854
SE	(0.957E-02)	(0.975E-02)	(0.978E-02)	(0.978E-02)
Significance	0.00	0.000	0.000	0.000

Best Model and Estimates of Loss per Prevalent Individual

To achieve a single loss estimate, we chose a best specification for each disorder on the basis of the results in tables 5.3B and 5.4B. A final model was estimated, by sex, combining the best model for each disorder. These results appear in table 5.5. Percentage loss per prevalent individual was estimated with the relevant timing measures (tables 5.1A to 5.2D) and the coefficients from table 5.5. These estimates appear in tables 5.6A and 5.6B, for men and women, respectively.

Table 5.3B   Estimates of Coefficients on Disorder Variables
for Alternative Timing Models of Income Loss for Men

Variable	Indicators of Disorder	Model 1	Model 2	Model 3
ALC				
Coefficient estimate	−0.103	−0.404E-02	−0.447E-04	−0.501E-04
SE	(0.352E-01)	(0.224E-02)	(0.692E-04)	(0.617E-04)
Significance[a]	0.002	0.036	0.259	0.208
DRGSEV				
Coefficient estimate	−0.758E-01	−0.108E-01	−0.116E-03	−0.481E-03
SE	(0.779E-01)	(0.929E-02)	(0.383E-03)	(0.364E-03)
Significance[a]	0.165	0.124	0.381	0.096
SCHDISOR				
Coefficient estimate	−0.508	−0.258E-01	−0.613E-03	−0.613E-03
SE	(0.994E-01)	(0.507E-02)	(0.154E-03)	(0.148E-03)
Significance[a]	0.000	0.000	0.000	0.000
AFFDISOR				
Coefficient estimate	0.339	0.158E-02	0.273E-03	0.227E-03
SE	(0.367E-01)	(0.431E-02)	(0.144E-03)	(0.128E-03)
Significance[a]	0.000	0.357	0.029	0.038
ANXDISOR				
Coefficient estimate	−0.106	−0.154E-02	−0.673E-04	−0.741E-04
SE	(0.402E-01)	(0.164E-02)	(0.399E-04)	(0.384E-04)
Significance	0.004	0.174	0.046	0.290
ASP				
Coefficient estimate	−0.417E-01	−0.215E-02	−0.563E-04	−0.279E-04
SE	(0.500E-01)	(0.196E-02)	(0.565E-04)	(0.503E-04)
Significance	0.202	0.136	0.159	0.290
SOMCOGA				
Coefficient estimate	−0.0993	−0.100	−0.126	−0.125
SE	(0.176)	(0.178)	(0.180)	(0.180)
Significance	0.278	0.287	0.243	0.243
Log-likelihood	−11,070	−11,120	−11,122	−11,122

[a]One-tailed significance level.

Which of these processes is most likely to describe the loss from
each disorder? The choice between descriptions of the impairment
processes is based on the results presented in tables 5.3B and 5.4B. In
almost every case, the model whose coefficient was most different
(statistically) from zero was chosen as "best" for each disorder. When
differences were very similar, other criteria were used. The discussion that follows indicates our thoughts on this selection process.

Alcohol Abuse and Dependency

The best model for men for alcohol is model 1. Losses from alcohol
abuse or dependency seem to be a function only of how long one

Table 5.4A   Estimates of Coefficients on Control Variables
for Alternative Timing Models of Income Loss for Women

Variable	Indicators of Disorder	Model 1	Model 2	Model 3
ONE				
Coefficient estimate	3.321	3.272	3.277	3.278
SE	(0.387)	(0.390)	(0.390)	(0.390)
Significance	0.000	0.000	0.000	0.000
AGE				
Coefficient estimate	0.259	0.263	0.262	0.263
SE	(0.0182)	(0.0184)	(0.0184)	(0.0184)
Significance	0.000	0.000	0.000	0.000
AGEGROUP2				
Coefficient estimate	6.068	6.132	6.127	6.130
SE	(0.499)	(0.502)	(0.502)	(0.502)
Significance	0.000	0.000	0.000	0.000
AGEGROUP3				
Coefficient estimate	6.913	7.009	6.974	6.981
SE	(0.432)	(0.434)	(0.434)	(0.434)
Significance	0.000	0.000	0.000	0.000
AGEGROUP4				
Coefficient estimate	7.363	7.488	7.412	7.415
SE	(0.835)	(0.841)	(0.842)	(0.842)
Significance	0.000	0.000	0.000	0.000
AGE*GROUP2				
Coefficient estimate	−0.249	−0.252	−0.251	−0.252
SE	(0.0211)	(0.0212)	(0.0212)	(0.0212)
Significance	0.000	0.000	0.000	0.000
AGE*GROUP3				
Coefficient estimate	−0.272	−0.275	−0.274	−0.275
SE	(0.0187)	(0.0188)	(0.0188)	(0.0188)
Significance	0.000	0.000	0.000	0.000
AGE*GROUP4				
Coefficient estimate	−0.279	−0.283	−0.281	−0.281
SE	(0.0222)	(0.0224)	(0.0224)	(0.0224)
Significance	0.000	0.000	0.000	0.000
MAR				
Coefficient estimate	−0.441	−0.460	−0.458	−0.460
SE	(0.0375)	(0.0377)	(0.0377)	(0.0377)
Significance	0.000	0.000	0.000	0.000
KIDS				
Coefficient estimate	−0.102	−0.104	−0.104	−0.104
SE	(0.890E-02)	(0.899E-02)	(0.900E-02)	(0.899E-02)
Significance	0.000	0.000	0.000	0.000
HRACE				
Coefficient estimate	−0.585	−0.619	−0.618	−0.619
SE	(0.0595)	(0.0595)	(0.0594)	(0.0594)
Significance	0.000	0.000	0.000	0.000
BRACE				
Coefficient estimate	0.0477	0.0257	0.0251	0.0245
SE	(0.0455)	(0.0458)	(0.0458)	(0.0458)
Significance	0.295	0.575	0.583	0.593

(continued)

Table 5.4A   (*Continued*)

Variable	Indicators of Disorder	Model 1	Model 2	Model 3
ORACE				
Coefficient estimate	−0.128	−0.126	−0.122	−0.125
SE	(0.0856)	(0.0848)	(0.0848)	(0.0848)
Significance	0.136	0.136	0.149	0.140
SICK				
Coefficient estimate	−0.457	−0.443	−0.453	−0.453
SE	(0.0821)	(0.0833)	(0.0835)	(0.0834)
Significance	0.000	0.000	0.000	0.000
TLY0				
Coefficient estimate	−0.789	−0.817	−0.813	−0.817
SE	(0.0752)	(0.0757)	(0.0758)	(0.0756)
Significance	0.000	0.000	0.000	0.000
TLY1				
Coefficient estimate	−0.681	−0.698	−0.694	−0.700
SE	(0.0917)	(0.0924)	(0.0925)	(0.0924)
Significance	0.000	0.000	0.000	0.000
TLH1				
Coefficient estimate	−0.784	−0.838	−0.841	−0.844
SE	(0.0787)	(0.0788)	(0.0788)	(0.0786)
Significance	0.000	0.000	0.000	0.000
TLD2				
Coefficient estimate	−0.494	−0.529	−0.529	−0.532
SE	(0.0798)	(0.0801)	(0.0801)	(0.0799)
Significance	0.000	0.000	0.000	0.000
TLD3				
Coefficient estimate	−0.268	−0.298	−0.303	−0.305
SE	(0.119)	(0.120)	(0.120)	(0.120)
Significance	0.024	0.013	0.012	0.011
TLL3				
Coefficient estimate	−0.123	−0.131	−0.130	−0.132
SE	(0.0727)	(0.0730)	(0.0732)	(0.0730)
Significance	0.090	0.073	0.076	0.070

experiences the alcohol abuse or dependency disorder. The male alcohol abuse or dependency coefficient (table 5.3B) is significant at the .036 level. Other models have estimates that are not statistically significant.

All of the models of alcohol impairment are estimated as significant for women. The most significant model for women ($p = .026$) is model 2 (table 5.4B). Model 1 is significant at the .05 level, and model 3 is significant at the .07 level. Although it is difficult to distinguish between these alternative processes taken at face value (as the full discussion to follow will show), this is the one case where we consider the model 2 estimates to be the best.

The difference between men and women in regard to this disor-

Table 5.4B   Estimates of Coefficients on Disorder Variables for Alternative Timing Models of Income Loss for Women

Variable	Indicators of Disorder	Model 1	Model 2	Model 3
ALC				
Coefficient estimate	−0.0747	−0.0131	−0.695E-03	−0.439E-03
SE	(0.0792)	(0.789E-02)	(0.357E-03)	(0.292E-03)
Significance[a]	0.173	0.048	0.026	0.067
DRGSEV				
Coefficient estimate	0.141	0.876E-02	0.377E-03	−0.195E-04
SE	(0.116)	(0.188E-01)	(0.109E-02)	(0.105E-02)
Significance[a]	0.112	0.321	0.365	0.493
SCHDISOR				
Coefficient estimate	−0.245	−0.513E-02	−0.359E-04	−0.892E-04
SE	(0.119)	(0.762E-02)	0.279E-03)	(0.243E-03)
Significance[a]	0.020	0.251	0.449	0.357
AFFDISOR				
Coefficient estimate	0.271	0.234E-02	0.110E-03	0.102E-03
SE	(0.0430)	(0.403E-02)	(0.142E-03)	(0.133E-03)
Significance[a]	0.000	0.281)	0.220	0.222
ANXDISOR				
Coefficient estimate	−0.188	−0.373E-02	−0.604E-04	−0.661E-04
SE	(0.0397)	(0.141E-02)	(0.329E-04)	(0.318E-04)
Significance	0.000	0.004	0.034	0.019
ASP				
Coefficient estimate	−0.108	−0.236E-04	0.611E-04	0.310E-04
SE	(0.105)	(0.425E-02)	(0.118E-03)	(0.109E-03)
Significance	0.150	0.498	0.302	0.338
SOMCOGA				
Coefficient estimate	−0.477	−0.459	−0.476	−0.482
SE	(0.174)	(0.176)	(0.176)	(0.176)
Significance	0.003	0.005	0.004	0.003
SIGMA				
Coefficient estimate	1.077	1.084	1.085	1.085
SE	(0.0173)	(0.0174)	(0.0175)	(0.0175)
Significance	0.000	0.000	0.000	0.000
Log-likelihood	−13,560	−13,587	−13,588	−13,588

[a]One-tailed significance level.

der is interesting. Recall that model 1 describes a loss process that occurs in the present and model 2 describes cumulative effects over the period during which an individual experiences a disorder. A possible sociological basis for men being described by current effects and women being described by current plus future effects is that alcohol abuse or dependence is less culturally acceptable for women than for men. Stigmatization influences assignment and responsibility and, hence, productivity. The fact that the stigmatization for women stops when the disorder stops probably has to do with the familiarity of the

Table 5.5   Regression Coefficients for Indicator Model and Final Model, by Sex

Disorder	Indicator Model[a]	Final Model[b]	Indicator Model[a]	Final Model[b]
ALCTIME		Model 1		Model 2
Coefficient estimate	-0.103	-0.00407	-0.075	-0.000621
SE	(0.035)	(0.00224)	0.079	(0.000357)
Significance[c]	0.005	0.035	0.17	0.04
DRGSTIME		Model 3		Model 3
Coefficient estimate	-0.076	-0.000336	0.141	0.000134
SE	(0.078)	(0.000381)	0.116	(0.00108)
Significance[c]	0.17	0.19	1.216[d]	0.124[d]
SCHTIME		Model 3		Model 1
Coefficient estimate	-0.508	-0.000557)	-0.245	-0.00583
SE	(0.099)	(0.000122)	(0.119)	(0.00753)
Significance[c]	0.000	0.000	0.02	0.22
AFFTIME		Model 1		Model 1
Coefficient estimate	0.339	0.00203	0.271	0.00202
SE	(0.037)	(0.00437)	(0.043)	(0.00402)
Significance[c]	9.167[d]	0.464[d]	6.3[d]	0.503[d]
ANXTIME		Model 3		Model 3
Coefficient estimate	-0.106	-6.60E-05	-0.188	-6.36E-05
SE	(0.040)	(3.807E-05)	(0.040)	(3.171E-05)
Significance[c]	0.004	0.04	0.000	0.02
ASPTIME		Model 1		Model 1
Coefficient estimate	-0.42E-01	-0.00238	-0.108	-0.000146
SE	(0.056)	(0.00195)	(0.105)	(0.00427)
Significance[c]	0.23	0.11	0.15	0.37
SOMCOGA		Indicator		Indicator
Coefficient estimate	-0.099	-0.109	-0.477	-0.466
SE	(0.176)	(0.180)	(0.174)	(0.176)
Significance[c]	0.29	0.27	0.003	0.004
SIGMA				
Coefficient estimate		0.854		1.085
SE		(0.101)		(0.0175)
Significance[c]		0.000		0.000

[a]Indicator coefficients are from table 5.3B.
[b]Timing coefficients are estimated.
[c]One-tailed significance level.
[d]These are t-values. The coefficient has the wrong sign.

disorder in the culture. "It is well known" that stopping drinking ends the disorder and that normal economic behavior can be resumed.

The loss associated with alcohol abuse or dependency in the final model is significant for both men and women (table 5.5). The loss for men ranges from a little over 1 percent for 18–24-year-olds to 9.8 percent for 55–64-year-olds (table 5.6A). These losses are statistically different from zero at the $p = .04$ level. Because women's losses are described by a cumulative model, they estimate as larger

Table 5.6A   Estimates of Loss per Prevalent Individual and Tests of Significance for Men, by Age Group

Timing Measure of ADM Disorder by Age Group[a]	(1)	(2) Loss per Prevalent Man[b]	(3) Standard Error of Loss per Prevalent Man[c]	(4) t-value of Loss per Prevalent Man[d]	(5) p-value of Loss[e]
ALCTIME					
18–24	3.56	−0.0145	0.008	−1.80	0.036
25–34	7.56	−0.0308	0.017	−1.81	0.035
35–54	13.88	−0.0565	0.031	−1.81	0.035
55–64	24.03	−0.0978	0.054	−1.80	0.035
DRGSTIME					
18–24	32.48	−0.0109	0.0127	−0.86	0.194
25–34	77.63	−0.0261	0.0298	−0.87	0.191
35–54	257.5	−0.0865	0.1008	−0.86	0.195
55–64		No prevalent individuals observed.			
SCHTIME					
18–24	133.2	−0.0742	0.0281	−2.64	0.004
25–34	155.7	−0.0867	0.0271	−3.21	0.000
35–54	631.7	−0.3519	0.1742	−2.02	0.022
55–64	2,657.0	−1.4799	0.3610	−4.10	0.000
AFFTIME		Positive coefficients estimated. Calculation not relevant.			
ANXTIME					
18–24	182.6	−0.0121	0.0071	−1.71	0.044
25–34	380.9	−0.0251	0.0146	−1.72	0.042
35–54	976.9	−0.0645	0.0375	−1.72	0.043
55–64	1,478.0	−0.0975	0.0572	−1.71	0.044
ASPTIME					
18–24	11.82	−0.0281	0.0231	−1.22	0.111
25–34	17.95	−0.0427	0.0350	−1.22	0.111
35–54	27.09	−0.0645	0.0529	−1.22	0.111
55–64	40.69	−0.0968	0.0797	−1.22	0.112

[a]Source: Tables 5.2A–5.2D.
[b]Source: Product of column (1) and final model coefficients from table 5.5.
[c]Computed as described in appendix 5.A, using statistics from tables 5.1A–5.1D and table 5.5.
[d]Column (2)/(3).
[e]Corresponds to the one-tailed test.

than men's. Women's losses from alcohol abuse or dependency start out at the same levels as men's losses (in percentage terms)—in the 1 percent range for 18–24-year-olds—but rise at a faster rate with age. Women's losses from alcohol abuse or dependency are a little under 3 percent for 25–34-year-olds, are almost 13 percent for 35–54-year-olds, and reach about 20.6 percent for 55–64-year-olds. As with men, these losses are statistically different from zero at about the $p = .05$ level (table 5.6B).

Table 5.6B   Estimates of Loss per Prevalent Individual and Tests of Significance for Women, by Age Group

Timing Measure of ADM Disorder by Age Group[a]	(1) Loss per Prevalent Woman[b]	(2) Standard Error of Loss per Prevalent Woman[c]	(3) t-value of Loss per Prevalent Woman[d]	(4) p-value of Loss[e]
	(1)	(2)	(3)	(4)	(5)
ALCTIME					
18–24	13.54	−0.0084	0.00524	−1.60	0.054
25–34	44.92	−0.0279	0.0166	−1.68	0.046
35–54	204.5	−0.1270	0.0755	−1.68	0.046
55–64	332.4	−0.2064	0.13134	−1.57	0.058
DRGSTIME	Positive coefficients estimated. Calculation not relevant.				
SCHTIME					
18–24	5.82	−0.0339	0.0445	−0.76	0.222
25–34	11.17	−0.0651	0.0893	−0.77	0.221
35–54	16.97	−0.0989	0.13122	−0.75	0.227
55–64	27.47	−0.160	0.21421	−0.75	0.227
AFFTIME	Positive coefficients estimated. Calculation not relevant.				
ANXTIME					
18–24	165.4	−0.0105	0.00529	−1.99	0.023
25–34	372.7	−0.0237	0.0119	−1.99	0.023
35–54	942.1	−0.0599	0.0300	−2.00	0.023
55–64	2,040.0	−0.1297	0.0649	−2.00	0.023
ASPTIME					
18–24	11.36	−0.00166	0.0486	−0.034	0.486
25–34	17.34	−0.00253	0.0741	−0.034	0.486
35–54	30.72	−0.00449	0.13129	−0.034	0.486
55–64	44.76	−0.00653	0.19167	−0.034	0.486

[a]Source: Tables 5.2A–5.2D.
[b]Source: Product of column (1) and final model coefficients from table 5.5.
[c]Computed as described in appendix 5.A, using statistics from tables 5.1A–5.1D and table 5.5.
[d]Column (2)/(3).
[e]Corresponds to the one-tailed test.

Drug Abuse and Dependency

For men, the best model describing the effect of drug abuse and dependency (and the severity condition) on market performance seems to be model 3 ($p = .096$ in table 5.3B), although the model 1 specification is nearly as significant ($p = .124$). Model 3's description implies that drug abuse and/or dependency has both cumulative effects over use and continuing effects beyond the time when drug abuse or dependency stops.

As table 5.4B shows, there is no statistically significant model of income loss associated with drug abuse and dependency for women. Although neither statistically significant nor significant in magnitude, model 3 does yield a negative point estimate on the drug severity measure.

The statistical significance of the estimated drug-related loss coefficient for men in the final model, as table 5.5 shows, is $p = .19$. This is compared to its estimate in the all-model 3 specification of $p = .096$ (table 5.3B). For women, the negative but not statistically significant point estimate in the model 3 specification estimated as positive in the final model. Table 5.6A shows the estimated instantaneous percentage loss per prevalent male for the three youngest age groups. No prevalent individuals were observed in the oldest age group (fifty-five to sixty-four years old). The estimated losses caused by recognized drug abuse or dependency were at about the same levels as the alcohol losses in the earlier years but, because model 3 is a cumulative model, drug losses exceeded the losses due to alcohol abuse and dependency in the later years. Loss estimates for drug abuse and dependency for males were 1.1 percent for 18–24-year-olds, 2.6 percent for 25–34-year-olds, and 8.65 percent for 35–54-year-olds. These losses were significant at about the .19 level of significance. Because of the positive point estimate associated with drug loss for women, no income loss estimate was calculated.

Why the lack of significance for women? The alcohol results suggest that there may be greater stigma associated with substance use by women than by men. Stigma associated with illegal activities should exceed stigma associated with legal activities. With such negative effect, the tendency to underreport drug use is probably greater for women. The effect of correctly reporting income, hypothesized as lower when there has been drug abuse or dependency, and underreporting drug abuse and dependency symptoms is to erase the relationship between income loss and drug use in the data set.

Schizophrenic Disorders

The effects of schizophrenic disorders in men are so statistically significant in every model that it is not possible to discriminate between the processes. Any of the three seems appropriate on empirical grounds. It is likely that more loss is appropriate here, and model 3 results are consistent with that situation. Because of the significance of the loss estimates for men, the insignificant results associated with women (table 5.4B) are puzzling. Model 1 for women seems the best guess, but it is significant only at the .25 level.

The coefficient on the model 3 schizophrenic-type disorder timing measure in the final model for men was also very significant ($p = .000$). The economic losses from a schizophrenic-type disorder start out at levels that are as bad as the worst losses from alcohol or drug abuse, at about 7.4 percent for 18–24-year-old men and 8.7 percent for 25–34-year-olds. As these individuals age, their disorder becomes increasingly devastating. By the time men are in the 35–54-year-old range they earn an estimated 35 percent less. They have virtually no economic life by the time they are 55–64 years old; their losses are reduced by 100 percent—a 148 percent loss was the actual figure estimated (an impossible figure). These losses were all significant at the $p = .02$ or better level. The estimates of loss reported in Rice et al. (1990) are based on "smeared" estimates of the coefficients presented in tables 5.6A and 5.6B (Duan 1983). The "smearing" transformation is: "smeared" coefficient $= (EXP[coefficient] - 1.0)$. Problems like a 148 percent reduction are resolved by this transformation.

For women, the model 1-specified coefficient in the final model was slightly more significant ($p = .22$) than in its model 1 specification ($p = .25$). Losses caused by schizophrenia for women (table 5.6B) were quite moderate by comparison with those of men suffering from a schizophrenic-type disorder. The youngest age group earned a little over 3 percent less; 25–34-year-olds earned 6.5 percent less; 35–54-year-olds earned about 10 percent less; and the oldest group earned 16 percent less. These losses were significant only at the $p = .22$ level, suggesting greater variation in the economic effects of schizophrenia on women than on men.

Affective Disorders

In the (comparative) indicator model, affective disorders were strongly associated with a large positive influence on income. This finding was severely reduced in the timing models, however. We do not accept the implication that, all other things equal, having an affective disorder diagnosis increases one's income. Rather, we conclude that the selection bias problem is particularly pronounced for affective disorders. Whether this results from the socioeconomic distribution of affective disorders or from the greater responsiveness of higher-income individuals to DIS questions yielding affective disorder diagnoses cannot be determined from this analysis. Therefore, the findings on affective disorders were not used in the income loss calculations.

Anxiety Disorders

Uncontroversially, for men, the cumulative models are superior to the simpler time-with-disorder model, and the more cumulative model 3 estimates are more significant ($p = .027$) than the model 2 estimates ($p = .046$). For women, the picture is a little different, as every model seems to describe the relation between anxiety and productivity loss (table 5.4B). In this case, anxiety for women is like schizophrenia for men. Although model 1 for women has a slightly more significant coefficient ($p = .004$), model 3 is significant at the $p = .02$ level and model 2 is significant at the $p = .034$ level. Model 3 was selected for the final specification to reproduce a similar form for men and women in the final model equation.

Table 5.5 shows that losses were estimated as significantly different from zero for both sexes. The p levels are .04 and .02 for men and women, respectively. For men, a 1.2 percent loss is associated with 18–24-year-olds; a 2.5 percent loss is associated with 25–34-year-olds; a 6.5 percent loss is associated with 35–54-year-olds; and a 9.8 percent loss is associated with 55–64-year-olds (table 5.6A). These estimates are all significant at about the .04 level. As the loss estimates of table 5.6B confirm, the losses associated with anxiety for women are about the same as those associated with anxiety disorders for men. They are a little more statistically different from zero (about $p = .02$). Women's losses start a little smaller than men's and end a little larger: 1.1 percent for 18–24-year-olds; 2.4 percent for 25–34-year-olds; 6.0 percent for 35–54-year-olds; and 13.0 percent for 55–64-year-olds.

Antisocial Personality Disorder

Antisocial personality is best estimated by model 1 for men (table 5.3B), although it is significant only at the $p = .136$ level. For women (table 5.4B), only model 1's coefficient has a negative point estimate; it is not close to statistical significance.

In the final model for men, the model 1 specification for antisocial personality proved slightly more significant ($p = .11$) than it had in the single-model specification. Losses for men were calculated to rise uniformly with age group: 2.8 percent for 18–24-year-olds to 9.7 percent for 55–64-year-olds. These losses are different from zero at the .11 level. In neither the single-form models nor the final model was the negative point estimate for females statistically different from zero. As table 5.6B shows, the magnitude of the antisocial personality disorder for women was small as well, starting at 0.2 percent for the youngest group and rising to 0.7 percent for the oldest group. The losses could be due to chance alone one-half of the time.

Somatization and Severe Cognitive Disorders

SOMCOGA is an indicator variable of either somatization or severe cognitive disorder. The prevalence rates for these disorders were quite low, and this aggregate disorder was meant to be a catchall category that was included in the specification to complete the disorder description. The results estimate the percentage of income loss by sex. No distinction is made by age group. The estimates for both sexes are negative, but the 10.9 percent loss for men is not statistically different from zero and the 46.6 percent loss for women is quite different from zero ($p = .004$).

Comparison with the Results of Previous Studies

A note of caution about direct comparison is in order. Different studies use different disorder definitions and aggregations, and these differences render their numerical results somewhat noncomparable. For example, this study employed a DSM-III definition of alcohol prevalence, whereas the RTI study employed a behavioral measure (problem drinking). These differing definitions may affect the measured population prevalence rates. This alone can affect the measured impairment rates, depending on whether the average prevalent individual is based on a restrictive or a more relaxed definition of prevalence. Second, other studies used a different specification. In other studies, the process translating disorders into productivity loss was exogenous to the analysis. Impairment was represented by an indicator of group membership. In this study, the process translating disorders into productivity loss was endogenous to the analysis. The impairment process was described with alternative functions of the time that it existed. Third, there are different levels of aggregation and consideration of other possible disorders. This study analyzed the income-depressive effects of six different categories of mental disorder, whereas others analyzed the effects of more aggregated mental disorders. This study simultaneously controlled for alcohol, drug, and mental disorders, whereas others did not. We here summarize the various findings on the three disorder categories, alcohol, drug, and mental disorders.

This study found alcohol impairment rates of 1–10 percent for men, depending on age, and 1–21 percent for women. In the RTI study, the corresponding alcohol impairment rate for both sexes combined was 21 percent, significantly higher than for this study, considering that male prevalence rates are more than double those for females in both studies. Mullahy and Sindelar (1988), studying twenty-five- to fifty-nine-year-old men from the ECA New Haven cohort, obtained a two-stage least squares estimate of 23 percent alcohol impairment with marginal statistical significance.

This study found drug impairment rates of 1–9 percent for men and positive coefficients for women at all ages. In contrast, the RTI found a highly significant 28 percent impairment rate for both sexes related to any lifetime episode of heavy marijuana use of one or more month's duration.

In this study there were various rates of impairment due to mental illness, depending on age, sex, and category of mental illness. For most mental illness categories the impairment rates are generally within the 1–12 percent impairment range, with the exception of schizophrenic disorders, for which the range is 7–100 percent for men and 3–16 percent for women.

Bartel and Taubman (1979, 1986) analyzed the effect of mental disorders on earnings of the National Academy of Science/National Research Council panel of twins. In the 1979 study, they reported a 24 percent reduction in 1973 earnings due to the presence of a psychiatric diagnosis made during the previous five years. In the 1986 study, distinguishing between psychosis and neurosis, they found 37 percent and 11 percent reductions, respectively, for diagnoses made during the previous five years. Overall earnings loss due to all mental disorders was estimated to be 24 percent.

Frank and Gertler (1987), using the Baltimore site data of the ECA survey, found a 26 percent reduction in personal income of eighteen- to sixty-four-year-old men as a result of "mental distress," defined as a composite of three different measures of psychiatric diagnosis.

In general, the results found in this study suggest lower rates of impairment than have been previously reported. (For a more extensive discussion of the differences between these and RTI findings, see Rice et al. 1990, 179–200.)

Summary and Conclusions

This chapter contains three principal sections. The first surveyed and reviewed the analytical development of models that estimate the impairment to worker productivity from a large class of health-related problems. The argument was made that, when the causal relationship between physical or cognitive capacities and specific health-related declinations are clear (e.g., spinal injury), the measure of productivity impairment is unambiguously allocatable to group membership. For ADM prevalences, only associative relationships exist. Additionally, the first section discussed some collateral statistical problems (simultaneity, selection bias) associated with measuring loss by group membership.

The aim of the second section was to develop methods to estimate the productivity loss from ADM disorders that can be unambiguously allocated to ADM disorders. Three models of the temporal distribution of impairment induced by ADM disorders were presented. The models yielded similar specifications of the relationship between the prevalence of ADM disorders and income loss. However, the separate processes are described by model-specific timing/duration measures of ADM disorders. Formulated for a cross-sectional microdata environment, these models use current income and incorporate information from individual disorder histories, the timing and duration of disorders within individual lifetimes. Demographic characteristics are used to estimate expected income in the absence of the prevalence of ADM disorders. This section further derived methods for consistent estimates of ADM impairment rates.

The third section presented and discussed estimated ADM impairment rates based on data from the 1980–84 NIMH epidemiological catchment area survey. In general, the rates found are lower than those previously reported. For impairment due to drug abuse among women and for affective disorders among both sexes, the results were the opposite of those expected, suggesting unmeasured simultaneous effects of income and prevalence (or the reporting of prevalence).

Gains were made in the translation of disorders by group membership into measures of impairment. Different individual ADM impairment rates were estimated for individuals within the same category of disorder who had different disorder histories.

Certainly, further research along these lines is warranted, as many of the results remain inconclusive. Research combining appropriate specification of the ADM impairment process with systems of simultaneous equations to correct simultaneity bias remains to be successfully accomplished.

Acknowledgments

Research reported in this chapter was partially supported by the Alcohol, Drug Abuse, and Mental Health Administration, contract 283-87-0007.

Appendix 5.A   Explanation of the Estimate of the Standard Error of the Percentage Loss per Prevalent Individual Based on the Timing Model

The percentage loss per prevalent individual based on the timing model is the product of two random variables: the estimated coefficient from the timing model (table 5.5), denoted here by b, and the average timing measure per prevalent individual in a sex-age group, denoted here by ATg for group g. The variance of a product of random variables is given by equation (5.19) (Chiang 1980, 18),

$$\text{Var}(b\,ATg) = \sigma^2_b \sigma^2_{ATg} + [E(ATg)]^2 \sigma^2_\beta + [E(\beta)]^2 \sigma^2_{ATg}, \qquad (5.19)$$

and is estimated by

$$S^2_{bATg} = S^2_b S^2_{ATg} + ATg^2 S^2_b + b^2 S^2_{ATg}. \qquad (5.20)$$

The estimate of the variance of the average timing measure, S^2_{ATg}, is given by the estimate of the variance of the timing measure divided by the sample size minus one, denoted by $ng - 1$, $S^2_{Tg}/(ng - 1)$. These estimates appear in tables 5.1 for men and tables 5.2 for women. Equation (5.21) illustrates the incorporation of this substitution into equation (5.20):

$$S^2_{bATg} = S^2_b S^2_{Tg}/(ng - 1) + ATg^2 S^2_b + b^2 S^2_{Tg}/(ng - 1) \qquad (5.21)$$

The standard error of the estimate of the timing-based loss per prevalent individual is, of course, the square root of the estimate of the variance of the timing-based loss per prevalent individual, computed by equation (5.21).

References

American Psychiatric Association Task Force on Nomenclature and Statistics. 1980. *Diagnostic and Statistical Manual of Mental Disorders*. 3d ed. Washington, D.C.: American Psychiatric Association.

Bartel, Ann, and Paul Taubman. 1979. "Health and Labor Market Success: The Role of Various Diseases." *Review of Economics and Statistics* 61:1–8.

———. 1986. "Some Economic and Demographic Consequences of Mental Illness." *Journal of Labor Economics* 4:243–56.

Becker, Gary. 1967. "Human Capital and the Personal Distribution of Income." Woytinsky Lecture No. 1, University of Michigan.

Berkowitz, Monroe. 1985. *Economic Consequences of Spinal Cord Injury*. Bureau of Economic Research Project No. NAO-384. New Brunswick, N.J.: Rutgers.

Berry, R. E., Jr., and J. P. Boland. 1977. *The Economic Cost of Alcohol Abuse.* New York: Free Press.

Chiang, Chin Long. 1980. *An Introduction to Stochastic Processes and Their Applications*, p. 18. New York: Robert E. Krieger Publishing.

Chiang, Chin Long, and Paul M. Conforti. 1989. "A Survival Model and Estimation of Time to Tumor." *Mathematical Biosciences* 94, no. 1:1–29.

Chirikos, Thomas N., and Gilbert Nestel. 1985. "Further Evidence on the Economic Effects of Poor Health." *Review of Economics and Statistics* 67:61–69.

Clark, W., and L. Midanik. 1982. "Alcohol Use and Alcohol Problems among U.S. Adults: Results of the 1979 National Survey." In *Alcohol and Health Monograph No. 1: Alcohol Consumption and Related Problems.* Rockville, Md.: National Institute on Alcohol Abuse and Alcoholism.

Cruze, A. M., H. J. Harwood, P. C. Kristiansen, J. J. Collins, and D. C. Jones. 1981. *Economic Costs to Society of Alcohol and Drug Abuse and Mental Illness, 1977.* Research Triangle Park, N.C.: Research Triangle Institute.

Duan, M. 1983. "Smearing Estimate." *Journal of the American Statistical Association* 78:605–10.

Eaton, William W., Charles E. Holzer III, Michael Von Korff, James Anthony, John E. Helzer, Linda George, M. Audry Burnam, Jeffrey H. Boyd, Larry Kessler, and Ben Z. Lucke. 1984. "The Design of the Epidemiologic Catchment Area Surveys." *Archives of General Psychiatry* 41:942–48.

Fein, R. 1958. *Economics of Mental Illness: A Report to the Staff Director, Jack R. Ewalt.* New York: Basic Books.

Frank, R., and P. Gertler. 1987. The Effect of Mental Distress on Income: Results from a Community Survey." Working Paper No. 2433. Cambridge, Mass.: National Bureau of Economic Research.

Greene, William H. 1986. *LIMDEP User's Manual.* New York: Econometric Software.

———. 1990. *Econometrics.* New York: Macmillan.

Hartunian, N. S., C. N. Smart, and M. S. Thompson. 1981. *The Incidence and Economic Costs of Major Health Impairments.* Lexington, Mass.: D. C. Heath.

Harwood, H. J., D. M. Napolitano, P. Kristiansen, and J. J. Collins. 1984. *Economic Costs to Society of Alcohol and Drug Abuse and Mental Illness: 1980.* Research Triangle Park, N.C.: Research Triangle Institute.

Heien, David M., and David J. Pittman. 1989. "The Economic Costs of Alcohol Abuse: An Assessment of Current Methods and Estimates." *Journal of Studies on Alcohol* 50:567–79.

Hu, T. W., and F. Sandifer. 1981. *Synthesis of Cost of Illness Methodology— Final Report.* Contract No. 233-79-3010. National Center for Health Services Research.

Inman, Robert P. 1984. "Disability Indices, the Economic Costs of Illness, and Social Insurance: The Case of Multiple Sclerosis." *Acta Neurologica Scandinavica* 70 (Suppl. 101):46–55.

Luft, Harold S. 1975. "The Impact of Poor Health on Earnings." *Review of Economics and Statistics* 58:43–57.

Malzberg, B. 1950. "Mental Illness and the Economic Value of Man." *Mental Hygiene,* no. 34:225–27.
Mitchell, J. M., and J. S. Butler. 1986. "Arthritis and the Earnings of Men." *Journal of Health Economics* 5:81–98.
Mullahy, J., and J. Sindelar. 1988. "Lifecycle Effects of Alcoholism on Education, Earnings and Occupation." Paper presented at the Fourth Biennial Conference on the Economics of Mental Health, National Institute of Mental Health, Asilomar, Calif., April 21–22, 1988.
Myers, Jerome K., Myra M. Weissman, Gary L. Tischler, Charles E. Holzer III, Philip J. Leaf, Helen Orvaschel, James C. Anthony, Jeffrey H. Boyd, Jack D. Burke, Jr., Morton Kramer, and Roger Stoltzman. 1984. "Six-Month Prevalence of Psychiatric Disorders in Three Communities." *Archives of General Psychiatry* 41:959–67.
National Institute of Mental Health (NIMH). 1988. *ECA Public Use Wave 1 Codebook,* January. Unpublished.
National Institute on Drug Abuse (NIDA). 1982. *Public Use Tapes, National Household Survey on Drug Abuse, 1982.* Rockville, Md.: U.S. Department of Health and Human Services.
Osterberg, Esa. 1983. "Calculating the Costs of Alcohol: The Scandinavian Experience," chapter 5. In M. Grant, M. Plant, and A. Williams (eds.): *Economics and Alcohol: Consumption and Controls.* New York: Gardner Press.
Parnes, H. S., and J. Meyer. 1971. "Withdrawal from the Labor Force by Middle Aged Men, 1966–67." Columbus: Center for Human Resource Research, Ohio State University, January. Mimeo. Quoted by Luft (1975).
Regier, D. A., J. K. Myers, M. Kramer, L. N. Robins, D. G. Blazer, R. L. Hough, W. W. Eaton, and B. Z. Lucke. 1984. "The NIMH Epidemiologic Catchment Area Program: Historical Context, Major Objectives, and Study Population Characteristics." *Archives of General Psychiatry* 41:934–41.
Rice, Dorothy P., Sander Kelman, Leonard S. Miller, and Sarah Dunmeyer. 1990. *The Economic Costs of Alcohol and Drug Abuse and Mental Illness: 1985.* Report submitted to the Office of Financing and Coverage Policy of the Alcohol, Drug Abuse, and Mental Health Administration, U.S. Department of Health and Human Services. San Francisco: Institute for Health & Aging, University of California.
Robins, Lee N. 1985. "The Development and Characteristics of the NIMH Diagnostic Interview Schedule." In M. Weissman, J. Meyers, and C. Ross (eds.): *Community Surveys of Psychiatric Disorders.* New Brunswick, N.J.: Rutgers.
Robins, L. N., J. E. Helzer, J. Groughan, and K. S. Ratcliff. 1981. "National Institute of Mental Health Diagnostic Interview Schedule: Its History, Characteristics and Validity." *Archives of General Psychiatry* 38:381–89.
Robins, Lee N., John E. Helzer, Myrna M. Weissman, Helen Orvaschel, Ernest Gruenberg, Jack D. Burke, Jr., and Darrel A. Regier. 1984. "Lifetime Prevalence of Specific Psychiatric Disorders in Three Sites." *Archives of General Psychiatry* 41:949–58.

Salkever, David S. 1988. "Morbidity Costs: National Estimates and Economic Determinants." In *Research and Human Capital Development,* vol. 5, pp. 237–88. Greenwich, Conn.: JAI Press.

Sherwood, G. E. F., and Angus E. Taylor. 1954. *Calculus.* Englewood Cliffs, N.J.: Prentice-Hall.

Stromsdorfer, Ernest W., and George Farkas. 1980. "Introduction." In Ernest W. Stromsdorfer and George Farkas (eds.): *Evaluation Studies, Review Annual,* Vol. 5. Beverly Hills, Calif.: Sage Publications.

6

Measurement Error in Self-evaluations of Mental Health: Implications for Labor Market Analysis

Elizabeth Savoca, Ph.D.

An individual's health, both physical and mental, is an important determinant of labor market outcomes such as income and earnings (Grossman and Benham 1973; Benham and Benham 1982; Bartel and Taubman 1979, 1986; Frank and Gertler 1987, 1989), occupational choice (Kemna 1987; Mullahy and Sindelar 1989), and labor force participation (Mullahy and Sindelar 1987, 1990; Stern 1989), especially among prospective retirees (Anderson and Burkhauser 1985; Berkovec and Stern 1988; Mitchell and Anderson 1989; Sickles and Taubman 1986). Careful econometric analyses of the role of health in labor market activities have been sensitive to the potential endogeneity of health. People's health may be partly determined by life-style preferences and time rates of preference that may also influence their labor market choices. Furthermore, the causality between labor market success and health may be two-way. That is, current health may be directly affected by income, labor force status, and the physical and mental stresses associated with different types of work.

Researchers have also been aware of the potential biases associated with measurements of health. Many important surveys of labor market behavior (e.g., National Longitudinal Survey, Panel Study of Income Dynamics, and Retirement History Survey) are limited to self-reported measures. These self-assessments may introduce an additional source of endogeneity through a reporting bias that is influenced by labor market status. The availability of disability and retirement benefits that are contingent on poor health may induce some nonworking individuals to understate their health. Some unemployed persons and non-labor-force participants may use poor health as an "excuse" for not working.

Self-reported health may also suffer from measurement error since, as laypersons, individuals may be unable to assess accurately their true health status. Additional measurement error may be introduced by differences in the interpretation of survey questions across individuals in a sample. Finally, if the true underlying health variable is a continuous latent index of illness severity, then the discrete nature of self-rated measures captures true health imperfectly.

Each of these issues has been the subject of careful investigations in recent years. Stern (1989) presented explicit tests of the exogeneity of self-evaluated health to the labor force participation decision. Butler et al. (1987) provided explicit estimates of the size of the measurement error by analyzing the correlation between a self-diagnosis of a physical disease (arthritis) and a simulated clinical diagnosis.

This chapter focuses on the measurement errors associated with self-evaluations of mental illness. It departs from prior work in an important way. Rather than assuming that the measurement error conforms to the classical model of errors in variables, it allows a systematic bias in self-rated health which may vary across demographic characteristics. This may be particularly relevant to self-assessments of mental health because people, perhaps fearing a perceived social stigma attached to mental illness, may be reluctant to admit their emotional problems. This attitude may vary with gender, race, age, and education.

The presence of a systematic bias in self-rated measures of health should be of critical concern to labor market researchers who are forced to rely on self-reported measures as proxies of true health. The econometric justifications for including a variable measured with error are straightforward when the proxy is an unbiased estimate of the true variable. For one, the direction of the bias in the coefficient of the proxy variable is known a priori (toward zero). Second, the biases on the coefficients of the other control variables are always reduced by the inclusion of the proxy (Judge et al. 1985). However, when the proxy varies not only with the true unobserved variable but also with other exogenous characteristics of the individual, then the inclusion of a proxy may actually increase the bias in the measured effect of the other variables on labor market outcomes (Maddala 1977).

Background

Economists have undertaken numerous attempts to assess the consequences for labor market analysis of measuring health with error.

Virtually all efforts have taken the indirect approach of estimating labor market models of earnings or labor force participation rates using alternative measures of health and comparing the estimated coefficients across equations.[1]

Much of this literature has focused on the labor supply decisions of prime-age men in an effort to understand the sharp decline in their participation rates during the post–World War II era. Early studies that examined the role of health frequently used self-rated measures. The most common was based on the answer to the question, "Does your health limit the kind or amount of work you can do?" Many of these studies concluded that health was a primary factor in the labor force participation decision, in some cases more important than the financial incentives of wages, unearned income, social security benefits, and other income support programs.

Parsons (1982) was one of the first to speculate that these studies may have understated the role of economic factors by using a health proxy whose measurement error may have been positively correlated with earnings. Since social security benefits replace a relatively high fraction of earnings for low-wage individuals, the incentive for them to understate their health to qualify for early retirement benefits is greater. Consequently, the regression estimates attribute the influence of low earnings on labor supply to the effect of poor health. Using mortality experience instead of a self-reported measure of disability, Parsons found that the estimated consequences of financial factors are much greater than were indicated by prior studies. He also found that, when health is omitted from the model, the estimated coefficients on economic variables remain close to the estimates using mortality experience. This led him to conclude that omitted variable bias may not be too severe.

Anderson and Burkhauser (1983, 1985) found that, in single equation models of labor force participation, when mortality rates replace self-ratings of health the estimated wage elasticity is five times larger. Bazzoli (1985) found that the estimated effect of economic factors on the decision to retire is greater when preretirement self-evaluations of health are used instead of postretirement self-assessments. This finding lends some support to the notion that retirees may use poor health as an "ex post rationalization" for labor force withdrawal.

Lambrinos (1981) examined how estimates of the income and wage elasticities of the labor supply of white men change when self-reported dichotomous measures of health are replaced with more objective measures (both discrete and continuous). He found practically no difference in estimated elasticities of substitution between market and nonmarket activities when a dichotomous objective dummy replaced a subjective dummy. However, when a discrete objective measure was replaced by a continuous objective measure the estimated elasticity of substitution fell.

More recently, researchers have focused on the potential specification errors arising from measurements of mental health. Frank and Gertler (1987), in a study of the influence of mental distress on income, assessed the measurement error bias associated with diagnosis-based measures of mental illness. By these measures individuals with mental disorders who did not seek professional help are misclassified as healthy. Since the use of mental health services is determined in part by income, diagnosis-based measures may be endogenous to a model of income determination. Their results suggest only a slight downward bias in the estimated effect of mental distress on income when diagnosis-based measures are used instead of population-based measures.

These studies are valuable for they give the readers a sense of how the conclusions of the analyses are affected by alternative treatments of health. However, this indirect evidence does not provide the reader with enough information to ascertain the extent to which differences in coefficients from using different measures of health arise from measurement error in the health variable or from other specification choices made by the researcher.[2]

Only recently have econometric studies provided explicit tests of the potential errors in self-rated health. Stern (1989) estimated a structural model of the joint determination of male labor market participation and self-evaluation of overall health allowing two-way causality as well as correlations between the unobserved factors affecting the decisions both to work and to report a disability. He found only weak evidence to support the hypothesis that self-rated health is endogenous to the decision to work. Furthermore, he found that labor market participants tend to report disability *more often* than do nonparticipants, *ceteris paribus*. Butler et al. (1987) provided evidence of the degree of measurement error in self-diagnoses of arthritis. Finding a strong correlation between the self-rating and a simulation of a physician diagnosis, they concluded that self-evaluations are legitimate measures of true health. Econometric evaluation of the relationship between self-evaluated mental health and more objective measures had not previously been undertaken.

Defining Mental Health

The position taken in this chapter is that a self-rating of mental health is a legitimate measure only to the extent that it agrees with psychiatric criteria for mental illness. This point of view is taken for three basic reasons.

First, some mental illnesses, by definition, are illnesses in which an individual's perception of reality is distorted. Some obvious examples are schizophrenia, paranoia, and hypochondria.

Second, medical sociologists argue that, even when individuals correctly perceive symptoms of psychological disorders, they may be reluctant to admit them for fear of a social stigma attached to mental illness (Scheff 1963). Epidemiological studies also report that patients tend to define their health status to a large extent in terms of the degree to which symptoms restrict their regular activities. As David Mechanic wrote, "Although physicians ordinarily focus on symptoms that are serious in their implications for future health, patients focus more often on symptoms that interfere in some obvious way with usual routines" (1982, 15).

The third reason derives from uncertainty over the interpretation of survey questions by individual respondents. The self-rating that I analyze in this chapter is the answer to the question, "How would you rate your present emotional health: excellent, good, fair, or poor?" Some people may read this question broadly as a question about their overall sense of well-being or overall satisfaction with life. This interpretation conforms to the opinions of many who regard the concept of mental illness as essentially a social concept rather than a pathological or clinical one.[3] Such views are reflected in the often-cited definition of health adopted by the World Health Organization: "Health is a state of complete physical, mental, and social well-being and not merely the absence of disease or infirmity" (World Health Organization 1948). But this perspective is of limited relevance to studies of labor market behavior whose objectives are to control for the effect of mental illness on, say, wages or labor force participation. This is because individuals may closely define their overall well-being in terms of their economic and social success. Consequently, use of such a self-reported measure would make it extremely difficult to disentangle the interrelations between mental health and labor market outcomes. Furthermore, if one wishes to draw policy conclusions about the effectiveness of increased expenditures on mental health services in enhancing earnings and employment stability, then a psychiatric evaluation seems the more appropriate control because it identifies illnesses that follow a clinical treatment path.[4]

Others may interpret this question more narrowly as a question about mental distress. Even then, however, individuals in any given sample may apply different standards against which they are evaluating their present health. Some may compare themselves to others; some may compare their present state to their past state.

The Data

The data for this study come from the first wave of a community survey of noninstitutionalized adults in the New Haven site of the NIMH's epidemiological catchment area program conducted in the early 1980s.[5] This survey included the typical questions eliciting the respondent's evaluation of his or her overall emotional health. Lay interviewers also administered the NIMH Diagnostic Interview Schedule, which was designed to enable the interviewers to simulate standard psychiatric diagnoses of several types of psychiatric disorders.[6] Detailed information is also available on the demographic and socioeconomic background of the survey respondents. As mentioned earlier, a self-reported measure of health is taken from the answer to the question, "How would you rate your present emotional health: excellent, good, fair, or poor?" This measure is compared to a dichotomous diagnostic measure of present emotional health which equals 0 if any psychiatric disorder was diagnosed as occurring within one year of the interview date and 1 if none is diagnosed.

Table 6.1 reports descriptive statistics on the variables used in this analysis. The ECA was designed to oversample the elderly. Consequently, the sample has a higher proportion of women than has the adult population in the United States. Additionally, because of cohort effects in educational attainment the sample has a smaller propor-

Table 6.1   Description of Variables

Variable Description	Mean	Standard Deviation
Mental Health Self-Rating		
Excellent	0.358	0.479
Good	0.468	0.499
Fair	0.146	0.353
Poor	0.029	0.166
DIS classification disorder present	0.170	0.376
Female	0.592	0.492
Age	55.742	20.307
White	0.887	0.317
Married with spouse present	0.501	0.500
Education		
No degree	0.372	0.483
High school graduate	0.449	0.497
College graduate	0.179	0.384

Table 6.2   Cross-tabulation of Clinical Diagnosis by Self-rating

Self-rating	Number	%	Self-rating	Number	%
No disorder	3,958	100.0	Disorder present	813	100.0
Excellent	1,540	38.9	Excellent	169	20.8
Good	1,867	47.2	Good	365	44.9
Fair	485	12.3	Fair	209	25.7
Poor	66	1.7	Poor	70	8.6

tion of high school and college graduates than has the population nationwide. A total of 5,034 individuals were surveyed. Observations with incomplete information on the set of variables of interest were dropped from the study, leaving a sample size of 4,771.

Table 6.2 contains a cross-tabulation of the two measures of mental health to give some indication of the degree of agreement. As one can easily see, there is an obvious association. The proportion of individuals who rated their emotional health as excellent was lower among those with a clinically diagnosed mental disorder, while the number who rated themselves as in fair or poor condition was considerably higher. However, a still fairly substantial fraction of individuals meeting diagnostic criteria for mental disorders considered themselves in excellent emotional health (21%). This suggests that individuals are using a standard different from the criteria that form the basis of the clinical diagnosis.

Econometric Estimation and Results

Econometric Model

I attempt a more systematic comparison between the two by estimating the econometric model developed in this section. It is assumed that both the self-report and the diagnostic measures of mental health are discrete outcomes of unobserved, continuous latent variables that are related in the following way:

$$I_i^* = Z_i^* + \eta_i \tag{6.1}$$

where I_i^* is a continuous latent index of mental health that varies according to the survey respondent's criteria, Z_i^* is a continuous latent variable measuring the degree of mental health according to professional diagnostic criteria, and η_i is a measurement error that consists of two components:

$$\eta_i = X_i\gamma + \upsilon_i \tag{6.2}$$

where X_i is a vector of exogenous characteristics of individual i and υ_i is a normally distributed, independent random error with zero mean and variance σ_υ^2.

In a classic model of errors-in-variables, the measurement error is assumed to be purely random. Equation (6.2), however, allows for two sources of error in the self-assessment of mental health—one that arises from purely random deviations from professional criteria (υ) and another that is related systematically to exogenous characteristics of the individual ($X\gamma$). This alternative perspective is influenced by a vast literature in sociology and psychology which argues that the ways in which individuals present and acknowledge symptoms of emotional distress are heavily influenced by cultural factors so that systematic biases that vary with ethnicity, social status, gender, and age may be present in self-evaluations of mental health. For example, there is a widespread impression that women are more open to discussions about emotional distress (Leaf and Bruce 1987). There are also many epidemiological studies that argue strong age cohort effects in the willingness to seek professional help and in the willingness to acknowledge mental distress, with elderly cohorts inclined to ignore and deny symptoms of psychological disorders (Leaf et al. 1988). The psychosocial literature on the relationship between social class and self-perceptions of mental illness has noted that individuals from the lower end of the social strata are more likely to present symptoms of psychological illness as physical ailments rather than emotional troubles (Mechanic 1982). Studies of ethnic differences in attitudes toward mental illness have shown that persons of Northern European ancestry are more likely to rate symptoms of psychiatric disorders as socially undesirable and hence may be more likely to suppress the admission of emotional distress (Dohrenwend 1966). Therefore, allowing for this nonstandard component to the error in self-reported health is appropriate. As we shall discover further on, estimates of any systematic bias of this nature are essential for determining the consequences of including self-rated health as a regressor in a labor market equation.

The clinical measure Z_i^* is also related to X_i according to

$$Z_i^* = X_i\theta + \mu_i \tag{6.3}$$

where μ_i is a normally distributed independent random variable with zero mean and variance σ_μ^2.

The variables I_i^* and Z_i^* have observed discrete indicators I and Z defined as

$$Z_i = 1 \quad \text{if } Z_i^* > 0 \tag{6.4}$$
$$ = 0 \quad \text{if } Z_i^* \leq 0 \quad \text{and}$$
$$I_i = j \quad \text{if } \delta_{j-1} < I_i^* < \delta_j \quad \text{for } j = 1, 2, 3, 4$$

where δ_j are unobserved thresholds in the distribution of I_i^* corresponding to the four categories of self-rated health (poor, fair, good, and excellent).

Substituting equations (6.2) and (6.3) into (6.1) yields

$$I_i^* = X_i(\theta + \gamma) + \omega_i \tag{6.5}$$

where $\omega_i = \mu_i + \upsilon_i$.

Equations (6.3), (6.4), and (6.5) form the basis of a discrete choice model that can be estimated simultaneously. Equation (6.5) follows an ordered-probit model.[7] Equation (6.3) follows the standard binary probit specification. Since true health Z^* and self-rated health I^* are unobserved, their units of measurement are necessarily arbitrary so that two identifying restrictions must be imposed. First, following the usual normalization σ_μ is set to 1 so that the estimable equations of the model are

$$Z_i^{**} = X_i(\theta/\sigma_\mu) + \mu_i/\sigma_\mu \tag{6.6}$$
$$I_i^{**} = X_i[(\theta + \gamma)/\sigma_\mu] + \omega_i/\sigma_\mu \tag{6.7}$$

with $Z_i^{**} = Z_i^*/\sigma_\mu$ and $I_i^{**} = I_i^*/\sigma_\mu$.

Second, one must either assume that at least one of the coefficients of the characteristics included in X is the same for both the diagnostic measure and the self-rated index or assume that the errors, υ and μ, are uncorrelated. The latter restriction is imposed because there are no apparent justifications for assuming that any particular characteristic will have an identical relationship to both measures. The assumption that the errors, υ and μ, are independent is equivalent to assuming that the respondents' random errors in their own assessment of mental health are independent of the errors in the DIS algorithm.[8]

Maximum likelihood estimation of equations (6.6) and (6.7) provides consistent estimates of θ/σ_μ, γ/σ_μ, $\sigma_\upsilon/\sigma_\mu$, δ_1/σ_μ, δ_2/σ_μ, and δ_3/σ_μ ($\delta_0 = -\infty$ and $\delta_4 = +\infty$). Given the assumptions of the model, μ/σ_μ and ω/σ_μ are jointly normal with zero means, variances 1 and $1 + \sigma_\upsilon^2/\sigma_\mu^2$, respectively, and correlation coefficient, $1/\sqrt{(1 + \sigma_\upsilon^2/\sigma_\mu^2)}$.

Results

The results are presented in table 6.3. With the exception of marital status the maximum likelihood estimates indicate that the relation-

Table 6.3   Maximum Likelihood Estimates of Mental Health Status

	Ordered-Probit Estimates of Self-evaluation $\hat{\theta} + \hat{\gamma}$	Binary Probit Estimates of Psychiatric Diagnosis $\hat{\theta}$
Female	−0.243[a]**	−0.050
	(0.095)	(0.046)
Age (÷ 10)	−0.111[b]***	0.142***
	(0.025)	(0.012)
White	0.496[b]***	−0.084
	(0.142)	(0.070)
Married	0.334***	0.251***
	(0.093)	(0.046)
High school degree	0.971[b]***	0.209***
	(0.118)	(0.055)
College degree	1.713[b]***	0.312***
	(0.171)	(0.067)
Constant		0.027
		(0.097)
Fair health threshold (δ_1)	−4.832***	—
	(0.352)	
Good health threshold (δ_2)	−2.082***	—
	(0.235)	
Excellent health threshold (δ_3)	1.624***	—
	(0.226)	
σ_υ	2.530***	—
	(0.167)	

Notes: The underlying latent indices of the model are positively related to mental health (i.e., increases in the indices imply improvements in mental health). Standard errors are in parentheses. All coefficient estimates are measured up to an unknown scalar σ_μ. $N = 4{,}771$. Log of the likelihood function = $-7{,}062.527$.
[a]Statistically different from psychiatric diagnosis at $<.05$.
[b]Statistically different from psychiatric diagnosis at $<.01$.
*$p < .10$.   **$p < .05$.   ***$p < .01$.

ship between each of these characteristics and the clinical simulation of a mental health diagnosis is quite different from the relationship between the characteristic and the self-report measure in both a statistical and a practical sense. In particular, the self-rating varies much more with gender, race, and education. According to both measures, mental health improves with education, but the increments are much larger for the self-evaluation. The estimated model detects no statistically significant difference in the prevalence of psychiatric disorders by gender and race, whereas whites and men tend to give themselves relatively high mental health ratings in their self-assessments. The self-rating varies less with age than does the clinical diagnosis but in the opposite direction. Mental health improves with age according to diagnostic criteria and worsens with age in the self-assessment.

Implications

The results presented thus far provide evidence that the deviations of self-evaluations of mental health from the more objective clinical measures vary with the demographic characteristics of the survey respondent. An important implication of this finding for labor market analysis can be revealed in reference to the following regression model: $y = X\beta + \alpha z + \epsilon$ where y is an $N \times 1$ vector of observations on the dependent variable, ϵ is an $N \times 1$ vector of random errors, X is an $N \times k$ matrix of exogenous characteristics measured without error, z is an unobservable continuous latent variable, and β and α are $k \times 1$ and 1×1 vectors of parameters to be estimated. Here let z represent true mental health, y represent an observed labor market outcome such as earnings and hours worked, X denote explanatory variables other than mental health (such as gender, race, and education), and ϵ denote a random error uncorrelated with X and z.[9]

Suppose that the variable z is proxied by p, a self-evaluation of mental health. Also, suppose that we wish to know whether the inconsistency in the least squares estimator of β is reduced or worsened by the inclusion of p as a control variable. It is well known that the inconsistency in the estimator $\hat{\beta}$ arising from the omission of mental health from the model is $\alpha\theta$ where θ is the plim of the least squares estimator of the coefficient vector from an auxiliary regression model: $z = X\theta + \mu$.

Suppose the proxy follows the classical errors in variables model: $p = z + \upsilon$ where υ has zero mean, variance σ_υ^2, and is uncorrelated with $\epsilon, X,$ and z. Then Judge et al. (1985) showed that the inconsistency in $\hat{\beta}$ arising from the inclusion of the proxy is proportional to the omitted variable bias, $\alpha\theta f$, where $f = \sigma_\upsilon^2/(\sigma_\upsilon^2 + \sigma_\mu^2)$ and σ_μ^2 is the residual variance of z from the regression of z on X. Since the proportion f is less than 1 the inconsistency in $\hat{\beta}$ will be lower when the proxy is included. The intuition behind this result is straightforward. Since the only systematic variation in the proxy p comes from variation in true health z, then including p eliminates some of the bias in $\hat{\beta}$ that results from the correlation between the omitted variable, mental health z, and the included nonhealth variables.

Assume, instead, that the proxy takes the form: $p = z + X\gamma + \upsilon$. Then, as shown by Maddala (1977) for the three-variable model and in the appendix for the case where more than one variable is included in X, the inconsistency in $\hat{\beta}$ resulting from adding the proxy p to the regression equation equals $\alpha[\theta f - (1 - f)\gamma]$. That is, the inconsistency is the sum of the measurement error bias ($\alpha\theta f$) resulting from the purely random deviations of p from z and the measurement error bias

$[-\alpha(1 - f)\gamma]$ arising from the independent correlations between p and X. In this case the inconsistency arising from including a health proxy is lower than the omitted variable bias only if $|[\theta f - (1 - f)\gamma]|$ is less than θ. Consequently, the usefulness of this proxy as a control variable depends critically on the size of the ratio of the variance of the random measurement error (σ_v^2) to the residual variance of true health (σ_μ^2), the size of the coefficient vector of X in a regression of z on $X(\theta)$, and the size of the coefficient vector of X in a regression of p on z and $X(\gamma)$.

Using the maximum likelihood estimates of θ/σ_μ, γ/σ_μ, and σ_v/σ_μ to approximate the relative magnitude of the critical regression coefficient vectors and residual variances, estimates of the inconsistencies in the coefficients on gender, age, race, marital status, and education which result from including a self-rated measure of mental health can be compared to estimates of the inconsistencies arising from omitting mental health from the model. Table 6.4 reports for each variable estimates of $[\theta f - (1 - f)\gamma]/\sigma_\mu$ and θ/σ_μ. Since these quantities are measured only up to an unknown scalar, the absolute sizes of the quantities are less important than the relative sizes and signs.

The estimates indicate that the inconsistency in the estimated effects of gender, marital status, and education on labor market outcomes is reduced by the inclusion of the self-rated health proxy. The negative estimates for women indicate that both approaches (omitting health and including self-rated health) impart a negative bias into gender differences in labor market outcomes, thus overstating gender differences in behavior. But the bias from omitting health is

Table 6.4   Estimated Size of Biases Arising
from Alternative Approaches toward the Treatment
of Mental Health in Labor Market Studies

Coefficient	Inconsistency from Excluding Health $\hat{\theta}$	Inconsistency from Including Self-rated Measure of Health $\hat{\theta}\hat{f} - (1 - \hat{f})\hat{\gamma}$
Female	−0.050	−0.017
Age	0.014	0.016
White	−0.084	−0.152
Married	0.251	0.205
High school degree	0.209	0.078
College degree	0.312	0.080

Note: Both numerical estimates are measured up to an unknown scalar, σ_μ.

worse. The positive estimates for education imply that both treatments of health lead to an overstatement of the effects of education on labor market outcomes, but again the inconsistency is more severe when health is excluded from the estimated model.[10]

The estimated inconsistencies for age indicate a higher inconsistency arising from including the self-rated proxy but one that is practically insignificant from the omitted variable bias. The estimates for race, however, indicate that the inconsistency from including a self-rated health proxy is much greater than the omitted variable bias. Furthermore, the direction of the bias is one which would lead to an understatement of racial differences in labor market outcomes if the self-rated measure is used.[11]

Alternative Interpretations

The implications drawn from the estimates thus far have been made from the point of view that the simulated clinical diagnosis is the true measure of health. The simulation, of course, may also be measured with error. If the measurement error in the DIS algorithm is purely random, then the interpretations are essentially unchanged.

A more problematic case arises when there is a systematic bias in the simulated clinical diagnosis. Indeed, the clinical diagnosis relies on the accuracy of the respondent's answers to a battery of questions regarding the manifestations of psychological disorders. To the extent that the measurement error in the DIS algorithm results from the respondent's efforts to conceal deep-rooted problems, the clinical simulation may suffer from the same biases as the self-assessment of overall emotional health. However, to the extent that the measurement error in the overall self-evaluation arises from the inability of the respondent to translate accurately any given set of acknowledged symptoms or limitations into an overall assessment of mental illness, the clinical simulation is a more accurate measure.

In a study appraising the reliability of the DIS classifications, Anthony et al. (1985) found that, when compared to direct diagnosis by psychiatrists, the DIS classifications led to an understatement of the most prevalent disorders—phobias and alcohol and drug abuse.[12] This implies that the aggregate measure of mental health based on the simulated clinical diagnosis used here may overstate "true" mental health.

If these deviations from the psychiatric reappraisal lead one to suspect that the error structure of the DIS may not be purely random but may follow, instead, a structure similar to the self-rating, then how might the implications in the previous section change? Let the error, μ_i, in equation (6.3) follow

$$\mu_i = X_i\lambda + \phi_i \tag{6.8}$$

where ϕ_i is a normal random variable with zero mean. Then equation (6.3) should be written as

$$Z_i^* = X_i(\theta + \lambda) + \phi_i. \tag{6.9}$$

This interpretation of equation (6.3) implies that the calculations of table 6.4 are not θ and $\theta f - (1 - f)\gamma$, as intended, but rather $(\theta + \lambda)$ and $(\theta + \lambda)f - (1 - f)(\gamma - \lambda)$.[13] That is, both columns of table 6.4 are off by the same factor, λ.[14] If we assume that the systematic errors in the self-rating and the DIS classification are of the same nature (i.e., they are both either positively or negatively related to particular background characteristics) and that the errors in the DIS are smaller than the errors in the self-report (i.e., $\gamma - \lambda > 0$ implies $\gamma > \lambda > 0$ and $\gamma - \lambda < 0$ implies $\gamma < \lambda < 0$), then the conclusions regarding the gains and losses from including a proxy rather than omitting mental health from the regression are essentially the same. For example, with the imposition of these two restrictions on the error structure of the DIS, the finding of the large positive contribution of race to the deviation between the self-rating and the DIS classification implies that, when compared to a direct psychiatric examination, whites tend to rate themselves higher than nonwhites on both the overall self-evaluation and the DIS categorization. Consequently, the numbers reported in table 6.4 for race are off by the same positive amount, λ.[15] Hence, the true biases for race are even more negative.

A further issue concerns the structural interpretation of the proxy variable model assumed in this analysis. This chapter takes as one point of departure the work of Stern (1989), who argued that the potential endogeneity of self-rated health should not be of serious concern to studies of labor market behavior. Consequently, the interpretations of the estimated coefficients on the exogenous individual characteristics are made largely from the perspective of noneconomic models of an individual's perceptions of his or her mental health.

Yet one might also argue that the proxy variable model estimated here is an approximation to the reduced form of a more general structural model of self-rated health which specifies labor market outcomes as causal variables, that is, $p = p(z, X, y)$. Consequently, the assumption of uncorrelated errors [$\text{cov}(v,\epsilon) = \sigma_{v\epsilon} = 0$], maintained in the calculations of the proxy variable bias reported in table 6.4, may not hold. It can be shown, however, that when v and ϵ are assumed to be correlated ($\sigma_{v\epsilon} \neq 0$) the inconsistency from including a self-rated measure of health becomes $\alpha[\theta f - (1 - f)\theta] - (\theta + \gamma)\sigma_{v\epsilon}/(\sigma_v^2 + \sigma_\mu^2)$.[16]

Although a precise measure of the covariance between self-rated mental health and various labor market outcomes is beyond the scope of this chapter, it seems reasonable to assume that it is positive. Therefore, the *sign* of the additional term in the expression for the proxy variable bias can be determined by the estimates of ($\theta + \gamma$). The signs of these estimated values imply that the estimated inconsistency reported for race in column 2 of table 6.4 becomes even more negative when $\sigma_{v\epsilon} > 0$, strengthening one conclusion of the analysis. The estimated inconsistencies resulting from including self-rated health for gender and education move closer to zero when $\sigma_{v\epsilon} > 0$. This suggests that the measurement error bias in these coefficients may be even less than the estimates reported in table 6.4.[17] For age, the bias from including self-evaluated health becomes more positive. Thus, the omitted variable bias in the coefficient on age may be, relative to the proxy variable bias, much smaller than what is indicated in table 6.4.

Summary and Conclusions

This chapter analyzed the effect of using a self-rated measure of mental health as an explanatory variable in analyses of labor market behavior from the perspective of an errors-in-variables problem. Medical sociologists have argued that the way in which an individual presents and acknowledges symptoms of both physical and mental distress is strongly influenced by cultural factors so that errors in self-evalutions may vary with the demographic characteristics of an individual. Econometric theory argues that, if errors in health variables take this form, then it may not be the case that including a health proxy yields more consistent estimates than omitting health from the model.

The econometric model developed in this chapter permits meaningful comparisons between two discrete indicators of mental health —one subjective and one based on standard psychiatric criteria. It also provides a set of statistics which can be used to decide which approach, omitting health or including a subjective proxy, leads to greater inconsistencies in the estimates of other control variables.

A major finding is that labor market studies which focus on race may obtain more reliable estimates of racial differences in labor market outcomes by omitting mental health from the model when the only available measure is an overall self-assessment. The estimated model shows no statistically significant racial difference in mental health according to professional diagnostic criteria. This suggests that omitted-variable bias is inconsequential. However, the estimates also indicate a relatively substantial racial difference in the deviation between self-rated mental health and clinically evaluated health. This deviation leads to a relatively large underestimate of racial differences in labor market outcomes when the self-rated health proxy is included as a control variable. This finding, though, does not apply to all other determinants of labor market activities. In particular, the results also imply that the inconsistencies in estimates of the effect of education on labor market behavior arising from the inclusion of self-rated mental health may be much smaller than the inconsistency resulting from omitting health from the model.

There are some natural directions in which this research can be advanced. For one, disaggregation by type of disorder may help in understanding why the difference between the self-rating and the clinical measure varies with the background characteristics of the individual. For example, the fact that women and the elderly tend to suffer disproportionately from depression, a condition characterized by feelings of hopelessness and despondency, may explain why their self-ratings are substantially lower than the self-evaluations of men and younger people. Men and youths, on the other hand, tend to suffer disproportionately from alcohol and drug abuse. The role of denial figures prominently in these diseases, thus partially accounting for the relatively high self-ratings of men and youths. Information about physical illness may also provide some explanations for the deviations. The psychosocial literature argues that perceptions of emotional health are intricately tied up with an individual's physical health. Poor physical health may account for the negative relationship between age and self-evaluations of mental health.

A third direction would add more structure to the model by including specific labor market outcomes as a third indicator of mental health. Such an approach could quantify more precisely the gains and losses from adding self-evaluated health to a model of labor market behavior.

Acknowledgments

I thank Martha Livingston Bruce, Martin Gaynor, John Mullahy, and Jody Sindelar for valuable feedback on earlier drafts. Financial support for this research came from National Institute of Mental Health grant 5 T32 MH15783.

Appendix 6.A   Consequences of Measurement Error
in Variables for Least Squares Estimates

This discussion extends the results of Maddala (1977) to the case where more than one right-hand-side variable is measured without error. Consider the regression model $\mathbf{y} = \mathbf{X}\boldsymbol{\beta} + \alpha\mathbf{z} + \boldsymbol{\epsilon}$ where $\mathbf{y}$ is an $N \times 1$ vector of observations on the dependent variable, $\boldsymbol{\epsilon}$ is an $N \times 1$ vector of random errors, $\mathbf{X}$ is an $N \times k$ matrix of exogenous characteristics measured without error, $\mathbf{z}$ is an unobservable continuous latent variable, and $\boldsymbol{\beta}$ and α are $k \times 1$ and 1×1 vectors of unknown parameters. The variable $\mathbf{z}$ is measured by the proxy variable $\mathbf{p} = \mathbf{z} + \mathbf{X}\boldsymbol{\gamma} + \boldsymbol{v}$ where $\mathbf{p}$ and $\boldsymbol{v}$ are $N \times 1$ vectors of random variables and $\boldsymbol{\gamma}$ is a $k \times 1$ vector of unknown coefficients. I derive in this appendix the inconsistency in the least squares estimates of $\boldsymbol{\beta}$ resulting from including $\mathbf{p}$ as a proxy for $\mathbf{z}$.

Assume that $\mathbf{z}$ and $\mathbf{X}$ are uncorrelated with the random variables, $\boldsymbol{\epsilon}$ and $\boldsymbol{v}$, and that $\text{cov}(\boldsymbol{\epsilon},\boldsymbol{v}) = 0$. Also assume that the following limits exist: $\text{plim}(\mathbf{X'X}/N) = \mathbf{M_{XX}}$, $\text{plim}(\mathbf{X'z}/N) = \mathbf{M_{Xz}}$, $\text{plim}(\mathbf{z'z}/N) = \mathbf{M_{ZZ}}$, $\text{plim}(\boldsymbol{v'v}/N) = \mathbf{M_{vv}}$, and $\text{plim}(\boldsymbol{\epsilon'\epsilon}/N) = \mathbf{M_{\epsilon\epsilon}}$. These assumptions imply that $\text{plim}(\mathbf{p'p}/N) = \mathbf{M_{pp}}$ and $\text{plim}(\mathbf{p'X}/N) = \mathbf{M_{pX}}$ also exist.

The estimated regression model using the proxy $\mathbf{p}$ is $\mathbf{y} = \mathbf{X}\boldsymbol{\beta} + \alpha\mathbf{p} + \omega$ where $\omega = \boldsymbol{\epsilon} - \alpha\boldsymbol{v} - \alpha\mathbf{X}\boldsymbol{\gamma}$. We are interested in the bias in our estimator of $\boldsymbol{\beta}$ which arises from the inclusion of $\mathbf{p}$ as compared to the inconsistency resulting from omitting $\mathbf{z}$ from the model. Letting $\mathbf{W} = (\mathbf{X}\ \mathbf{p})$ and $\boldsymbol{\delta} = \begin{pmatrix} \boldsymbol{\beta} \\ \alpha \end{pmatrix}$, the least squares estimator of $\boldsymbol{\delta}$ is $\boldsymbol{\delta} = (\mathbf{W'W})^{-1}\mathbf{W'y}$ and $\text{plim}(\hat{\boldsymbol{\delta}} - \boldsymbol{\delta}) = \text{plim}\begin{bmatrix} \hat{\boldsymbol{\beta}}-\boldsymbol{\beta} \\ \hat{\alpha}-\alpha \end{bmatrix} = \text{plim}\ ((\mathbf{W'W})^{-1}\mathbf{W'}\omega)$.

Now, $\text{plim}\left(\dfrac{\mathbf{W'W}}{N}\right) = \text{plim}\begin{bmatrix} \mathbf{X'X}/N & \mathbf{X'p}/N \\ \mathbf{p'X}/N & \mathbf{p'p}/N \end{bmatrix} = \begin{bmatrix} \mathbf{M_{XX}} & \mathbf{M'_{pX}} \\ \mathbf{M_{pX}} & \mathbf{M_{pp}} \end{bmatrix}$ and

$\text{plim}\left(\dfrac{\mathbf{W'}\omega}{N}\right) = \text{plim}\begin{bmatrix} \mathbf{X'}(\boldsymbol{\epsilon} - \alpha\mathbf{X}\boldsymbol{\gamma} - \alpha\boldsymbol{v})/N \\ \mathbf{p'}(\boldsymbol{\epsilon} - \alpha\mathbf{X}\boldsymbol{\gamma} - \alpha\boldsymbol{v})/N \end{bmatrix} = -\alpha \begin{bmatrix} \mathbf{M_{XX}}\boldsymbol{\gamma} \\ \mathbf{M_{pX}}\boldsymbol{\gamma} + \mathbf{M_{vv}} \end{bmatrix}$.

So $\text{plim}\begin{pmatrix} \hat{\boldsymbol{\beta}} - \boldsymbol{\beta} \\ \hat{\alpha} - \alpha \end{pmatrix} = -\alpha \begin{bmatrix} \mathbf{M_{XX}} & \mathbf{M'_{pX}} \\ \mathbf{M_{pX}} & \mathbf{M_{pp}} \end{bmatrix}^{-1} \begin{bmatrix} \mathbf{M_{XX}}\boldsymbol{\gamma} \\ \mathbf{M_{pX}}\boldsymbol{\gamma} + \mathbf{M_{vv}} \end{bmatrix}$. Using the properties of the inverse of a partitioned matrix, the $\text{plim}(\hat{\boldsymbol{\beta}} - \boldsymbol{\beta}) =$

$$-\alpha\ [\mathbf{M_{XX}^{-1}} + \mathbf{M_{XX}^{-1}}\mathbf{M'_{pX}}\mathbf{D}^{-1}\mathbf{M_{pX}}\mathbf{M_{XX}^{-1}} - \mathbf{M_{XX}^{-1}}\mathbf{M'_{pX}}\mathbf{D}^{-1}]\begin{bmatrix} \mathbf{M_{XX}}\boldsymbol{\gamma} \\ \mathbf{M_{pX}}\boldsymbol{\gamma} + \mathbf{M_{vv}} \end{bmatrix}$$

where $\mathbf{D} = \mathbf{M_{pp}} - \mathbf{M_{pX}}\mathbf{M_{XX}^{-1}}\mathbf{M'_{pX}}$. It can be shown that $\mathbf{D} = \mathbf{M_{vv}} + \mathbf{M_{\mu\mu}} = \sigma_v^2 + \sigma_\mu^2$, where σ_μ^2 is the population variance of the error in a regression of $\mathbf{z}$ on $\mathbf{X}$: $\mathbf{z} = \mathbf{X}\boldsymbol{\theta} + \boldsymbol{\mu}$, $\boldsymbol{\theta}$ is the $k \times 1$ vector $\mathbf{M_{XX}^{-1}}\mathbf{M_{XZ}}$, and σ_v^2 is the population variance of $\boldsymbol{v}$. Thus

$$\text{plim}(\hat{\beta} - \beta) = -\alpha \left[\gamma - \frac{M_{XX}^{-1} M_{pX}' M_{vv}}{D} \right].$$

Since $M_{XX}^{-1} M_{pX}' = M_{XX}^{-1}[M_{Xz} + M_{XX}\gamma]$ and $M_{XX}^{-1} M_{Xz} = \theta$, then $M_{XX}^{-1} M_{pX}' = \theta + \gamma$. Therefore, the plim $(\hat{\beta} - \beta) = \alpha \left[\dfrac{\theta \sigma_v^2 - \gamma \sigma_\mu^2}{\sigma_v^2 + \sigma_\mu^2} \right]$.

The inconsistency is $\hat{\beta}$ arising from omitting health from the regression model is $\alpha\theta$. Thus, including a health proxy worsens the inconsistency in $\hat{\beta}$ only if $\left| \dfrac{\theta \sigma_v^2 - \gamma \sigma_\mu^2}{\sigma_v^2 + \sigma_\mu^2} \right|$ exceeds θ.

Notes

1. See Manning, Newhouse, and Ware (1982) for an analysis of the relationship between alternative measures of health and the demand for medical care.

2. More explicitly, suppose that the researcher makes specification choices that result in correlations between some of the nonhealth control variables and the equation errors. Then it can be shown that the differences in the coefficients across equations using alternative measures of health may not be due solely to measurement errors in the health variables.

3. See Ware et al. (1979) for a discussion of the various approaches toward defining mental health.

4. Proponents of the theory of physician-induced demand may argue that there are economic incentives for psychiatrists to overstate the prevalence of mental disorders. Thus, psychiatric evaluations of mental health may have a systematic bias toward mental illness. Recently, the economics literature has tended to discount the relevance of this notion for the field of psychiatry. Evidence of intense competitive pressures faced by psychiatrists from nonmedical providers ("New Paths to Mental Health" 1990) implies that such behavior is unsustainable in the long run. Frank (1985), providing formal indicators of the degree of competition in the market for psychiatrists' services, concluded that "competitive" is an appropriate characterization of this market.

5. See Mullahy and Sindelar (1984) for a more detailed discussion of the ECA survey at the New Haven site.

6. See American Psychiatric Association (1980) for a discussion of the criteria followed by the DIS.

7. See Maddala (1983) or Amemiya (1985) for a discussion of ordered-probit models.

8. An alternative restriction would normalize σ_v to 1. But that would make comparisons between the two health measures meaningless, since they would be normalized to two different unknown scalars.

9. An interesting feature of the analysis in this section is that one does not need to specify y, only the set of exogenous X variables that affect y.

Therefore, the discussion that follows can also be applied to other models of behavior which specify health as a control variable, in particular, models of utilization of mental health services.

The variable y might also denote an unobservable latent index of an individual's propensity toward, say, labor force participation, which has a dichotomous 0-1 outcome. The econometric results of this chapter are derived only for least squares estimators of the labor market equation. But Griliches and Yatchew (1985) showed that, at least for a simple two-variable linear model, the least squares result regarding measurement error bias holds for maximum likelihood estimators of discrete choice models as long as the random variables in the model are normally distributed.

10. These inferences assume that mental health has a positive effect on labor market outcomes such as labor force participation, hours worked, and wages ($\alpha > 0$), whereas the coefficient on a sex dummy (FEMALE = 1) is usually negative and the coefficient on educational attainment is usually positive.

11. Here I assume that the coefficient on a race dummy (WHITE = 1) is usually positive in equations for labor market outcomes.

12. Anthony et al. compared the prevalence of disorders that were judged to be present within one month before the lay DIS interview with the prevalence rates implied by one-month psychiatric diagnoses. They attributed much of the differences between the two to disagreements in the recency of the disorder—the DIS applying more stringent criteria. They also found that a large number of disparities between the two stemmed from different classifications of the disorder, not from disagreements over whether a disorder exists. Hence, the use of a DIS-based one-year diagnosis of the presence of any disorder as an indicator of current mental health may eliminate much of the deviation between the DIS classifications and a psychiatric diagnosis.

13. In the construction of table 6.4, the maximum likelihood estimates of the coefficient vector of X in the probit equation for the clinical measure were used to measure θ. Under this alternative interpretation about the error structure of the DIS, the parameter estimates of X are measuring $\theta + \lambda$, not θ. Similarly, in table 6.4 the difference between the parameter estimates for the self-rating and the estimates for the psychiatric diagnosis were used to estimate γ. Under this alternative assumption, the difference measures $(\theta + \gamma) - (\theta + \lambda) = \gamma - \lambda$, not γ.

14. Note that $(\theta + \lambda)f - (1 - f)(\gamma - \lambda) = \theta f - (1 - f)\gamma + [\lambda f - (1 - f)\lambda] = \theta f - (1 - f)\gamma + \lambda$.

15. That is, we infer from the $\gamma - \lambda > 0$ finding for whites that $\gamma > \lambda > 0$.

16. See Maddala (1977) for the derivation of this result for the case of the three-variable model.

17. However, this inference should be made cautiously, since the proxy variable bias could conceivably become largely positive for gender and largely negative for education. In this case, the inconsistency arising from including self-rated health may be worse than the omitted variable bias. Without a measure of $\sigma_{v\epsilon}$ this issue cannot be resolved.

References

Amemiya, T. 1985. *Advanced Econometrics*. Cambridge: Harvard University Press.

American Psychiatric Association. 1980. *Diagnostic and Statistical Manual of Mental Disorders*. 3d ed. Washington, D.C.: American Psychiatric Association.

Anderson, K. H., and R. V. Burkhauser. 1983. "The Importance of the Measure of Health in Empirical Estimates of the Labor Supply of Older Men." *Economic Letters* 16:375–80.

———. 1985. "The Retirement Health Nexus: A New Measure of an Old Puzzle." *Journal of Human Resources* 20:315–30.

Anthony, J. C., M. Folstein, A. Romanoski, M. R. Von Korff, G. R. Nestadt, R. Chahal, A. Merchant, C. H. Brown, S. Shapiro, M. Kramer, and E. M. Gruenberg. 1985. "Comparison of the Lay Diagnostic Interview Schedule and a Standardized Psychiatric Diagnosis." *Archives of General Psychiatry* 42:667–75.

Bartel, A., and P. Taubman. 1979. "Health and Labor Market Success: The Role of Various Diseases." *Review of Economics and Statistics* 61:1–8.

———. 1986. "Some Economic and Demographic Consequences of Mental Illness." *Journal of Labor Economics* 4:243–56.

Bazzoli, G. J. 1985. "The Early Retirement Decision: New Empirical Evidence on the Influence of Health." *Journal of Human Resources* 20:214–34.

Benham, L., and A. Benham. 1982. "Employment, Earnings, and Psychiatric Diagnosis." In V. Fuchs (ed.): *Economic Aspects of Health*, pp. 203–20. Chicago: University of Chicago Press.

Berkovec, J., and S. Stern. 1988. "Job Exit Behavior of Older Men." Charlottesville: University of Virginia. Mimeo.

Butler, J. S., R. V. Burkhauser, J. M. Mitchell, and T. P. Pincus. 1987. "Measurement Error in Self-Reported Health Variables." *Review of Economics and Statistics* 69:644–50.

Dohrenwend, B. P. 1966. "Social Status and Psychological Disorder: An Issue of Substance and an Issue of Method." *American Sociological Review* 31:14–34.

Frank, R. G. 1985. "Pricing and Location of Physician Services in Mental Health." *Economic Inquiry* 23, no. 1:115–34.

Frank, R. G., and P. A. Gertler. 1987. "The Effect of Mental Distress on Income: Results from a Community Survey." National Bureau of Economic Research Working Paper No. 2433.

———. 1989. "The Effect of Medicaid Policy on Mental Health and Poverty." *Inquiry* 26:283–90.

Griliches, Z., and A. Yatchew. 1985. "Specification Error in Probit Models." *Review of Economics and Statistics* 67:134–39.

Grossman, M., and L. Benham. 1973. "Health, Hours, and Wages." In M. Perlman (ed.): *The Economics of Health and Medical Care*, pp. 205–47. New York: John Wiley.

Judge, G. G., W. E. Griffiths, R. C. Hill, H. Lutkepohl, and T. Lee. 1985. *The Theory and Practice of Econometrics*. 2d ed. New York: John Wiley.

Kemna, H. J. M. I. 1987. "Working Conditions and the Relationship between Schooling and Health." *Journal of Health Economics* 6:189–210.

Lambrinos, James. 1981. "Health: A Source of Bias in Labor Supply Models." *Review of Economics and Statistics* 63:81–98.

Leaf, Philip J., and Martha Livingston Bruce. 1987. "Gender Differences in the Use of Mental Health-related Services: A Re-examination." *Journal of Health and Social Behavior* 28:171–83.

Leaf, Philip J., Martha Livingston Bruce, Gary L. Tischler, Daniel H. Freeman, Myrna Weissman, and Jerome K. Myers. 1988. "Factors Affecting the Utilization of Specialty and General Medical Mental Health Services." *Medical Care* 26:1–18.

Maddala, G. S. 1977. *Econometrics*. New York: McGraw-Hill.

———. 1983. *Limited-Dependent and Qualitative Variables in Econometrics*. Cambridge: Cambridge University Press.

Manning, W. G., J. P. Newhouse, and J. E. Ware. 1982. "The Status of Health in Demand Estimation: Or Beyond Excellent, Good, Fair or Poor." In V. Fuchs (ed.): *Economic Aspects of Health*, pp. 143–83. Chicago: University of Chicago Press.

Mechanic, D. 1982. "The Epidemiology of Illness Behavior and Its Relationship to Physical and Psychological Distress." In D. Mechanic (ed.): *Symptoms, Illness Behavior, and Help-Seeking*, pp. 1–24. New York: PRODIST.

Mitchell, J., and Anderson, K. 1989. "Mental Health and the Labor Force Participation of Older Workers." *Inquiry* 26:262–71.

Mullahy, J., and J. Sindelar. 1987. "Economic Consequences of Mental Illness." Medical Economics Group. Yale Working Paper No. 21.

———. 1989. "Life-cycle Effects of Alcoholism on Education, Earnings, and Occupation." *Inquiry* 26:272–82.

———. 1990. "Gender Differences in the Effects of Mental Health on Labor Force Participation." In I. Sirageldin (ed.): *Research in Human Capital and Development: Female Labor Force Participation*, pp. 125–46. Greenwich, Conn.: JAI Press.

"New Paths to Mental Health Put Strains on Some Healers." 1990. *New York Times*, 17 May, p. 1.

Parsons, D. O. 1982. "The Male Labor Force Participation Decision: Health, Reported Health, Economic Incentives." *Economica* 49, no. 193:81–91.

Scheff, T. J. 1963. "The Role of the Mentally Ill and the Dynamics of Mental Disorder." *Sociometry* 26:436–53.

Sickles, R. C., and P. A. Taubman. 1986. "An Analysis of the Health and Retirement Status of the Elderly." *Econometrica* 54:1339–57.

Stern, S. 1989. "Measuring the Effect of Disability on Labor Force Participation." *Journal of Human Resources* 24:361–95.

Ware, J. E., S. A. Johnston, A. Davies-Avery, and R. H. Brook. 1979. *Concep-*

tualization and Measurement of Health for Adults in the Health Insurance Study. Vol. 3, *Mental Health.* R-1987/3-HEW. Santa Monica, Calif.: Rand Corporation.

World Health Organization. 1948. *Constitution.* In *Basic Documents.* Geneva: World Health Organization.

7

The Effects of Physical and Mental Health on Female Labor Supply

Christopher J. Ruhm, Ph.D.

H ealth problems are likely to raise the disutility of work and to lower marginal products. It is therefore not surprising that poor health is associated with significant reductions in work hours and participation rates in virtually every study that considers it. Nonetheless, we have little information on the effect of specific ailments or on the overall influence of health status, as compared with economic and demographic factors, in determining the labor supply.

This continuing uncertainty results largely from the paucity of health data available in most surveys. Researchers have typically been forced to rely on questions asking whether "health limitations" prevented the respondent from working in the recent past or if the respondent's health is better or worse than average (either for similarly aged individuals or for the entire population). These measures suffer from two serious shortcomings. First, the reported responses may vary with labor market status. Second, no single indicator can adequately capture the multiple facets of health.

In this chapter I utilize a unique data source containing information on the regular usage of fifteen distinct types of medications and on a clinically tested indicator of mental depression for women between the ages of forty-five and fifty-seven. The detailed nature of the data allows investigation of a number of questions receiving limited attention in previous work. These include (1) the relationship between specific health problems and labor supply, (2) the importance of health versus economic and demographic factors in labor force decisions, and (3) the relative effects of physical and mental health problems.

This study is one of the first to focus on middle-aged women. Women in their middle years are of special interest for two reasons.

First, since labor force participation rates among women in this age group have approximately doubled during the last forty years, factors influencing their participation decisions have important effects on aggregate labor supply.[1] Second, despite this increase, female participation and employment rates remain around twenty percentage points below those of similarly aged men.[2] This implies that many women continue to have greater discretion in their work decisions, which suggests that poor health has a larger potentially negative effect on their labor supply than on that of men.

Three major findings are highlighted below. First, the regular use of medications or high depression scores are frequently associated with large reductions in labor force participation and employment. The influence on labor supply varies substantially across types of ailments, however, which suggests limitations in previous research using general indicators of health. Second, although only somewhat sketchy supporting data are available, mental illness seems to be of key importance. For example, large reductions in participation and employment rates are observed for persons suffering from mental depression. Third, relatively few sample members experience the types of health problems which significantly decrease labor supply. As a result, economic and demographic characteristics explain a larger portion of economywide variations in labor supply than does ill health.

Previous Research

Previous researchers typically obtained information on health status from questions asking (1) whether "health limitations" had prevented the respondent from working in the recent past or had otherwise limited daily activities or (2) whether the respondent's health was better, the same, or worse than that of average individuals of the same age.[3] These health measures contain a number of well-known problems. First, there is reporting bias if response errors differ systematically with labor market status. This is likely both because health problems are a socially more acceptable reason for not working than is the desire for leisure and because eligibility for some transfer programs (i.e., disability) depends upon health status.[4] Second, general measures fail to capture the multifaceted aspects of health. For example, the effect of chronic arthritis is likely to differ from that of acute (but treatable) heart conditions.

Two primary methods have been used to correct for reporting bias. Some researchers (e.g., Lee 1982; Sickles and Taubman 1986) have modeled self-classified health and labor force status as being jointly determined. Such structural models represent an improvement over standard reduced form estimates but are critically dependent on strong identifying restrictions.

A more common approach has been to replace self-reported status with "objective" indicators of health. The latter include hours or weeks of previous illness (Boskin 1977; Burkhauser 1979), future mortality rates (Parsons 1980, 1982; Program Analysis Staff 1982; Anderson and Burkhauser 1985), or health status reported during a previous period when the respondent was working (Bazzoli 1985). Unfortunately, each of these is likely to measure true health rather imprecisely. Retrospective recall of sickness is quite poor, and previous transitory illnesses do not indicate current health status. Subsequent mortality rates imperfectly indicate health status because some deaths result from accidents or sudden illnesses, which are not correlated with prior labor force participation, while other chronic health problems impose serious work limitations but have little effect on life expectancies. Previously reported health status similarly fails to capture the influence of unexpected deteriorations in health.[5]

A number of researchers used detailed health data to examine the extent of reporting and selection biases in self-classified measures of general health. Lambrinos (1981) employed principle component analysis to construct proxy measures of underlying health using information on nine activity, two sensory, and sixteen psychological limitations, plus seven symptoms. The Fillenbaum-Maddox health impairment index, which utilizes data on mobility and activity limitations as well as on various self-assessed health variables, was included in Bazzoli's 1985 study. Chirikos and Nestle (1985) combined information on functional impairments and self-defined overall status to evaluate the effects of changes in a dichotomous health variable on earnings and work hours. Finally, Butler et al. (1987) contrasted a self-reported dichotomous indicator of arthritis with a simulated clinical diagnosis based on symptom reports. This research indicates that self-classifications of health status overstate the dampening effect of ill health on labor supply but that a smaller negative influence remains when "objective" measures are used.

Interestingly, none of these studies used the available information to show explicitly the effects of specific health problems on labor supply. Research that has done so generally looked at only a narrow subset of ailments. Eight distinct diseases were investigated by Bartel and Taubman (1979), who found that recent diagnoses of some illnesses correlated with 20 to 30 percent reductions in earnings. These results must be interpreted cautiously, however, because their data set (the National Academy of Science/National Research Council twin sample) is restricted to white veteran male twins born in the United States and suffers from a number of shortcomings in data collection. Other studies focusing on the role of specific health problems are more limited in scope. Bartel and Taubman (1986), Frank and Gertler (1988), and Mitchell and Anderson (1989) examined the economic effect of mental illness but with few controls available on physical health. Inman (1987) analyzed the effects of multiple sclerosis but had no information on other measures of health.

The Data and the Sample

Data for this investigation were obtained from the New England Research Institute's Massachusetts Womens' Health Study (MWHS). The MWHS sampled women born from 1926 through 1936 from Massachusetts Street Lists using a two-stage, stratified cluster-sampling design, with selection probabilities proportional to size at the first stage and simple random sampling at the second. The original baseline survey took place in 1981–82. A cohort of 2,500 women identified as premenopausal (menses during the last three months) were reinterviewed six times at nine-month intervals.

A core questionnaire and one of three randomly assigned rotating instruments were administered at each follow-up interview. One of the rotating instruments contained questions used to construct an index of depression. Data for each respondent from the baseline survey and the first follow-up interview, which included the depression questions, were used.[6] Respondents who had never held a paid job or who dropped out of the survey before the relevant follow-up interview were excluded from the analysis. These restrictions reduced the final sample size to 2,399. At the time of the follow-up survey, 74.4 percent of this group participated in the labor force, 71.4 percent were employed, and 49.3 percent worked more than thirty-five hours per week.[7]

The presence of specific health ailments or conditions was measured by the use of medications taken to treat these ailments. Dummy variables were constructed to indicate weekly or more frequent usage of medicines treating problems relating to the heart, cholesterol, blood pressure, migraine headache, pain, diabetes, thyroid conditions, allergies, hormones, arthritis or rheumatism, other muscles/joints, the stomach, sleeping, depression, and tension. The list of the questions used to construct these variables is included in appendix 7.A.

Medication usage imperfectly captures the presence of health problems for at least two reasons. First, the treatment may sometimes eliminate or control the ailment such that it has no effect on labor supply. Second, it is not possible to distinguish persons with the health condition who do not use the medication from those without the condition. As a result, the negative effects of untreated health ailments on labor supply may be understated. Ideally, variables indicating the presence of the condition would be available in addition to those identifying medication usage. Despite this limitation, the specificity of health data in this analysis far surpasses that which has typically been available to previous researchers.

There has been little previous effort to estimate separately the effects of physical and mental health problems on employment or labor force participation. The detailed health information provided in the MWHS allows such a distinction. An immediate problem occurs, however, when classifying medications as treating physical or mental illnesses. Medications for heart, cholesterol, diabetes, thyroid, arthritis, or muscle/joint problems almost certainly relate to physical disorders, whereas the use of sleeping pills, antidepression medications, diazepam (Valium), or chlordiazepoxide hydrochloride (Librium) probably indicates mental distress. Drugs taken for allergies, migraine headaches, and hormone or stomach problems were somewhat arbitrarily categorized as treating physical ailments, although each of these may have a mental health component. As shown below, these medications generally have little effect on labor supply and so their assignment is probably not critical.

The medication variables contain considerably more detailed data on physical than on mental illness. To obtain additional information on the latter, we constructed three dummy variables indicating ranges of scores on the Center for Epidemiological Studies— Depression (CESD) scale. The CESD scale consists of twenty self-reported items representing major components in the clinical syndrome of depression such as depressed affect, feelings of worthlessness and hopelessness, psychomotor retardation, loss of appetite, and the absence of positive affect. Higher scores indicate more severe depression. The complete set of questions and the algorithm for constructing the CESD score are contained in appendix 7.B. Previous studies (e.g., Radloff 1977) indicated that the CESD score has high internal consistency and correlates well with clinical assessments of depression.[8]

Dummy variables were constructed indicating CESD scores in the ranges 9–15, 16–23, and 24+ (with the excluded group having scores of less than 9). The lower end of each of these ranges corresponds to approximately the eightieth, ninetieth, and ninety-fifth sample percentiles, respectively.[9] Even with the inclusion of the CESD variables, the indicators of mental illness refer primarily to depression or other neuroses and may miss potentially severe psychotic disorders. As a result, the relative importance of mental illness probably remains understated.

Regressors indicating age (at baseline), education, marital and ethnic status, family size, birthplace, and whether dependents live in the home were included in the analysis. Economic data are less satisfactory. Respondents were questioned about their labor force participation and if they worked full- or part-time. Unfortunately, little information was available on wage rates or nonearned income. Dummy variables for the current or previous one-digit occupation of the respondent and the current occupation of her husband (if any) were included to proxy these factors.

Reporting biases are minimized in this study by the nature of MWHS and the particular questions utilized. The stated purpose of the survey was to collect *health* (rather than employment) information, and the vast majority of questions referred specifically to health. The few that addressed labor supply issues were located at the end of the questionnaire and were clearly of secondary interest. As a result, it is unlikely that respondents considered their employment status when answering even fairly general health questions. Response errors to the specific questions used in this analysis (e.g., "do you take insulin?") are even less likely to depend systematically upon employment status. The specificity of the information also avoids the need to rely on general measures of health.

Tables 7.1–7.3 present summary information on medication usage and depression scores. Among respondents, 14.5 percent were treated for high blood pressure but fewer than 5 percent were treated for any other ailment (table 7.2). Nonetheless, more than one-third (35.0 percent) of the sample took at least one medication and 11.0 percent regularly used two or more medicines (table 7.1). Given that the survey data nonparticipation and employment rates were 26 and 29 percent, respectively, sample variation in health status is *potentially* sufficient to explain a significant proportion of the observed variations in labor supply.

Cross-tabular analysis suggests that health is of at least some importance in determining participation and employment probabilities. Among women using no medications, 76.5 percent partici-

Table 7.1   Number of Medications Used

Number of Medications Used	Sample Probability	Conditional Probability Labor Force Participation	Employment	Full-time Employment
0	0.650	0.765	0.734	0.496
1	0.240	0.715	0.696	0.516
2	0.078	0.709	0.676	0.473
≥3	0.032	0.592	0.553	0.316
1 or more—physical	0.327	0.701	0.679	0.491
1 or more—mental	0.062	0.616	0.575	0.390

Table 7.2   Type of Medications Used

Type of Medicine	Probability of Using Specified Medication	Probability of Using at Least One Other Medication Conditional on Use of Specified Medication
Physical Problem		
Heart	0.027	0.730
Cholesterol	0.003	0.857
Blood pressure	0.145	0.382
Pain	0.021	0.735
Insulin	0.017	0.550
Thyroid	0.049	0.452
Arthritis	0.031	0.639
Muscle/joint	0.013	0.700
Migraine	0.013	0.613
Hormone	0.040	0.419
Allergy	0.049	0.474
Stomach	0.030	0.586
Mental Problem		
Sleeping pills	0.016	0.676
Valium/Librium	0.039	0.696
Depression	0.018	0.756

pated in the labor force. Of this group, 73.4 percent and 49.6 percent, respectively, were employed and worked full-time. Among respondents taking three or more medications, the corresponding percentages were only 59.2 percent, 55.3 percent, and 31.6 percent (table 7.1). The negative relationship between ill health and labor supply seems particularly strong when considering medications treating mental rather than physical illness.

Comorbidity, as measured by the use of multiple medications, is also important. As shown in table 7.2, between 38 and 86 percent of

Table 7.3   Medication Use Related to Depression Score

Depression Score	Probability of Specified CESD Score	Probability of Using Medication	
		Any	Mental Health
0–8	0.802	0.320	0.038
9–15	0.099	0.407	0.113
16–23	0.049	0.518	0.149
≥24	0.050	0.556	0.265

persons using each of the fifteen specified medicines takes at least one other medication and at least 70 percent of those treated for heart, cholesterol, muscle/joint, pain, or depression problems does so.[10] The resulting collinearity of the health covariates may make it difficult to ascertain independent effects of specific health problems. This issue is particularly salient when considering previous research examining the relationship between mental health and labor supply (e.g., Mitchell and Anderson 1989), since surveys providing information on mental distress have generally provided quite limited data on physical problems. The measured impact of the former is therefore likely to indicate the combined effect of physical and mental illness. This can be seen by noting that fully 63.0 percent of MWHS respondents using one or more mental health medications also take at least one medicine treating a primarily physical problem. Conversely, only 12.0 percent of those treated for physical ailments use mental health medications.

Table 7.3 shows that medication usage is positively correlated with the CESD score. Among women with depression scores of 8 or less, 32.0 percent used at least one medication, as compared to 40.7, 51.8, and 55.6 percent of respondents with scores of 9–15, 16–23, and 24+, respectively. Corresponding percentages treated with at least one of the mental health pharmaceuticals were 3.8, 11.3, 14.9, and 26.5 percent. This indicates that the depression score and the medication variables capture overlapping but nonidentical components of health status.[11]

The Framework for Analysis

The model for subsequent econometric analysis is derived from standard static labor supply theory. The individual's constrained maximization problem is

$$\max U(C,H,\mathbf{V},\mathbf{Z}) \tag{7.1}$$
$$\text{subject to } C = wH + I,$$

where U is utility, C is a representative consumption good (with price normalized to one), H is hours worked, $\mathbf{V}$ and $\mathbf{Z}$ are vectors of observed and unobserved characteristics, respectively, w is the real wage, and I represents nonwage income. First-order conditions for utility maximization yield optimum hours worked, H^*, which fulfill

$$w = m(C,H^*,\mathbf{V},\mathbf{Z}) = -U_H/U_C.$$

Thus, workers set labor supply such that the real wage equals the (negative of the) marginal rate of substitution of work hours for consumption goods.

From the first-order conditions, we can define the reservation wage $r = m(C,H,\mathbf{V},\mathbf{Z})$ which, when substituted into the budget constraint, gives the reservation wage function:

$$r = r(I,\mathbf{V},\mathbf{Z}). \tag{7.2}$$

Market wages depend upon observed and unobserved characteristics,

$$w = w(\mathbf{V},\mathbf{Z}), \tag{7.3}$$

and the individual participates in the labor force if

$$w(\mathbf{V},\mathbf{Z}) - r(I,\mathbf{V},\mathbf{Z}) \geq 0. \tag{7.4}$$

The econometrician estimates the market and reservation wages with error as

$$w^* = \mathbf{V}\,\beta_w = w + \epsilon_w \tag{7.5a}$$

and

$$r^* = \mathbf{V}\,\beta_r + I\,\gamma_r = r + \epsilon_r. \tag{7.5b}$$

The probability of the individual being in the labor force is therefore

$$\begin{aligned} P &= Pr(\epsilon_w - \epsilon_r \leq w^* - r^*) \\ &= Pr(\mu \leq X\,\beta) \\ &= F(X\,\beta), \end{aligned} \tag{7.6}$$

where $\mu = \epsilon_w - \epsilon_r$, $X\beta = \mathbf{V}(\beta_w - \beta_r) + I\,\gamma_r$, and $F(.)$ is the cumulative density function of μ. Notice from equation (7.6) that unexpectedly low reservation wages ($\epsilon_r > 0$) or high market wages ($\epsilon_w < 0$) raise participation probabilities.

Observed outcomes for the ith individual can be described by the dichotomous variable Y_i, which equals one (zero) if μ_i is less than or equal to (greater than) $X_i\beta$. If μ is normally distributed, it is therefore appropriate to estimate

$$Y_i = X_i\beta + \mu_i \tag{7.7}$$

as a binary probit model.

The market wage equation specified by (7.3) refers to expected wages conditional on individual characteristics. To distinguish between labor force participation and employment, we can specify an offer wage equation, which differs from the market wage equation by an additional error term. For instance, the disturbance may be negative for persons working in sectors with transitory reductions in demand. The individual will be employed if offer wages exceed reservation wages and the right-hand side of the probit equation is identical to equation (7.7).[12]

The probability that an individual works full-time (more than thirty-five hours per week) can be modeled by assuming that

$$H^* = h[w(\mathbf{V},\mathbf{Z}) - r(I,\mathbf{V},\mathbf{Z})] = X\beta - \mu, \tag{7.8}$$

with $h(0) = 0$ and $h' \geq 0$, and defining a full-time work dummy variable,

$$F_i = \begin{matrix} 0 \\ 1 \end{matrix} \quad \text{if} \quad \mu_i \begin{matrix} > \\ \leq \end{matrix} X_i\beta - 35.$$

We can again estimate the structural probit model described in equation (7.7), with F_i replacing Y_i as the dependent variable.

Alternatively, we can consider nonemployment, part-time employment, and full-time employment simultaneously by defining the ranked trichotomous variable,

$$S_i = \begin{matrix} 0 \\ 1 \\ 2 \end{matrix} \quad \text{if} \quad \begin{matrix} \mu_i > X_i\beta \\ X_i\beta - 35 < \mu_i \leq X_i\beta, \\ \mu_i \leq X_i\beta - 35 \end{matrix}$$

and estimating an ordered-probit model.

One assumption underlying this analysis is that causation runs from health to employment status. It is possible, however, that the health and labor supply are *simultaneously determined*. For instance, nonemployment could cause (as well as be caused by) poor health, in which case the health coefficient captures the combined effect. This type of reverse causation has received little attention in previous studies and is an important subject for future research.[13]

The Regression Results

In this section I present the results of binary and ordered-probit models estimated by maximum likelihood. Three dichotomous dependent variables indicate labor force participation, employment, and full-time employment (at least thirty-five hours per week). The trichotomous variable used in the ordered-probit model is set to zero, one, or two, respectively, for nonemployed women, part-time workers, and full-time employees. For ease of exposition, the demographic and health coefficients will be discussed separately, although (except where noted) both sets of controls are included in all regressions.

Table 7.4 displays probit coefficients for the nonhealth variables.[14] The findings are quite standard and warrant only brief comment. Labor force participation and employment probabilities are lower for older, currently married, and less educated women and slightly higher for those born outside the United States. Respondents with two children are most likely to work; those with a single child least frequently do so. If children still reside in the home, participation and full-time employment probabilities are reduced.[15]

The effect of health, as measured by medication usage and depression scores, is considered next. One issue deserving attention is that schooling and occupational attainment are endogenous in a life-cycle context. Previous research (e.g., Grossman 1975) suggested that poor health at young ages has negative effects on cognitive development scores and years of completed schooling. Similarly, women with histories of ill health may disproportionately work (or have worked) in occupations where labor force attachments are relatively weak. If so, inclusion of education and occupation controls may bias the estimated health coefficients toward zero.

To examine the importance of this type of endogeneity, I estimated the labor force participation model both with and without the education and occupation covariates. Results of these estimates, which are detailed in the first three columns of table 7.5, suggest that the health coefficients are only slightly altered by inclusion of the occupation and education regressors. Prescription pain medication provides an example of the typical pattern. The associated regression coefficient is -0.582 when both education and occupation are excluded, -0.570 when schooling covariates are added, and -0.531 when occupations are also controlled for. The medication most sensitive to the inclusion of education and occupation is sleeping pills, where the coefficient increases from -0.170 to -0.056 with the addition of education and occupation regressors.

These findings suggest that health problems are negatively correlated with schooling and occupational attainment but that the relationship is typically quite weak. Corroborating evidence is obtained by noting that the inclusion of medication regressors has almost no influence on the estimated effect of education.[16] Since education and occupation have a strong effect on labor supply, both directly and because they proxy earnings, they are included throughout the subsequent analysis.

The fourth column of table 7.5 presents estimates for a participation equation that includes the depression score dummy variables but excludes the three medications associated with mental distress. The physical health coefficients are typically larger (in absolute value) than the corresponding estimates in column 3, but the change is usually small. The difference probably occurs because persons treated for mental illness frequently have physical problems and more detailed data on mental health are obtained from the medication variables than from the CESD score.

Estimated health coefficients for the binary and ordered-probit models are displayed in table 7.6. Each column displays the results of two separate regressions. The medication coefficients are obtained from an equation that excludes the three depression score dummy variables; the CESD coefficients are obtained from specifications that exclude the mental health pharmaceuticals but include treatments for physical problems. Demographic covariates are included in all cases.

Ill health is typically associated with reduced labor supply. Thirteen of the fifteen medication coefficients have negative signs in the participation and ordered-probit models; ten and twelve, respectively, in the employment and full-time employment equations. Given the small number of respondents using some of the medications and the frequency of comorbidities, it is not surprising that many of the coefficients fail to reach statistical significance. Nevertheless, the (negative) coefficient exceeds its standard error for eight medications in the participation regression, for seven each in the employment and ordered-probit models, and for six medicines in the full-time work equation. Interestingly, two of the three medication categories consistently having a statistically significant negative effect on labor supply (Valium/Librium and antidepressives) treat primarily mental rather than physical ailments. The only physical medications that approach or reach statistical significance are those prescribed for pain or elevated cholesterol.

Further evidence of the negative effects of mental illness are obtained from the CESD variables. The pattern of coefficients indicates monotonic reductions in labor supply as the depression score rises, with particularly strong decreases for the 5 percent of the sample with scores exceeding 23. (The excluded category are workers with depression scores of 8 or less.) There is also evidence of reductions in work hours for the group with scores of 16–23.

Table 7.4 Regression Coefficients for Nonhealth Covariates

Regressor	Sample Average	Binary Probit Estimates			Ordered-Probit Estimates
		Labor Force Participation	Employment	Full-time Employment	
Age (years)	48.207	0.832	0.835	0.412	-0.199
		(2.11)	(2.16)	(1.11)	(2.05)
Age squared	2,330.545	-8.7E-3	-8.7E-3	-4.4E-3	
		(2.18)	(2.22)	(1.15)	
Education					
High school dropout	0.121	-0.308	-0.372	-0.284	-0.290
		(3.29)	(4.05)	(3.10)	(3.72)
Some college	0.430	0.333	0.316	0.250	0.264
		(4.94)	(4.82)	(4.06)	(4.73)
Marital Status					
Never married	0.064	0.448	0.669	0.847	0.838
		(2.23)	(3.45)	(4.72)	(5.50)
Divorced	0.124	0.508	0.295	0.648	0.532
		(4.31)	(2.71)	(6.43)	(5.89)
Widowed	0.051	0.375	0.300	0.476	0.418
		(2.39)	(1.99)	(3.50)	(3.31)

Number of Children

	Mean	Labor force participation	Employment	Full-time employment	Ordered-probit
1	0.057	-0.288 (1.55)	-0.129 (0.74)	-0.115 (0.67)	-0.141 (0.94)
2	0.205	0.070 (0.43)	0.275 (1.82)	0.099 (0.69)	0.151 (1.22)
≥3	0.636	-0.083 (0.53)	0.105 (0.72)	-0.057 (0.41)	7.1E-3 (0.06)

Relative Living at Home

	Mean	Labor force participation	Employment	Full-time employment	Ordered-probit
Parents	0.055	-0.064 (0.45)	-8.2E-3 (0.06)	0.102 (0.77)	0.755 (0.64)
Children	0.684	-0.119 (1.54)	-0.036 (0.49)	-0.142 (2.01)	-0.86 (1.35)

Birthplace

	Mean	Labor force participation	Employment	Full-time employment	Ordered-probit
Outside U.S.	0.063	0.130 (1.02)	0.152 (1.21)	0.161 (1.38)	
Outside Massachusetts	0.184	-0.074 (0.92)	-0.056 (0.72)	-0.159 (2.13)	

Notes: Models are estimated by maximum likelihood. $N = 2{,}339$; absolute value of t statistics are in parentheses. Dependent variable means are 0.7435, 0.7144, and 0.4930 for labor force participation, employment, and full-time employment, respectively. Also included in regressions are variables indicating ethnic status, the survey follow-up, the spouse's (if any) occupation, and medication usage. The dependent variable in the ordered-probit model is equal to 0, 1, or 2, respectively, if the respondent is nonemployed, working less than thirty-five hours per week, or working at least thirty-five hours per week. Ethnic status, age squared, and birthplace variables are excluded from the ordered-probit model because of their high collinearity with other covariates.

Table 7.5   Sensitivity of Estimated Health Coefficients
to Alternative Specifications of Labor Force Participation Model

Regressor	Coefficient Estimate			
Medicines—Physical				
Heart	−0.267	−0.252	−0.238	−0.311
	(1.49)	(1.39)	(1.29)	(1.73)
Cholesterol	−0.781	−0.807	−0.752	−0.836
	(1.53)	(1.54)	(1.43)	(1.59)
Blood pressure	−0.133	−0.097	−0.102	−0.117
	(1.59)	(1.14)	(1.18)	(1.36)
Pain	−0.582	−0.570	−0.531	−0.545
	(2.92)	(2.84)	(2.61)	(2.66)
Insulin	−0.053	0.026	−0.032	−0.034
	(0.23)	(0.11)	(0.14)	(0.15)
Thyroid	0.123	0.095	0.080	0.089
	(0.87)	(0.68)	(0.57)	(0.64)
Arthritis	0.008	−0.025	−0.024	−0.048
	(0.05)	(0.15)	(0.14)	(0.28)
Muscle/joint	−0.326	−0.382	−0.401	−0.400
	(1.29)	(1.50)	(1.55)	(1.55)
Migraine	−0.116	−0.171	−0.204	−0.280
	(0.47)	(0.69)	(0.82)	(1.14)
Hormone	−0.013	−0.020	−0.043	−0.055
	(0.09)	(0.13)	(0.28)	(0.36)
Allergy	−0.118	−0.154	−0.179	−0.195
	(0.89)	(1.15)	(1.33)	(1.44)
Stomach	0.164	0.192	0.181	0.166
	(0.93)	(1.07)	(0.99)	(0.91)
Medicines—Mental				
Sleeping pills	−0.170	−0.080	−0.056	
	(0.73)	(0.34)	(0.24)	
Valium/Librium	−0.354	−0.346	−0.327	
	(2.41)	(2.33)	(2.18)	
Depression	−0.469	−0.496	−0.442	
	(2.18)	(2.27)	(2.00)	
Depression Score				
9–25				0.052
				(0.51)
16–23				−0.039
				(0.27)
≥24				−0.275
				(2.08)
Education Variables	No	Yes	Yes	Yes
Occupation Variables	No	No	Yes	Yes

Note: See note to table 7.4.

Positive coefficients, indicating greater work propensities, are occasionally obtained. With two exceptions, however, the estimated effects are small and imprecisely measured. The first is that persons taking stomach medications are more likely than their counterparts to participate in the labor force. There is no difference, however, in their propensities to work and, if anything, they are less likely to be employed full-time. This pattern may be explained by stress associated with unemployment or involuntary part-time work. The second exception is the positive coefficient for thyroid medication. Although the effect is small for labor force participation and employment, the coefficient is large and statistically significant in the full-time employment and ordered-probit models. This may occur because full-time workers can least afford to fall asleep during the day, a primary effect of thyroid conditions, and so are more likely to obtain treatment for this ailment.

Since probit coefficients are difficult to interpret, predicted labor supply effects of selected medications and depression scores are presented in table 7.7. The odd-numbered columns show expected employment or participation probabilities for individuals not using the medication or having the specified CESD score. The even-numbered columns display the corresponding probabilities if the medication is used or the CESD score falls in the specified range. Entries in parentheses indicate changes in predicted probabilities, with negative values representing health-related reductions in labor supply. These estimates are obtained from the binary probit models with regressors, other than the specific health variable in question, evaluated at the sample means.

Some ailments are associated with extremely large reductions in labor supply. The use of cholesterol-lowering medicines reduces the predicted probabilities of participation, employment, and full-time employment by 27.6, 41.0, and 14.2 percentage points, respectively; these correspond to decreases of 36, 56, and 28 percent.[17] The decline among persons taking prescription pain medications is 18.7, 18.0, and 7.4 percentage points, respectively, or 24, 24, and 15 percent. Decreases for the other physical health medications are smaller but often exceed 10 percent.

As already noted, mental illness substantially reduces predicted labor supply. Use of antidepressive medications correlates with reductions of 15.3, 16.3, and 12.7 percentage points (20, 22, and 25 percent) in labor force participation, employment, and full-time employment, respectively. Women taking Valium or Librium are 14–17 percent less likely than their counterparts to participate in the labor force or be employed, and they work full-time almost 30 percent less often. Compared to women with CESD scores of less than 9, predicted participation, employment, and full-time employment probabilities of women with depression scores above 23 are reduced by 12, 15, and 26 percent (9.1, 11.3, and 13.2 percentage points). There is also an 18 percent reduction in the probability of full-time employment for

Table 7.6 Regression Coefficients for Medication and Depression Covariates

| Regressor | Binary Probit Estimates | | | Ordered-Probit Estimates |
	Labor Force Participation	Employment	Full-time Employment	
Medicines—Physical				
Heart	-0.238	-0.187	-0.261	-0.244
	(1.29)	(1.03)	(1.41)	(1.45)
Cholesterol	-0.752	-1.081	-0.364	-0.677
	(1.43)	(2.00)	(0.68)	(1.72)
Blood pressure	-0.10	-0.066	-0.028	-0.414
	(1.18)	(0.77)	(0.35)	(0.56)
Pain	-0.531	-0.492	-0.186	-0.363
	(2.61)	(2.44)	(0.90)	(2.12)
Insulin	-0.032	0.053	-0.170	-0.093
	(0.14)	(0.23)	(0.79)	(0.47)
Thyroid	0.080	0.109	0.318	0.239
	(0.57)	(0.79)	(2.46)	(2.05)
Arthritis	-0.024	0.047	0.051	0.028
	(0.14)	(0.28)	(0.31)	(0.19)
Muscle/joint	-0.401	-0.311	-0.441	-0.378
	(1.55)	(1.21)	(1.66)	(1.56)

Migraine	-0.204	-0.091	-0.332	-0.235
	(0.82)	(0.37)	(1.36)	(1.08)
Hormone	-0.043	0.026	-8.9E-3	-5.2E-3
	(0.28)	(0.17)	(0.06)	(0.04)
Allergy	-0.179	-0.227	0.017	-0.087
	(1.33)	(1.73)	(0.13)	(0.76)
Stomach	0.181	0.028	-0.170	-0.052
	(0.99)	(0.16)	(1.00)	(0.33)
Medicines—Mental				
Sleeping pills	-0.056	-0.072	-0.167	-0.077
	(0.24)	(0.31)	(0.69)	(0.36)
Valium/Librium	-0.327	-0.368	-0.389	-0.390
	(2.18)	(2.48)	(2.56)	(2.99)
Depression	-0.442	-0.447	-0.323	-0.410
	(2.00)	(2.05)	(1.45)	(2.12)
Depression Score				
9–15	0.052	-0.018	-0.083	-0.056
	(0.51)	(0.19)	(0.88)	(0.67)
16–23	-0.039	-0.093	-0.226	-0.168
	(0.27)	(0.68)	(1.74)	(1.39)
≥24	-0.275	-0.320	-0.334	-0.314
	(2.08)	(2.47)	(2.57)	(2.88)

Notes: See note to table 7.4. Also included in regressions are demographic characteristics and a dummy variable for the survey follow-up. Medication coefficients were obtained from a regression that excludes CESD variables. CESD coefficients were obtained from a regression that excludes mental health medications.

Table 7.7   Predicted Effects of Selected Medication Usage
or Depression Score on Labor Force Participation and Employment

Medication or Depression Score	Predicted Probability					
	Labor Force Participation		Employment		Full-time Employment	
	$X_j = 0$	$X_j = 1$	$X_j = 0$	$X_j = 1$	$X_j = 0$	$X_j = 1$
Medicine—Physical						
Heart	0.770	0.692	0.737	0.673	0.502	0.399
	(−0.078)		(−0.064)		(−0.103)	
Cholesterol	0.769	0.493	0.736	0.327	0.500	0.358
	(−0.276)		(−0.410)		(−0.142)	
Pain	0.771	0.584	0.739	0.559	0.501	0.427
	(−0.187)		(−0.180)		(−0.074)	
Muscle/joint	0.770	0.632	0.737	0.626	0.501	0.331
	(−0.138)		(−0.110)		(−0.170)	
Migraine	0.769	0.702	0.736	0.705	0.501	0.371
	(−0.067)		(−0.031)		(−0.130)	
Allergy	0.771	0.713	0.739	0.660	0.499	0.506
	(−0.058)		(−0.079)		(0.007)	
Medicine—Mental						
Valium/Librium	0.772	0.662	0.740	0.609	0.505	0.354
	(−0.110)		(−0.131)		(−0.152)	
Depression	0.770	0.617	0.738	0.575	0.502	0.375
	(−0.153)		(−0.163)		(−0.127)	
Depression Score						
16–23	0.771	0.759	0.742	0.712	0.514	0.424
	(−0.012)		(−0.031)		(−0.090)	
≥24	0.771	0.680	0.742	0.630	0.514	0.382
	(−0.091)		(−0.113)		(−0.132)	

Notes: Predicted probabilities are calculated from binary probit regressions with covariates (other than X_j) evaluated at their sample means. Changes in predicted probabilities are shown in parentheses. For the depression score, predicted changes are compared to those of persons with CESD scores of 8 or less.

women with scores of 16–23, with smaller decreases in the other labor supply variables.

Economywide Effects

Although health problems have large effects on individual employment decisions, it is not obvious whether the types of ailments associated with reduced labor supply are sufficiently prevalent that ill health has a substantial negative effect on aggregate participation or employment rates. For example, although women treated for elevated cholesterol work relatively infrequently, only 0.3 percent of the sample suffer from this ailment; thus, it is likely to account for only a small portion of total nonemployment.

In this section I examine the economywide influence of ill health on labor supply by decomposing the total explanatory power of each binary probit model into "pure" health and demographic effects and "covariances" or "interactions" between the two. The effect of health is then divided into its physical and mental health components. In the linear model, such decompositions would be obtained by using the squared correlation coefficient to measure goodness-of-fit and by applying analysis of variance. It is less clear, however, which goodness-of-fit criterion is most appropriate when considering qualitative response models (such as probit).

The decomposition in this chapter is based on a statistic, suggested by McFadden (1974), measuring the increase in the log-likelihood resulting from the inclusion of the vector of covariates, as compared to the intercept-only model. This is defined as

$$\pounds = 1 - [\ell(X)/\ell(0)],$$

where $\ell(0)$ and $\ell(X)$ are the maximized log-likelihoods of the intercept-only and full models; $\pounds$ is bounded between 0 and 1.[18] To maximize explanatory power, I include the full set of medication covariates *and* the three CESD variables in X.

Even with the large number of covariates, the model is poorly specified. As shown in row 1 of table 7.8, $\pounds$ is less than 0.10 in the participation and employment equations and only 0.12 for the full-time employment model. Further, demographic effects account for between 82 and 90 percent of the explained increase in the log-likelihood and health accounts for only 7–16 percent, with the remaining 2–4 percent due to interactions between health and demographic characteristics (see rows 2 through 4). These findings are consistent with recent research suggesting that economic and demographic factors, rather than health limitations, are the primary determinants of labor supply.

Physical Health versus Mental Health

The distinction between physical and mental health is interesting both in its own right and because of the differential treatment by medical providers and third-party payers. Health insurance policies, for example, typically provide more limited coverage of treatments for mental illness than for physical care. This is the case even though mental health problems are quite common. For example, data from

Table 7.8   Explanatory Power of Demographic and Health Effects
on Labor Force Participation and Employment

	Dependent Variable		
	Labor Force Participation	Employment	Full-time Employment
Explained increase in log-likelihood (£)	0.0973	0.0921	0.1214
Percentage of Total Increase Explained by:			
Demographic variables	82.91%	82.44%	89.27%
Health variables	13.97	15.78	6.87
Interaction	3.12	1.77	3.86
Percentage of Health Increase Explained by:			
Physical health	48.42%	41.91%	45.56%
Mental health	33.63	39.85	38.13
Covariance	17.95	18.24	16.31

Note: £ = 1 − [ℓ(X) − ℓ(0)], where ℓ(0) and ℓ(X) are the maximized log-likelihoods of the intercept only and of full models, respectively.

the Epidemiologic Catchment Area Program indicate that 16.6 percent of women suffer from one or more mental disorders in any given month, with 2.9 percent experiencing a major depressive episode during the same period (Reiger et al. 1988).[19]

Despite the considerably greater detail provided in the survey on physical problems, mental illness accounts for a substantial portion of health-related reductions in labor supply. In the participation equation, physical ailments are responsible for 48 percent of the total health effect and mental distress is responsible for 34 percent (table 7.8, rows 5 and 6). Given the frequency of comorbidities, it is not surprising that covariance between physical and mental health is also substantial—accounting for the remaining 18 percent (row 7). Mental illness becomes even more important in the employment and full-time employment models, explaining between 38 and 40 percent of the total health effect, with a continuing large covariance and a decline in the relative explanatory power of physical health.

Older Women

To investigate the possibility that the small economywide effect of health problems on labor supply is due to the relatively young age of the sample, the decomposition of health and demographic effects was repeated for women who were at least fifty years old at the time of the baseline survey.[20] As shown in table 7.9, the total explanatory power of the included covariates and the portion attributed to ill health is larger for this subgroup. £ rises to between 0.148 and 0.173 (see row 1), which is 43 to 64 percent greater than for the corresponding equation in table 7.8. Health accounts for 16–27 percent of the reduction in the log-likelihood (row 3); this is 1.5–2.3 times as important as the "pure" health effect in the full sample (row 3). Nonetheless, economic and demographic factors continue to be two to five times as important.

The explanatory power of both physical and mental health rises with age. The increase in the former is larger than that of the latter, however, with the result that the relative contribution of mental illness falls moderately with the exclusion of women under fifty. Among the older subsample, physical ailments account for between 60 and 73 percent of the total health effect, and mental illness accounts for less than 30 percent (rows 5 and 6).[21] The covariance between physical and mental health remains of some importance, accounting for 4–11 percent of the total health effect (row 7). Interestingly, the decline in the relative explanatory power of mental health is least pronounced when attention is restricted to full-time employment.

Table 7.9   Explanatory Power of Demographic and Health Effects on Labor Force Participation and Employment for Women ≥50 Years Old

| | Dependent Variable | | |
	Labor Force Participation	Employment	Full-time Employment
Explained increase in log-likelihood (£)	0.1481	0.1506	0.1732
Percentage of Total Increase Explained by:			
Demographic variables	71.70%	75.61%	78.63%
Health variables	26.93	24.20	15.71
Interaction	1.36	0.19	5.66
Percentage of Health Increase Explained by:			
Physical health	72.84%	71.82%	60.58%
Mental health	21.69	24.34	27.99
Covariance	5.47	3.84	11.43

Note: See note to table 7.8.

Summary and Conclusions

Middle-aged women regularly using medications or having high depression scores are less likely to work or participate in the labor force than are their healthier counterparts. The health effect varies widely across specific ailments, however, with large reductions for women suffering from elevated cholesterol, muscle or joint problems, pain, depression, or anxiety.[22] Surprisingly, women treated for thyroid disorders are more likely than their counterparts to work full-time. Previous research has typically utilized general indicators of health status. In addition to reporting bias problems, the disparity of health effects suggests that such measures fail to capture adequately the multifaceted aspects of health.

The importance of health problems for individual labor supply decisions does not translate into a significant economywide effect. Although health plays a larger role for the oldest sample members, even for this group the explanatory power of a wide array of health variables is less than one-half as large as that of the included demographic and economic characteristics. Although better indicators of health could raise its measured importance, the data source used for this analysis contains far more detailed information than was available to most earlier researchers, and only modest increases would be expected from still more comprehensive data.

This investigation has also separately considered the effects of physical and mental illness. Despite the limited information available on the latter, the results provide a strong indication that mental distress has a significant negative influence on individual labor supply decisions and accounts for an important share of health-related nonemployment, especially among younger sample members. This information is relevant for the current debate on the provision and financing of mental health services.

Acknowledgments

Partial funding for this research was received from the Heller School at Brandeis University under National Institute of Mental Health grant MH16846-08. I thank the New England Research Institute for providing me with data, which was collected under National Institutes of Health grant AG0311-08. This chapter was improved by helpful comments from Nancy Avis, Donald Brambilla, Randy Ellis, Richard Frank, Michael Grossman, Tom McGuire, Sonja McKinlay, and workshop participants at Brandeis and Boston Universities. Research assistance was provided by Jean Lecot.

Appendix 7.A   Questions on Medication Usage in the MWHS Survey Which Were Used for This Analysis

"We also need to know about how often you use medications. I am going to read you a list of common medications. For each one, please let me know if you are currently taking the medication daily, at least once a week, less than once a week, or not at all."

a. Medicine for your heart   [HEART]*
b. Medicine for cholesterol or fats in your blood [CHOLESTEROL]
c. Medicine for your blood pressure   [BLOOD PRESSURE]
d. Medication prescribed for migraine headaches   [MIGRAINE]
e. Any other pain reliever needing a prescription   [PAIN]
f. Insulin   [INSULIN]
g. Thyroid pills   [THYROID]
h. Hormone pills for menopause or aging symptoms (Premarin, DES, Estrace, Ogen, etc.)   [HORMONE]
i. Medicine for allergies (including injections)   [ALLERGY]
j. Medicine for an upset stomach   [STOMACH]
k. Prescription medication for arthritis or rheumatism [ARTHRITIS]
l. Prescription medication for other muscle/joint problems (Indocin, Robaxin)   [MUSCLE/JOINT]
m. Sleeping pills   [SLEEPING PILLS]
n. Pills to relax you (Valium, Librium) needing a prescription   [VALIUM/LIBRIUM]
o. Medication for depression   [DEPRESSION]

*The name of the corresponding dummy variable is shown in brackets.

Appendix 7.B   Construction of CESD Score

The CESD score is constructed as the sum of individual scores from a list of twenty questions, each of which is valued on a scale of 0 to 3. The minimum score is 0, and the maximum is 60. The number shown to the right of the actual question represents the CESD score attributed to that response. The survey text is as follows:

"I am going to read you a list of ways you might have felt or behaved. Please tell me on *how many different days* you have felt this way *during the past week.*"

	On at most 1 day	On up to 2 days	On 3–4 days	On 5–7 days
a. I was bothered by things that usually don't bother me.	0	1	2	3
b. I did not feel like eating; my appetite was poor.	0	1	2	3
c. I felt that I could not shake off the blues even with help from my family or friends.	0	1	2	3
d. I felt I was just as good as other people.	3	2	1	0
e. I had trouble keeping my mind on what I was doing.	0	1	2	3
f. I felt depressed.	0	1	2	3
g. I felt that everything I did was an effort.	0	1	2	3
h. I felt hopeful about the future.	3	2	1	0
i. I thought my life had been a failure.	0	1	2	3
j. I felt fearful.	0	1	2	3
k. My sleep was restless.	0	1	2	3
l. I was happy.	3	2	1	0
m. I talked less than usual.	0	1	2	3
n. I felt lonely.	0	1	2	3
o. People were unfriendly.	0	1	2	3
p. I enjoyed life.	3	2	1	0
q. I had crying spells.	0	1	2	3
r. I felt sad.	0	1	2	3
s. I felt that people dislike me.	0	1	2	3
t. I could not get "going."	0	1	2	3

Notes

1. In 1948, 36.9 percent of women thirty-five to forty-four years old and 35.0 percent of women forty-five to fifty-four years old participated in the

labor force; by 1988 the participation rates of these groups had risen to 75.2 and 69.0 percent, respectively (U.S. Department of Labor 1989, 26–27).

2. In 1988, 94.5 and 90.9 percent of men thirty-five to forty-four and forty-five to fifty-four years old, respectively, participated in the labor force (U.S. Department of Labor 1989, 26).

3. A partial listing of recent studies using these measures includes Quinn (1977), Boskin and Hurd (1978), Gordon and Blinder (1980), Burkhauser and Quinn (1983), Hanoch and Honig (1983), and Diamond and Hausman (1984).

4. Lambrinos (1981) provided a careful discussion of this and related issues.

5. Bound (1989) argued that, given the low signal-to-noise ratio of these measures, it may actually be preferable to use self-reported health status.

6. Further information on the survey instrument or sampling procedure is available upon request.

7. Respondents were defined as labor force participants if they claimed to be employed for pay, unemployed with a job to return to, or unemployed and looking for work. They were classified as nonparticipants if they were employed without pay or were not working because they were full-time homemakers, unemployed and not looking for work, retired through age or choice, full-time students, or disabled or ill.

8. In initial validation studies (see Radloff 1977), the mean CESD score for the general population ranged between 7.94 and 9.25, that for residents of a private psychiatric facility was 24.42, and that among outpatients treated for severe depression (scores of 7 or higher on the Raskin Depression Rating Scale) was 39.11. The average CESD score for the MWHS sample is 9.01.

9. In clinical research, CESD scores of 16 and above have been (somewhat arbitrarily) taken to indicate depression. There is no evidence, however, of the appropriate cutoff points for determining the relationship between depression and labor supply.

10. This is an imperfect measure of comorbidity, however, since some individuals could take two or more types of medications to treat the same illness.

11. This is not surprising. Depression is only one component of mental illness, and the CESD scale measures the *current* level of symptoms, which may vary over time.

12. The individual will be unemployed if market wages exceed reservation wages which, in turn, are greater than offer wages.

13. Even studies jointly estimating health and participation equations (e.g., Lee 1982; Sickles and Taubman 1986) generally assume that nonemployment has no causal effect on health. The study of Haveman, Stone, and Wolfe (1988) is an exception. These authors allowed causality to run from work hours to health as well as from health to hours worked but found no evidence that the hours of work caused health.

14. Respondent occupations are excluded from these regressions to avoid collinearity between the sector of employment and other demographic variables. As shown for labor force participation in columns 2 and 3 of table 7.N.1,

Table 7.N.1 Sensitivity of Estimated Demographic Coefficients to Alternative Specifications of Labor Force Participation Model

	Coefficient Estimates		
Regressor	Labor Force Participation	Employment	Full-time Employment
Age (years)	0.834	0.832	0.765
	(2.14)	(2.11)	(1.92)
Age squared	−8.8E-3	−8.7E-3	−8.1E-3
	(2.22)	(2.18)	(1.99)
Education			
High school dropout	−0.322	−0.308	−0.245
	(3.49)	(3.29)	(2.50)
Some college	0.329	0.333	0.182
	(4.93)	(4.94)	(2.42)
Marital Status			
Never married	0.405	0.448	0.433
	(2.05)	(2.23)	(2.12)
Divorced	0.416	0.508	0.500
	(3.66)	(4.31)	(4.19)
Widowed	0.298	0.375	0.378
	(1.96)	(2.39)	(2.37)
Number of Children			
1	−0.283	−0.288	−0.258
	(1.54)	(1.55)	(1.38)
2	0.097	0.070	0.087
	(0.61)	(0.43)	(0.53)
≥3	−0.063	−0.083	−0.071
	(0.41)	(0.53)	(0.45)
Relative Living at Home			
Parents	−0.053	−0.064	−0.060
	(0.38)	(0.45)	(0.42)
Children	−0.118	−0.119	−0.107
	(1.55)	(1.54)	(1.37)
Birthplace			
Outside U.S.	0.149	0.130	0.123
	(1.18)	(1.02)	(0.94)
Outside Massachusetts	−0.074	−0.074	−0.099
	(0.94	(0.92)	(1.22)
Medication Variables	No	Yes	Yes
Occupation Variables	No	No	Yes

Notes: See note to table 7.4.

the main effect of including occupation variables is to decrease slightly the age effect and reduce dramatically the influence of education. This implies that educated persons work in occupations with sustained high rates of labor force attachment. The likelihood function of the ordered-probit model did not converge when the full set of demographic covariates was included. Convergence was obtained by excluding the quadratic term on age and the dummy variables on ethnic status and birthplace.

15. Coefficients not shown indicate that females of Portuguese origin and, to a lesser extent, blacks have unusually strong labor force attachments. Labor supply is also relatively high for women married to blue collar workers and low when the spouse works in professional, teaching, or sales occupations. When controls for the respondent's occupation are added, high participation and employment probabilities are observed for managerial, professional, administrative, teaching, or health occupations, whereas attachments are low for laborers and construction or mining workers.

16. As shown in columns 1 and 2 of table 7.N.1, adding the medication variables slightly raises the coefficient on less than twelve years of education (from -0.322 to -0.308) and has essentially no effect on that for schooling in excess of twelve years (increasing it from 0.329 to 0.333). If health and education were strongly related, the returns to schooling would decline dramatically with the inclusion of medication regressors.

17. This result should be interpreted cautiously because less than 0.3 percent of respondents (seven women) take medication for high cholesterol and there is a possibility that treatment for elevated cholesterol is spuriously correlated with some other factor or condition that reduces labor supply.

18. The term £ measures the actual increase in ℓ as a proportion of the potential increase. With two uncorrelated and independent subclasses of regressors, X_i and X_j, the explained increase could be decomposed into the portions due to each class as $£ = £_i + £_j$. If X_i and X_j are correlated, $£ < £_i + £_j$. If interactions are important, $£ > £_i + £_j$. Two alternative goodness-of-fit measures were considered in preliminary work. The first, Efron's R^2, is analogous to the squared correlation coefficient in the linear model. The second, Somer's D_{yx}, is a rank correlation coefficient measuring the probability that, for a randomly chosen ordered pair $\{i,j\}$, where $Y_i = 1$ and $Y_j = 0$, $\hat{y}_i > \hat{y}_j$, for $\hat{y}$ the predicted values from the probit model. The rank order of the three criteria were identical across seven alternative model specifications and the numerical values of Efron's R^2 and £ were extremely similar.

19. Lifetime prevalence rates are typically two to three times larger than one-month rates.

20. This subgroup consisted of 687 women, of whom 492 participated in the labor force, 472 were employed, and 329 worked full-time.

21. In part, this may occur because mental illness becomes less common as women reach late adulthood. One-month prevalence rates of any mental disorder are 19.2, 14.6, and 13.6, respectively, for women twenty-five to forty-four, forty-five to sixty-four, and over sixty-five years of age. The age-related reduction in major depressive episodes is even more dramatic, with one-month prevalence rates of 3.9, 2.6, and 0.9 percent for the three age groups (Reiger et al. 1988).

22. Caution should be exercised in generalizing these results to younger women. Given the age range of the sample, relatively few respondents are likely to have small children living at home. The presence of such children is an important correlate of labor supply and may interact with health ailments.

References

Anderson, Kathryn, and Richard Burkhauser. 1985. "The Retirement-Health Nexus: A New Measure of an Old Puzzle." *Journal of Human Resources* 20:315–30.

Bartel, Ann, and Paul Taubman. 1979. "Health and Labor Market Success: The Role of Various Diseases." *Review of Economics and Statistics* 61:1–8.

———. 1986. "Some Demographic and Economic Consequences of Mental Illness." *Journal of Labor Economics* 4:243–56.

Bazzoli, Gloria. 1985. "The Early Retirement Decision: New Empirical Evidence on the Influence of Health." *Journal of Human Resources* 20:214–34.

Boskin, Michael J. 1977. "Social Security and Retirement Decisions." *Economic Inquiry* 15:1–25.

Boskin, Michael J., and Michael D. Hurd. 1978. "Effect of Social Security on Early Retirement." *Journal of Public Economics* 10:361–77.

Bound, John. 1989. "Self-Reported vs. Objective Measures of Health in Retirement Model." National Bureau of Economic Research, Working Paper No. 2997.

Burkhauser, Richard. 1979. "The Pension Acceptance Decision of Older Workers." *Journal of Human Resources* 14:63–75.

Burkhauser, Richard, and Joseph Quinn. 1983. "Is Mandatory Retirement Overrated? Evidence from the 1970's." *Journal of Human Resources* 18:337–58.

Butler, J., Richard Burkhauser, Jean Mitchell, and Theodore Pincus. 1987. "Measurement Bias in Self-Reported Health Variables." *Review of Economics and Statistics* 69:644–50.

Chirikos, Thomas, and Gilbert Nestle. 1985. "Further Evidence on the Economic Effects of Poor Health." *Review of Economics and Statistics* 67:61–69.

Diamond, Peter, and Jerry Hausman. 1984. "The Retirement and Unemployment Behavior of Older Men." In Henry Aaron and Gary Burtless (ed.): *Retirement and Economic Behavior,* pp. 97–132. Washington, D.C.: Brookings.

Frank, Richard, and Paul Gertler. 1988. "An Assessment of Measurement Error Bias in Estimating the Effect of Mental Distress on Income." Johns Hopkins University. Mimeo.

Gordon, Roger, and Alan Blinder. 1980. "Market Wages, Reservation Wages and Retirement Decisions." *Journal of Public Economics* 14:277–308.

Grossman, Michael. 1975. "The Correlation between Health and Schooling." In Nestor E. Terleckyj (ed.): *Household Production and Consumption,* pp. 147–211. New York: Columbia University Press (for the National Bureau of Economic Research).

Hanoch, Gioria, and Marjorie Honig. 1983. "Retirement Wages, and Labor Supply of the Elderly." *Journal of Labor Economics* 1:131–51.

Haveman, Robert, Mark Stone, and Barbara Wolfe. 1988. "Market Work, Wages, and Men's Health." University of Wisconsin. Mimeo.

Inman, Robert. 1987. "The Economic Consequences of Debilitating Illness: The Case of Multiple Sclerosis." *Review of Economics and Statistics* 69:651–60.

Lambrinos, James. 1981. "Health: A Source of Bias in Labor Supply Models." *Review of Economics and Statistics* 63:206–12.

Lee, L. 1982. "Health and Wage: A Simultaneous Equations Model with Multiple Discrete Indicators." *International Economic Review* 23:199–222.

McFadden, Daniel. 1974. "Conditional Logit Analysis of Qualitative Behavior." In P. Zarembka (ed.): *Frontiers in Econometrics*, pp. 105–42. New York: Academic Press.

Mitchell, Jean, and Kathryn Anderson. 1989. "Mental Health and the Labor Force Participation of Older Workers." *Inquiry* 26:262–71.

Parsons, Donald. 1980. "The Decline in Male Labor Force Participation." *Journal of Political Economy* 88:117–34.

———. 1982. "The Labor Force Participation Decision: Reported Health and Economic Incentives." *Economica* 49:81–91.

Program Analysis Staff. 1982. "Mortality and Early Retirement." *Social Security Bulletin* 45 (December).

Quinn, Joseph. 1977. "Microeconomic Determinants of Early Retirement: A Cross-sectional View of White Married Men." *Journal of Human Resources* 12:329–46.

Radloff, Lenore. 1977. "The CES-D Scale: A Self-Report Depression Scale for Research in the General Population." *Applied Psychological Measurement* 1:385–401.

Reiger, Darrel, Jeffrey Boyd, Jack Burke, Donald Rae, Jerome Myers, Morton Kramer, Lee Robins, Linda George, Marvin Karno, and Ben Locke. 1988. "One Month Prevalence of Mental Disorders in the United States." *Archives of General Psychiatry* 45:977–86.

Sickles, Robin, and Paul Taubman. 1986. "An Analysis of the Health and Retirement Status of the Elderly." *Econometrica* 54:1339–56.

U.S. Department of Labor. 1989. *Handbook of Labor Statistics*, Bulletin 2340. Washington, D.C.: U.S. Government Printing Office.

8

Linkages among Deviance in Adolescence, Antisocial Personality Disorders in Adulthood, and Work Behavior

Jean M. Mitchell, Ph.D.

A
ntisocial disorders, defined as the repeated violation of social norms, frequently affect the behavior of many school-aged children and adolescents. Conduct-disordered (antisocial) children and adolescents tend to engage in common activities: fighting, truancy, stealing, vandalism, and substance abuse (Loeber 1985). Not surprisingly, individuals who exhibit such behaviors are apt to experience academic difficulties and as a result frequently drop out of high school. This phenomenon has developed into a major national concern as statistics indicate that the high school graduation rate in the United States declined significantly throughout the 1980s; in 1988, for example, the high school dropout rate was close to 30 percent.

The deviant activities of children and adolescents also contribute significantly to the rising crime rates that plague many urban areas. To illustrate, in 1986 more than 1.4 million juveniles were arrested for nonindex crimes such as vandalism, drug abuse, or running away. Nearly another 900,000 were arrested for index crimes including larceny, robbery, theft, and rape (Patterson, DeBaryshe, and Ramsey 1989). Indeed, these statistics imply that the deviant activities of children and adolescents have serious socioeconomic consequences for both the individuals involved and society.

Psychologists contend that conduct-disordered children and adolescents are prone to develop antisocial personality disorders as adults (Patterson, DeBaryshe, and Ramsey 1989). Although some clinical evidence supports this hypothesis, these findings may not be generalized because the analyses are based on small selected samples of juvenile delinquents or alcoholics. Although other studies have also examined the behavioral problems of high school students, these analyses are frequently biased because they tend to exclude individuals from high-risk groups (i.e., dropouts and absentees). To my knowledge, no study has examined data from a large representative sample to assess whether deviant behaviors that affect children and adolescents persist over the life cycle and develop into antisocial personality disorders when these individuals enter adulthood. Moreover, it is unclear how antisocial personality disorders affect an individual's work behavior. These relationships have not been considered previously because reliable information regarding mental health disorders is generally not collected in large-scale surveys.

In this chapter I use data from the NIMH Epidemiologic Catchment Area Program to assess first whether misconduct and delinquency during childhood and adolescence are precursors of antisocial personality disorders during adulthood. A second objective is to ascertain whether antisocial personality disorders adversely affect work behavior. The ECA data are ideal for examining the persistence of deviant behaviors over the life cycle because this survey contains detailed information on conduct disorders that occur during childhood and adolescence as well as psychiatric disorders that are diagnosed during adulthood.

Recognizing whether deviant behaviors persist over the life cycle has important policy implications because clinical follow-up studies of conduct-disordered children show that these individuals are likely to experience chronic unemployment, divorce, accidents, alcoholism, and other psychiatric disorders (Caspi, Elder, and Bem 1987; Farrington 1983). If deviance during childhood and adolescence is a significant predictor of antisocial behavior during adulthood, then interventions and treatments designed to address these behavioral problems when they arise during the early years of the life cycle are likely to yield significant economic gains for both the individuals involved and society.

Background and Literature Review

The *Diagnostic and Statistical Manual of Mental Diseases* (American Psychiatric Association 1980) defines conduct disorder as "a repetitive and persistent pattern of conduct in which either the basic rights of others or major age-appropriate societal norms or rules are violated." The conduct is more serious than the ordinary mischief and pranks of children and adolescents (Clarke and Clarke 1988). Antisocial behaviors are generally classified as either overt or covert. Actions against people (e.g., aggression and noncompliance) are viewed as overt antisocial behaviors. In contrast, covert behaviors are typically abusive actions involving either property or oneself (i.e., vandalism, substance abuse).

Some psychologists have noted that deviance which begins during childhood is likely to persist into adolescence and adulthood (Patterson, DeBaryshe, and Ramsey 1989). A number of clinical studies report findings supporting this hypothesis. For example, West and Farrington (1973) conducted a fourteen-year follow-up study of aggressive, antisocial boys. Their findings showed that aggressive children are apt to become violent, delinquent adolescents. In another study, Moore, Chamberlain, and Mukai (1979) found that young boys who were prone to stealing had more than an 80 percent chance of being apprehended by the police before these boys reached the age of fourteen. A longer-term follow-up study of the same boys by Patterson (1986) revealed that more than two-thirds of these boys became chronic, repeated offenders.

Other deleterious consequences of deviant behavior during childhood have been documented as well. Several clinical studies demonstrated that deviant behavior during childhood adversely affects educational attainment (Hawkins and Lishner 1987). Antisocial behavior during childhood has also been associated with increased rates of alcoholism (Zucher and Gomberg 1986).

Indeed, extensive clinical evidence identifies the types of deviant behaviors frequently exhibited by antisocial children. Other clinical evidence demonstrates that early and later antisocial behaviors are linked and that these activities have adverse long-term consequences for the individuals involved. Several psychologists contend that the development of effective identification, prevention, and treatment strategies will require information from longitudinal investigations on the sequence and progression of antisocial behaviors (Kazdin 1985; Nicol 1985; Loeber 1985). Nonetheless, despite this recognition, reliable longitudinal research documenting the linkages between antisocial behaviors over the life cycle and the socioeconomic consequences of these disorders is sparse.

To my knowledge, only one study has examined data from a large representative sample to identify the longitudinal relationships between antisocial behaviors in early adolescence and substance abuse in the same individuals four years later. In this study, Windle (1990) found that substance involvement in early adolescence was a significant predictor of late-adolescent alcohol and drug use. Given the limited evidence on this issue, further research using reliable population-based data is needed to examine whether these relationships persist over the life cycle and whether these disorders have deleterious economic consequences for both the affected individuals and society.

The Data

This study uses data from the NIMH Epidemiologic Catchment Area Program, a multisite community-based survey designed to assess the prevalence of mental health disorders in the general population. This data set contains high-quality information regarding the presence of symptoms of mental health disorders as well as socioeconomic information. The data on mental health problems are derived from the Diagnostic Interview Schedule, a highly structured instrument that can be administered by trained lay interviewers. Validity tests revealed that administration of this instrument by psychiatrists and lay persons yields similar results (Robins et al. 1981). The measures of mental health derived from this questionnaire are more comprehensive than traditional diagnosis-based indicators because they are constructed from the responses to questions asked of all survey participants. Hence, these indicators are not subject to the measurement error problems that are likely to arise from incorrectly classifying individuals with some mental health disorders as healthy simply because these conditions have not been diagnosed by a health care provider.

Several DIS/DSM-III diagnoses can be assessed. The diagnoses and symptoms relevant to this analysis include childhood and adolescent conduct disorders and antisocial personality disorders during adulthood. The DIS evaluates symptoms on a lifetime basis to establish whether the diagnoses are active or in remission. Minimum severity thresholds identify clinically significant events from routine stresses of daily life.

The survey was conducted at five sites: New Haven, Connecticut (Yale University); Baltimore, Maryland (Johns Hopkins University); St. Louis, Missouri (Washington University); Durham, North Carolina (Duke University); and Los Angeles, California (UCLA). About three thousand noninstitutionalized persons were interviewed at each site. The questioning comprised two face-to-face interviews conducted approximately one year apart.

This analysis is based on core data from the first wave of interviews gathered at three of the five sites: Baltimore, Durham, and Los Angeles. New Haven and St. Louis have been excluded because of idiosyncrasies in the data collected at these sites. The Hopkins site covers an area in the eastern one-third of Baltimore City. The Duke site comprises one urban county (Durham) and four rural counties. More than one-third of the population in each of these sites is black. The Los Angeles site encompasses two areas situated in Los Angeles county; about 30 percent of the combined population is Hispanic.

Empirical Model and Estimation Procedures

An empirical model is estimated to examine whether deviant behaviors during childhood and adolescence are significant predictors of antisocial personality disorders during adulthood. Symptoms of antisocial personality disorder include job troubles, negligence toward children, nontraffic arrest, violence, marital/relationship problems, trouble with debts, vagrancy, and lying. The DIS instrument contains a series of detailed questions regarding these symptoms which are used to diagnose the presence of antisocial personality disorder.

The dependent variable is dichotomous and indicates whether the respondent ever met the criteria for the DSM-III diagnosis of antisocial personality disorder. Application of ordinary least squares in this situation results in biased coefficients, heteroscedasticity, and imprecise predictions. For this reason the model is estimated using logistic regression. The logit coefficients show how a change in an independent variable affects the log of the odds ratio and therefore indicate the direction but not the magnitude of changing an independent variable. The elasticities are calculated to demonstrate the magnitude of the change in the likelihood of being diagnosed as antisocial personality disordered for a given change in a specific independent variable. The magnitude depends on the steepness of the cumulative distribution function at the point of evaluation. The steeper the cumulative distribution function, the greater will be the effect of a change in an explanatory variable.

Clinical evidence from psychological studies reveals that demographic characteristics such as race, neighborhood, and parental education, income, and occupation are related to the incidence of antisocial behavior during childhood and adolescence (see, e.g., Elliott, Huizinga, and Ageton 1985). Stressful circumstances such as unemployment, family violence, marital discord, and divorce also contribute to child adjustment problems. Unfortunately, such detailed longitudinal information on family history, parental traits, and behavioral characteristics of individuals during childhood and adolescence is not collected in large scale surveys.

The ECA survey is unique, however, because it contains several questions regarding symptoms of conduct disorders which occurred during childhood and adolescence. These indicators are used to control for individual behavioral characteristics that may persist over the life cycle and precipitate the onset of antisocial personality disorder. Symptoms of conduct disorders include poor grades, misbehavior in school, truancy, expulsion or suspension from school, frequent fighting either at home or at school, stealing, vandalism, juvenile arrest, and an episode of running away overnight.

Clinical studies show that deviant behavior during childhood and adolescence has adverse effects on educational attainment. The model includes the number of years of formal schooling to isolate the effects of deviant behavior from the effect of education. Failure to incorporate the level of schooling in the model may cause one to overstate the influence of adolescent deviance on the likelihood of developing an antisocial personality disorder. This variable also provides a test of the Grossman hypothesis that more educated individuals demand more health and, for this reason, are less prone to develop antisocial personality disorders.

Control variables for race are included to recognize that minorities tend to have worse mental health than their white counterparts. Binary variables for site are incorporated to capture geographic influences that may explain differences in the incidence of mental health disorders.

A labor force participation equation is estimated to ascertain whether a diagnosis of antisocial personality disorder has negative effects on work behavior. The dichotomous dependent variable equals 1 if the individual is working in the current period. The work equation is estimated with logistic regression. The independent variables include the indicator of antisocial personality disorder and the determinants of the wage offer and the reservation wage typically used in models of labor force participation. These variables include age, education, race, marital status, geographic location, and veteran status.

Empirical Results

The analysis is based on a sample of 2,174 men twenty-five to sixty-four years old who reported complete information on all variables. Women are excluded from the analysis to maintain comparability with existing studies in the psychology literature, which have been confined to boys. The variable definitions, means, and standard deviations are reported in table 8.1. Approximately 9 percent of the sample met the criteria for the DSM-III diagnosis of antisocial per-

Table 8.1   Definitions of Variables

Variable	Definition
ANTSP	1 if individual ever met criteria for DMS-III diagnosis of antisocial personality disorder ($\mu = 0.087$, $\sigma = 0.282$)
WORK	1 if individual is currently working ($\mu = 0.776$, $\sigma = 0.417$)
GRADE	years of schooling completed ($\mu = 11.869$, $\sigma = 3.857$)
LOWMARKS	1 if individual either repeated a grade or school marks were poor and teachers felt that individual could have performed better ($\mu = 0.337$, $\sigma = 0.473$)
TRSCHOOL	1 if individual was frequently in trouble with the teacher for misbehaving in school ($\mu = 0.147$, $\sigma = 0.354$)
EXPELLED	1 if individual was ever expelled or suspended from school ($\mu = 0.190$, $\sigma = 0.392$)
TRUANT	1 if individual ever played hooky from school ($\mu = 0.399$, $\sigma = 0.490$)
FIGHTS	1 if individual started fights that led to trouble more than once, either a school or at home ($\mu = 0.111$, $\sigma = 0.315$)
RUNAWAY	1 if individual ever ran away overnight ($\mu = 0.091$, $\sigma = 0.315$)
LYING	1 if individual lied a lot ($\mu = 0.163$, $\sigma = 0.369$)
STEALING	1 if individual swiped or stole things ($\mu = 0.286$, $\sigma = 0.452$)
VANDALISM	1 if individual intentionally damaged someone's car or if individual destroyed or damaged someone's property ($\mu = 0.092$, $\sigma = 0.290$)
JARREST	1 if individual was ever arrested as a juvenile ($\mu = 0.083$, $\sigma = 0.276$)
WHITE	1 if race is white; the omitted category is Hispanic and others ($\mu = 0.626$, $\sigma = 0.484$)
BLACK	1 if race is black; the omitted category is Hispanic and others ($\mu = 0.193$, $\sigma = 0.395$)
NEAST	1 if site is Baltimore; the omitted category is Los Angeles ($\mu = 0.279$, $\sigma = 0.448$)
SOUTH	1 if site is Durham; the omitted category is Los Angeles ($\mu = 0.356$, $\sigma = 0.479$)
AGE	age of individual in years ($\mu = 41.82$, $\sigma = 12.72$)
SQAGE	square of age ($\mu = 1,910.92$, $\sigma = 1,139.37$)
MARRIED	1 if individual is married and living with spouse; the omitted category is never married ($\mu = 0.590$, $\sigma = 0.492$)
FORMER	1 if individual is either divorced or separated; the omitted category is never married ($\mu = 0.198$, $\sigma = 0.3981$)
VET	1 if individual ever served in the military ($\mu = 0.393$, $\sigma = 0.488$)

Source: Variables are derived from core data reported in the Epidemiologic Catchment Area Survey.

sonality disorder. Moreover, a large proportion of these men reported that they had engaged in deviant behaviors during childhood and adolescence. For example, nearly 34 percent of the sample indicated that they had performed poorly in school, and another 40 percent reported that they had played hooky at least once. Stealing or petty theft was another common problem, reported by close to 29 percent of the sample.

The results of the logistic regression for the antisocial personality disorder equation are presented in table 8.2. The χ^2 statistic of

Table 8.2   Logit Estimates Predicting the Development
of an Antisocial Personality Disorder

Independent Variable	Coefficient	Standard Error	Elasticity
GRADE	−0.024	0.016	−0.259
LOWMARKS	0.133	0.103	0.041
TRSCHOOL	0.130	0.113	0.020
EXPELLED	0.416*	0.108	0.072
TRUANT	0.491*	0.113	0.151
FIGHTS	0.461*	0.112	0.047
RUNAWAY	0.416*	0.120	0.034
LYING	0.595*	0.104	0.088
STEALING	0.494*	0.104	0.129
VANDALISM	0.657*	0.117	0.055
JARREST	0.546*	0.118	0.041
WHITE	0.170	0.148	0.097
BLACK	0.144	0.189	0.025
NEAST	−0.507*	0.138	−0.127
SOUTH	−0.194	0.140	−0.057
CONSTANT	2.877*	0.231	—

Notes: The omitted categories are Hispanic, site—Los Angeles, and no symptoms of
deviant behavior. Dependent variable, ANTSP = 1 if individual ever met criteria for
DSM-III diagnosis of antisocial personality disorder, $N = 2,174$. $\chi^2 = 1,186.98$.
*$p < .01$.

1186.98 indicates that the variables included in the model have a
significant ability to predict whether an individual will develop an
antisocial personality disorder. The results lend support to the hypothesis that deviant behavior during childhood and adolescence increases the likelihood that an individual will be diagnosed as antisocial personality disordered in adulthood. Eight of the ten indicators
of deviance have the correct sign and are statistically significant at
conventional levels. The elasticities associated with each of these
measures of deviance are reported in the last column of table 8.2.
Since deviant behavior during adolescence may adversely affect
schooling (which is also included in the equation), these coefficients
and elasticities represent conservative or lower-bound estimates. The
elasticities for the eight significant indicators of deviance range from
0.034 for runaways to 0.15 for truant individuals. Truancy, stealing,
and lying seem to have the largest effects on the likelihood of being
diagnosed as antisocial personality disordered. The elasticities associated with truancy, stealing, and lying are 0.15, 0.13, and 0.09, respectively.

The results also suggest that individuals with more years of
formal schooling are less prone to develop antisocial personality disorders. This finding, while only marginally significant, is consistent
with the Grossman hypothesis that more educated people demand

more health than do less educated persons. Surprisingly, race seems to have no effect on the probability of developing an antisocial personality disorder. In contrast, geographic location is a significant determinant of whether a man is diagnosed as having an antisocial personality disorder. In particular, men residing in Baltimore are less prone to these disorders than are men living in either Los Angeles or Durham.

The logit estimates predicting the probability of working are presented in table 8.3. Nearly all of the variables in the work equation are statistically significant and have the anticipated signs. Of particular interest is the finding that a diagnosis of antisocial personality disorder significantly reduces the probability of working. Nonetheless, the elasticity for this variable, reported in the last column of table 8.3, indicates that the magnitude of the decrease in the probability of employment is very small. Moreover, this finding is not surprising given that about 78 percent of the sample is working. In contrast, age and education have the largest effects on whether an individual works. For example, the increase in the log odds ratio of employment associated with a 1 percent increase in the level of schooling is 0.12. These results are consistent with the human capital theory that education and experience are the primary determinants of whether an individual works.

Summary and Conclusions

The results of this study imply that symptoms of conduct disorders during childhood and adolescence persist over the life cycle and precipitate the onset of antisocial personality disorder in adulthood. These findings, based on a large representative sample of individuals, corroborate evidence from clinical follow-up studies of conduct-disordered children showing that these individuals are prone to develop psychiatric disorders in adulthood.

Other clinical research indicates that the persistence of behavioral problems into adulthood has detrimental socioeconomic consequences for the affected individuals. The findings of this analysis suggest that a diagnosis of antisocial personality disorder decreases the probability of working, but the magnitude of this effect is very small. Considering that many individuals who develop antisocial personality disorders tend to have educational deficiencies, it is likely that these disorders have much larger adverse effects on occupational choice and earnings. If future research demonstrates that this is the case, then intervention strategies designed to address these be-

Table 8.3   Logit Estimates Predicting the Probability of Working

Independent Variable	Coefficient	Standard Error	Elasticity
ANTSP	−0.345**	0.097	−0.007
AGE	0.121**	0.021	1.113
SQAGE	−0.0017**	0.0002	−0.316
GRADE	0.044**	0.008	0.115
WHITE	0.234**	0.106	0.032
BLACK	−0.159**	0.120	−0.007
MARRIED	0.518**	0.082	0.067
FORMER	0.173*	0.092	0.008
VET	0.009	0.066	0.001
NEAST	−0.212**	0.092	0.013
SOUTH	−0.215**	0.092	0.004
CONSTANT	3.120**	0.000	—

Notes: The omitted categories are Hispanic, site—Los Angeles, never married, non-veteran, and no DSM-III diagnosis of antisocial personality disorder. Dependent variable, work = 1 if individual is currently working, $N = 2,174$. $\chi^2 = 2,174.02$.
$*p < .10.$ $**p < .01.$

havioral problems when they arise in childhood are apt to have significant economic benefits for the affected individuals and society.

References

American Psychiatric Association. 1980. *Diagnostic and Statistical Manual of Mental Diseases.* 3d ed. Washington, D.C.: American Psychiatric Association.

Caspi, A., G. H. Elder, and D. J. Bem. 1987. "Moving against the World: Life Course Patterns of Explosive Children." *Developmental Psychology* 23:308–13.

Clarke, A. M., and A. D. Clarke. 1988. "The Adult Outcomes of Early Behavioral Abnormalities." *International Journal of Behavioral Development* 11(1):3–19.

Elliott, D. S., D. Huizinga, and S. S. Ageton. 1985. *Explaining Delinquency and Drug Use.* Beverly Hills, Calif.: Sage Publications.

Farrington, D. P. 1983. "Offending from 10 to 25 Years of Age." In K. T. Van Dusen and S. A. Mednick (eds.): *Prospective Studies of Crime and Delinquency,* pp. 17–37. Boston: Kluwer-Nijhoff.

Hawkins, J. D., and D. M. Lishner. 1987. "Schooling and Delinquency." In E. H. Johnson (ed.): *Handbook on Crime and Delinquency Prevention,* pp. 179–221. New York: Greenwood Press.

Kazdin, A. 1985. *Treatment of Antisocial Behavior in Children and Adolescents.* Homewood, Ill.: Dorsey Press.

Loeber, R. 1985. "Patterns of Development of Antisocial Children." *Annals of Child Development* 2:77–116.

Moore, D., P. Chamberlain, and L. Mukai. 1979. "Children at Risk for Delinquency: A Follow-up of Aggressive Children and Adolescents Who Steal." *Journal of Abnormal Child Psychology* 7:345–55.

Nicol, A. 1985. *Longitudinal Studies in Child Psychology and Psychiatry.* New York: John Wiley.

Patterson, G. R. 1986. "Performance Models for Antisocial Boys." *American Psychologist* 86:852–75.

Patterson, G. R., D. B. DeBaryshe, and E. Ramsey. 1989. "A Developmental Perspective on Antisocial Behavior." *American Psychologist* 44:329–35.

Robins, L. N., J. E. Helzer, J. Croughan, and Kathryn Ratcliff. 1981. "National Institute of Mental Health Diagnostic Interview Schedule: Its History, Characteristics, and Validity." *Archives of General Psychiatry* 38:381–89.

West, D. J., and D. P. Farrington. 1973. *Who Becomes Delinquent?* London: Heinemann.

Windle, M. 1990. "A Longitudinal Study of Antisocial Behaviors in Early Adolescence as Predictors of Late Adolescence Substance Use: Gender and Ethnic Group Differences." *Journal of Abnormal Psychology* 99, no. 1:86–91.

Zucher, R. A., and E. S. L. Gomberg. 1986. "Etiology of Alcoholism Reconsidered." *American Psychologist* 41:783–93.

PART III

Insurance and the Demand for Mental Health Care

The area in the field of economics and mental health that has seen the greatest concentration of research is concerned with insurance and the demand for mental health services. This topic has been studied using the full array of data sets and study designs available to the applied economist. Natural experiments have most commonly been used to study the effect of insurance coverage on the demand for mental health care. The RAND Health Insurance Experiment randomly assigned households to insurance plans to take account of biased selection in choice of insurance plan. Other studies compared utilization levels among large insured populations. A consensus has emerged that the demand for ambulatory mental health services is more responsive to cost sharing than is general medical care.

There remain many important unanswered questions. Information on demand response to coverage and supply response to reimbursement policy is the critical element of research that is needed for the purposes of designing insurance plans. Compulsory insurance is once more on the public policy agenda in the 1990s. Mandated insurance laws continue to be hotly contested policies throughout the nation. Addressing the legitimate concerns of all parties interested in the design of insurance plans and insurance regulation calls for detailed information on the utilization of mental health services under varying forms of insurance coverage.

The next generation of research on insurance and demand will be called upon to answer a large number of detailed questions regarding the response to demand. For example: Are all mental health services equally responsive to coverage? Do all populations of patients respond equally to the terms of coverage? Previous research has provided a strong basis for the analyses that will deliver the answers. Theoretical and empirical tools of demand analysis are now well developed, although a number of problems specific to developing models of the demand for mental health services remain to be solved. Chapter 9, by Willard Manning and Richard Frank, focuses on what has been learned about using econometric techniques for obtaining estimates of demand response to insurance in the mental health sector. They identify several of the difficult issues that should be more fully studied in the next round of empirical research. A number of promising approaches to ongoing problems are reviewed, and the research tradeoffs are clearly spelled out.

In chapter 10, Jeffrey Rubin, Virginia Wilcox-Gök, and Partha Deb begin the task of providing estimates of demand response for special populations facing specific coverage options. They examine the effect of supplemental insurance coverage on the utilization of health care by Medicare enrollees who are mentally disabled. This is a population that is severely and persistently mentally ill and that places large financial demands on the health care system. Developing a detailed understanding of their utilization of services carries a great deal of policy significance.

Using existing research to provide systematic policy assessments for the design of health insurance plans and insurance regulation is a task that researchers have too often neglected. Researchers are increasingly being challenged to present their results in a manner that is usable to the policy community. Too often, policy implications are an obligatory ending to a research report. Chapter 11, by Thomas McGuire, makes use of the best of what is known on the demand for mental health services to construct a simulation model that can be used by a legislature to assess various proposals for structuring insurance coverage of mental health services in private insurance. McGuire demonstrates the power of the simulation model by assessing a set of proposals under consideration by the state of Connecticut for altering their mandated mental health insurance statute.

The emerging research on the demand for mental health services promises to provide precise estimates of specific types of demand response. Old difficulties stemming from the complex structure of coverage for mental health services will be addressed using new econometric approaches. Finally, economists in the mental health area will contribute to the design of new insurance plans for mental health care and will provide to policy makers the tools for assessing the various options.

9

Econometric Issues in the Demand for Mental Health Care under Insurance

Willard G. Manning, Jr., Ph.D.,
and Richard G. Frank, Ph.D.

O ver the past few years, there has been much concern about the role of cost sharing in the design of insurance coverage for mental health care. Interest in the design of health insurance for mental health care stems from several competing concerns. First, there is a desire to use insurance to reduce or remove financial barriers that may impede access to mental health services, especially for those who are sick and poor.

Second, there is a concern that generous coverage for mental health care may be extremely costly. The utilization of mental health services is more sensitive to cost sharing than are other types of health care (Frank and McGuire 1986; Keeler, Manning, and Wells 1988; Taube, Kessler, and Burns 1986). Thus, there is a reluctance on the part of employers and insurers to offer extensive coverage for mental health. As a result, limits on both inpatient and outpatient coverage are common (American Psychiatric Association 1989). Day limits of thirty to sixty days per inpatient episode or per year are most frequent. Outpatient care typically has limits on total expenses of $1,000 to $2,000. Moreover, outpatient mental health care usually carries a 50 percent coinsurance rate, which is less generous than the coverage for outpatient general medical care.

Finally, there is the traditional interest in designing insurance that protects individuals and families against financial risk associated with the onset of a major mental disorder. This desire for protection must be balanced against the weakened incentives to consume prudently and a tendency to make the costs of coverage excessive.

A critical ingredient for designing a responsible insurance plan that balances these competing concerns about coverage for mental health care is the effect of the out-of-pocket price on the demand for that care. If the demand for outpatient mental health care is very responsive to out-of-pocket price, then lowering the cost sharing in an insurance plan should encourage many more people to use care. However, that increase in use may be quite expensive. If the increase is large, it may partially or completely offset the gains from any additional protection against financial risk. Several dimensions must be assessed to characterize the demand response of mental health care to price. These can be summarized as a set of three questions:

- Does lowering out-of-pocket price increase the likelihood that mental health care will be used?
- How much do insurance premiums increase with reduced cost sharing for mental health care?
- How do utilization and risk change as out-of-pocket prices change?

In this chapter, we focus on the effect of out-of-pocket price per se on the demand for mental health care. We review the suggestions of economic theory about the response to insurance and discuss the implications for the estimation of the effect of insurance on the use of mental health services. Although we discuss some empirical results, our primary concern here is the juncture of economic theory and econometrics. For a recent review of the empirical literature, we recommend the article by Frank and McGuire (1986).

Economic Theory

Most studies of the demand for mental health care have used data where prices vary because the out-of-pocket price faced by consumers differs across insurance plans. Within each of these plans, the out-of-pocket price also varies because the policy has different unit prices for different quantities. A typical insurance plan covering mental health care would have a deductible specific to mental health (say $200) and a 50 percent coinsurance rate up to a maximum plan cost of $1,500 (which implies thirty visits at a fee of $100 per visit). Beyond the maximum, the patient would pay the full price of care out of pocket.[1] Figure 9.1 displays the case of a typical insurance plan with three "price" blocks. For quantities of less than Q_0, the family pays the full price of care, p, out of pocket. For quantities above Q_0 but below Q_1, the family pays cp (where $0 < c < 1$ is the coinsurance rate) for each unit between Q_0 and Q_1. Above Q_1, the family pays the full price p per unit.[2] At the beginning of the next accounting year, the family begins this process afresh.

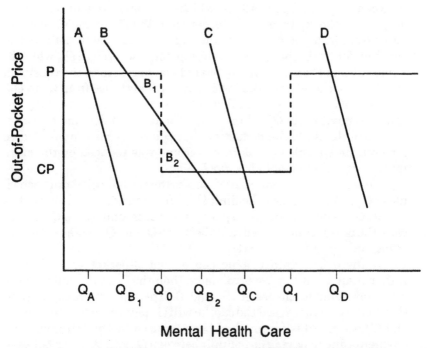

Mental Health Care

Figure 9.1   Demand under a typical mental health insurance plan.

Economic theory provides two ways of describing the family's response to such price schedules. In one case, it is assumed that the family has perfect foresight and knows where its demand curve will be. In the other case, uncertainty about future mental health care needs is introduced into the family's decision making.

Perfect Foresight

Consider the demand curves for individuals A, B, C, and D in figure 9.1. Consumer A's demand curve crosses the price schedule at Q_A. She will consume that quantity because her consumer surplus (the area between [above] the price schedule and the demand curve) is maximized by choosing to pay the full price.[3]

Similarly, consumer C will choose to operate along the second block at point Q_C, paying the marginal price cp for the last unit. However, consumer C also must pay a higher price for each of the first Q_0 units. Because these units were $(1 - c)p$ more expensive, he will act as if his income had fallen by the amount $(1 - c)\, p\, Q_0$.

Consumer B's choice is more complicated because his demand curve crosses the price schedule along two sections. He will choose between Q_{B1} and Q_{B2} based on whichever maximizes his consumer surplus. If the B_1 triangle is larger than the B_2 triangle, then the gains from facing a lower unit price (cp) beyond Q_0 will not compensate him for the higher price per unit (p) for Q_{B1} through Q_0, which he values at less than p. If the B_2 triangle is larger, then the consumer surplus associated with the lower out-of-pocket price from Q_0 to Q_{B2} (the area of triangle B_2) is sufficient to cover the loss in surplus for the inframarginal units Q_{B1} through Q_0. Should that demand curve cut the schedule above the deductible but below the maximum covered amount, he will also act *as if* his income was reduced by the extra inframarginal payment $(1 - c)pQ_0$.

Consumer D's demand curve crosses the out-of-pocket price schedule at Q_D, which is above the limit Q_1 on insured or covered visits. As a result, she pays the full price per visit for each unit above Q_1. In her case, the presence of insured units between Q_0 and Q_1 acts as a transfer of income equal to $(1 - c)p(Q_1 - Q_0)$.

If there is a catastrophic cap on out-of-pocket expenditures, rather than a limit on covered visits, then the logic is similar to the cases for demand curves A, B, and C. The one difference is that, should the patient exceed the cap, he will (1) pay a zero marginal price and (2) act as if his income had been reduced by the inframarginal payments due to paying cp per unit between Q_0 and Q_1 and p between 0 and Q_0:

$$p Q_0 + (1 - c) p (Q_1 - Q_0).$$

In each case, the relevant price for the consumer is the marginal price where the demand curve crosses the out-of-pocket price schedule *and* income has changed by the extent that he has paid more or less than the marginal out-of-pocket price for the preceding units. See Buchanan (1952–53), Gabor (1955), Oi (1971), Taylor (1975), Phlips (1983), and Hausman (1985) for a more detailed description.

There are two special cases worth noting. The first applies to consumer B. If his demand curve cuts the out-of-pocket price schedule such that area B_1 *equals* area B_2, then he will be indifferent between operating at price p and price cp, between consuming Q_{B1} and Q_{B2} units. In this case, there is neither a determinant marginal price nor quantity. However, this case should be relatively rare because it requires that the two areas exactly equal each other (which has a probability very near zero).

The second special case is more problematic. Patient D's demand curve could cut the out-of-price schedule in the gap at Q_1. In fact, there are many possible demand curves that could fall into this gap. Thus, for a range of demand curves, the quantity will be Q_1 but the marginal price will be indeterminant—between cp and p.

Imperfect Foresight

In most health applications, the assumption that families know the exact location of their ex ante demand curve may be inappropriate. On January 1, the consumer may not know with certainty whether she will be sick enough at some time during the year so that her mental health care demand will exceed the deductible—she is uncertain whether her demand curve is that given by A, B, C, or D in figure 9.1.

The nature of her demand response will depend on how and when she can make decisions. If she must make a once-and-for-all decision on January 1 and if she is risk neutral, then her optimal choice is to act as if she faced a marginal price equal to the expected marginal price (Keeler, Newhouse, and Phelps 1977; Ellis 1986). If she is generally healthy and has not previously made use of mental health services, then she will act as if she faced a price slightly less than p. The difference is due to the small probability that she may use enough services to exceed the deductible Q_0 and operate in the range from Q_0 to Q_1, where the coinsurance rate is less than one. However, if she has previously received psychotherapy, she may expect to exceed the deductible but not the limit on covered visits. In this case, she will act as if the relevant price is close to but above cp. If she has a persistent mental health problem (major recurrent depression), she may expect to exceed her limit on coverage, and thus the expected price will again be close to p.

If her decisions are for large, lumpy pieces of care (e.g., hospitalization), she may follow a similar course because a single event would be sufficient to exceed the deductible. A more likely scenario includes a number of smaller, discrete events (Keeler, Newhouse, and Phelps 1977). If the patient is healthy on January 1 and expects to be so throughout the year, she may act as if the marginal price is close to the full price p. As the year proceeds, she may become sick and the bill for the treatment of that illness will reduce the distance remaining to the deductible. The smaller the deductible remaining, the more likely that some chance event will move her demand curve out beyond the deductible. On the other hand, the less time remaining in the calendar year, the less likely is the possibility that such an event will occur. However, if she has large expenditures early in the year, she may expect that insurance will not cover her needs for the full year because she knows that there is a high probability that the limit Q_1 will be exceeded.

This story suggests that the price the consumer faces "changes" during the year within a plan; out-of-pocket price initially falls from the full price, early in the year, toward cp as illness brings the consumer closer to Q_0 and then rises if she is a heavy enough user to approach Q_1. The consumer's choice becomes a complex, dynamic programming problem under uncertainty. This is the problem addressed by Keeler, Newhouse, and Phelps (1977).

Statistical Methods

The preceding model of choice is correct from the perspective of microeconomic theory. However, the ordinary least squares (OLS) implementation of the model can lead to biased estimates that may seriously misstate the price responsiveness of demand (see Newhouse, Phelps, and Marquis 1980 for more details).[4] The problem is that the ex post marginal price is negatively correlated with the quantity demanded and with the error term if the insurance policy has declining marginal prices. It can lead to an upward bias if the policy has increasing marginal prices. Either of these correlations violates one of the assumptions necessary for OLS estimates to be consistent.

To the extent that income, mental health status, and other factors affect demand for mental health care, the estimated elasticities for these variables will also be inconsistently estimated. For example, if the onset of depression increases the demand for mental health services, it will lower the marginal price of those services. Thus, depression and marginal price are correlated, and marginal price is correlated with the error term. Thus, the OLS bias is transmitted from the coefficient for marginal price to the coefficient of the measure of depression.[5]

The first of these problems can be clearly illustrated with an extreme, but telling, example of an insurance plan with a deductible followed by a coinsurance rate. Assume that the demand for mental health services is perfectly inelastic and that customers face the insurance policy depicted in figure 9.2A. The resulting price/ quantity combinations observed will look like the *heavy dots* on the insurance/price schedule in figure 9.2A. If we were to estimate the model via ordinary least squares for those points, the result would be the *dashed line* in figure 9.2B. That line is not perfectly inelastic because the marginal price changes (in steps) with price. Adding covariates may reduce but will not eliminate the bias in the price coefficient, unless those variables can explain all of the variation in demand.

The coverage for mental health care is typically more complicated than figure 9.2. For mental health insurance, there is typically

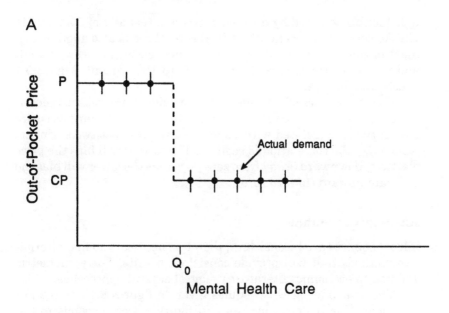

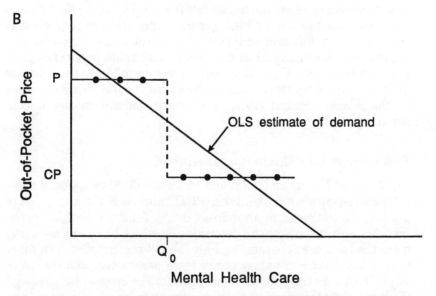

Figure 9.2   *A*, actual demand under a simple insurance plan. *B*, OLS estimate of demand under a simple insurance plan.

a deductible followed by a coinsurance rate (usually of 50 percent). Unlike coverage for general medical care, there is also another segment of the price schedule where patients reach the coverage limit and the coinsurance rate changes back to 100 percent. Figure 9.1 illustrates this case.

For these types of arrangements, the sign of the bias is indeterminant, a priori. In the first two segments (below Q_1), marginal price is negatively correlated with quantity. Over the last two segments (above Q_0), the correlation is positive. The former will bias the price elasticity downward (away from zero), whereas the latter will bias the estimate upward (toward zero).

Alternative Solutions

If least squares are inconsistent, then it is necessary to find alternative methods that will provide consistent results. The econometric and health economics literatures suggest several approaches.

The consumer price schedules given in figures 9.1 and 9.2 are nonlinear. The budget constraint in figure 9.3 corresponds to the price schedule in figure 9.1. The budget constraint will have two "kinks" and is referred to as a piece-wise linear budget constraint. One kink occurs where the deductible is exceeded (Q_0 on the horizontal axis), and the second kink occurs where the coverage limit is reached (Q_1 on the horizontal axis). Each of the approaches to modeling the nonlinear budget constraint discussed below breaks the problem into two parts. First, the models attempt to locate the relevant budget segment for the consumer. Next, the models locate the point on the relevant budget segment where the patient chooses to consume.

Full Information Maximum Likelihood

Burtless and Hausman (1978) and Hausman (1985) suggested a full information maximum likelihood (FIML) approach. For a given set of preferences (reflected in an indirect utility function) with an unobservable error term, one can determine on which block or linear segment the consumer operates and his level of consumption as a function of the unknown values of the taste parameters and the error term. With a distributional assumption for the error structure (e.g., the error term is normally distributed with unknown variance), one can then estimate the model's parameters by FIML. Burtless and Hausman did this for labor supply with individuals facing a progressive, piece-wise linear income tax. They assumed an indirect utility

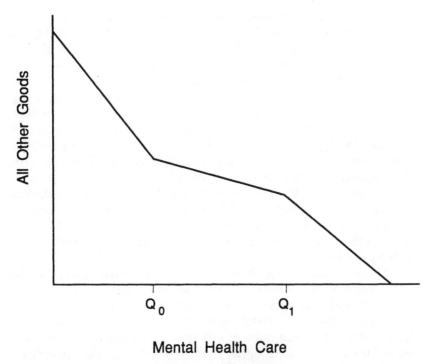

Mental Health Care

Figure 9.3   Budget constraint under insurance.

function that corresponds to the constant elasticity demand case and a homoscedastic normal error distribution.

Their FIML estimates have the advantage that they can in principle deal with the two special cases noted at the end of the economic theory section: (1) patient B in figure 9.1 if B is indifferent between the first and second segments and (2) a number of patients whose demand intersects the out-of-pocket price schedule at the gap above Q_1 in figure 9.1.

Moffitt's (1989) examination of the expenditures on food stamps extended this FIML model to allow for measurement error in the observed consumption. If the quantity consumed is measured with error, then the analyst could infer that the individual was located on a linear budget segment other than the one on which he actually was. This might occur commonly with either survey or claims data used in the economics of mental health if there were reporting errors or missing claims. Given stigma and the resulting tendency to underreport use, this may often occur in mental health survey data. We might thereby infer that an individual was below a coverage limit when he was actually above it.

Applied econometricians may react to the economic choice problem of selecting a block of the price schedule and then choosing how much to consume as suggestive of an estimation strategy like the Heckman selection model (1979). The first step would model the "choice" of budget-line segment, while the second step would estimate the quantity demand conditional on the choice of budget segment, correcting for the obvious "selection bias." Moffitt's 1986 review, however, noted that the response to a nonlinear price schedule (such as the typical insurance policy) does not satisfy the assumptions of separation in the likelihood function that is necessary to use the Heckman selection model (1979).

These various FIML approaches should avoid the bias inherent in OLS. OLS estimates are biased because the observed marginal price is correlated with the error. FIML estimates avoid this bias because they rely on the exogenous prices on each and every segment of the price schedule.

However, to avoid this bias, the FIML approach requires that the analyst specify the indirect utility function (or some equivalent representation of tastes) and the error distribution. Thus, the potential weakness is that the model relies very heavily on the functional forms assumed for the indirect utility function and on the distribution of the error term. If either is misspecified, the parameter estimates may be inconsistent.

We know of no study of the robustness of these methods to departures from the underlying assumptions about either the error structure or the specification of individual tastes. Knowing something about the robustness of these FIML methods would be essential before proposing their application to a mental health problem. We are cautious in proposing the use of the FIML approach because of the characteristics of utilization of mental health care in large insured populations. Over 90 percent of insured individuals do not use any mental health services during a year. Among users of outpatient mental health services, approximately 90 percent use fewer than fifteen visits. Within the 10 percent of users who exceed fifteen visits, some are very heavy users (over fifty visits). We doubt that this typical pattern of utilization can be characterized by any simple parametric distribution.

Limited Information Maximum Likelihood and Other Approaches

Ellis (1986) proposed an alternative method that builds on the microeconomic foundations of Keeler, Newhouse, and Phelps (1977). He tested this model using data on outpatient mental health services where the insurance coverage was characterized by increasing block pricing (no deductible, a coinsurance rate $c < 1$, and a limit on covered visits). Ellis showed that, if the consumer is risk-neutral and operating in a world without wealth effects, the consumer responds as if facing the expected end-of-the-year price. Using suitable qualitative choice methods (e.g., a logistic regression for a price schedule with two levels for prices), one can estimate the probability that the consumer will be on various blocks of the insurance policy at the end of the year. Using the estimated probabilities from that model, one can then construct an instrumental variable for the expected price. The expected price in that case would be equal to the weighted sum of the prices on each block, where the weights are the estimated probabilities for those blocks. Ellis and McGuire (1986) applied the technique developed by Ellis to data on mental health claims for Blue Cross of Massachusetts. They calculated price elasticities of demand for outpatient mental health care based on the "expected" out-of-pocket price. The point estimate for 50 percent copayment was estimated to be −0.37.

Terza and Welch (1982) proposed a two-step FIML version of the Heckman selection model procedure, extended to allow for multiple blocks of the tariff. Their method differs from the usual two-step approach in that (1) the Heckman correction includes terms for each block and (2) they subtract this correction from the dependent measure. However, given Moffitt's (1986) comment regarding the use of selection models for data such as these, the selection model is probably not appropriate.

Manning and Marquis (1989) proposed another limited information maximum likelihood alternative to this problem. Their method views the decision to exceed the deductible or a cap as a way of inferring key elements of the underlying demand for health care, such as the price elasticity. If the household chooses the block that yields the highest feasible utility, one can reformulate the estimation problem as follows: For a given indirect utility function, one can specify the indirect utility function for each block as a function of its marginal price and income (net of inframarginal payments). Because the household takes the segment with the higher indirect utility, one can rearrange the patient's decision as the difference in the two indirect utilities—the indirect utility on the upper block minus that on the lower block. If the difference is positive, the family consumes on the upper block. This difference can be expressed as a function of the indirect utility function parameters, the two marginal prices, and the two (net) incomes. This difference can be rearranged into a dichotomous choice model and estimated. For example, if the indirect utility function corresponds to the constant elasticity case and the error term for unobserved shift parameters is normally distributed, the difference can be specified as a probit regression model. In this case, most of the underlying indirect utility function and hence the demand function parameters can be recovered from the equation for the choice of block.

The methods of Ellis, Terza and Welch, and Manning and Marquis have some inherent limitations. Unlike the approach of Burtless and Hausman, they do not fully use the underlying economic theory and data to obtain their estimates. Ellis's expected price submerges the details of the out-of-pocket price schedule. Terza and Welch similarly simplify the setup. Both approaches lose part of the statistical information on demand that could be gleaned from the decision to exceed the deductible or the coverage limit. Manning and Marquis look at the decision to exceed the deductible but ignore the information in the decision about how much to consume, above or below the deductible.

All three approaches do not fully address the two special cases that can be addressed by FIML. The case of patient B, where the two triangles are exactly equal, is probably too rare to worry about, but a patient like D, cutting through the gap at the limit on covered visits, could be relatively common.

These methods cannot be applied to subcategories of services covered by a common set of coinsurance rates and internal limits unless some strong assumptions are made about tastes and error terms. Manning and Marquis could estimate the demand for health care in the HIE, but not the demand for mental health care separately.

Episodic Models

Keeler and Rolph (1988) used episodes of care to implement empirically the theoretical model of demand under insurance with uncertainty about future events described by Keeler, Newhouse, and Phelps (1977). They assumed that, at the beginning of each spell of illness, the consumer knows how much time and expenditure lies between the current position and the next block of the insurance policy. Keeler and Rolph examined demand during periods when the consumer was far, near, or beyond the upper limit on out-of-pocket expenditures.[6] Chronic and foreseeable health care use (e.g., ongoing psychotherapy) was dated to the beginning of the year or when first knowable. Consumption during the period when the patient is far from the upper limit should reflect demand when the effective or expected price approximately equals the price in the first block. Thus, the price elasticity in this range approximates the pure price elasticity that would occur if price were constant.

As an individual approaches the cap, demand reflects an effective price that is a mix of the price in the first block and the increasing possibility of free care (zero price) beyond the limit.[7] Demand in this segment also reflects any differences in sickliness that occur, because only the more sickly individuals will enter this region.[8]

This method will work well if the episode sizes are small relative to the distance remaining between the patient's initial position and the cap on out-of-pocket expenses. It may not work well if the episodes are large and lumpy, like hospitalizations, relative to the limit. In such cases, a single decision to be hospitalized may be sufficient to carry the individual beyond the cap on out-of-pocket expenses. For this reason, the consumption pattern typical for mental health use may be problematic; we return to the mental health case below.

This episodic model is more appealing than most of the alternatives because the estimation follows from the underlying behavior for decisions that occur over time. Its primary shortcoming is that it requires detailed data on the timing and spending for each episode of treatment within the course of the year. A secondary difficulty is that it requires the ability to link different visits into both clinically and economically coherent episodes of treatment. Unfortunately, few data sets contain the level of detail necessary to implement this method.

Keeler, Manning, and Wells (1988) applied a somewhat different model of episodes to the estimation of the demand for outpatient mental health services. They found that those patients with multiple mental health episodes had about the same annual spending on mental health care as those with single episodes. Thus, the fewer episodes were almost completely offset by higher costs per episode. This was quite different from medical care, where Keeler and Rolph found relatively constant cost per episode. As a result, the Keeler and Rolph approach was inapplicable to mental health care.

Instead, Keeler, Manning, and Wells looked at "one episode": when it started and the rate of spending during the episode. They used a Weibull regression model to estimate the time to first treatment in the year based on insurance plan, the amount of dollars remaining to the cap on out-of-pocket expenses, and other covariates. They also estimated the cost for the one episode based on the plan's copayment rate and the amount of dollars remaining to the cap. The period when $400 remained to the cap was deemed to be "far" from the cap and to represent a pure price response.[9]

Their results indicate that the pure price elasticity of demand for outpatient mental health care has an arc elasticity of −0.59 in the range of coinsurance rates from 0 to 95 percent, whereas the corresponding elasticity for ambulatory general medical care is −0.34. The arc elasticities based on the coinsurance rate for the plan (including the effect of the cap) are −0.40 and −0.27, respectively.[10]

The use of survival methods to estimate the likelihood of any care enhances the precision in the work of Keeler, Manning, and Wells. Simple dichotomous variable methods (e.g., logit or probit) are less precise because they lose the information about when events occur within the year. However, this gain in precision requires that the analyst know when the first use of mental health care occurred during the year. Such information may be readily available from detailed claims data, but not from surveys or aggregated claims data.

All of the methods discussed, except for that of Ellis (1986), were studied in the context of declining block pricing. As we have mentioned, this is not the typical form of coverage for mental health. The microeconomic theory underlying the estimators should be applicable to both increasing and decreasing block pricing. The distribution of services utilization under coverage limits may lead to a clustering of observations around the coverage limits. This may complicate the application of some of the estimation approaches.

Discussion

Several methods now exist for the consistent estimation of demand models in the face of insurance plans with nonlinear pricing schedules. Each of these methods requires some strong modeling assumptions in order to estimate the price elasticity. The robustness of these methods to the requisite assumptions and the distribution of the underlying data need to be explored carefully using Monte Carlo methods. We would like to see particular attention paid to the trade-off of precision from more restrictive models (e.g., a Burtless-Hausman model applied to mental health care) against the lack of bias in more robust methods (e.g., Ellis's expected price approach). We hope that the next few years will also see some direct comparisons of these methods so that we can evaluate their performance in real-world situations involving mental health care, with insurance policies that have deductibles, coinsurance rates, and limits on covered services.

Survival Methods

While those evaluations are being conducted, we encourage the expanded use of survival or failure time models in analysis of the demand for mental health care. First, the substitution of survival methods for the usual dichotomous methods should generate more precise estimates of the annual probability of any use of mental health, as well as the timing of such events. Similarly, one can use survival methods as a dual approach to count-based approaches. For example, if the episodes of mental health care follow a Poisson distribution, the interarrival time is exponential; if the count follows a negative binomial distribution, the interarrival is Weibull. Looking at interarrival times will be more precise than looking at counts. Third, the use of such methods is a natural generalization of the microeconomic theory of demand facing an insurance policy and some uncertainty about future events.

Although the work of Keeler, Manning, and Wells (1988) and of Wells, Keeler, and Manning (1990) is a step in that direction, they did not fully exploit the potential of survival methods. Mental health episodes occur rarely, but when they do their treatment can be lengthy, often spanning several years. Thus, a more behaviorally complete model might require the use of data and methods that would examine the amount of time that individuals stay out of treatment (REMISSION) and the amount of time that individuals are in treatment (ILLNESS). Because treatment occurs over a span of time rather than at a point in time, we need to model the length of treatment; the economic, clinical, and other factors influencing the initiation and termination of treatment; and its cost. At the beginning of each year, the individual will face the full cost of care until the deductible is satisfied, the coinsurance rate thereafter, and free care beyond any catastrophic cap or the full price beyond any limit on coverage. Thus, the generosity of coverage (i.e., the marginal price) becomes a time-varying parameter in an empirical extension of the Keeler, Newhouse, and Phelps (1977) dynamic programming model to multiple years.

For many mental disorders the onset of a particular illness affects the probability of a recurrence and the severity of the recurrence. For one example of such a mental disorder, see chapter 12 by Kamlet et al. (this volume).

The labor literature on spells of employment and unemployment provides a prototype for such a model. Heckman, Singer, and others examined these issues using variants of the proportional hazard model; see Heckman and Singer (1985) for reviews and examples.

Some Additional Thoughts on Demand Modeling

Distributional Problems

The econometric modeling of mental health care must deal explicitly with two attributes of the distribution of outpatient mental health care utilization and expenditures if the results are to be robust. First, in any one year only a small proportion of the population (about one in twenty) will receive any mental health care from specialty providers, an equally small fraction will see a general medical care provider for a mental health problem, and an even smaller proportion (fewer than one in one hundred) receive any inpatient mental health care. Second, among those individuals who do receive mental health care, the amount of use is quite skewed—whether we measure demand and use by visits or by dollars.

Simple OLS models or even one- or two-parameter Box-Cox models will not necessarily be robust to either the large number of zeros or the extreme skewness among the users. Although this proposition has not been demonstrated for mental health care, results on the modeling of general medical care from the Health Insurance Experiment indicate that the magnitude of estimated differences among participants randomly assigned to health insurance plans can differ widely depending on the statistical methods used (Duan et al. 1983). Since the underlying distributional problems are more severe for mental health than for general medical care, we would expect the sensitivity of the results to be even greater for the analyses of mental health care than for those of general medical care.

A number of researchers have used variants of the two-part model described by Cragg (1971) to deal with these twin distributional problems. The first part is a dichotomous dependent-variable regression model, such as logistic or probit regression, to deal with the no-use versus any-use problem. The second part is an OLS (conditional) regression with the log of visits or dollars as the dependent measure. The predicted use rate is the predicted probability times the exponentiated prediction from the conditional model times the smearing factor (the average of the exponentiated residuals). The last term is included because the expected value of the exponentiated error is not zero—the arithmetic mean of the raw variable is higher than the geometric mean for most health care.[11]

Another alternative would be the Tobit model. Unfortunately, that model is not robust to even minor departures from its underlying assumptions (Goldberger 1980; Hurd 1979; Maddala 1983). Given the extreme characteristics of mental health care use and expenditures, the Tobit model is probably an unreliable choice of estimator.

Biased Selection
The second statistical issue that should concern mental health analysts is the possibility of adverse selection in observational studies. Few people receive mental health care, and when they do it can be large amounts of care for several years. Anticipation of high financial losses creates a strong financial incentive to find health insurance plans with generous insurance coverage, as long as the premiums are not so high as to make the selection unrewarding. Families can make such choices even in a world of group (employer/union)-provided insurance. Many employees can choose among several plans at the same employer. The federal employee plans studied by Reed (1974) and others are probably the most extreme example. Another opportunity is available to families with two or more wage earners, each of whom can elect dependent coverage through work. Families in either circumstance can elect to put healthy members on less generous plans and sicker ones on more generous plans. The result is that poor mental health status becomes correlated with insurance generosity. In the absence of precise measures of mental health status, part of the effects of unmeasured sickliness will be attributed to insurance. This will overstate the effect of insurance coverage on demand for mental health care.

Early studies, by Reed (1974, 1975), of the Federal Employees Health Benefit Plan (FEHBP) suggested an enormous effect of mental health coverage on demand. There was almost a fourfold variation in use between the high- and low-option plans, two plans with only minor differences in coinsurance rates and other internal limits. In contrast, Keeler et al. projected a ratio between no insurance and full insurance (no out-of-pocket costs) of 2.5 using HIE data. The FEHBPs allow for adverse selection, whereas the HIE's random assignment and other design features should eliminate such a possibility. There were, however, other significant differences between the HIE and FEHBP populations that may in part account for differential response rates.

The biases from selection effects need not be so extreme but still have important policy implications. All other things being equal, the higher the price elasticity of demand, the greater will be the cost increases stemming from expanded coverage. Optimal insurance design suggests that the larger the price elasticity, the less generous the insurance coverage should be. Thus, a set of estimates of price sensitivity that overstate the true effect of cost sharing on the use of mental health care services could lead to overly restrictive coverage.

The Forgotten Benefit
The question of demand response is not the only issue to be considered in studies of mental health demand and the design of insurance benefits. Cost increases stemming from demand response are the adverse effect of health insurance. The gains from reducing each family's financial risks constitute the "benefit" side. As long as the incremental risk-pooling gains from reduced cost sharing more than offset the incremental increases in costs from demand response, we should expand mental health coverage. Zeckhauser (1970) and Besley (1988) provided some theoretical elaborations of these propositions. Keeler et al. (1988), Buchanan et al. (1991), and Manning et al. (1989) provided some implementations for general medical care and for outpatient mental health care. Health economists should focus more attention on the tradeoffs between risk gains and deadweight losses, rather than just focusing on the latter.

Notes

1. An upper limit on out-of-pocket expenditures (e.g., a catastrophic cap), followed by free care, while common for overall health care, is much less common for mental health care.
2. If there were a catastrophic cap or stop loss, the price above Q_1 would be zero.
3. Choosing the block that maximizes consumer surplus is an approximation to maximizing utility. However, for small budget shares, as are common in mental health, the approximation should be more than adequate.
4. Another popular method for characterizing the generosity of an insurance plan is to replace price by the average out-of-pocket price = the ratio of out-of-pocket expenses to total expenses. This approach also leads to overestimates of demand. By construction, the price variable is inversely correlated with quantity and, hence, the error term. See Horgan (1986) and Taube, Kessler, and Burns (1986) for examples of this approach.
5. Megdal's (1987) Monte Carlo study demonstrates the least squares bias for the price and other covariates.
6. They used data from the HIE, where there was a coinsurance rate followed by a cap on out-of-pocket expenses. Because the cost per episode was relatively constant, they examined visit and admission rates using a negative binomial regression model.

7. HIE plans had a coinsurance rate followed by free care beyond a catastrophic cap on out-of-pocket expenses.

8. See Keeler et al. (1988) for how this sickliness phenomenon was handled.

9. This was $400 in dollars from the mid- and late 1970s.

10. Thus, the plan effect tends to understate the pure price effect in this case, with prices declining as consumption increases.

11. If the conditional error term were normally distributed, then we could use $\exp(\sigma^2/2)$. However, use of mental health care does not seem to be exactly lognormal among users. Instead, we suggest Duan's (1983) nonparametric smearing factor.

References

American Psychiatric Association. 1989. *Coverage Catalog.* 2d ed. Washington, D.C.: American Psychiatric Press.

Besley, T. J. 1988. "Optimal Reimbursement Health Insurance and the Theory of Ramsey Taxation." *Journal of Health Economics* 7:321–36.

Buchanan, J. L. 1952–53. Theory of monopolistic quantity discounts. *Review of Economic Studies* 10:119–28.

Buchanan, J. L., E. B. Keeler, J. E. Rolph, and M. R. Holmer. "Simulating Health Expenditures under Alternative Insurance Plans." *Management Science* 37:1067–90.

Burtless, G., and J. A. Hausman. 1978. "The Effect of Taxation on Labor Supply." *Journal of Political Economy* 86:1103–30.

Cragg, J. 1971. "Some Statistical Models for Limited Dependent Variables with Application to the Demand for Durable Goods." *Econometrica* 39:829–44.

Duan, N. 1983. "Smearing Estimate: A Nonparametric Retransformation Method." *Journal of the American Statistical Association* 78:605–10.

Duan, N., W. G. Manning, C. N. Morris, and J. D. Newhouse. 1983. "A Comparison of Alternative Models for the Demand for Medical Care." *Journal of Business and Economic Statistics* 1: 115–26.

Ellis, R. P. 1986. "Rational Behavior in the Presence of Coverage Ceilings and Deductibles." *Rand Journal of Economics* 17:158–75.

Ellis, R. P., and T. G. McGuire. 1986. "Cost Sharing and Patterns of Mental Health Care Utilization." *Journal of Human Resources* 21:359–80.

Frank, R. G., and T. G. McGuire. 1986. "A Review of Studies of the Impact of Insurance on the Demand and Utilization of Specialty Mental Health Services." *Health Services Research* 21:241–65.

Gabor, A. 1955. "A Note on Block Tariffs." *Review of Economic Studies* 45:32–41.

Goldberger, A. S. 1980. "Abnormal Selection Bias." Workshop Series 8006. Social Systems Research Institute, University of Wisconsin.

Hausman, J. A. 1985. "The Econometrics of Nonlinear Budget Sets." *Econometrica* 53:1255–82.

Heckman, J. 1979. "Sample Selection as a Specification Error." *Econometrica* 47:153–61.

Heckman, J. J., and B. Singer. 1985. *Longitudinal Analysis of Labor Market Data.* Cambridge: Cambridge University Press.

Horgan, C. M. 1986. "The Demand for Ambulatory Mental Health Services from Specialty Providers." *Health Services Research* 21:291–319.

Hurd, M. 1979. "Estimation in Truncated Samples When There Is Heteroscedasticity." *Journal of Econometrics* 11:247–58.

Keeler, E. B., J. Buchanan, J. Rolph, and J. Hanley. 1988. "Demand for Episodes of Medical Treatment in the Health Insurance Experiment." Rand Corporation Report R-3454-HHS. *Journal of Health Economics* 7:369–92.

Keeler, E. B., W. G. Manning, and K. B. Wells. 1988. "The Demand for Episodes of Mental Health Services." *Journal of Health Economics* 7:369–92.

Keeler, E. B., J. P. Newhouse, and C. E. Phelps. 1977. "Deductibles and the Demand for Medical Care Services: The Theory of a Consumer Facing a Variable Price Schedule under Uncertainty." *Econometrica* 45:641–56.

Keeler, E. B., and J. E. Rolph. 1988. "The Demand for Episodes of Treatment in the Health Insurance Experiment." *Journal of Health Economics* 7:337–67.

Maddala, G. S. 1983. *Limited-Dependent and Qualitative Variables in Econometrics.* Cambridge: Cambridge University Press.

Manning, W. G., and M. S. Marquis. 1989. "Health Insurance: The Tradeoff between Risk Pooling and Moral Hazard." Rand Report R-3729-HHS. Santa Monica, Calif.: Rand Corporation.

Manning, W. G., K. B. Wells, J. L. Buchanan, E. B. Keeler, R. B. Valdez, and J. P. Newhouse. 1989. "Effects of Mental Health Insurance: Evidence from the Health Insurance Experiment." Rand Report R-3815-NIMH/HCFA. Santa Monica, Calif.: Rand Corporation.

Megdal, S. B. 1987. "The Econometrics of Piecewise-Linear Budget Constraints." *Journal of Business and Economic Statistics* 5:243–48.

Moffitt, R. 1986. "The Econometrics of Piecewise-Linear Budget Constraints: A Survey and Exposition of the Maximum Likelihood Method." *Journal of Business and Economic Statistics* 4:317–28.

———. 1989. "Estimating with Value of an In-Kind Transfer: The Case of Food Stamps." *Econometrica* 57:385–409.

Newhouse, J. P., C. E. Phelps, and M. S. Marquis. 1980. "On Having Your Cake and Eating It Too: Econometric Problems in Estimating the Demand for Health Services." *Journal of Econometrics* 13:365–90.

Oi, W. Y. 1971. "A Disneyland Dilemma: Two-Part Tariffs for a Mickey Mouse Monopoly." *Quarterly Journal of Economics* 85:77–90.

Phlips, L. 1983. *The Economics of Price Discrimination.* Cambridge: Cambridge University Press.

Reed, L. S. 1974. "Utilization of Care for Mental Disorder under the Blue Cross and Blue Shield Plan for Federal Employees, 1972." *American Journal of Psychiatry* 13:964–75.

————. 1975. *Coverage and Utilization of Care for Mental Health Conditions under Health Insurance: Various Studies, 1973–1974.* Washington, D.C.: American Psychiatric Association.

Taube, C. A., L. G. Kessler, and B. J. Burns. 1986. "Estimating the Probability and Level of Ambulatory Mental Health Services Use." *Health Services Research* 21:321–40.

Taylor, L. D. 1975. "The Demand for Electricity: A Survey." *Bell Journal of Economics* 6:74–110.

Terza, J. V., and W. P. Welch. 1982. "Estimating Demand under Block Rates: Electricity and Water." *Land Economics* 58:181–88.

Wells, K. B., E. Keeler, and W. G. Manning. 1990. "Patterns of Outpatient Mental Health Care over Time: Some Implications for Estimates of Demand and for Benefit Design." *Health Services Research* 24:773–90.

Zeckhauser, R. J. 1970. "Medical Insurance: A Case Study of the Trade-off between Risk Spreading and Appropriate Incentives." *Journal of Economic Theory* 2:10–26.

10

Private Health Insurance and the Use of Medical Care by Disabled Mentally Ill Medicare Enrollees

Jeffrey Rubin, Ph.D.,
Virginia Wilcox-Gök, Ph.D.,
and Partha Deb, Ph.D.

S tudies of mental health markets often assess the level of utilization and the elasticity of demand for mental health services in
populations with some form of private health insurance. This
type of study fails to address an important public policy question:
what is the extent of access to health insurance and medical services
among people who have a severe disabling chronic mental illness?

Access problems arise in various ways. Some individuals lose
private health insurance coverage after the loss of a job. Lack of
employment, in turn, makes it more difficult to continue coverage
with private payments. Others, perhaps because of a preexisting
health condition, are unable to obtain insurance coverage. Still others with a serious psychiatric illness may exceed coverage limits.

Some access problems are overcome, in part, with government
assistance. For example, government spending is often used to em-
ploy staff to provide services to eligible clients. In other instances
government subsidizes purchases with a combination of cash transfers and publicly financed health insurance. Within government programs, access is affected by two additional factors: the eligibility
rules used to screen applicants and the benefits accorded eligible
persons. Finally, access to both health services and health insurance
can be affected by the willingness of providers to supply their services and products.

One population in which it is possible to study questions of access
to health insurance and health services is people under sixty-five who

are enrolled in Medicare as a consequence of a disabling mental disorder. Unfortunately, this group falls far short of the entire population of chronically mentally ill persons. Most notably, mentally ill persons who do not have the requisite work experience or family circumstances do not qualify for Medicare coverage. Also, persons whose condition is not so severe as seriously to impair their ability to work, persons whose condition is of recent origin, and persons whose mental disorder is expected to persist for just a short period are also excluded. Nonetheless, the remaining group is a substantial segment of the overall chronically mentally ill population. They are persons who place great demands on the social and health services in a community, as well as on their own families.

In addition to gaining new information on access, studies of the Medicare population can shed light on how eligibility rules and benefit structures might be changed. Medicare benefits and costs are subject to manipulation through legislative action. Before instituting policy reforms it is important to understand how a particular group of enrolled persons behave under the current arrangement.

At the end of 1988 almost 620,000 people were receiving Social Security Disability Insurance (SSDI) benefits as a result of a mental disorder (other than mental retardation).[1] This is the largest single diagnostic group, representing nearly 22 percent of all disabled workers collecting benefits. Those with mental disorders predominate in the younger age groups. Approximately 36 percent of disabled workers under age thirty have a mental disorder and 38.9 percent of those thirty to thirty-nine years old have a mental disorder. Among the oldest persons (age sixty to sixty-four years old) eligible for SSDI only 12.4 percent have a mental disorder.

Among persons newly awarded benefits in 1987, 19.5 percent had a mental disorder. In 1988 the proportion of new enrollees (70,000 out of 412,700) with a mental disorder fell to 18.4 percent. About 64 percent of new enrollees were men, and 17.9 percent had a mental disorder. Among the 36 percent of new female disabled workers receiving SSDI in 1988, 19.4 percent had a mental disorder.

Data on the racial makeup of the group receiving newly awarded disabled worker benefits are available for 1987. About 14.6 percent of disabled worker beneficiaries were black, 77.6 percent were white, and 7.8 percent were categorized as other. Among blacks 24.6 percent had a mental disorder, among whites the proportion was 18.1 percent, and among "others" it was 23.2 percent.

Eligibility for SSDI benefits is important to disabled persons for two reasons. First, cash benefits are paid to persons who meet the employment and functional impairment criteria required to qualify for SSDI. (The average monthly benefit to new SSDI disabled worker beneficiaries in 1987 was $523.) The second important benefit associated with qualifying for SSDI is that, after being eligible for benefits for twenty-four months, an individual automatically is covered under Medicare. Although Medicare does not provide unlimited benefits for mental health services and participation in part B of Medicare requires the payment of a premium, the program does provide protection from certain health care expenses facing disabled persons.

Program data provide some evidence of the level of benefits received by disabled enrollees in Medicare. As of 1987 just over three million people qualified for Medicare either as a result of being on SSDI or because of kidney disease. About 70 percent of disabled Medicare enrollees received some medical service costing Medicare just under $8.5 billion or about 11.2 percent of total Medicare reimbursements.

Medicare program data are not typically reported by disabling condition. Only limited information is available on the use of psychiatric services among Medicare enrollees under age sixty-five. In 1988 there were 51,200 admissions to psychiatric hospitals among this population. This number represents a decline over the absolute number of admissions in each of the three previous years, when admissions averaged about 60,000. The rate of psychiatric admissions per 1,000 disabled enrollees also fell from 21.1 in 1987 to 16.6 in 1988.

Other research on Medicare and the use of mental health services offers evidence of Medicare expenses for mental health services without distinguishing between payments for the aged and payments for those enrolled in Medicare subsequent to qualifying for SSDI. One report suggested that in 1986 Medicare spent about $1.4 billion for mental health care in general hospitals and "other organized facilities" (Scallet 1990). Others indicated that "less than 3 percent of the Medicare dollar is spent on mental health" (Lave and Goldman 1990, 20). This figure is for mental health services and does not necessarily reflect the amount spent on persons with a severe mental disorder. Moreover, it includes the combined disabled and aged Medicare populations. Lave and Goldman noted that "approximately 11 percent of all Medicare hospital discharges were disabled, whereas about 39 percent of Medicare discharges with a mental illness diagnosis were disabled" (1990, 20).

Other studies also provided some data on health care use by the disabled (Lubitz and Pine 1986; Bye, Riley, and Lubitz 1987). Unfortunately, these studies lumped persons with mental illness with persons with mental retardation. Moreover, the data are aggregated and are no more recent than 1981. To overcome some of these deficiencies and gaps in knowledge, we used microdata to examine both the private health insurance coverage and the health care utilization of disabled Medicare enrollees.

The Model

Medicare does not provide complete coverage for all health care costs. Individual enrollees remain responsible for certain deductibles and copayments.[2] Moreover, there are limits on some benefits, especially in regard to mental health services (Lave and Goldman 1990). The presence of such features means that individuals must bear some of the costs of receiving medical care covered under Medicare and, for forms of care not covered by Medicare, individuals may have to bear the entire cost of care.

Firms in the private insurance market have responded to the gaps in Medicare coverage by offering Medigap insurance to Medicare enrollees. It is possible that the presence of this additional coverage affects the use of medical care by Medicare recipients. In this chapter we focus on the presence of private health insurance, including Medigap insurance, and the use of medical care by Medicare enrollees who are disabled due to a mental or emotional illness.

To understand the effect of private health insurance coverage on utilization, we must control for other factors that could explain observed differences in use. Because the demand for medical care may be correlated with the decision to purchase private health insurance, it is necessary to incorporate the insurance decision into the utilization model and to incorporate the level of utilization into the private health insurance model. Although a number of studies have examined the factors that affect the purchase of private health insurance, most have not extended the analysis to determine how utilization affects the likelihood of having private health insurance nor how the presence of private health insurance influences utilization (Garfinkel, Bonito, and McLeroy 1987; Long, Settle, and Link 1982; Rice and McCall 1985; Cafferata 1985). Furthermore, these studies all focus only on aged Medicare enrollees.

A few studies do link the demand for health insurance with the use of medical care. Cameron et al. (1988) studied the effects of public health insurance programs in Australia on the utilization of medical care. However, in the analysis of the Australian programs an important step in the utilization process, the decision to enter the medical care system, was ignored. We postulate that observed utilization is the outcome of two distinct decisions: (1) the individual makes the decision to enter treatment and seeks treatment by a physician; (2) after the initial contact, the individual decides whether to continue with further treatment.[3] Within this framework, we anticipate that economic factors, including both household income and the presence of private health insurance, affect the initial decision to seek care. However, once the individual has entered the medical care system, we anticipate that medical need will continue to be important in decisions about the quantity of medical care while economic factors will be less influential than in step 1.

Others have estimated health care demand using a multistep process. Coffey (1983) distinguished among the decision to choose a public or private provider, the decision to seek care, and the decision about the quantity of care. Hu, Huang, and Cartwright (1988) used a two-step decision model in studying elderly Medicare recipients. However, they applied the model to medical care expenditures rather than medical care utilization. None of the prior literature examined the use of private health insurance and medical care by mentally ill Medicare enrollees.

The relationship between medical care use and the presence of private health insurance coverage may be due either to simultaneity or to unobserved factors common to both the choice of private health insurance and the use of medical care. Before discussing our treatment of simultaneity and common unobserved factors, we discuss the variables assumed to influence access to private health insurance in addition to Medicare coverage and the utilization of medical care.

Both demand and supply factors may be associated with the presence of private health insurance at the time of the survey and the utilization of medical care. Accordingly, our specifications must be interpreted as reduced form rather than structural equations. Definitions of all variables used in the analysis are given in table 10.1, and means and standard deviations are shown in table 10.2.

Private Health Insurance

Factors expected to be associated with the presence of private health insurance at the time of the survey (PRIVATE) include household income, health status, and expected utilization. Although household income affects an individual's ability to afford private health insurance, it also partially determines an individual's eligibility for Medicaid.[4] In turn, Medicaid eligibility is expected to affect an individual's decision to have private health insurance. The endogeneity of Medicaid enrollment for disabled Medicare enrollees was established by Rubin and Wilcox-Gök (1991). Because our focus in this chapter is on the role of private health insurance supplements to Medicare, we control for the endogeneity of Medicaid status simply by using the predicted probability of Medicaid status in our analysis.[5] To avoid multicollinearity between income and Medicaid enrollment, we use the probability of Medicaid enrollment (MEDICAIDHAT) and an interaction term between the probability of not enrolling in Medicaid and family income (INTERACTION).

An individual's current health status (POOR HEALTH), the number of functional limitations (LIMIT), and the presence of mental or emotional illness (MENTAL&EMOT) may indicate health care needs and thereby also affect the likelihood of having additional private health insurance. These variables may proxy the anticipated level of medical care use (doctor visits or hospital care) and thereby positively influence the demand for private health insurance, *ceteris paribus*. However, it is also possible that health insurers attempt to exclude applicants with health conditions that are associated with high costs of medical care. This supply-side effect would cause a negative relationship between poor health and the probability of having private health insurance. Other personal characteristics hypothesized to be associated with the presence of private health insurance include AGE, race (WHITE), gender (FEMALE), marital status (MARRIED), and education (HIGH SCHOOL).

Because a disabled person with Medicare coverage may have private health insurance through another family member who is employed, a variable indicating whether any family member is employed (WORKER) is included.[6] Also included is a dummy variable indicating whether the enrollee resides in the NORTHEAST. This variable is included to control for a possible regional differential in the cost of private health insurance other than a differential caused by differing utilization of medical care (which is captured in the predicted utilization variable). These two variables are important in the simultaneous equations context in that they are omitted from the utilization equations and therefore identify the utilization equations. WORKER is not expected to influence utilization of medical care beyond its influence in determining whether the Medicare enrollee has private health insurance.[7] Similarly, although the cost of selling and providing private health insurance may differ between the Northeast and other areas of the country and affect utilization of medical care because of a higher or lower predicted probability of having private insurance (PRIVATEHAT), living in the Northeast is not expected to have an independent effect on utilization of medical care.

Table 10.1   Definitions of Variables

Variable	Definition
Dependent Variables	
DOCTOR VISIT (Y/N)	Dummy variable = 1 if the individual has at least one visit with a physician over a 12-month period
LOG OF DOCTOR VISITS	Log of physician visits over a 12-month period
HOSPITAL STAY (Y/N)	Dummy variable = 1 if the individual has at least one hospital stay over a 12-month period
LOG OF HOSPITAL DAYS	Log of hospital days over a 12-month period
MEDICAID	Dummy variable = 1 if the individual is enrolled in Medicaid
PRIVATE	Dummy variable = 1 if the individual has private health insurance in addition to Medicare
Independent Variables	
AFDC CUTOFF	State AFDC eligibility cutoff in thousands of dollars
AGE	Years of age
BEDS	Number of hospital beds per 1,000 population in the state
DOCS	Number of doctors per 1,000 population in the state
FEMALE	Dummy variable = 1 if the recipient is female
HIGH SCHOOL	Dummy variable = 1 if the recipient has a high school diploma. The omitted category contains individuals who have not completed high school.
INCOME	Monthly household income in thousands (weighted by size of household and averaged over four months)
INTERACTION	Interaction variable = (1 − Medicaidhat) × (monthly household income)
LIMIT	Number of functional limitations
LOGDAYSHAT	Predicated log of the number of hospital days during the previous 12 months
LOGVISITSHAT	Predicted log of the number of doctor visits during the previous 12 months
MARRIED	Dummy variable = 1 if the recipient is currently married (includes persons married with spouse absent)
MEDICAIDHAT	Predicted value of MEDICAID
MEDICALLY NEEDY STATE	Dummy variable = 1 if the individual lives in a state in which Medicaid eligibility includes medical need
MENTAL&EMOT	Dummy variable = 1 if individual is mentally ill or has a nervous, emotional, alcohol, or drug problem
METRO	Dummy variable = 1 if a family member lives in a metropolitan area
NORTHEAST	Dummy variable = 1 if the individual lives in Connecticut, Delaware, District of Columbia, Maine, Maryland, Massachusetts, New Hampshire, New Jersey, New York, Pennsylvania, Rhode Island, or Vermont

(*continued*)

Table 10.1   (*Continued*)

Variable	Definition
OWN HOUSE	Dummy variable = 1 if respondent owns home
POOR HEALTH	Dummy variable = 1 if self-reported health status is poor
PRIVATEHAT	Predicted value of PRIVATE
PRSTAYHAT	Predicted probability of a hospital stay during the previous 12 months
PRVISITHAT	Predicted probability of visiting a doctor during the previous 12 months
WHITE	Dummy variable = 1 if the recipient is white
WORKER	Dummy variable = 1 if a family member is employed

Table 10.2   Means and Standard Deviations
of Regression Variables

Variable	Mentally Ill Population			Non–Mentally Ill Population		
	N	Mean	SD	N	Mean	SD
DOCTOR VISIT (Y/N)	146	0.86	0.35	1,621	0.88	0.33
DOCTOR VISITS	126	6.98	8.32	1,422	13.75	18.14
LOG OF DOCTOR VISITS	126	1.46	0.99	1,422	2.02	1.10
HOSPITAL STAY (Y/N)	146	0.28	0.45	1,621	0.33	0.47
HOSPITAL DAYS	41	59.15	52.11	544	16.44	18.14
LOG OF HOSPITAL DAYS	41	3.59	1.15	544	2.25	1.09
MEDICAID	146	0.31	0.46	1,621	0.23	0.42
PRIVATE	146	0.29	0.46	1,621	0.44	0.50
AFDC CUTOFF	146	0.34	0.10	1,621	0.33	0.09
AGE	146	49.66	12.59	1,621	52.43	11.02
BEDS	146	5.75	0.74	1,621	5.68	0.93
DOCS	146	2.00	0.47	1,621	1.98	0.53
FEMALE	146	0.47	0.50	1,621	0.41	0.49
HIGH SCHOOL	146	0.58	0.49	1,621	0.42	0.49
INCOME	146	1.24	0.81	1,621	1.28	0.93
LIMIT	146	1.76	1.94	1,621	3.05	2.40
MARRIED	146	0.31	0.46	1,621	0.53	0.50
MEDICALLY NEEDY STATE	146	0.05	0.21	1,621	0.19	0.39
METRO	146	0.62	0.49	1,621	0.66	0.47
NORTHEAST	146	0.23	0.42	1,621	0.23	0.42
OWN HOUSE	146	0.58	0.50	1,621	0.72	0.45
POOR HEALTH	146	0.24	0.43	1,621	0.55	0.50
WHITE	146	0.89	0.31	1,621	0.79	0.41
WORKER	146	0.39	0.49	1,621	0.46	0.50

Utilization of Medical Care

Utilization of medical care is represented by four variables. Two dummy variables indicating whether the individual had at least one visit to a doctor [DOCTOR VISIT (Y/N)] or at least one stay in a hospital [HOSPITAL STAY (Y/N)] during the year before the survey are used. In addition, the number of visits to a doctor (LOG OF DOCTOR VISITS) and the number of hospital days (LOG OF HOSPITAL DAYS) during the year before the survey are used.

In the utilization regressions, AGE, gender (FEMALE), race (WHITE), and education (HIGH SCHOOL) are characteristics of the individual typically thought to influence the demand for medical care. The variables representing chronic limiting conditions (LIMIT), general health status (POOR HEALTH), and mental or emotional illness (MENTAL&EMOT) capture the effects of an individual's specific health status on the demand for care. The level of medical insurance (Medicare only, Medicare plus private health insurance [PRIVATE], or Medicare plus Medicaid [MEDICAIDHAT]) is included to indicate the cost of care to the individual. Private health insurance generally lowers the cost of a physician visit or a hospital stay and changes the relative costs of inpatient and outpatient care.

Finally, variables indicating whether the individual lives in an urban area (METRO) and the per capita number of doctors (DOCS) or hospital beds (BEDS) are proxies for factors influencing the supply of medical care in a state or metropolitan area. These variables are important in the context of the simultaneous equations in that they are omitted from the private health insurance and therefore identify the private insurance probits. As indicators of the supply of medical care and therefore arguments in the predicted value of medical care use, these variables may influence whether an individual has private health insurance. However, it is not expected that the supply of medical care would also have an independent effect on whether a disabled Medicare enrollee has private insurance.

Data and Estimation Methods

The Data

To examine differences in the health insurance coverage and medical care utilization by the mentally and emotionally ill and other disabled Medicare enrollees, we used a sample of 420 observations of disabled Medicare enrollees under age sixty-five from wave 3 (1984) of the Survey of Income and Program Participation (SIPP). The survey provides extensive data on individual characteristics, as well as information on private and public health insurance and health care use. This survey, like most others, excludes the institutionalized population. Thus, it will not yield a truly representative sample of all disabled Medicare enrollees. Nonetheless, a large proportion of the eligible population comprises noninstitutionalized individuals, and SIPP does provide sufficient information to analyze the patterns of health insurance coverage and health care utilization among the majority of disabled Medicare enrollees.

Among the 420 observations of disabled Medicare enrollees, 36 people reported a mental or emotional disorder, 371 had at least one doctor visit, and 119 had at least one hospital stay.[8] This sample, however, does not reflect the true proportions of these individuals in the population. Although sample weights are provided for SIPP observations, standard weighted regression estimation procedures are not appropriate for the models estimated in this chapter. To obtain estimates that reflect the behavior of a representative sample of the disabled, a new sample that reflects the true proportions in the population is created by replicating the observations in the original sample. The number of replications for each observation is proportional to its SIPP sample weight. This replication procedure yields a representative sample of 1,767 observations.

Estimating Models

Individuals enter the health care system by seeking the care of a physician. We use probit analysis to determine the factors influential in whether an individual had at least one visit to a physician [DOCTOR VISIT (Y/N)] and at least one hospital stay [HOSPITAL STAY (Y/N)] during the past year.

We next examine the quantity of medical care received, given that an initial contact has been made. This is measured by (1) the number of visits made to a physician (given at least one visit) and (2) the number of days of hospital care (given at least one hospital stay) during the past year. Because the distributions of these variables are highly skewed, LOG OF DOCTOR VISITS and LOG OF HOSPITAL DAYS are used as the dependent variables.

The nature of the relationship between the use of medical care and the presence of private health insurance is not known a priori. We therefore consider models with simultaneity, with jointly distributed error terms (caused by unobserved factors common to both equations), and with both simultaneity and jointly distributed error terms. A more detailed description and comparison of similar models for elderly Medicare recipients is found in Wilcox-Gök and Rubin (1992).

Jointly Distributed Errors

It is possible that a correlation between the purchase of health insurance and the use of medical care occurs because individuals have unobserved characteristics that cause some individuals to demand more health insurance coverage than that provided by Medicare and also to use more medical care than do other individuals. These individuals do not have private health insurance in addition to Medicare because they anticipate greater use of medical care. Rather, there are underlying factors that cause them to demand more of both goods.[9]

In this situation, the effects of the unobserved characteristics are common to the error terms of the insurance and utilization equations. Our first approach is to use a joint error estimation model to capture the cross-equation correlation in the error terms. Specifically, we assume that the errors have a standard bivariate normal distribution. Bivariate probit regressions are used to estimate the coefficients of the joint decision to have private health insurance (PRIVATE) and to visit a physician [DOCTOR VISIT (Y/N)] and the joint decision to have private health insurance and to go to a hospital [HOSPITAL STAY (Y/N)]. A probit and conditional OLS regression (with error terms having bivariate normal distributions) are used to estimate the coefficients of the joint decision to have private insurance (PRIVATE) and to make multiple visits to a physician (LOG OF DOCTOR VISITS) and the joint decision to have private health insurance (PRIVATE) and to have multiple hospital stays (LOG OF HOSPITAL DAYS).[10]

Simultaneity

If individuals anticipate a need for medical care and purchase health insurance in advance to meet this need, then the choice of private health insurance is simultaneously determined with the demand for medical care. While individuals cannot perfectly predict their future demands for medical care, they may have information about their health which leads them to expect greater demand. Thus, not only are the probabilities and levels of utilization dependent upon an individual's health insurance coverage, but the level of coverage may be dependent upon (anticipated) utilization.

Because simultaneity and jointly distributed errors are not mutually exclusive, we estimate a second version of our model of insurance and medical care utilization assuming the presence of both.[11] For proper estimation of the coefficients of factors affecting the utilization of medical care with simultaneity, a three-stage, full information maximum likelihood estimating model is used.

Our use of instruments for the choice of health insurance coverage (PRIVATEHAT, MEDICAIDHAT) in the estimation of medical care utilization is similar to the approach used by Cameron et al. (1988). The estimation of medical care utilization consists of a regression for each of the four utilization measures. A probit analysis is performed for whether the individual had at least one visit to a physician [DOCTOR VISIT (Y/N)] and whether the individual had at least one stay in a hospital [HOSPITAL STAY (Y/N)]. Conditional regressions are performed for the number of visits to a physician (LOG OF DOCTOR VISITS) and the number of days in a hospital (LOG OF HOSPITAL DAYS). The error terms of each pair of second-stage equations are assumed to have the standard bivariate normal distribution. The identification of the utilization equations is assured by the inclusion of WORKER and NORTHEAST in the private insurance probit.

For proper estimation of the coefficients of factors influencing whether an individual had a private health insurance policy, a predicted value of each type of utilization is obtained from the second-stage probits and regressions. These are used in the third-stage probits for private health insurance. Again, the error terms of each pair of second-stage equations are assumed to have the standard bivariate normal distribution. The identification of the private insurance equations is assured by the inclusion of METRO and DOCS or BEDS in the utilization equations.

The choice of models for the utilization regressions is discussed by both Maddala (1985) and Duan et al. (1983).[12] Because our model describes individuals as entering the medical system sequentially, we run the probits of DOCTOR VISIT (Y/N) and HOSPITAL STAY (Y/N) on the full sample and the regressions with quantity-dependent variables on the subsample of individuals who have at least one doctor visit or one hospital stay, respectively.[13]

Empirical Results

Likelihood ratio tests were used to evaluate the models with joint errors (JEE) and the models with simultaneity and joint errors (S&JEE). For DOCTOR VISIT (Y/N), LOG OF DOCTOR VISITS, and LOG OF HOSPITAL DAYS, the S&JEE model performs significantly better than does the JEE model. For HOSPITAL STAY (Y/N), the JEE and S&JEE models perform equally well.[14] We therefore report the coefficient estimates of the S&JEE models in table 10.3.

The top half of table 10.3 reports coefficient estimates for the

Table 10.3   Coefficient Estimates from Analysis
of Private Insurance and Medical Care Utilization
with Simultaneity and Joint Errors

Variable	(1) Prob. of a Doctor Visit	(2) Log of Doctor Visits	(3) Prob. of a Hospital Stay	(4) Log of Hospital Days
Private Insurance Equation				
POOR HEALTH	0.123	0.340	0.381	-1.983
	(0.277)	(0.648)	(0.484)	(1.508)
LIMIT	-0.027	-0.049	-0.016	-0.328
	(0.034)	(0.043)	(0.064)	(0.266)
MENTAL&EMOT	-0.363	-0.316	-0.302	-6.984
	(0.279)	(0.407)	(0.275)	(5.487)
AGE	-0.010	0.001	-0.005	0.055
	(0.015)	(0.017)	(0.013)	(0.049)
FEMALE	0.558*	0.507*	0.609*	0.374
	(0.173)	(0.185)	(0.185)	(0.388)
WHITE	0.183	0.078	0.158	-2.294
	(0.251)	(0.388)	(0.249)	(1.915)
MARRIED	0.276	0.319	0.425	0.919**
	(0.239)	(0.202)	(0.268)	(0.530)
HIGH SCHOOL	0.263	0.355	0.395	-0.404
	(0.173)	(0.317)	(0.373)	(0.520)
MEDICAIDHAT	-1.939*	-1.404	-1.775**	2.799
	(0.829)	(1.144)	(1.050)	(3.410)
INTERACTION	0.262*	0.347	0.301*	0.573
	(0.115)	(0.211)	(0.149)	(0.383)
NORTHEAST	0.379*	0.370**	0.379*	-0.017
	(0.194)	(0.204)	(0.183)	(0.411)
WORKER	0.317**	0.253	0.295**	-0.033
	(0.183)	(0.192)	(0.179)	(0.337)
PRVISITHAT	1.074			
	(1.689)			
LOGVISITSHAT		-0.156		
		(0.880)		
PRSTAYHAT			-0.601	
			(2.139)	
LOGDAYSHAT				4.693
				(3.719)
INTERCEPT	-1.301	-0.763	-0.797	-10.820
	(1.310)	(1.076)	(1.039)	(8.090)
Utilization of Medical Care				
POOR HEALTH	1.096*	0.800*	0.552*	0.407
	(0.275)	(0.149)	(0.179)	(0.273)
LIMIT	-0.012	0.016	0.070*	0.068**
	(0.062)	(0.028)	(0.032)	(0.040)
MENTAL&EMOT	0.185	-0.309	0.069	1.472*
	(0.360)	(0.245)	(0.290)	(0.490)
AGE	0.012	0.012*	0.005	-0.013
	(0.013)	(0.006)	(0.011)	(0.013)
FEMALE	0.406	0.130	0.064	0.147
	(0.294)	(0.277)	(0.224)	(0.392)

(continued)

Table 10.3   *(Continued)*

Variable	(1) Prob. of a Doctor Visit	(2) Log of Doctor Visits	(3) Prob. of a Hospital Stay	(4) Log of Hospital Days
WHITE	−0.331	−0.288**	0.144	0.505
	(0.268)	(0.158)	(0.192)	(0.324)
MARRIED	0.930*	0.108	0.188	−0.007
	(0.407)	(0.192)	(0.215)	(0.341)
HIGH SCHOOL	0.425	0.368*	0.400*	0.100
	(0.315)	(0.170)	(0.185)	(0.328)
PRIVATEHAT	−2.186	−0.704	0.514	−0.686
	(1.412)	(0.969)	(0.941)	(1.736)
MEDICAIDHAT	−1.450	0.393	1.332	−0.931
	(1.159)	(0.677)	(0.818)	(1.052)
INTERACTION	0.274	0.244	0.110	0.157
	(0.279)	(0.153)	(0.126)	(0.390)
METRO	0.158	0.209	−0.217	0.048
	(0.236)	(0.143)	(0.158)	(0.243)
DOCS	0.525	0.013		
	(0.334)	(0.149)		
BEDS			−0.022	0.064
			(0.081)	(0.083)
INTERCEPT	−0.370	0.592	−2.064*	1.881**
	(1.199)	(0.654)	(0.920)	(1.099)
RHO	0.249	−0.140	0.019	0.002
	(0.194)	(0.087)	(0.100)	(0.185)
Number of observations	1767	1548	1767	585
Log-likelihood	−1,413.29	−3,015.84	−1,946.85	−1,130.36
Model df	29	29	29	29

Note: Asymptotic standard errors are in parentheses.
*$p < .05$.
**$p < .10$.

probits of whether an individual had private health insurance.[15] Although the coefficients cannot be interpreted as derivatives of the dependent variables with respect to the independent variables, the signs of the coefficients indicate the sign of the derivative. Because a probit for private health insurance must be run with each of the utilization equations, four probits are reported. Probit 1 was run with the probit for DOCTOR VISIT (Y/N). Probit 2 was run with the conditional regression of the LOG OF DOCTOR VISITS. Probit 3 was run with the probit for HOSPITAL STAY (Y/N). Probit 4 was run with the conditional regression of the LOG OF HOSPITAL DAYS.

The first three independent variables of table 10.3 are indicators of health status: POOR HEALTH, LIMIT, and MENTAL&EMOT. None of these indicators is consistently associated with private health insurance.[16] Among personal characteristics, being female increases the likelihood that an individual has private health insurance. There is also some support for the view that being married increases the likelihood of having private insurance. Higher household income (larger value of the INTERACTION variable) is positively and significantly associated with the probability of private health insurance. In two of the probits, a higher probability of Medicaid coverage (MEDICAIDHAT) is significantly related to a lower probability of private health insurance. The presence of a family member who is employed (WORKER) is positively and significantly related to the probability of having private health insurance in two of the four probits. Living in the NORTHEAST is positively and significantly related to the probability of having private health insurance in addition to Medicare in three of the four probits. Finally, none of the predicted values of utilization was significantly related to the probability of having private health insurance.

The bottom half of table 10.3 reports coefficient estimates for the utilization probits and regressions. As expected, poor health (POOR HEALTH) increases an individual's utilization of all types of medical care. The number of chronic limiting conditions (LIMIT) significantly increases the utilization of hospital care but is not significantly associated with doctor visits. We find that persons with a mental illness or emotional disorder (MENTAL&EMOT) have significantly more hospital days than other disabled Medicare enrollees.

Several personal characteristics are significantly associated with utilization: Older disabled recipients (AGE) have more doctor visits.[17] Being white (WHITE) is negatively and significantly associated with the number of doctor visits. Being married (MARRIED) significantly increases the probability of a visit to the doctor. Having at least completed high school (HIGH SCHOOL) significantly increases the number of doctor visits and the probability of a hospital stay.

The predicted probability of having private health insurance (PRIVATEHAT) is not significantly related to any of the utilization measures.

Summary and Conclusions

Disabled Medicare enrollees with a mental illness or an emotional disorder are no less likely than other disabled Medicare enrollees to have private health insurance. Persons with a mental illness or emotional disorder, once admitted to a hospital, have a longer length of stay.[18] The negative, though insignificant, coefficient on doctor visits and the positive coefficient on hospital days may be due to Medicare's reimbursement policies. Because Medicare limits outpatient coverage for psychiatric care but provides close to full coverage for care in psychiatric units in general hospitals, physicians may be more likely to hospitalize someone with a mental or emotional disorder than other disabled Medicare enrollees, all else being equal.

If the benefit structure in Medicare is causing a substitution of inpatient for outpatient care, it may be necessary to consider changes in Medicare.[19] A review of studies of substitution in mental health care pointed to the potential deleterious effects on patient functioning and costs when inpatient care rather than outpatient care is provided (Goldstein and Horgan 1988).

The findings indicate that poor health is an important determinant of the decision to seek medical care and subsequent decisions concerning the quantity of doctor visits. However, for disabled Medicare enrollees health status is not an influential determinant of whether an individual has private health insurance.

A higher household income increases the probability that an individual will have private health insurance but does not have a significant effect on utilization. It is possible that a Medicare enrollee has private health insurance through family coverage offered by a family member's employer. A dummy variable indicating the presence of an employed family member is included in the model and is found to increase the probability of having private health insurance.

Some low-income disabled Medicare enrollees may be able to obtain Medicaid coverage. Hence, Medicaid status is treated endogenously in the model. As expected, the higher the probability of Medicaid enrollment, the lower is the probability of having private health insurance.

These findings on insurance coverage and health care utilization among a subgroup of disabled Medicare enrollees leave some important research questions unanswered while also suggesting that some policy reforms could improve the plight of the chronically and seriously mentally ill. The presence of a mental or emotional illness did not have a statistically significant effect on the probability of having private health insurance. Nonetheless, the sign on the variable (MENTAL&EMOT) was negative in all four cases. The available data do not allow us to explore some interesting questions related to these results. For example, it is possible that subgroups of the population with mental and emotional disorders have a particularly difficult time obtaining private coverage. Furthermore, because we lack data on the source of private coverage, we cannot determine whether the seriously mentally ill find it more difficult than other disabled persons in attempting to purchase health insurance to supplement Medicare coverage.

The apparent bias in Medicare toward inpatient care is indicative of the kind of problem facing disabled Medicare enrollees with a mental or emotional illness. Attempts to address this problem are constrained by pressures to contain Medicare costs. In this environment proposals that are cost-neutral with respect to Medicare are more likely to receive serious consideration.

One possibility is to incorporate added outpatient benefits for the treatment of psychiatric conditions into private supplemental health insurance policies. It is clear that mentally ill Medicare enrollees have different health service needs than other disabled and elderly beneficiaries. As efforts are made to regulate the market for supplemental health insurance policies and to identify model benefit plans, some consideration should be given to structuring a policy better suited to the needs of the younger mentally ill population.

One important feature of new supplemental policies would be a special emphasis on creating incentives for outpatient care. Unfortunately, very little of the research on the demand for mental health care would apply to the particular population eligible for SSDI and Medicare coverage. Hence, it is uncertain how these policies should be priced and whether costs would be so high as to prevent people from purchasing coverage. It is possible that expanded access to mental health care could lead to offsetting reductions in other health care financed by Medicare. If this can be documented, there is a case for using Medicare funds to subsidize private insurance purchases for this group.

Another option, making Medicare involvement more direct, would be to establish a part C under Medicare. Benefits under this option would be primarily for outpatient mental health care. Only persons qualifying for SSDI benefits on the basis of a psychiatric condition would be eligible to purchase this extended coverage. The supplemental benefits provided under a part C policy could be fully funded with premiums or partially funded through premiums with the remaining cost financed from the Medicare trust fund and/or general revenues. The size of any Medicare subsidy could be based on evidence of offsetting reductions in covered Medicare services.

Improvements in access to health care and changes in the service mix will alleviate only some of the problems facing persons with severe and chronic mental illness. Much work remains to be done in developing comprehensive programs that address the social, housing, employment, and other needs of the chronically mentally ill.

Acknowledgments

Support from National Institute of Mental Health grant NH 43450-01 is gratefully acknowledged. Dr. Wilcox-Gök also received support from Rutgers University Research Council grant 2-02306. The authors thank John Mullahy, Richard Frank, Willard Manning Jr., and participants at the Fifth Biennial Conference on the Economics of Mental Health for their comments.

Notes

1. The data in this section on the Medicare program and disabled populations are from the "Annual Statistical Supplement, 1989" (Social Security Administration 1989).

2. See Garfinkel, Bonito, and McLeroy (1987) for a detailed description of the Medicare program.

3. Of course, to be even more realistic, the entire process of treatment of an episode of illness could be handled as a sequential decision-making process. However, the important distinction is that, after the initial decision to seek medical care, decisions about the level of care are made jointly with medical professionals.

4. Key features of Medicaid and its importance in mental health markets are discussed by Taube, Goldman, and Salkever (1990).

5. The probability of Medicaid enrollment is predicted from a probit reported in table 10.N.1.

6. The Medicare enrollee's private health insurance may be any type of private insurance and is not necessarily Medigap insurance.

7. It is possible that the employment of family members raises the time cost of using medical care if the disabled Medicare enrollee requires that a family member accompany him or her to medical facilities. However, an alternative specification did not support this conjecture.

8. Too few Medicare enrollees in the sample have mental disorders to separate those with mental disorders from those with emotional disorders.

9. One possibility is that unmeasured aspects of an individual's health status affect both utilization and private health insurance coverage.

10. Because we expect that the individual alone makes the decision to visit a physician, while the decision to go to the hospital is greatly influenced by a physician's recommendation, we do not expect the same coefficient estimates for the two bivariate probits. Similarly, the coefficient estimates of the regressions of the quantity of care may differ greatly.

11. A simple simultaneous equations model was also estimated. As indicated in table 10.N.2, for physician care the models with joint error terms dominate this simple model.

12. The specification of the model reported in the results has been

checked in numerous ways. Several formulations of the health variables were considered, including a categorical indicator of general health and separate consideration of mental disorders. Alternative formulations of the education variable were also considered. The income interaction variable was created to replace a simple income variable used in earlier specifications. Finally, the robustness of the identification restrictions was checked by trying an alternative specification of WORKER, alternately dropping WORKER and NORTHEAST, and dropping BEDS or DOCS.

13. The data do not allow us to distinguish between cases in which an individual was admitted to a hospital after a doctor visit and those in which a doctor visit occurred after hospital admission. For this reason, we do not limit the population for the probit of HOSPITAL STAY (Y/N) to individuals with at least one doctor visit. Tobit estimation would be appropriate if the entire distribution were used and displayed self-censoring. However, because we have intentionally truncated the distributions of the continuous dependent variables, it is not appropriate to use tobit estimations of the coefficients in these regressions.

14. Chi-squared values are reported in table 10.N.2 for likelihood ratio (LR) tests between the JEE and S&JEE models. The dominance of the S&JEE model for LOG OF DOCTOR VISITS is only weakly statistically significant (approximate 75 percent confidence interval). Table 10.N.2 also supports our assumption of endogeneity between private health insurance and utilization. Because PRIVATE is a dichotomous form of a latent continuous variable, the standard Hausman-Wu test of exogeneity is not appropriate. However, if the error terms in the independent equations (IE) model are correlated, it follows that the latent variable is not orthogonal to usage (i.e., private insurance is endogenous). The LR tests between the IE and the JEE and S&JEE models reported in table 10.N.2 overwhelmingly reject the orthogonality of the latent private insurance variable and utilization.

15. The standard errors in tables 10.3 and 10.N.1 have been corrected for the weighted replication of the data. However, the standard errors reported for the coefficient estimates may be upwardly biased. In the usual two-stage simultaneous equations estimation procedure, unbiased standard errors may be obtained for the coefficient estimates by correcting for the heteroscedasticity of the second-stage regression error term. Like the simpler two-stage estimation, the standard errors of the coefficient estimates in the third stage of our estimating model may be upwardly biased, but the correction used in the two-stage estimation procedure is not appropriate.

16. In other studies of elderly Medicare enrollees, researchers found that the presence of chronic conditions has a positive and significant effect on the likelihood of having private insurance. See, for example, Garfinkel, Bonito, and McLeroy (1987).

17. Recall that all persons eligible for Medicare as a result of a disability are younger than 65. Our data indicate that persons with a mental illness or emotional disorder are only slightly younger (49.7) than other disabled persons (53.4). Program data indicate that, at the end of 1988, the average age of all disabled workers was 51.3 and the average age of all disabled workers with a mental disorder was 46.9.

Table 10.N.1   Coefficient Estimates from Probit of Medicaid Enrollment

Variable	Coefficient	Asymptotic Standard Error
AGE	−0.039*	0.009
FEMALE	0.183	0.164
WHITE	−0.223	0.222
HIGH SCHOOL	−0.444*	0.196
MARRIED	−0.390*	0.183
INCOME	−0.424*	0.132
OWN HOUSE	−0.577*	0.175
MED NEEDY STATE	0.339	0.215
AFDC CUT OFF	1.999	1.050
INTERCEPT	1.815*	0.605
Number of observations	1767	
Log-likelihood	−735.77	
Model df	10	

*$p < .05$.

Table 10.N.2   Specification Tests of Models of Private Health Insurance and Utilization of Medical Care

Variable	Simultaneous Equations	Joint Error Equations	Simultaneous & Joint Error Equations
DOCTOR VISIT (Y/N)			
Independent equations	19.56[a] (2)	11.14[a] (1)	27.08[a] (3)
Simultaneous equations		[−0.94]	7.52 (1)
Joint error equations			15.94[a] (2)
LOG OF DOCTOR VISITS			
Independent equations	2.24 (2)	13.70[a] (1)	16.38[a] (3)
Simultaneous equations		[18.79]	14.14[a] (1)
Joint error equations			2.68 (2)
HOSPITAL STAY (Y/N)			
Independent equations	3.44 (2)	0.22 (1)	2.00 (3)
Simultaneous equations		[4.26]	1.44 (1)
Joint error equations			1.78 (2)
LOG OF HOSPITAL DAYS			
Independent equations	22.22[a] (2)	0.03 (1)	22.22[a] (3)
Simultaneous equations		[−15.83]	0.001 (1)
Joint error equations			22.20[a] (2)

Notes: Chi-squared values from likelihood ratio tests are reported for LR tests between the IE and simultaneous equation (SE) models, IE and JEE models, IE and S&JEE models, and SE and S&JEE models, since all of these are nested. The degrees of freedom are shown in parentheses. The Schwarz criterion is used between the SE and JEE models because they are not nested. The numbers in brackets are the Schwarz criterion values for the JEE model versus the SE model.
[a]The LR test indicates that models differ significantly at the 5 percent level. There is no significance test for the Schwarz criterion.

18. It is possible that the greater number of days results from multiple periods of hospitalization and not from longer lengths of stay. However, both program data and SIPP data indicate that individuals with a mental disorder have longer average hospital stays than other disabled Medicare enrollees.

19. Some changes in Medicare since the SIPP data were collected have enhanced the outpatient coverage of mental health care (Lave and Goldman 1990).

References

Bye, B., G. Riley, and J. Lubitz. 1987. "Medicare Utilization by Disabled Worker Beneficiaries: A Longitudinal Analysis." *Social Security Bulletin* 50(12):13–28.

Cafferata, G. L. 1985. "Private Health Insurance of the Medicare Population and the Baucus Legislation." *Medical Care* 23:1086–96.

Cameron, A., P. Trivedi, F. Milne, and J. Piggott. 1988. "A Microeconometric Model of the Demand for Health Care and Health Insurance in Australia." *Review of Economic Studies* 55:85–106.

Coffey, R. 1983. "The Effect of Time Price on the Demand for Medical Care Services." *Journal of Human Resources* 18:408–24.

Duan, N., W. Manning, C. Morris, and J. Newhouse. 1983. "A Comparison of Alternative Models for the Demand for Medical Care." *Journal of Business and Economic Statistics* 1:115–26.

Garfinkel, S. A., A. J. Bonito, and K. R. McLeroy. 1987. "Socioeconomic Factors and Medicare Supplemental Health Insurance." *Health Care Financing Review* 9, no. 1:21–30.

Goldstein, J. M., and C. M. Horgan. 1988. "Inpatient and Outpatient Psychiatric Services: Substitutes or Complements?" *Hospital and Community Psychiatry* 39:632–36.

Hu, T.-W., L.-F. Huang, and W. S. Cartwright. 1988. "Supplemental Health Insurance Enrollment, Premium Payment, and the Effects of Insurance on Health Care Expenditures among the Elderly." University of California at Berkeley. Photocopy.

Lave, J. R., and H. H. Goldman. 1990. "Medicare Financing for Mental Health Care." *Health Affairs* 9, no. 1:19–30.

Long, S. H., R. F. Settle, and C. R. Link. 1982. "Who Bears the Burden of Medicare Cost Sharing?" *Inquiry* 19:222–34.

Lubitz, J., and P. Pine. 1986. "Health Care Use by Medicare's Disabled Enrollees." *Health Care Financing Review* 7(4):19–32.

Maddala, G. S. 1985. "A Survey of the Literature on Selectivity Bias as It Pertains to Health Care Markets." *Advances in Health Economics* 6:3–18.

Rice, T., and N. McCall. 1985. "The Extent of Ownership and the Characteristics of Medicare Supplemental Policies." *Inquiry* 22:188–200.

Rubin, J., and V. Wilcox-Gök. 1991. "Health Insurance Coverage among Disabled Medicare Enrollees." *Health Care Financing Review* 12(4):27–37.

Scallet, L. J. 1990. "Paying for Public Mental Health Care: Crucial Questions." *Health Affairs* 9, no. 1:117–24.
Social Security Administration. 1989. "Annual Statistical Supplement, 1989." SSA Pub. No. 13-11700. *Social Security Bulletin* 52:283–301.
Taube, C. A., H. H. Goldman, and D. Salkever. 1990. "Medicaid Coverage for Mental Illness: Balancing Access and Costs." *Health Affairs* 9, no. 1:5–18.
Wilcox-Gök, V., and J. Rubin. 1992. "Health Insurance and the Utilization of Medical Care by the Elderly." Rutgers University. Photocopy.

11

Estimating the Costs of a Mental Health Benefit: A Small-Employer Mandate

Thomas G. McGuire, Ph.D.

S tate regulation of insurance coverage through mandates has been an important influence on mental health coverage available to employees and dependents. As states (and the federal government) turn attention to the uninsured, all mandated benefits have been put under close scrutiny. Regulations that increase the cost of purchased health insurance may work against the goal of universal coverage by increasing the financial burden of new state regulations requiring employers to offer insurance to workers. Small employers are at the center of this debate. Almost one-half of the working uninsured are employed in firms with fewer than twenty-five employees (ICF, Inc. 1987). When small employers do offer insurance, they pay much more for the same health insurance than do larger firms.[1] The cost of cost-increasing insurance regulation will be of particular concern to small employers.

Connecticut recently included mental health coverage in compulsory health insurance legislation covering small employers. The law also requires the cost of the mental health coverage to be monitored and the wisdom of including the coverage within the mandate to be reconsidered. The Connecticut case is an example of a tradeoff facing many states and the federal government when considering legislation to cover the uninsured. While there may be general agreement that coverage for the currently uninsured should be a "no-frills" benefit package, reaching a consensus on what is a "frill" will not be easy. As a practical approach, insurance industry representatives in Connecticut and some researchers (Jensen and Gabel 1989) recommended exempting small firms from coverage mandates. The mental health community in Connecticut opposed an exemption.

In this chapter, I estimate the cost of including coverage for mental health services within a state compulsory health insurance plan for small employers in Connecticut, based on presently available data. The cost implications to employers and workers of eliminating and modifying the mandate are considered. Data from the small-employer sector in Connecticut are combined with data from research studies to forecast the costs of various outpatient mental health coverages. Taken separately, data from a particular plan and data from research each have major limitations for the purposes of cost forecasting. Information from a plan is typically very incomplete. Data and experience drawn from the research literature are concerned with the general or representative case and not with a particular application. In this chapter, information on patterns of use from research is used to complement the limited information available directly from the plan. Thus, for example, in addition to information on "demand response," an assumption about the distribution of users around a mean level of use reported in the plan is based on research findings. This chapter serves two purposes: (1) the specific purpose of estimating costs for policy options in Connecticut and (2) the general purpose of illustrating a method for bringing research on mental health services to bear on payment system design issues in a new way.

Mandating the inclusion of mental health coverage in a minimal package designed to cover presently uninsured workers and their dependents involves many of the same issues that have been discussed for some time in the debate over mandates. There are some important differences, however, in both the social benefits and the costs in this form of regulation.[2] In this chapter I do not deal with all of these costs and benefits but instead confine attention to the source of the drawbacks of mandating coverage: the health insurance costs imposed on smaller employers by including mental health coverage within a minimum insurance package.

State Insurance Regulation and Small Employers

Health insurance contracts are a magnet for state and federal regulation. In a recent count, states have enacted 730 mandates, requiring coverage for newborn care (forty-six states), mental health care (twenty-eight states), alcohol abuse treatment (twenty-nine states), and many other categories of benefits (Blue Cross and Blue Shield Association 1989). The number of mandates has doubled in ten years. Newer regulations address the "uninsured problem." Thirty-three states require a continuing coverage provision in employer health insurance, and twelve tax health insurance plans to help finance a state risk pool to pay for the "uninsurable" (Gabel and Jensen 1989). The U.S. Congress, in 1986, enacted the Consolidated Omnibus Budget Reconciliation Act (COBRA), requiring employers with twenty or more employees to offer eighteen months of coverage to terminated employees. Finally, health insurance contracts are used as a revenue source. All states tax commercial health insurance policies, typically at 2–3 percent of premiums, and twenty-six states tax Blue Cross and Blue Shield plans.

Large employers and their employees may be affected by these regulations—in the form of altered benefit packages or wage/fringe mix or in the decision to self-insure—but large employers do not drop health insurance because of regulation. In a survey conducted for the Small Business Administration, ICF Inc. (1987) found that 98 percent of employers with 100–499 workers and 100 percent of employers with 500+ workers offer health insurance as a fringe benefit.

Many small employers, however, are on the margin about whether to offer health insurance at all and may be affected in a more profound way by cost-increasing regulation. In the Small Business Association survey, 78 percent of employers with ten to twenty-four employees offered health insurance, and only 46 percent with nine or fewer employees offered health insurance. While it is true that small employers account for a relatively small share of total employment, workers and families from small firms nonetheless account for a large share of the uninsured. Although there are no data to support the speculation that small firms are less likely today than previously to offer health insurance, there is no doubt that, because employment is growing more rapidly among smaller firms, small firms' reluctance to offer health insurance is a contributor to the rolls of the uninsured.

Connecticut mandates numerous coverages in private health insurance. Section 38-174d of the Connecticut Statutes contains the required benefits for mental illness costs: 50 percent ambulatory coverage up to a $2,000 covered limit and sixty days per year of inpatient care (with partial hospitalization days to count against the inpatient day benefit at two to one). As described in public act 88-110, this mandate applies to health insurance policies issued to employers in Connecticut with at least 51 percent of their workers in Connecticut. The mandate therefore misses three categories of workers: (1) those with employers self-insuring and not subject to regulation of insurance contracts, (2) those with employers purchasing health insurance with a majority of employees outside the state, and (3) those employers not offering health insurance at all. Group 3 includes the employed uninsured, who along with their dependents have been estimated to constitute more than 70 percent of the uninsured (U.S.

General Accounting Office 1989). The recent changes in Connecticut extend the mental health mandate to employers (with as few as ten employees) who are newly required to offer health insurance.

Some recent research has focused on the possible effect of mandated benefits on small employers. Jensen and Gabel (1989) (results summarized in Gabel and Jensen 1989) studied health insurance provision in response to state insurance regulation in a sample of 1,320 small businesses in 1985. This study is directly relevant to the subject here because the empirical work distinguished among the effects of different forms of state regulation. The decision to offer insurance was modeled as a function of work-force composition, the corporate form and size of the employer, and nine measures of state regulation. The strongest negative effects on a firm's decision were found when there was a continuation of coverage rule ($t = 2.7$), premium taxes ($t = 1.7$), or risk-pool taxes ($t = 1.6$), all forms of regulation that impose costs without providing direct benefits to the firms' employees.[3] Interestingly, mandated benefits *did not* seem to decrease the likelihood of coverage. Counts of the total number and of recently enacted mandates had small and insignificant negative effects (t statistics of 0.4 and 1.0, respectively). Jensen and Gabel added separate indicators for mandates for substance abuse and mental health care because these are the mandates that, according to the authors, "businesses often complain about." Although no estimated coefficient of the four measures was statistically significant, on balance the presence of these mandates *increased* the likelihood of insurance.[4]

On the basis of these results, there seems to be an important distinction between state regulations that are mainly cost increasing without directly benefiting the firm and workers, such as taxes to finance risk pools, and regulations that impose costs but confer benefits, such as mandated coverage laws. Adverse effects of mandates on small employers' decisions to offer health insurance seem to be due to the cost-increasing/no-benefit form of regulation.

Predicting the Cost of a Mental Health Benefit Change

Three approaches to predicting the cost of a mental health benefit change can be identified. The first uses a simulation model based upon a research study. The second compares plans with different features and attributes cost differences to differences in coverages (controlling for other factors where possible). The third does what benefits consultants do: forecasts benefit changes based on proprietary formulas.

A great deal of research in health and mental health services has been concerned with the question of how demand or expenditures change with insurance coverage. The Health Insurance Experiment conducted by researchers at the Rand Corporation in the mid-1970s is the best known of the hundreds of studies of insurance and demand. Published research on demand for health and mental health care has centered around economists' interest in demand elasticities. A tenet of insurance theory is that services with a higher demand elasticity should have higher cost sharing to balance the gains from risk protection against the loss from moral hazard (Zeckhauser 1970). Most research in mental health services has been concerned with the question of whether demand for mental health care is more elastic than is demand for other health care, which generally it has been found to be (Keeler et al. 1986; Manning et al. 1987; McGuire 1989).

Researchers at Rand constructed a simulation model to estimate the costs of alternative benefit designs in private health insurance, based on patterns of use and observed responses to cost sharing in the HIE (Buchanan et al. 1991). The model has been used to forecast costs of mandated benefits for employees (Marquis et al. 1989). The patterns of use are calibrated to be nationally representative of current expenditures (based on the patterns of episode use during the mid-1970s in the HIE). The model is set up to analyze "HIE-type" plans with declining-block pricing, insurance being characterized by deductibles, a cost-sharing range defined in terms of total expenditures, and a stop loss after which all care is free. The model is presently not suitable for subnational cases, nor is it applicable to mental health. Mental health use is combined with "acute care" in the model with the same demand response as other medical care. Also, the insurance designs the model analyzes are the opposite of the typical case in mental health, where cost sharing most frequently increases, not decreases, with the level of use.

Another kind of benefit cost forecasting is employed by Jensen and Morrisey (1990), who used "premium regressions" to estimate the marginal effect on total insured costs of various benefit provisions, including a number in the mental health and substance abuse area. A premium regression takes as a dependent variable the insurance premium paid for a group of employees (the total of employer and employee contribution). This is regressed against characteristics of the covered group, local and regional medical market conditions, and plan coverage features. The virtue of the premium regression is that it in principle is able to take account of the direct and indirect effects of a benefit change. In the case of home health care, for example, use of this covered service might substitute for inpatient hospital care in ways that would be hard to measure except at the level of the total premium. Jensen and Morrisey used data on nine thousand plans from larger employers in 1981–84 to estimate the marginal effect on premium of a number of plan features. They controlled for characteristics of the plan group in the form of variables for percentage of males, percentage of nonwhites, and region of the country and in the form of insurance contract.

Results for the three mental health benefit variables (among seven total plan features) used in the regression were as follows: the family premium increased by 8.8 percent with coverage for substance abuse, 12.8 percent with psychiatric hospital stays, and 11.8 percent with psychologists' visits. These findings are highly implausible. It is inconceivable that these selective features of a mental health benefit, over and above more standard coverage such as psychiatrist visits and hospitalization in general hospitals, could increase premiums by 33.4 percent.

Although the authors referred to their empirical method as a "hedonic price" equation, another way to view what Jensen and Morrisey did is as an estimation of a quantity index of average demand as a function of population covered and coverage features. Seen in this way, serious drawbacks of their approach are evident. Population characteristics and regional variables typically dominate health care expenditure regressions. The authors had very few variables positioning the demand curve, missing even an age measure, probably the most important single variable. There was no control for adverse selection. As acknowledged by the authors, the choice of a few plan characteristics—mental health and substance abuse accounting for three of the seven—made it likely that these proxied the presence of a generous plan overall. The authors may mistakenly have attributed to the singled-out variables the effect of many plan design features. There was no distinction between the cost-shifting effect of coverage and the demand-response effect in terms of influence on premiums. Finally, coverages were measured in a simple "yes-or-no" form. The "premium regression" was actually a form of average health care demand equation, with many familiar specification problems.[5] These specification problems are so fundamental that it is unlikely that a premium-regression approach can be helpful in estimating the cost of coverage features.

In most circumstances, an employer concerned about the cost of a benefit change would not refer to a published simulation model or to a regression equation but would discuss the matter with benefit consultants employed by the carrier or from the specialized benefit consulting industry. These consultants combine knowledge of the employer with "experience" in related cases to give advice to the employer. It is difficult to criticize or commend these methods because the formula for making predictions and even the experience behind the estimates are not usually divulged.[6] The method used in this chapter is akin to the benefit consulting approach, although the methods used here are described in detail. As much information as possible (within time and resource limitations) was gained about a representative set of small employers in Connecticut. This was combined with "experience" in other cases to develop estimates. The assumptions and sources of data used here are set out in the next section.

Combining Plan and Research Data

This section contains a description of a method for forecasting the effects of changes in payment systems for mental health services on the use and cost of mental health services, applied in this chapter to the case of a mandated benefit for ambulatory mental health care for small employers in Connecticut.[7] In the material that follows, "services" refers to mental health services including substance abuse services (except where explicitly noted). A "plan" is a services payment system comprehensively defined to include elements of demand-side cost sharing such as deductibles, coinsurance, and limits; provider payment policies such as price limits and prospective payment; and administrative policies such as prior authorization. A "study population" is the members of a single payment system. Examples of possible study populations are federal employees and dependents enrolled in a Blue Cross/Blue Shield High Option Plan, employees and dependents of a private firm enrolled in the same health plan, or a group of Medicare beneficiaries. In this chapter the study population is the covered employees and dependents of small employers in Connecticut.

The method consists essentially of two steps. The first step is calibration of a model of demand for services. In this step (described in more detail below), information about the study population is combined with information about patterns of service use from research studies to make up a description of demand for services by the study population. Information about a study sample is always limited and is always less than the researcher would need to make fully accurate forecasts. The calibration step takes advantage of whatever information is available for the study population, supplementing study population data where necessary with information from outside research. For example, it might be known that in the existing plan, paying 50 percent of costs to a covered limit of $2,000 per year, the average annual expenditure on ambulatory services was $500 per user. Interest is in predicting the effect of an increase in the covered limit per year from $2,000 to $3,000. To estimate the cost effect of this change requires information about the distribution of users around the mean of $500. This distributional information would be drawn from research studies. In this example, the calibration step combines data from the study population about mean use with data from research about distribution to develop a more complete picture of demand. The calibration step is taken once for each study population.

The second step in the method is simulation of the effect of a plan change, for example, the effect of an increase in the covered limit from $2,000 to $3,000 for ambulatory services. Simulation uses the model of demand calibrated in the first step to forecast the effects. The base level of demand is determined in the first step. This, together with assumptions about demand response, is the basis of predictions about the effects of plan changes. Continuing the example, information about mean use (from the study population) and the distribution of users around the mean (from research studies) gives information about how many users are to be affected by an increase in the limit. An assumption about demand response then leads to a prediction of how much the affected users change their behavior. Assumptions about demand response are made based on research on mental health services use. The simulation step can be taken many times for each study population, once for each plan change of interest. Multiple changes in a plan can be examined at once.

Both the calibration and the simulation steps in the forecasting model are based on the general presumption that the underlying patterns of service use in a study population can be characterized by certain regularities, information about which has been gained from services research. In the calibration step, primary interest is in using outside information to compile a more complete description of the underlying patterns of demand. In the simulation step, outside information is used as a basis for predicting response to plan changes.

The simulation model is capable of forecasting the effects of demand-side coverage policies, supply-side payment policies, and administrative practices. (Alternative coverages for ambulatory mental health care are the only policies addressed in this analysis.) Assumptions about the effects of a plan change are necessary to forecast its effects on the study population. It is recognized that, although the information about some behavior responses is reasonably good (such as the response of demand for ambulatory services to changes in coverage), the information about many important responses is weak.

To choose one among many possible examples, there is little basis for a confident estimate of the effect of a change in coverage for ambulatory services on demand for inpatient services.

The basic structure of the forecasting method is summarized in figure 11.1.

Calibration: Describing the Underlying Pattern of Demand

Typically, a decision maker must forecast the effect of plan changes when *only certain statistics on service use are known* for a recent year. The decision maker might know total inpatient care costs, number of admissions by DRG, average LOS by DRG, ambulatory care costs, number of ambulatory users, and average price per ambulatory visit. Different information is available for different study populations. For some study populations, no DRG breakdowns may be available, for example. For other study populations, all that may be available is total number of inpatient admissions, total costs, and total LOS. The model described here is designed to make use of this readily available (but incomplete) information by supplementing it with information from other studies to help describe likely patterns of use in the study population, improving the accuracy of the forecasts.

Complete information about a study population can be obtained only by direct access to all services used (whether covered or uncovered by the current plan). It might be important, for example, in analysis of a plan change to know the distribution of the total number of inpatient days per person per year or the frequency with which persons use both inpatient and ambulatory services in the same year. Data on these aspects of use could be accessed directly from service records. Unfortunately, such data, and many other characteristics of use by persons in a plan, are not usually available.

In the best of real-world circumstances, the researcher has access to a claims file for the study population, has a large budget, and is under no time pressure. Claims files have many limitations. All data pertinent for forecasting benefit changes are not contained on claims, and claims files do not generally contain information about uncovered services. Finally, claims files are expensive and time consuming to analyze.

In more typical situations calling for predicting effects of plan changes for public policy or policy by private payers, some summary information of the type listed above is available from claims experience, and the researcher has a small budget and limited time. Use of outside information in these circumstances can be helpful. The incorporation of outside information with "known facts" about use in a plan is referred to here as *calibration*.

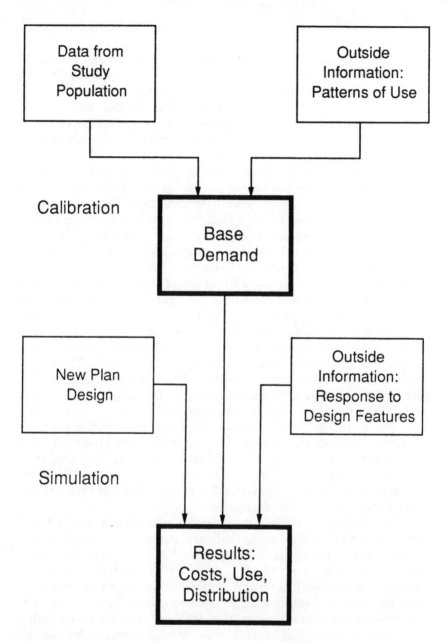

Figure 11.1   The structure of the forecasting model

One of Connecticut's large private insurance companies supplied data on the experience of mental health benefits costs to the Connecticut Department of Mental Health. These data were made available to this project on the condition that the carrier and the employers remain unidentified. Data are in the form of a "standard study of mental health claims" produced by the carrier. Utilization data are from approximately thirty-five hundred employees and dependents. All employers have twenty-five employees or fewer, and all have the minimum mental health benefits, 50 percent to $2,000 covered limit and sixty inpatient days per year (described above). Summary utilization data are provided in table 11.1. These firms voluntarily provide insurance and are subject to the state's mental health mandate.

Psychiatric and substance abuse amounted to about 18 percent of total charges and payments by the carrier. Covered charges for inpatient psychiatric care made up 70 percent of total covered charges and an even higher share of payments. All figures reported here can be regarded as estimates for ongoing costs because they reflect one year's use by a relatively small population. Inpatient psychiatric and substance abuse costs can be expected to vary greatly year by year because of the relatively low frequency of these events. There were only a total of nine claims for inpatient care processed during 1989 for the study sample. Thus, estimates for inpatient care should be regarded as carrying large standard errors.

For all categories of treatment for inpatient care, payments account for almost all covered costs, reflecting the plan's generous coverage of inpatient costs. Beneficiaries bear significant cost sharing for outpatient and office-based claims. Payments are 52 percent of covered costs for psychiatric outpatient facility and office claims, and 83 percent for other diagnoses.

To calculate average cost per user of office-based care, we need the number of persons using that care. According to the data supplied to the Connecticut Department of Mental Health, there were 103 persons who made an office claim for psychiatric care without making an inpatient claim and 20 persons who made an outpatient facility claim without making an inpatient claim. Six persons made an inpatient psychiatric claim. Some of these would have used office or outpatient care. The maximum number of users of what we call office-based care is thus $103 + 20 + 6 = 129$. This assumes no overlap of the office-based and outpatient-based users and that all inpatient users used some office or outpatient care. The minimum number is 103, assuming complete overlap with the outpatient category and that no inpatient users use any office or outpatient care. We make a conservative assumption (to keep use per person high) and assume

Table 11.1 Cost Summary for Small Employers in Connecticut, 1989

Category	Inpatient		Outpatient Facility and Office		Total	
	Covered	Paid	Covered	Paid	Covered	Paid
Psychiatric	$147.9	$144.3	$63.8	$33.0	$211.7	$177.3
	(21.1%)	(21.5%)	(8.1%)	(5.2%)	(14.2%)	(13.6%)
Substance abuse	$44.5	$42.7	$11.5	$11.0	$56.1	$53.7
	(6.4%)	(6.4%)	(1.5%)	(1.7%)	(3.8%)	(4.1%)
Other diagnoses	$507.1	$484.1	$712.7	$589.2	$1,219.9	$1,073.2
	(72.5%)	(72.1%)	(90.3%)	(93.0%)	(82.0%)	(82.3%)
Total	$699.5	$671.1	$788.1	633.2	$1,487.7	$1,304.2
	(100.0%)	(100.0%)	(100.0%)	(100.0%)	(100.0%)	(100.0%)

Notes: Money amounts are in thousands of dollars; the percentages within each column are in parentheses. The source of the data is a private insurance company covering a number of small employers. Data are made available through the Connecticut Department of Mental Health. Figures are for claims processed in 1989. Inpatient care includes physician charges associated with care and partial hospitalizations. Data are for active employees and dependents. (Two claims for a total of $264 in the other diagnoses category are for retirees.) Payments are what the carrier would pay before the application of coordination of benefits rules. Psychiatric diagnoses include ICD-9 codes (from the *International Classification of Diseases,* Ninth Edition) in the ranges 290–302, 306–319, V40, V61–V62, and V71.0. Substance abuse diagnoses are ICD-9 costs in the 303–305 range.

that there is overlap in 10 of 20 outpatient facility users and that 5 of 6 inpatient users make some contact with the outpatient facility or office sector. Thus, the total number of users is estimated to be 103 + (20 − 10) + (6 − 5) = 114. For psychiatric use, 87 percent of the outpatient facility and office-based costs were office based, so these claims will hereafter be referred to as "office" claims, and outpatient and office-based users will be referred to as "office" users. With the number of office users at 114 and the total office claims covered at $63,768 and paid at $33,008, the average covered costs per user were $559 and the average payments per user were $289. Office-based mental health payments are about 2.5 percent of total plan payments. The simulation model was calibrated to lead to a plan-paid cost of $33,008 with 114 users.

It should be clear that the information available is incomplete. Most importantly, the frequency of high- and low-cost users is not known. This information is critical when plan changes are contemplated with different effects on persons dependent on their level of use. A deductible hits nearly everyone, but the plan savings are not $200 per user because some users will not use $200 and some who would use more may be discouraged from seeking any treatment at all. The increase in the covered limit from $2,000 to $3,000 will affect only those who would use more than $1,000. The effect on the plan will depend on how much more these people would use.

Although the distribution of users across ranges of visits and costs for the study population is not known to the forecaster, a good deal of experience has accumulated about the distribution of use in research studies and other plans. Use of this experience can help in making more accurate estimates of the effects of changes on the study population. Our specific calibration approach here is to take the shaping parameter (a standard deviation from a lognormal) from outside research and use the study population to position the distribution of users. Based on a review of several studies, it seems that populations differ mostly in the rate of use and the mean demand. The shape of the distribution around the mean is roughly constant.

The most thoroughly studied users of health care were the four thousand people who spent up to five years participating in the Rand Health Insurance Experiment during the 1970s. Although this is a relatively small group of people in which to study a low-frequency event such as ambulatory mental health use, this research study has some important compensating advantages. First, the sample population was chosen to be nationally representative and was followed for three to five years. Second, very detailed information is available about this group, with a minimum of inaccuracy introduced by non-reporting of use. Third, although the Rand population was divided into many insurance plans, all plans were relatively generous in coverage of ambulatory mental health care. All plans had a family stop-loss feature of no more than $1,000 for all health expenses, after which all care was free.

Information about the distribution of users in year 2 of the HIE was used to calibrate the model of demand (Wells et al. 1982). During the second year of the HIE, 163 persons used a mental health service. The distribution of users across ranges of visits is shown in figure 11.2. About 61 percent of users made one to ten visits. How can this be used to help with our problem of forecasting the effect of the benefit change for the study population?

Information from the HIE can be summarized in the form of a functional distribution of users. The shape of the distribution of health care use is generally skewed. There are many users with small amounts of expenditures, visits, or other measures of use, but the distribution has a long tail signifying that there are a few heavy users. A number of families of distributions can fit this general shape. In this model, conditional on being positive, the annual distribution of expenses (or visits) for ambulatory care is lognormal.

Specifically,

$$y = \ell n(x),$$

where y is expenditures for ambulatory care and x is normal (μ, σ).

The exact shape of the lognormally distributed y will depend on the choice of the two parameters μ and σ (the mean and standard deviation of the normally distributed variable x).

We seek the μ and σ that give the best summary or fit to the year 2 data from the HIE. Fit is measured by a grouped R^2 statistic, defined as follows.

Letting i $= 1, \ldots, N$ be the number of categories,
f_i $=$ the actual relative frequency in the category,
$\hat{f_i}$ $=$ the fitted relative frequency in the category,
R^2 $= 1 - RSS/TSS$, where
$TSS = f_i(f_i - 1/N)^2$
$RSS = f_i(f_i - \hat{f_i})^2$.

The best-fitting lognormal distribution is one with $\mu = 1.9$ and $\sigma = 1.4$, shown in figure 11.2 and compared with the actual data from the HIE. The best-fitting lognormal is a close fit for some groups and not so close for others. Keep in mind that the observed distribution for the HIE was based only on 163 users—the 4.9 percent of the users who used forty-one to fifty visits corresponds to only 8 people. The shape of the actual data from the HIE would therefore change from

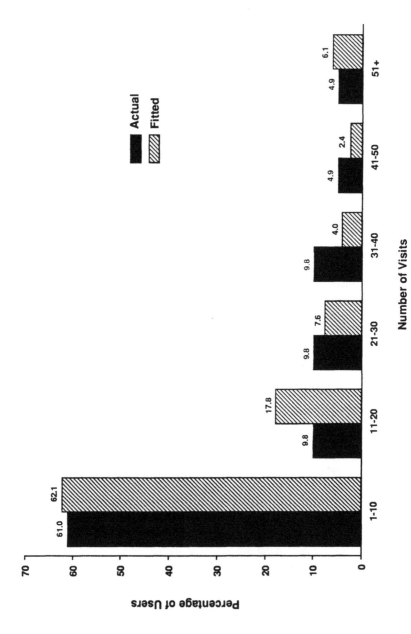

Figure 11.2   The fitted and actual distribution of ambulatory visits

year to year as a different group of users appeared, even if the underlying process for generating use was unchanged.

Data from several other populations were also fit with a lognormal. In the case of federal employees with the high-option plan and two proprietary data sources, the μ parameter providing the best fit varies considerably, from 1.4 to 2.3, but the best-fitting σ is relatively constant at 1.3, 1.4, 1.3.

Data from these research studies and from the Connecticut application can now be combined. Based on the research studies, the shape of the distribution is assumed to be described by a lognormal with a variance parameter $\sigma = 1.3$. The curve will be positioned by the Connecticut mean. This is done using the simulation model. For any (μ,σ) and benefit plan (with up to three linear segments), the model generates the relative frequency of users at visits 1–60 and 60+. (This will be described in more detail below). Then, given a price and a number of users, it is straightforward to compute plan costs. The process for finding the μ for the Connecticut application is to work backward, knowing that the total plan-paid costs for the ambulatory mental health benefit are $33,008. By iterative methods, in the presence of the actual Connecticut benefit at a price of $85 per visit and $\sigma = 1.3$, μ is adjusted until the distribution of demand is such as to just yield a plan cost of $33,008. The μ that solves this is μ = 1.56675.

At this point, we have an estimated *distribution of visits and expenditures,* not just a mean and total cost. Specifically, each visit between the first and the sixtieth is associated with a probability. These initial probabilities are consistent with the calibrated lognormal so that, in the presence of the actual benefit, the observed costs are implied. Thus, the distribution gives back the mean we know to be true, and its shape is consistent with the shape of distributions observed from other studies.

Demand Response

There are several considerations that are important for modeling demand response. A change in cost sharing affects the level of use. A benefit can be characterized by deductibles, a cost-sharing range, and a limit on coverage. A change in cost sharing will generally affect the number of users as well as the level of use. The assumptions made to account for these considerations are described here.

Demand, given use, is linear in cost sharing. Response is a parameter, chosen here to be 0.5. A 0.5 means that demand with no insurance is 50 percent of demand with full insurance. This is chosen (in conjunction with the effect of cost sharing on the number of users) to be in line with the demand response observed in the HIE. If, for example, for users at a certain point in the distribution of use, the cost sharing rises from 25 to 50 percent, the number of visits would fall by 12.5 percent (=[0.50 − 0.25]*0.5).

Demand-side cost sharing can be specified in the model with up to three linear segments, thereby accommodating deductibles and limits. Segments are set in dollar terms. Quantity demanded is consistent with utility maximization. For users at each part of the distribution, quantity is calculated by first finding the quantity demanded at each of the three prices possible. Then, "consumer surplus" is figured for each price. Finally, quantity is determined by the price-demand equality that is associated with the maximum consumer surplus. This multistage procedure is necessary because it is not possible to tell in advance which segment of the benefit schedule will be relevant to utility maximization. With declining-block pricing, there may be more than one local maximization, and total conditions must be checked.

The number of users can be affected by cost sharing. Some simple assumptions are made about this for three groups of users, the "high users," the "intermediate users," and the "low users." The rationale for the approach is that there are some fixed nonmonetary costs associated with entering treatment that vary across persons. For high users, these fixed costs are small in relation to the total value of treatment, so changes in cost sharing affect only level of use, not the use decision itself. For some low users, the fixed costs are significant and, unless cost sharing is generous, the low users would not undergo treatment at all. The intermediate users fall in between.

It is assumed first of all that anyone who is willing to demand at least twenty visits at a zero price will be a user no matter what the cost sharing. Some intermediate users who would be at eleven to twenty visits with no cost sharing may drop out altogether. This is made dependent on the *total cost* to the user of fifteen visits. The total cost is the relevant measure in the use/no-use decision, because it is the total cost of the range of visits contemplated (such as fifteen) that affects the consumer surplus associated with using. In this formulation, a deductible of $200 would have the same effect on the use/nonuse of the intermediate level users, those around fifteen visits, as would copayment that led to a $200 out-of-pocket (OOP) cost for the same level of visits. Although this makes sense from a theoretical point of view, there is little empirical evidence for how the form of cost sharing affects the use decision.

Specifically, for intermediate users, a change in OOP costs at fifteen visits is assumed to have a linear effect on the number of users. A value is chosen, here, 0.25, equal to the fraction of users who would drop use altogether if the benefit plan changed from complete coverage to no coverage. The reduction in users is in proportion to the change in OOP costs for fifteen visits.

A similar assumption is made for the low users, those who would make up to ten visits with no cost sharing. They are more likely to drop out of treatment, so the value of 0.5 is chosen to say that, if cost sharing goes from complete coverage to no coverage, 50 percent of the low users will stop treatment.

In sum, a change from no to complete cost sharing has three effects: 25 percent of intermediate users stop using; 50 percent of low users stop using; and, for all users, quantity demanded falls 50 percent. Each of these three values was chosen to be consistent with research evidence and theory. To give an idea of the overall magnitude of the effect of cost sharing in this model with these parameter values, in the Connecticut data a full-coverage plan would have 136 users and a total cost of $109,360. With no coverage, there would be 91 users and a total cost of $44,834. Full coverage increases demand about 2.5 times. This is a large demand response that is justified on the basis of mental health services research.

Results and Discussion

With the present coverage, I estimate OOP costs to be $34,504 and total costs to be $67,512. OOP costs are slightly higher than plan-paid costs because a few users exceed $2,000 per year. Eliminating coverage would decrease total costs by about one-third, while of course reducing plan-paid costs to zero. OOP costs would increase about 30 percent to $44,834, as shown in table 11.2.

The consequences of one benefit reduction and one benefit expansion are also summarized in table 11.2. Changing the dollar limit on coverage to $1,000 saves 21 percent of costs for the plan. Savings are much less than 50 percent because most users stop before $1,000 of use even with the $2,000 limit. The increase in OOP costs is small because, although users pay more per visit after $1,000, this is partly offset by the reduction in use brought about by the OOP price increase.

The benefit expansion considered is a reduction in the cost sharing to 20 percent, for the first $1,000. Although total costs increase only 16 percent as the result of this change, the benefit expansion is expensive to the plan, increasing its costs by 73 percent to $57,065.

Table 11.2 Effects of Coverage Changes in Ambulatory Mental Health Benefits

Variable	Users		Plan Costs		OOP Costs		Total Costs	
	Number	% Change	Amount	% Change	Amount	% Change	Amount	% Change
Present coverage: 50% to $2,000	114		$33,008		$34,504		$67,512	
Eliminate benefit	91	−20.2	$0	−100.0	$44,834	+29.9	$44,834	−33.6
Reduce limit: 50% to $1,000	113	−0.9	$25,902	−21.5	$35,220	+2.1	$61,123	−9.5
Reduce cost sharing: 0–$1,000: 20% $1,001–2,000: 50%	127	+11.4	$57,065	72.9	$24,959	−39.3	$78,022	+15.6

The plan bears most of the cost of the increased use and the cost shift from OOP payments because of the cost-sharing reduction.

The costs of a benefit change in the small employer sector in Connecticut are dominated by the effects on the low-level user. Any change in the covered limit up or down has little effect on costs, but a change in the cost sharing (either in the form of a copayment change or a deductible) would have large cost consequences. The high copayment requirement is effective in keeping costs down. There seem to be few opportunities for savings in relation to the present mandated benefit of 50 percent coverage to $2,000. The most obvious possible benefit reduction, decreasing the covered limit to $2,000, would save only 21 percent of costs to the plan, with some of these savings, of course, taking the form of costs shifted to employees.

Prediction of the cost of a benefit change requires integration of data from research with data from the plan under analysis. At minimum, behavioral response information must be added from outside. Usually, more outside information is needed because data on present patterns of use within plans are very incomplete. An analyst is often confronted with averages when distributions are called for. Outside information can be used in these circumstances, as the method used in this chapter illustrates. There are broad similarities in patterns of mental health use that can be the basis for estimates in applications.

The case considered here is the possible mandating of mental health benefits within compulsory insurance for small employers in Connecticut. The basis for cost estimates was the health insurance experience of small employers who voluntarily cover workers. The number of users and average cost per user from the insurer were supplemented with data on patterns of use from research populations to allow analysis of the effects of alternative coverage designs.

The method described in this chapter is intended to be useful to public- and private-sector decision makers who do not have the time or financial resources to conduct detailed plan-specific empirical investigations before making policy. In some cases, decision makers, such as employers or representatives of a state, do not have direct access to relevant data and must rely on insurers for data summaries. Making best use of the available information requires combining it with data on responses and patterns from earlier studies.

Acknowledgments

Support for this research was provided by National Institute of Mental Health grant 1K05MH00832-01. The assistance of Michael

Hogan, Commissioner, and Susan Essock, Director of Psychological Services, at the Connecticut Department of Mental Health was essential to this research. I am grateful to Randy Ellis, Barry Friedman, and Will Manning for comments on an earlier draft.

Notes

1. The Congressional Research Service (1988) estimated administrative costs for the smallest firms to be 35–40 percent of claims paid for the smallest firms (fewer than ten employees) compared to only 5–8 percent for firms with twenty-five hundred or more employees. Furthermore, restrictive underwriting practices have exacerbated the cost problem for small employers forced to buy insurance at "community rates" (Nadel 1989).

2. An important difference, discussed by Frank and McGuire (1990), is in how the cost of the legislation should be understood. In the mandate literature, *cost* has meant the increase in health insurance cost due to the required coverage. Labor market effects were ignored. This limited view of cost is justified in the usual mandate context because a mandate for mental health imposes a small change in a firm's required fringe benefit contribution in the region of the freely chosen level of fringes. The net effect on a firm's compensation costs is thus likely to be small and could be disregarded.

This argument does not work in the case of required mental health coverage within a mandate for health insurance for small firms. An imposed increase in fringe benefits in conjunction with a forced increase in fringes in the form of mandated health insurance may not have merely a second-order effect on compensation costs. Furthermore, if some affected employees are paid near the minimum wage, the firm may not be able to reduce wages to compensate for the required increase in fringe benefit costs. The labor market effects can probably be safely neglected in the case of a mandate applying to firms that have freely chosen to offer health insurance; these effects cannot be safely ignored when the incremental coverage is added to health insurance imposed on firms that, in the absence of regulation, offer no coverage at all.

3. The continuation of coverage provisions does provide to workers a kind of insurance against job loss. The cost of this regulation to the employers may be much less than its value to the workers if workers have other options, such as a spouse's coverage or Medicaid, after employment termination.

4. The four measures, their signs, and their significance were a mandate for psychologists' services ($-$, $t = 0.7$), inpatient, mental health coverage ($+$, $t = 0.1$), alcoholism treatment ($+$, $t = 0.1$), and drug abuse treatment ($+$, $t = 1.6$).

5. The classic discussion of econometric problems in nonexperimental studies of health insurance and demand is Newhouse, Phelps, and Marquis (1980).

6. Sharfstein, Muszynski, and Myers (1984) included two examples of explicit methods used by benefits consultants to forecast mental health coverage costs. Hay Associates used a model that is based on the costs of coverage for federal employees, simulating the effects of various coverage features. In a second model, Health Data Associates developed a point system rating various features of coverage. The source of the points was not described.

7. This section describes the model's capabilities only as they are relevant to forecasting ambulatory mental health care use. A more complete description of the simulation model is available from the author.

References

Blue Cross and Blue Shield Association. 1989. *Mandated Coverage Laws Enacted through 1988*. Washington, D.C.: Blue Cross/Blue Shield.

Buchanan, Joan L., Emmett B. Keeler, John E. Rolph, and Martin R. Holmer. 1991. "Simulating Health Expenditures under Alternative Insurance Plans." *Management Science* 37:1067–91.

Congressional Research Service, Library of Congress. 1988. *Cost and Effects of Extending Health Insurance Coverage*. Washington, D.C.: U.S. Government Printing Office.

Frank, Richard G., and Thomas G. McGuire. 1990. "Compulsory Employer-based Health Insurance and Coverage for Mental Health Services." *Health Affairs* 9, no. 1:32–42.

Gabel, Jon R., and Gail A. Jensen. 1989. "The Price of State Mandated Benefits." *Inquiry* 26:419–31.

ICF, Inc. 1987. *Health Care Coverage and Costs in Small and Large Businesses*. Report prepared for the U.S. Small Business Administration, April.

———. 1989. "State Mandated Benefits and the Small Firm's Decision To Offer Insurance." March. Typescript.

Jensen, Gail A., and Michael A. Morrisey. 1990. "Group Health Insurance: A Hedonic Approach." *Review of Economics and Statistics* 72:38–44.

Keeler, Emmett B., Kenneth B. Wells, Willard G. Manning, J. David Rumpel, and Janet M. Hanley. 1986. *The Demand for Episodes of Mental Health Services*. Report R-3432-NIMH. Santa Monica, Calif.: Rand Corporation. October.

Manning, Willard G., Kenneth B. Wells, Joan L. Buchanan, R. Burciaga Valdez, and Joseph P. Newhouse. 1987. "Effects of Mental Health Insurance: Evidence from the Health Insurance Experiment." Santa Monica, Calif.: Rand Corporation, December. Typescript.

Marquis, M. Susan, Joan L. Buchanan, Emmett B. Keeler, John E. Rolph, and Manbing Sze. 1989. *Mandating Health Insurance Benefits for Employees: Effects on Health Care Use and Employers' Costs*. Rand Note N-2911-DOL. Santa Monica, Calif.: Rand Corporation, June.

McGuire, Thomas G. 1989. "Financing and Reimbursement for Mental Health Services." In Carl Taube and David Mechanic (eds.): *The Future of Mental Health Services Research,* chapter 6, pp. 87–111. Washington, D.C.: National Institute of Mental Health.

Nadel, Mark V. 1989. "Health Insurance: Availability and Adequacy for Small Businesses." Statement before the Subcommittee on Health and the Environment, Committee on Energy and Commerce, House of Representatives, October 16, published as GAO/T-HRD-90-02. Washington, D.C.: U.S. Government Printing Office.

Newhouse, Joseph P., Charles E. Phelps, and M. Susan Marquis. 1980. "On Having Your Cake and Eating It Too: Econometric Problems in Estimating the Demand for Health Services." *Journal of Econometrics* 13:365–90.

Sharfstein, Steven S., Sam Muszynski, and Evelyn Myers. 1984. *Health Insurance and Psychiatric Care: Update and Appraisal.* Washington, D.C.: American Psychiatric Association.

U.S. General Accounting Office. 1989. *Health Insurance: An Overview of the Working Uninsured.* GAO/HRD-89-45. February.

Wells, Kenneth B., Willard G. Manning, Jr., Naihua Duan, John Ware, Jr., and Joseph P. Newhouse. 1982. *Cost Sharing and the Demand for Ambulatory Mental Health Services.* R-2960-HHS. Santa Monica, Calif.: Rand Corporation, September.

Zeckhauser, Michael. 1970. "Medical Insurance: A Case Study of the Trade-off between Risk Spreading and Appropriate Incentives." *Journal of Economic Theory* 2:10–26.

PART IV

Experimentation

ontrolled experiments have long been a primary tool in clinic research. Performing experiments with services delivery systems and insurance plans is considerably more complicated (and costly) than is the typical randomized clinical trial. Nevertheless, research and demonstration programs can be the source of valuable learning for the design of mental health services systems. The recognition of this significant payoff to research demonstrations has led to wider use of this research vehicle by mental health services researchers.

Demonstration research involves a large number of practical difficulties. Such challenges range from maintaining randomization to being able to locate subjects for follow-up. Because demonstrations are introduced into the natural environment of the patient population, a great deal of the control found in clinical trials is not present. The challenge to researchers is to design their studies to take advantage of existing technologies, such as management information systems and to minimize the problems associated with incomplete control over the study environment.

To date, some of the most significant findings in the area of mental health services research have emerged from research demonstrations. The RAND Health Insurance Experiment has produced convincing results on the demand response to cost sharing for ambulatory mental health services. The Training in Community Living project, in Madison, Wisconsin, led to the finding that the so-called PACT (Program in Assertive Community Treatment) was a cost-effective approach to organizing services for individuals with severe mental illness.

Researchers who perform randomized clinical trials are increasingly aware that the interventions they study must pass a cost-effectiveness test in addition to a clinical efficacy test. This is because health care payers need to be convinced of the wisdom of an investment in new technology. Thus, if a technology is to be adopted into mainstream clinical practice, cost-effectiveness issues must be addressed.

The chapters in this section reflect both the use of research demonstrations to test models of organizing and financing mental health services and the introduction of cost-effectiveness analysis into clinical trials. Chapter 12, by Mark Kamlet, Martcia Wade, David Kupfer, and Ellen Frank, uses data from a long-term clinical trial for the treatment of recurrent depression to examine the cost effectiveness of various interventions over the life course. The chapter presents both a new method and important substantive findings.

The two research demonstrations reported on here focus on the effect of capitation and the HMO organizational form for treating individuals with severe mental illness who are supported by public health care programs. The report from Minnesota (chapter 13, by Michael Finch, Nicole Lurie, Jon Christianson, and Ira Moscovice) describes mental health and substance abuse treatment in a traditional HMO setting. The report from Rochester, New York (chapter 14, by Haroutun Babigian, Olivia Mitchell, Phyllis Marshall, and Sylvia Reed), presents an approach to introducing capitation into a traditional public mental health services system. In chapter 15, Robert Schmitz reports on an experiment conducted under CHAMPUS. The experiment tests the effect on mental health use of a contracted provider network.

These chapters, taken as a group, offer a set of approaches to learning about mental health services that has not been widely used by economists working on economics and mental health. The chapters illustrate the rich potential offered by research demonstrations for studying basic questions of economic policy in the mental health services system.

12

Cost-Utility Analysis of Maintenance Treatment for Recurrent Depression: A Theoretical Framework and Numerical Illustration

Mark S. Kamlet, Ph.D.,
Martcia Wade, Ph.D.,
David J. Kupfer, M.D.,
and Ellen Frank, Ph.D.

C linical depression affects 1–3 percent of the U.S. population during any six-month period, according to conservative estimates (Myers et al. 1984).[1] The lifetime incidence of depression is over 15 percent. Depression is a debilitating illness that, as described by Stoudemire et al. (1987),

> usually leads to withdrawal from social, work, and family activities, decreased motivation, feelings of hopelessness, low self-esteem, pessimism, and self-blame. Withdrawal from family relationships can result in separation, divorce, and parent-child problems. Irritability, anger, and withdrawal can cause depressed patients to become isolated in their misery as others are driven away by their despair. Depression may lead to poor work performance, absenteeism, and unemployment. The cognitive impairments (difficulty in concentrating and memory loss) can resemble a form of dementia. . . . Depressed individuals have a high rate of physical complaints, especially pain, headaches, insomnia, and digestive problems.

Depression is linked not only to morbidity but also to mortality. Monkoff et al. (1973) suggested that 60 percent or more of people who commit suicide have clinically significant depression as the primary psychiatric disorder, accounting for about sixteen thousand deaths per year (Stoudemire et al. 1987).

For many people, depression is a recurrent phenomenon. It has been estimated that 50 percent of those suffering one depressive episode will suffer another within the ensuing ten years and that those who have experienced two depressive episodes have almost a 90 percent chance of experiencing a third. Once the disorder has become recurrent, rates of relapse are high. Keller et al. (1982a, 1982b) indicated that individuals with three or more lifetime episodes of depression may have relapse rates as high as 40 percent within fifteen weeks after recovery from a given episode. Klerman (1978) indicated that 65 percent of recurrent depressives have some degree of relapse within the first year if untreated.

Given the debilitating nature of depression and the high rate of relapse, attention has focused recently on ways to treat patients between depressive episodes. These "maintenance treatments" are intended to lower the probability, frequency, or duration of future episodes. Early research on maintenance treatments involved the use of lithium carbonate (e.g., Coppen et al. 1971), although this generally proved less effective than hoped (Glen, Johnson, and Shepherd 1984). Subsequent research indicated that imipramine is more effective than lithium carbonate in protecting against depressive recurrences, particularly for individuals with severe index episodes (Prien et al. 1984).

There has been substantial interest not only in drug maintenance therapies for recurrent depression, but also in psychotherapy. Klerman et al. (1984) suggested that, while medication affects neurovegetative symptoms of depression, such as sleep and appetite, psychotherapy affects aspects of depression like mood, self-esteem, and social functioning. Based on the premise that depression develops in a psychosocial context, recent research examined the effects of interpersonal therapy (IPT) as a maintenance treatment. IPT helps the patient understand and renegotiate difficult interpersonal relations. It is thought to be instrumental in recovery from depressive episodes and also may help prevent future episodes. This approach helps the patient develop more effective strategies for dealing with social and interpersonal problems associated with the onset of depression. In several studies IPT was found to be effective in relieving depressive symptoms and in delaying or preventing recurrences (DiMascio et al. 1979; Weismann 1979, 1984; Prusoff et al. 1980; Klerman et al. 1974), but all of these studies involved follow-up periods of one year or less.

In view of the promise of maintenance drug and therapy treatment, some have recommended maintenance treatment as generally desirable for recurrent depression. Angst (1984), for instance, suggested that long-term medication should be initiated to treat unipolar depression after the third episode, especially when the interval between the latest two episodes is relatively short. However, there are costs as well as benefits to drug maintenance treatment. Apart from monetary costs, the drugs often have side effects such as blood pressure and electrocardiogram changes, as well as potential interactions with other medications. Many individuals under imipramine drug treatment report continued sexual dysfunction. Over one-quarter experience unwanted weight gain (Fernstrom, Krowinski, and Kupfer 1986). Constipation, lethargy, and dry mouth can be other side effects of the medication.

In this chapter we present a theoretical framework for a cost-utility analysis of three maintenance treatments for recurrent depression: imipramine, IPT, and a combination of the two. Our framework is demonstrated using illustrative data from the first eighteen months of the Pittsburgh Study of Maintenance Therapies on Recurrent Depression (Frank, Kupfer, and Perel 1989), a study being conducted at the Western Psychiatric Institute and Clinic, University of Pittsburgh, under principal investigators Dr. Ellen Frank and Dr. David Kupfer and funded by the National Institute of Mental Health.

The Pittsburgh Study subjects meet DSM-III criteria for recurrent depression. They entered the protocol during a clinical episode. They were stabilized and needed to remain stable for a twenty-week period before entering the maintenance phase of the experiment. They were then randomly assigned to one of five maintenance treatment protocols: imipramine drug therapy, maintenance IPT psychotherapy (IPT-M) with a placebo drug, IPT-M without a placebo, IPT-M and imipramine drug therapy, and placebo. Subjects continue maintenance treatment for three years or until they have a recurrence of a depressive episode. A total of 128 individuals entered the maintenance phase of the research.

The data on the efficacy of the different maintenance treatments for the second eighteen months of the experiment, which are just now beginning to be analyzed, differ in important ways from the patterns displayed during the first eighteen months. As a result, the numerical results should be considered purely illustrative of the technique of cost-utility analysis and not a substantive analysis of the given maintenance treatments for recurrent depression that are analyzed. In the future we hope to be able to provide a cost-utility analysis based on the full three years of data.

A State-Transition Model for Analyzing Recurrent Depression

For analysis of the efficacy of IPT-M, imipramine treatment, and the combination of the two from an economic perspective, the health benefits that result from them must be converted into measures that are meaningful in terms of the quality and length of life for the individuals receiving maintenance treatment. Additionally, the costs associated with each treatment must be identified and measured. Finally, a comparison must be made between the costs of the treatment and the health effects that result from them.

To do this, we adopt a cost-utility analysis (CUA) approach. CUA evaluates a health intervention by comparing the incremental societal costs of a health intervention and the incremental health benefits that result from it. Typically, the outcome of a CUA is expressed as a ratio, with the units being dollars per quality adjusted life years ($/QALYs).

CUA in health care dates back to such works as Weinstein and Stason (1977). Although they used the term *cost-effectiveness analysis* (CEA) to describe the method they employed, the concept of cost effectiveness has taken on multiple other meanings over time. These range from "saving money while not impairing health" to "the lowest cost way of achieving a given set of health outcomes" (Gramlich 1981; Office of Technology Assessment 1980; Rapoport, Robertson, and Stuart 1982) to "the best way to achieve whatever objectives a decision maker is pursuing."[2] Following the lead of Anderson et al. (1986), Torrance (1986), and Drummond, Stoddart, and Torrance (1987), we use the term *cost-utility analysis* to distinguish the approach here from these other meanings of CEA. Nonetheless, as shorthand we will sometimes use the term *cost effective* to mean that a given health intervention is desirable from a CUA perspective. Similarly, we will sometimes use the term *cost-effectiveness ratio* to refer to the ratio of costs to health effects that result from a health intervention.

CUA has evolved over time toward a well-defined set of methodological procedures for analyzing the efficacy of health interventions from an economic perspective, but several controversies remain in the literature.[3] One concerns the use of discount rates. The issue is not only what discount rate to use but also whether both health outcomes and costs or only costs should be discounted. We choose several discount rates, 0, 3, and 5 percent, and examine the results obtained when discounting both costs and health outcomes and when discounting only costs.

Another controversy in the CUA literature occurs when, as is the case here, the effect of a health intervention involves more than direct medical costs and more than health narrowly conceived. Here, there are effects of maintenance treatment on the social functioning of individuals, on their work, and on their amount of leisure. As discussed in Kamlet (1991), these effects can in principle be either costed out and included in the costs of the health intervention (the numerator of the CUA cost-effectiveness ratio) or measured in terms of their effect on quality of life and included in the quality of life measure (the denominator of the cost-effectiveness ratio). Following the recommendations of Kamlet (1991), we include direct medical costs and the money equivalent of leisure devoted to treatment (measured in terms of the willingness to pay of the individual for the time involved) as costs in the numerator of the cost-effectiveness ratio. We measure the remaining effects, including the so-called indirect costs of the illness on the ability to work and on productivity at work, in terms of quality of life in the denominator of the cost-effectiveness ratio. We do, however, reexamine the results of our analysis from several of the other approaches that might be adopted on this issue.

When one conducts a CUA of the maintenance treatments considered here, costs and health outcomes must be considered in a dynamic context because they occur continually over the life of a subject. A simple state-transition model is presented for recurrent depression. For any maintenance treatment, an individual at any given time can be in any of three states: (A) not depressed and under the specified maintenance treatment, (B) depressed, or (C) dead. An individual can move from state A to state B—a recurrence; from state A to state C—death by natural causes; from state B to state A—stabilization; or from state B to state C—death by suicide.

The amount of time the individual is in states A and B is stochastic. Given that a state transition is to occur, the model is Markovian in the sense that the probabilities of transitions from state A to state B, state A to state C, and state B to state A are independent of the past history of the individual.

The time line of analysis for a given subject begins when a subject enters the maintenance treatment. The subject is by definition in state A at this initial time. The individual remains stable for a period of time, Y. Then there is a recurrence of depression (i.e., a move from state A to state B). There is some probability, p, that the subject commits suicide during this depressive episode (i.e., moves from state B to state C). If not, the individual remains depressed for a period of time, X, after which there is again stabilization (i.e., subject moves from state B to state A). Let Z denote the expected life-span, assuming that the individual does not die as a result of future depressive episodes (i.e., does not commit suicide). The above process then repeats itself until the individual either commits suicide or survives Z years, at which time the subject dies of natural causes (moves from state A to state C).[4]

In this framework, maintenance treatment is intended to increase Y, the time interval between recurrences. It may also shorten the length and dampen the magnitude of future episodes. The literature offers no direct evidence on these latter possibilities, however, and to be conservative we will restrict the effect of maintenance to its effect on Y.

Quality of life in our model depends on the presence or absence of depression and on the specific maintenance treatment. To be sure, the relationship between quality of life and the specific pattern of depressive episodes is much more complex. The effects of a depressive episode on an individual's social functioning often persist long after the episode itself, particularly in marital and close interpersonal relationships (Bothwell and Weismann 1977). Therefore, if maintenance treatment reduces the frequency of recurrences, it may well improve the quality of life for the individual even during periods of stabilization. But, again, to be conservative we will consider maintenance treatment only as it affects the frequency of episodes.

Adopting this perspective, let ϕ be the quality of life when depressed. The value of ϕ is between 0 and 1, where 0 is death and 1 is perfect health, and ϕ reflects a von Neumann-Morgenstern (VNM)-utility rating of quality of life. As discussed above, it encompasses effects of depression on health, social functioning, work, and leisure. Let β be the quality of life when stable. Like ϕ, β also reflects VNM-utility and is between 0 and 1, where 0 is death and 1 is perfect health.

The direct costs of maintenance treatment include the time of the health professionals involved in the treatment, the use of office space, the cost of any medication and lab work, and the patient's time. Let D represent the direct cost per unit time associated with maintenance treatment while the patient is stable. There are also, of course, medical costs associated with treating depressive episodes. Let T represent the direct cost per episode.

While the state-transition model presented here is simple, it captures the key health, quality of life, and financial aspects required for a CUA of maintenance treatment. At the same time, it makes a variety of simplifying assumptions beyond those that have already been highlighted. The model assumes that there are only two states of mental well-being, healthy and depressed, with no intermediate ground or levels of severity. In fact, many individuals do not return to full quality of life after a depressive episode but may improve only to a certain level of functioning. We also assume that individuals who have a recurrence and are treated do stabilize if they do not commit suicide, although, in fact, some remain chronically depressed. Although some patients have no symptoms and no impairment in social functioning during the intervals between episodes, others do have symptoms. Again, the assumption is such as to make any estimates of the benefits of maintenance treatment conservative.

Additionally, we assume that individuals who are depressed seek professional treatment unless they commit suicide. Weismann and Myers (1978) suggested that fewer than one-quarter of the patients who have clinically significant depressive symptoms ever see a mental health professional (although they estimate that more than 80 percent see a general physician and nearly 60 percent receive psychotropic drugs). Frank and Kamlet (1989), using data from the Baltimore Epidemiological Catchment Area, found that an individual's decision to seek treatment is influenced by such factors as age, marital status, employment status, physical health status, and insurance coverage, as well as mental health status per se. Frank and Gertler (1988), also using data from the Baltimore Epidemiological Catchment Area, reported that only 54 percent of those with mental distress sought a health care provider for their illness. In light of these findings, the assumption that a depressed individual seeks treatment may seem unrealistic. However, it also probably lends a conservative bias to our overall conclusion. While those who do not seek treatment and stabilize spontaneously do not incur treatment costs, they undoubtedly suffer longer and more severe depressions which, in the overall cost-utility analysis, would most probably dominate any reductions in direct costs from not seeking treatment.

Modeling the Cost-Effectiveness Ratio

The time-line framework described above allows us to derive a formula for a cost-effectiveness ratio for maintenance treatment. Initially, assume a deterministic value for X and Y, the length of a depressive episode and the time to recurrence, set in each case equal to their expected values.

Let N be the maximum number of recurrences an individual can experience until the expected life-span is reached. N can be shown to be

$$N = \text{greatest integer less than } [(Z - Y)/(X + Y)]. \qquad (12.1)$$

Let L be the individual's expected life-span upon beginning maintenance treatment, allowing for the possibility of suicide. L can be shown to be

$$L = Y[1 - (1 - p)^N] + (X + Y)[(1 - p) - (1 - p)^N]$$
$$+ (1 - p)^N Z \text{ (for } N > 0). \tag{12.2}$$

Let B be the expected number of nonfatal recurrences the individual will experience. B can be shown to be

$$B = [(1 - p) - (1 - p)^{N+1}]/p. \tag{12.3}$$

Let S be the expected amount of time the individual will be alive and nondepressed. S can be shown to be

$$S = L - BX. \tag{12.4}$$

Let the subscript MT refer to the values of the above variables for an individual experiencing maintenance treatment, and let the subscript SQ represent the values of the same variables for someone who receives no maintenance treatment. Then, without discounting, the direct costs associated with maintenance treatment over the course of the patient's life are

$$S_{MT}D + B_{MT}T. \tag{12.5}$$

The analogous direct costs associated with no maintenance treatment are

$$B_{SQ}T, \tag{12.6}$$

where it is assumed there are no direct costs during stabilized periods under the status quo of no maintenance treatment.

The expected number of quality-adjusted life years after the beginning of maintenance treatment, again without discounting, is

$$\phi B_{MT}X + \beta S_{MT}. \tag{12.7}$$

The analogous expected number of quality-adjusted life years for the same individual not having maintenance treatment is

$$\phi B_{SQ}X + S_{SQ}, \tag{12.8}$$

where it is assumed that quality of life is equal to 1 when stable under the status quo.

Having derived these relationships, a formula for the cost-effectiveness ratio can now be given. It is

$$[S_{MT}D_{MT} + (B_{MT} - B_{SQ})T]/[\phi(B_{MT} - B_{SQ})X + \beta S_{MT} - S_{SQ}]. \tag{12.9}$$

It is straightforward to derive similarly a cost-effectiveness ratio for one maintenance treatment compared to another maintenance

treatment. Let the subscripts $MT1$ and $MT2$ refer to two maintenance treatments. Then, the cost-effectiveness ratio of MT1 relative
to MT2 is

$$[S_{\mathrm{MT1}}D_{\mathrm{MT1}} - S_{\mathrm{MT2}}D_{\mathrm{MT2}} + (B_{\mathrm{MT1}}$$
$$- B_{\mathrm{MT2}})T]/[\phi(B_{\mathrm{MT1}} - B_{\mathrm{MT2}})X + \beta_{\mathrm{MT1}}S_{\mathrm{MT1}} - \beta_{\mathrm{MT2}}S_{\mathrm{MT2}}]. \qquad (12.10)$$

Treating X and Y as deterministic, it is also possible to derive an
analytic equation for the cost-effectiveness ratios (12.9) and (12.10)
that allows for discounting of health outcomes and/or costs. To do so,
let the average direct cost per year incurred by the individual alive
and under maintenance treatment be C_{MT} and that under no maintenance treatment be C_{SQ}. These figures average both costs incurred
while the patient is stable, if any, and costs when the individual is
depressed, weighted by the respective time the individual is in each
state. Then, using a discount rate of r, the numerator of the cost-
effectiveness ratio can be written

$$C_{\mathrm{MT}}e^{-rt}dt - C_{\mathrm{SQ}}e^{-rt}dt = C_{\mathrm{MT}}/r(1 - e^{-rLMT}) - C_{\mathrm{SQ}}/r(1 - e^{-rLSQ}).$$

Similarly, let QOL_{MT} be the average quality of life of the individual when alive under maintenance treatment (averaged between periods in which the individual is stable and periods in which the individual is depressed), and let QOL_{SQ} be the comparable value under
the status quo. Then the numerator of the cost-effectiveness ratio can
be written

$$QOL_{\mathrm{MT}}e^{-rt}dt - QOL_{\mathrm{SQ}}e^{-rt}dt =$$
$$QOL_{\mathrm{MT}}/r(1 - e^{-rLMT}) - QOL_{\mathrm{SQ}}/r(1 - e^{-rLSQ}).$$

So, the cost-effectiveness ratio becomes

$$[C_{\mathrm{MT}}/(1 - e^{-rLMT}) - C_{\mathrm{SQ}}/(1 - e^{-rLSQ})]/[QOL_{\mathrm{MT}}/(1 - e^{-rLMT})$$
$$- QOL_{\mathrm{SQ}}/(1 - e^{-rLSQ})]. \qquad (12.11)$$

It is not straightforward, however, or ultimately even analyt-
ically tractable to relax the assumption that X and Y are deterministic. To deal with this, we derive our estimates of cost-effectiveness
ratios using Monte Carlo analysis. The distributions for X and Y are
specified and an individual's life experience is simulated, with results
for X and Y for each episode and period of stabilization drawn from
these distributions. By doing this a sufficiently large number of times
(generally one thousand in our simulations), one can make accurate
estimates of the expected costs and health outcomes associated with
given maintenance treatments. This Monte Carlo analysis keeps a
running track of costs and health outcomes over time for each simulation. In this setting, it is very easy to account for discounting by

simply weighing each cost and health outcome by the appropriate amount (based on the time of occurrence and the discount rate being employed) and converting it into a present value equivalent. All of our illustrative empirical results presented below are based on these Monte Carlo analyses.

Assigning Numerical Values to the Empirical Parameters of the Model

The various parameters defined above now must be assigned numerical values. We assume that the patient is a 40-year-old woman. This implies that Z, life expectancy contingent on the individual not committing suicide, is 36 years.

IPT-M involves one therapy session each month. Each session lasts sixty minutes. Therapist time at Western Psychiatric Institute, where the sessions are held, is billed at $95 per hour. This is used as a first approximation of the costs of therapists and of the administrative overhead involved in the session. In addition to these costs are the time costs to the patient, which, including transportation, amount to approximately two hours per month. Most empirical studies place an hour of transportation time at 60–80 percent of an average hour of pay, or between $4.95 and $6.60 in 1986 dollars. Including $2 for parking or bus fare, this leads to an opportunity cost of about $14 per visit for the patient and a total direct cost of approximately $110 per month or $1,320 per year for IPT-M.

Drug therapy is estimated to cost approximately $550 per year. This is based on an estimated cost of $0.30 per 50 mg of imipramine, an average daily dose of 200 mg per day, and $120 per year associated with blood work and physician visits.

It is difficult to assign a utility value for ϕ, the quality of life associated with being depressed. Several studies in the literature, however, provide some guidance about reasonable values. Sackett and Torrance (1978) presented brief scenarios of various chronic health states to individuals in the general public. They used the "time tradeoff" method to calibrate the VNM-utility associated with each health state. One of the chronic illnesses considered was a three-month episode of depression. On a scale where 1 represented full health and 0 represented death, the mean daily utility for depression was .44, with a standard error of .024. It is interesting to note the severe diminution of quality of life that depression represents in this rating. Compared with other three-month illnesses, the mean daily utility for depression was lower than that for tuberculosis or dialysis.

It also was rated as lower than having a kidney transplant, a mastectomy for injury, or a mastectomy for breast cancer.

Torrance, Boyle, and Horwood (1982) provided a multiattribute scale of the utility of health states, based again on preferences of the general public. Their scale involves the multiplicative interaction of scales for physical functioning, role functioning, and social-emotional functioning. One of the social-emotional functioning categories is "being anxious or depressed some or a good bit of the time and having very few friends and little contact with others." This condition, accompanied by full physical functioning and full functioning in terms of self-care and being able to work, yields a utility value of .45, with a standard error of .053, where 1 corresponds to a life at full health and 0 to death shortly after birth. Insofar as the emotional functioning of chronically depressed individuals is at least as bad as the category description and is associated with less than full physical, self-care, and occupational functioning, this .45 rating can be seen as an upper boundary for recurrent depression.

Kaplan and Anderson (1988) summarized fifteen years of research on the development of the Quality of Well-being Scale. This scale, based also on preferences of the public toward health states, uses an additive set of subscales for mobility, physical activity, and social activity, weighted by a severity scale based on symptom and problem complexes. It too ranges from 0 to 1. The authors indicated that individuals with depression have a Quality of Well-being Scale score of either .68 or .61, depending on whether they are outpatients or inpatients.

Wells et al. (1989) reported on the functioning and well-being of depressed patients. Depressed individuals were assessed in terms of physical, role, and social functioning as well as perceived overall current health. On scales ranging from 0 to 100, depressed individuals had ratings of 78, 81, and 73 for physical, social, and role functioning, respectively. This was a lower rating on all three scales than for other chronic illnesses such as hypertension, diabetes, arthritis, gastrointestinal problems, and back problems. On the overall health scale, depressed individuals scored 58.7 on a 0 to 100 scale, lower than the above chronic conditions and also lower than advanced coronary artery disease and angina.

Taken as a whole, the literature on the quality of life of depressed individuals provides a relatively consistent picture in which depression is judged to be among the most severe chronic illnesses. We chose a utility value of .45 as a baseline value for ϕ, the quality of life associated with being depressed. We also chose values of .3 and .7 as "reasonably pessimistic" and "reasonably optimistic" values.

Here and throughout, "reasonably optimistic" is defined as a parameter value that makes depression less bad (and therefore makes maintenance treatments less cost effective), and "reasonably pessimistic" is defined conversely.

It is also difficult to assign a value to p, the probability per episode that someone with major depression commits suicide. As indicated above, it has been estimated that some 60 percent of suicides have clinically significant depression as the primary psychiatric disorder. Stoudemire et al. (1987) estimated that some 20,000 deaths per year are secondary to depression. Assuming a 2 percent, six-month prevalence rate for depression, this is about a .0025 chance of suicide per depressive episode. It is unclear whether such a rough calculation is applicable to recurrent depression. Nonetheless, .0025 seems a reasonable base-case value. We use .001 and .01 as the optimistic and pessimistic range for this variable.

Stoudemire et al. (1987) estimated the direct costs of depression to be about $2.1 billion in the aggregate for the United States for 1980. Using a 2 percent, six-month prevalence rate, this implies about $250 (in 1980 dollars) per episode in direct costs. If, for example, two-thirds of those who are depressed seek some form of treatment within six months, this would be about $375 (in 1980 dollars) in direct costs per treated episode, or about $500 per episode in current dollars.

Such overall averages are, again, somewhat misleading. Different choices of provider lead to different direct costs. The direct costs are probably less in the general mental health care sector than in the specialty mental health care sector. Moreover, interviews with experienced health professionals suggest that this $500 figure is quite low. Nonetheless, to be conservative, we chose $500 per episode as our base-case value, using $1,500 and $200 per episode as our range.

Finally, it is also very difficult to assign a value to β, the utility associated with imipramine drug treatment. As described above, a subset of patients on maintenance drug therapy experience side effects. In some instances these side effects are sufficiently severe that they are a significant deterrent to the patient remaining on the maintenance therapy. The magnitude of these side effects, however, remains hard to calibrate and seems to vary substantially across patients. As a result, the analyses of the drug and of the drug and therapy maintenance treatments assign a wide variety of values for β, with cost-effectiveness ratios computed for each of these values.

The values for Y_{MT} and Y_{SQ} are based on the results of the first eighteen months of the Pittsburgh Recurrent Depression Maintenance Project. We analyzed the distribution of recurrences across protocols using a hazard analysis statistical model of the following form:

$$T = \exp(Xb + e)T_0, \tag{12.12}$$

where T is the time to recurrence, X is a vector of dummy variables representing the different treatment cells, b are parameters indicating differences across treatment cells in expected time to recurrence, e is an error term representing unobserved influences on T, and T_0 is a normalization constant.

The distribution of e was specified as a Weibull distribution. The Weibull distribution has a cumulative distribution function:

$$F(t) = \exp(-at^g). \tag{12.13}$$

The Weibull distribution allows the probability of recurrence to be a function of the time already spent under maintenance treatment. Depending on the value of g, the probability of a recurrence can increase or decrease over time. In the former case, recurrences display a "ticking time bomb" time pattern, with the odds of recurrence in a given time interval (e.g., in the next month) being higher the longer the interval since entering maintenance treatment. In the latter case, the probability of recurrence in a given time interval decreases the longer the subject has been in maintenance. This is consistent with a "threshold" time pattern for recurrences, where the longer one is stable the less likely is a recurrence.

The Weibull distribution can also encompass the case in which the probability of a recurrence in a given future time interval is independent of the time since stabilization. This case, which divides the "ticking time bomb" from the "threshold" pattern of recurrences, occurs when g equals 1. With g equal to 1, the Weibull distribution becomes an exponential distribution with a cumulative distribution function:

$$F(t) = \exp(-at). \tag{12.14}$$

Equation (12.14) is the cumulative distribution function for the so-called "proportional hazards model" in which the odds of a recurrence in a given future time interval are independent of the time since the prior episode.

Equation (12.12) was used to construct a likelihood function. The data to estimate the model's parameters were from the first eighteen months of the study. Anyone still in maintenance at eighteen months was treated as a right-censored observation. The few subjects who left the study during the first eighteen months for reasons other than recurrence were also treated as right censored. The parameters (and their associated asymptotic standard errors) of the model were then estimated using maximum likelihood.

The estimate of g was .998, with a standard error of .11, and thus the hypothesis that $g = 1$ cannot be rejected. The stochastic pattern of recurrences under maintenance treatments for depression, therefore, appears consistent with a proportional hazards model with an exponential hazard distribution. Under this assumption, the odds of a recurrence in a given future time period appear the same regardless of the time since the last recurrence, and the expected time to the next recurrence is the same regardless of the time already spent in maintenance treatment.

The parameter estimates for the treatment cell effects were all statistically significant at a 99 percent confidence level. They lead to the following expected time to recurrence under the different treatment protocols: $Y_{SQ} = 0.51$ year, Y_{DRUG} is 1.93 years, Y_{IPT-M} is 1.36, and $Y_{IPT-M\&DR}$ is 3.42, where the subscript $DRUG$ refers to imipramine maintenance treatment, the subscript $IPT-M$ refers to maintenance interpersonal therapy, and the subscript $IPT-M\&DR$ refers to the combination of imipramine and interpersonal therapy maintenance treatment.

These estimates indicate that imipramine drug therapy, IPT-M, and the combination of the two are all effective in delaying the onset of recurrence. The combination of the two is particularly effective in these estimates. As indicated earlier, however, the pattern for the next eighteen months of the experiment differs somewhat from the pattern of the first eighteen months. In particular, it appears that the imipramine drug therapy becomes increasingly effective while the incremental benefit of combining the drug treatment with IPT-M diminishes substantially. Again, this means that the empirical example provided below must be viewed as only illustrative of the method and not as a substantive evaluation of the given maintenance treatments analyzed.

Table 12.1 summarizes the parameter values used in the empirical analysis.

Empirical Results

IPT-M versus No Maintenance Treatment

Table 12.2 displays the empirical results of the Monte Carlo analysis comparing IPT-M and the status quo of no maintenance treatment. Under the base case, IPT-M reduces the cumulative probability of

Table 12.1   Parameter Values for CUA of Therapy Maintenance Treatment for a Forty-Year-Old Woman

Variable	Baseline Value
$Y_{IPT\text{-}M}$	1.36 years
Y_{SQ}	0.51 year
Y_{DRUG}	1.93 years
$Y_{IPT\text{-}M\&DRUG}$	3.42 years
Z	36 years
$D_{IPT\text{-}M}$	$1,320/year
D_{DRUG}	$600/year
D_{SQ}	$0/year
$D_{IPT\text{-}M\&DR}$	$1,920/year
β_{SQ}	1
$\beta_{IPT\text{-}M}$	1
β_{DR}	Variable values
$\beta_{IPT\text{-}M\&DR}$	Variable values

Variable	Pessimistic Value	Baseline Value	Optimistic Value
X	0.6 year	0.4 year	0.2 year
ϕ	0.3	0.45	0.7
T	$1,500/episode	$500/episode	$200/episode
p	.01	.0025	.001

where

- Y = expected time to recurrence
- Z = expected life-span assuming no suicide upon entering maintenance treatment
- D = direct cost per unit time of maintenance treatment while patient is stable
- X = duration of depressive episode
- ϕ = quality of life while being depressed
- β = quality of life while stable under maintenance treatment
- T = direct costs of treating a depressive episode
- p = probability of suicide per episode
- IPT-M = interpersonal therapy maintenance treatment
- DRUG = imipramine drug maintenance treatment
- IPT-M&DR = imipramine drug and interpersonal therapy maintenance treatment
- SQ = status quo of no maintenance treatment

suicide from 8.8 to 4 percent and in so doing saves an average of 0.89 years of life per individual. By increasing the amount of time during which the individual is stable, IPT-M leads to an average increase of 3.71 QALYs. The expected lifetime (undiscounted) costs associated with treating depression decline under IPT-M from $18,643 to $9,815. This savings of approximately $9,000 in direct treatment costs, however, is less than the (undiscounted) lifetime costs of IPT-M of $36,351.

Table 12.2   Empirical Results for IPT-M Compared to the Status Quo

	Discount Rate		
Variable	0%	3%	5%
Placebo Base Case			
Expected QALY	26.35	15.83	11.86
Maintenance costs	$0		
Cumulative probability of suicide	.088		
Expected life-span	74.49		
Expected lost years of life from suicide	1.51		
Direct costs of episodes	$18,643	$11,384	$8,625
IPT Base Case			
Expected QALY	31.06	17.78	12.92
Maintenance costs	$36,351	$20,650	$14,938
Cumulative probability of suicide	.040		
Expected life-span	75.40		
Expected lost years of life from suicide	.60		
Direct costs of episodes	$9,815	$5,948	$4,483
Placebo Optimistic Case			
Expected QALY	32.20	19.27	14.40
Maintenance costs	$0		
Cumulative probability of suicide	.045		
Expected life-span	75.10		
Expected lost years of life from suicide	.90		
Direct costs of episodes	$9,694	$5,916	$4,479
IPT Optimistic Case			
Expected QALY	34.46	19.61	14.21
Maintenance costs	$41,416	$23,422	$16,900
Cumulative probability of suicide	.017		
Expected life-span	75.81		
Expected lost years of life from suicide	.19		
Direct costs of episodes	$4,380	$2,662	$2,011

IPT-M, thus, does not in this illustration seem to save in total direct costs. The health improvements that result from the increase in costs, however, are substantial. The incremental cost per quality adjusted life year is $7,419 with a 0 percent discount rate, $7,802 with a 3 percent discount rate, and $10,185 with a 5 percent discount rate. (The value decreases to $4,101 and $2,745 discounting costs at 3 percent and 5 percent, respectively, and not discounting QALYs.) These are very low ratios, indicating that IPT-M is very cost effective compared to a wide variety of other common health interventions. Typically, values between $40,000 and $75,000 are cited in the literature as reasonable thresholds for cost-effectiveness ratios. Such values are consistent with "value of life" figures of $1 million to $2 million for middle-aged men, a range typical in cost-benefit analyses in health care.

As can be seen, these general results are quite robust to sensitivity analysis. In particular, under the optimistic assumptions, the cost-effectiveness ratio increases to only $15,974 (with zero discounting).

The conclusion that maintenance treatment leads to increased costs is quickly modified if earning effects—so-called indirect costs—are included as costs along with direct costs. Including future earning changes as part of the costs of an illness derives from the "human capital" approach for valuing life and health. The human capital approach stands in some contrast to the emphasis of cost-utility analysis on quality of life, as well as to the "willingness to pay" approach that has come to dominate most cost-benefit analyses in health care. Making such a modification leads to many difficulties in CUA, including a need in principal to value nonmonetary benefits of work and to value leisure for those who do not work. In addition, the definition of QALYs becomes problematic. Now, full quality of life does not mean full health including a full ability to partake of social, leisure, individual, and occupational activities, but means some more restrictive concept.

Nonetheless, for readers attracted to the human capital approach, it is worth considering the effect of maintenance treatment on the sum of direct and indirect costs. It is quickly apparent that there is an absolute savings when direct and indirect costs are summed together. Stoudemire et al. (1987) estimated $1,180 in decreased wages per depressive episode in 1980 dollars. Updating this figure to 1990 dollars, IPT-M in this illustration leads to a savings of about $9,000 (at a 0 percent discount rate) in direct plus indirect costs. This figure is, itself, extremely conservative. It does not take account of lost future wages from suicide or the substantial decreases in productivity that are associated with an individual who is depressed but continues to work.

Imipramine versus No Maintenance Treatment

Table 12.3 presents results for the base case comparing the imipramine maintenance treatment with the status quo of no maintenance treatment. Imipramine drug maintenance treatment in this illustration reduces the cumulative probability of suicide from 8.8 to 3.5 percent and, because of this, leads to an average increase of 0.91 years of life per individual. Despite this increase in length of life, the cost-effectiveness of drug maintenance treatment is very dependent on the value of β, the quality of life when stable but taking the drug. In the baseline case, if β is less than .81, then drug maintenance

Table 12.3   Empirical Results for Imipramine
Maintenance Treatment

	Discount Rate		
Variable	0%	3%	5%
Expected QALY, β = 0.7	23.24	12.87	9.17
Expected QALY, β = 0.8	26.34	14.57	10.37
Expected QALY, β = 0.9	29.23	16.18	11.54
Expected QALY, β = 1.0	32.34	17.84	12.68
Maintenance costs	$16,266	$8,909	$6,307
Cumulative probability of suicide	.048		
Expected life-span	75.26		
Expected lost years of life from suicide	0.74		
Direct costs of episodes	$7,105	$4,305	$3,246

treatment is iatrogenic, leading to increased costs and decreased overall QALYs. Since one important benefit of drug maintenance treatment is decreased suicide, the benefits of which are weighted toward the future, the higher the discount rate the less beneficial is drug maintenance treatment in terms of QALYs relative to the status quo. For instance, with β equal to .9, drug treatment leads to an increase of 2.89 QALYs without discounting but a decrease of 0.31 QALYs compared to no maintenance treatment at a 5 percent discount rate.

As with IPT-M, the direct costs associated with drug maintenance treatment are sufficiently large that they exceed savings in direct treatment costs for the depressive episodes experienced by an individual. However, the total increase in direct costs is sufficiently small that, whenever β is great enough for drug maintenance treatment to lead to an increase in QALYs, the drug maintenance treatment quickly becomes very cost effective. With β equal to .9, the cost-effectiveness ratio of drug maintenance treatment is $1,691/QALY at a 0 percent discount rate and $5,427 at a 3 percent discount rate (although, as noted above, the ratio is negative—positive costs and negative health outcomes—at a 5 percent discount rate). With β equal to 1, the cost-effectiveness ratio of drug maintenance treatment is $814/QALY, $972/QALY, and $1,148/QALY at 0, 3, and 5 percent discount rates, respectively.

Imipramine and IPT-M versus No Maintenance Treatment

Table 12.4 presents results for the base case comparing the combination of imipramine and IPT-M with the status quo of no maintenance treatment. The cumulative probability of suicide in these illustrative

Table 12.4   Empirical Results for Imipramine and IPT-M

	Discount Rate		
Variable	0%	3%	5%
Expected QALY, β = 0.7	24.07	12.53	8.61
Expected QALY, β = 0.8	27.30	14.18	9.74
Expected QALY, β = 0.9	30.28	15.65	10.72
Expected QALY, β = 1.0	33.46	17.33	11.89
Maintenance costs	$59,504	$30,448	$20,726
Cumulative probability of suicide	.030		
Expected life-span	75.52		
Expected lost years of life from suicide	0.48		
Direct costs of episodes	$4,609	$2,792	$2,103

results declines to 3.0 percent. The cost effectiveness of the imipramine and IPT-M therapy is again quite sensitive to β, the quality of life while stable under drug maintenance treatment, and the discount rate.

At a 0 percent discount rate for health and cost outcomes, the threshold value for β is .77. For any value of β below .77 in this illustration, the maintenance treatment results on average in fewer QALYs and greater costs. This is slightly less than the 0 percent discount threshold for β of .81 for imipramine treatment alone. This threshold increases with the discount rate, rising to .91 at 3 percent and to .997 at 5 percent.

Once the threshold value for β is passed, however, the combination of imipramine and IPT-M quickly becomes cost effective relative to the status quo of no maintenance treatment for conventional cost-effectiveness ratios. At a 0 percent discount, the cost-effectiveness ratio is $11,540/QALY for β equal to .9 and $6,386 for β equal to 1. At a 3 percent discount rate, the cost-effectiveness ratio is $14,473/QALY for β equal to 1.

Imipramine versus IPT-M

Comparing IPT-M and imipramine drug maintenance treatment, the results are again quite sensitive to β in this illustration. Insofar as IPT-M provides some degree of reduction in suicide and insofar as reduction in suicide was central in the overall cost effectiveness of drug maintenance treatment, higher levels of β are required for drug maintenance treatment to lead to an increase in QALYs compared to IPT-M. Now, the threshold for β in this regard is .93. For any value of β below .93, IPT-M leads to greater QALYs, even at a 0 percent discount rate, than does imipramine. Once β increases above .93, however, imipramine is cost-effective relative to IPT-M. This is because imipramine drug maintenance treatment involves lower total direct costs than does IPT-M. Indeed, from a cost-effectiveness perspective, imipramine can be preferred to IPT-M at values of β of less than .93 because the decrease in overall health saves a sufficient amount in direct costs. For instance, at β equal to .9, drug maintenance treatment leads to a decrease in QALYs by 0.82 but saves $22,635 in direct costs (at a 0 percent discount rate). For any cost-effectiveness threshold ratio below $27,604, it would be cost effective to forsake the additional QALYs in exchange for the decrease in costs.

Imipramine and IPT-M versus IPT-M

Comparing the combination of imipramine and IPT-M versus IPT-M alone, the combination results in an expected increase in direct costs of $17,947 (at a 0 percent discount rate) in this illustration. Whether this additional expenditure is cost effective depends largely on β. For a β of less than .92, the IPT-M and imipramine maintenance treatment leads to fewer expected QALYs than does IPT-M alone. Once β exceeds .93, the combination of IPT-M and imipramine quickly becomes cost effective relative to IPT-M alone. At β equal to 1, the cost-effectiveness ratio of IPT-β and imipramine compared to that of IPT-M alone is $7,480/QALY.

Imipramine and IPT-M versus Imipramine

Comparing the combination of imipramine and IPT-M versus imipramine alone, the combination results in an expected increase in direct costs of $40,722 in this illustration. At any level of β, however, this additional expenditure leads to an increase in expected health. This increase ranges from about 0.9 to 1.1 QALYs, depending on the value of β. Thus, the cost-effectiveness ratio of the combination of imipramine and IPT-M versus imipramine alone is approximately $40,000.

Summary and Conclusions

Cost-utility analysis is increasingly used as a method for assessing the societal health benefits from a health intervention with societal costs of that health intervention. It offers the potential to compare the cost effectiveness of quite diverse health interventions using a common metric. It has been very difficult to apply CUA in mental health care, however. This is because the etiology of mental illnesses and the clinical efficacy of treatment are often subject to substantial uncertainty. Also, mental illnesses are often chronic and require dynamic consideration of the effect of a health intervention across the life-span of an individual.

In this chapter, we addressed each of these difficulties in presenting a cost-utility analysis of maintenance treatment for recurrent depression. Data from the Pittsburgh Study of Maintenance Therapies in Recurrent Depression were used to illustrate the clinical efficacy of different maintenance treatments. A state-transition model allows the lifetime history of an individual under different maintenance treatments to be modeled, using Monte Carlo simulation to derive the empirical results from the model.

We used the illustrative results for the efficacy of the different maintenance treatments from the first eighteen months of the Pittsburgh Recurrent Depression Project for a prototypical case of a 40-year old woman. For each of the maintenance treatments, estimates were generated using the model for the cumulative probability of suicide, the direct costs, the indirect costs, and the expected number of quality-adjusted life years. For treatments involving drugs, this latter variable is conditional upon the severity of the side effects of the imipramine medication.

These basic results can be used to compare each maintenance treatment to the status quo in terms of direct cost savings, indirect cost savings, expected changes in the length of life, expected changes in quality-adjusted life years, and cost effectiveness measured in terms of dollars per quality-adjusted life year. The different maintenance treatments can be compared to one another on these same dimensions.

Although the results must be viewed as illustrative and not substantive analyses of the cost effectiveness of these particular maintenance treatments, they reveal the potential power of cost-utility analysis to provide an important complement to evaluation based purely on clinical efficacy of treatment and prevention efforts in mental health.

Acknowledgments

This research was supported in part by National Institute of Mental Health grants MH29618-10 and MH30915-14.

Notes

1. Attempts to gauge the prevalence of depression by measuring symptoms of depression (versus using structured interviews and standard diagnostic criteria) typically lead to higher estimates of the prevalence of depression. Weissman and Myers (1978) estimated prevalence to be 16–20 percent, whereas Boyd and Weissman (1981) estimated a prevalence of 9–20 percent.

Those who seem to be at high risk of depression include persons with first-degree relatives who suffer from alcoholism, sociopathy, or depression (Andreason and Winokur 1979); persons who are under extreme stress or who have suffered losses, as from divorce, bereavement, or job loss (Lloyd 1980; Clayton, Halikas, and Maurice 1972); persons who have histories of early parent loss and childhood bereavement; and persons who have major medical illnesses (Stoudemire 1985). The risk of depression seems greater for women, younger persons, the separated and divorced, and those who are socioeconomically disadvantaged.

2. Reflecting this view, Hatziandreu et al. (1988) wrote that "cost-effectiveness is a relative and subjective concept defined as 'having an additional benefit' worth the additional cost." Warner and Luce (1983) expressed a similar view of CEA.

3. Kamlet (1991) provided a more detailed discussion of the history and development of CUA as a method for summarizing the effectiveness of different treatment options in health care from an economic perspective.

4. A more refined model would allow an individual in state A to have transitions to either state B or state C, with the transition to state C representing death by natural causes (i.e., other than a suicide). Similarly, individuals should be able to die of natural causes while depressed. In practice, the assumption that individuals live until their ex ante expected life-span upon entering maintenance treatment affects the empirical results only marginally. In future versions of this model, however, a refinement of this assumption as suggested here will be adopted.

References

Anderson, J. P., J. W. Bush, Milton Chen, and Danielle Dolenc. 1986. "Policy Space Areas and Properties of Benefit-Cost/Utility Analysis." *Journal of the American Medical Association* 255:795–97.

Andreason, N. C., and G. Winokur. 1979. "Secondary Depression: Familial, Clinical or Research Perspectives." *American Journal of Psychiatry* 136:62–66.

Angst, J. 1984. "Prospective Study on the Four Affective Disorders." Presented at the Consensus Development Conference Program.

Bothwell, S., and M. M. Weismann. 1977. "Social Impairments Four Years after an Acute Depressive Episode." *American Journal of Orthopsychology* 47:231–32.

Boyd, J. H., and M. M. Weissman. 1981. "Epidemiology of Affective Disorders." *Archives of General Psychiatry* 38:1039–46.

Clayton, P. J., J. A. Halikas, and W. L. Maurice. 1972. "The Depression of Widowhood." *British Journal of Psychiatry* 121:71–78.

Coppen, A., R. Noguera, J. Bailey, B. H. Burns, M. S. Swani, E. H. Hare, R. Gardner, and R. Maggs. 1971. "Prophylactic Lithium in Affective Disorders." *Lancet* 2:275–79.

DiMascio, A., M. M. Weissman, B. A. Prusoff, C. Neu, M. Zwilling, and G. L. Klerman. 1979. "Differential Symptom Reduction by Drugs and Psychotherapy in Acute Depression." *Archives of General Psychiatry* 36:1450–56.

Drummond, Michael F., Greg L. Stoddart, and George W. Torrance. 1987. *Methods for the Economic Evaluation of Health Care Programmes*. New York: Oxford University Press.

Fernstrom, M. H., R. L. Krowinski, and D. J. Kupfer. 1986. "Chronic Imipramine Treatment and Weight Gain." *Psychiatric Research* 17:269–73.

Frank, E., D. J. Kupfer, and J. M. Perel. 1989. "Early Recurrence in Unipolar Depression." *Archives of General Psychiatry* 46:397–400.

Frank, R. G., and P. J. Gertler. 1988. "An Assessment of Measurement Error Bias for Estimating the Effect of Mental Distress on Income." Johns Hopkins University. Typescript.

Frank, R. G., and M. S. Kamlet. 1989. "Provider Choice for the Treatment of Mental Disorder: The Impact of Health and Mental Health Status." *Journal of Health Services Research* 24:83–103.

Glen, A. I. M., A. L. Johnson, and M. Shepherd. 1984. "Continuation Therapy with Lithium and Amitriptyline in Unipolar Depressive Illness: A Randomized, Double Blind, Controlled Trial." *Psychological Medicine* 14:37–50.

Gramlich, E. 1981. *Benefit-Cost Analysis of Government Programs*. Englewood Cliffs, N.J.: Prentice-Hall.

Hatziandreu, E. I., J. P. Kaplan, M. C. Weinstein, C. J. Caspersen, and K. Warner. 1988. "A Cost Effectiveness Analysis of Exercise as a Health Promotion Activity." *American Journal of Public Health* 78:214–28.

Kamlet, M. S. 1991. *A Framework for Cost-Utility Analysis of Government Health Care Programs*. Washington, D.C.: Office of Disease Prevention and Health Promotion, U.S. Public Health Service.

Kaplan, R. M., and J. P. Anderson. 1988. "A General Health Policy Model: Update and Applications." *Journal of Health Services Research* 23:203–35.

Keller, M. B., R. W. Shapiro, P. W. Lavori, and N. Wolfe. 1982a. "Recovery in Major Depressive Disorder: Analysis with Life Tables and Regression Models." *Archives of General Psychiatry* 39:905–10.

———. 1982b. "Relapse in Major Depressive Disorder: Analysis with Life Table." *Archives of General Psychiatry* 39:905–10.

Klerman, G. L. 1978. *Manual for Short Term Interpersonal Psychotherapy*. Unpublished.

Klerman, G. L., A. DiMascio, M. Weissman, B. Prusoff, and E. S. Paykel. 1974. "Treatment of Depression by Drugs and Psychotherapy." *American Journal of Psychiatry* 131:186–91.

Klerman, G. L., M. M. Weissman, B. J. Roundsaville, and E. S. Chevron (eds.). 1984. *Interpersonal Psychotherapy of Depression*. New York: Basic Books.

Lloyd, C. 1980. "Life Events and Depressive Disorder Reviewed." *Archives of General Psychiatry* 37:541–48.

Monkoff, Kenneth, Eric Bergman, Aaron T. Beck, and Roy Beck. 1973. "Hopelessness, Depression, and Attempted Suicide." *American Journal of Psychiatry* 130:455–59.

Myers, J. K., M. M. Weismann, G. L. Trischler, C. E. Holzer III, P. J. Leaf, H. Orraschel, J. Anthony, J. H. Boyd, J. D. Burke, Jr., M. Kramer, and R. Stoltzman. 1984. "Six-Month Prevalence of Psychiatric Disorders in Three Communities: 1980–1982." *Archives of General Psychiatry* 41:959–67.

Office of Technology Assessment, U.S. Congress. 1980. *The Implications of Cost-Effectiveness Analysis of Medical Technology*. Washington, D.C.: U.S. Government Printing Office, September.

Prien, R. F., D. J. Kupfer, P. A. Mansley, J. G. Small, V. B. Tucson, C. B. Voss, and W. E. Johnson. 1984. "Drug Therapy in the Prevention of Recurrences in Unipolar and Bipolar Affective Disorders: A Comparison of Lithium, Imipramine, and a Lithium Combination." *Archives of General Psychiatry* 41:1096–1104.

Prusoff, B. A., M. M. Weissman, G. L. Klerman, and B. J. Roundsaville. 1980. "Research Diagnostic Criteria Subtypes of Depression: Their Role as Predictors of Differential Response to Psychotherapy and Drug Treatment." *Archives of General Psychiatry* 37:796–801.

Rapoport, J., R. Robertson, and B. Stuart. 1982. *Understanding Health Economics*. Rockville, Md.: Aspen.

Sackett, D. L., and G. W. Torrance. 1978. "The Utility of Different Health States as Perceived by the General Public." *Journal of Chronic Diseases* 31:697–704.

Stoudemire, A. 1985. "Depression in the Medically Ill." In J. O. Cavenar (ed.): *Psychiatry*, Vol. 2, pp. 1–8. New York: Lippincott.

Stoudemire, A., R. Frank, M. Kamlet, and N. Hedemark. 1987. "Depression." In Robert W. Amler and H. Bruce Dull (eds.): *Closing the Gap: The Burden of Unnecessary Illness*, pp. 65–71. New York: Oxford University Press.

Torrance, G. W. 1986. "Measurement of Health State Utilities for Economic Appraisal: A Review." *Journal of Health Economics* 5:1–30.

Torrance, G. W., M. H. Boyle, and S. P. Horwood. 1982. "Application of Multiattribute Utility Theory To Measure Social Preferences for Health States." *Operations Research* 30:1043–67.

Warner, K. E., and B. R. Luce. 1983. *Cost-Benefit and Cost-Effectiveness Analysis in Health Care*. Ann Arbor, Mich.: Health Administration Press.

Weinstein, M. C., and W. B. Stason. 1977. "Foundations of Cost-Effectiveness

Analysis for Health and Medical Practices." *New England Journal of Medicine* 296:716–21.

Weismann, M. M. 1979. "The Psychological Treatment of Depression: Evidence for the Efficacy of Psychotherapy Alone, in Comparison with, and in Combination with Pharmacotherapy." *Archives of General Psychiatry* 36:1216–69.

————. 1984. "The Psychological Treatment of Depression: Update of Clinical Trials." In J. B. W. Williams and R. L. Spitzer (eds.): *Psychotherapy Research: Where Are We and Where Should We Go?*, pp. 89–105. New York: Guilford Press.

Weismann, M. M., and J. K. Myers. 1978. "Rates and Risks of Depressive Symptoms in a United States Urban Community." *Acta Psychiatrica Scandinavica* 57:219–31.

Wells, K. B., A. Stewart, R. D. Hayes, W. R. Bumam, M. Daniels, S. Berry, S. Greenfield, and J. Ware. 1989. "The Functioning and Well-being of Depressed Patients: Results from the Medical Outcomes Study." *Journal of the American Medical Association* 262:914–19.

13

The Treatment of Alcohol and Drug Abuse among Mentally Ill Medicaid Enrollees: The Utilization of Services in Prepaid Plans versus Fee-for-Service Care

Michael Finch, Ph.D.,
Nicole Lurie, M.D., M.S.P.H.,
Jon B. Christianson, Ph.D.,
and Ira S. Moscovice, Ph.D.

I n 1982, the Health Care Financing Administration authorized six states to enroll Medicaid beneficiaries in prepaid health plans on a demonstration basis. Hennepin County, Minnesota (containing Minneapolis), was selected as an urban site in this demonstration. It was the only site in which Medicaid recipients were randomly assigned to prepaid versus fee-for-service care and also the only site in which Medicaid recipients classified as disabled due to mental illness were enrolled in prepaid plans.

The primary purpose of this chapter is to compare the utilization of services for alcohol and drug abuse treatment by chronically mentally ill individuals in prepaid plans versus fee-for-service Medicaid. The findings reported here are drawn from a larger evaluation effort that addressed aged, dual-eligible (Medicare/Medicaid), as well as chronically mentally ill recipients and measured outcomes related to access, satisfaction, physical and mental health, functional status, and costs, in addition to utilization.

Background

Although the exact numbers vary widely depending on the study populations (Pulver et al. 1989), there now seems to be considerable evidence that the coexistence of substance abuse and other psychiatric disorders is relatively common (Kofoed et al. 1986). Epidemiologic Catchment Area studies suggest that 21 to 39 percent of substance abusers in the community also meet widely accepted criteria for psychiatric disorders. Various studies of patients in psychiatric settings similarly find a high percentage (25–40 percent) who are substance abusers (Kofoed et al. 1986). Some studies of select samples of patients suffering from schizophrenia found even higher proportions with "dual disorders." For example, Miller and Tanenbaum (1989) reviewed the psychiatric inpatient records of 55 male schizophrenic patients consecutively admitted to the psychiatric division of a general hospital and concluded that 30 had abused one or more drugs (including alcohol). Drake, Osher, and Wallach (1989) analyzed alcohol use among 115 schizophrenic patients discharged from a state hospital and participating in an after-care program. They found that 22 percent were clearly abusing alcohol.

Data from previous studies indicate that patients suffering from dual disorders are typically younger, more often male, and of a lower socioeconomic status than other psychiatric patients (Kay, Kalathara, and Meinzer 1989; Drake, Osher, and Wallach 1989). Patients with dual disorders also typically have a more severe course of illness than other psychiatric patients because substance abuse distorts symptoms and impedes the identification of the clinical condition (Caton et al. 1989). Kofoed et al. (1986) noted that these patients are "over represented in problematic patient groups, including those who demand irregular discharges from psychiatric hospitals; those seen in emergency rooms, where substance abuse contributes to fully half of psychiatric emergencies; and those who are considered treatment failures in substance abuse treatment programs" (p. 867). Also, according to Drake and Wallach (1989), they "have difficulty managing the practical aspects of their lives, maintaining stable housing, and avoiding institutionalization in hospitals and jails" (p. 1041). In a study of schizophrenic patients in an after-care program, Drake, Osher, and Wallach (1989) found that even minimal drinking, at levels not considered to be alcohol abuse, was a predictor of rehospitalization during a one-year follow-up period. In a companion article, Drake and Wallach (1989) reported that dual-disorder patients were nearly twice as likely to be rehospitalized during a one-year follow-up period. Among 187 chronically mentally ill patients living in the community, 59 had a dual diagnosis of substance abuse. Of these 59 patients, 35 were rehospitalized.

The high use of inpatient and other services by dual-disorder patients is naturally a concern of the public programs that finance their care. This concern is heightened by relatively pessimistic assessments of the ability of present treatment systems to meet the needs of these patients effectively. Ridgely, Goldman, and Talbott (1989) observed that "state-of-the-art in treating chronic mentally ill young adults is not well advanced. When one considers the additional problem of addressing substance abuse (programmatically) among chronically mentally ill young adults, it would be more accurate to describe the development of treatment as in its infancy, characterized more by trial-and-error than by implementation of established treatment protocols" (p. 288). They noted that these patients frequently abandon structured treatment programs and seek services in emergency rooms and other crisis facilities (p. 291). There is considerable debate about whether the benefits that dual disorder patients obtain from hospital-based treatment programs are sustained when they move out of the hospital's insulating environment. There is also relatively little empirical evidence concerning the effectiveness of programs that serve "gatekeeping" functions for dual-disorder patients (Ridgely, Goldman, and Talbott 1989).

Analysts of prepaid health plans for the general population point out that they centralize financial incentives, leading to a more conservative use of treatment resources, particularly with respect to expensive inpatient care (Luft 1981). Many prepaid plans actively attempt to "manage" the resource use of high-utilizing members by employing gatekeepers and limiting self-referrals and emergency room treatment. These characteristics suggest that enrolling dual-disorder patients in prepaid plans could improve the coordination of their care while at the same time reducing cost for public programs. However, individuals with chronic mental disorders complicated by substance abuse may be less able to protect themselves against the underservice that could occur if prepaid plans are overaggressive in constraining resource use. Schlesinger (1986), in particular, expressed concern that Medicaid beneficiaries who have a chronic mental illness might fare poorly in prepaid plans. At present, there is no empirical evidence about the effect of prepaid plans on the utilization of services by dual-disorder patients. The Hennepin County demonstration provides an opportunity to address this issue.

Hennepin County Demonstration

In Hennepin County, 35 percent of all Medicaid beneficiaries were randomly assigned to receive services from prepaid health plans. An independent broker managed the enrollment process, and individuals who did not choose a plan within sixty to ninety days after assignment to the prepaid group were randomly assigned to a plan. Unless beneficiaries requested a change of health plan within sixty days of initial enrollment, they were required to remain in their health plan for one year. They were not given the option of returning to fee-for-service Medicaid, so there is no possibility of selection bias within the randomized design of the demonstration. Enrollment of individuals in the aged, blind, and disabled category, from which the analytic sample in this study was drawn, was accomplished on a month-to-month basis between November 1986 and April 1987, with service delivery for early enrollees beginning on January 1, 1987.

Four prepaid plans contracted with the state of Minnesota to enroll beneficiaries in the blind/disabled category, which included severely, chronically mentally ill individuals. Three plans were IPA model HMOs, and one was a network plan. Their sponsoring organizations were Blue Cross/Blue Shield, Hennepin County, the University of Minnesota, and an independent organization. Capitated rates for reimbursing the plans were determined for seventy-four rate cells based on age, sex, Medicare participation, institutional versus non-institutional residence, and eligibility status. Rates did not vary across plans and were set at 95 percent of projected costs for aged, blind, and disabled beneficiaries. (See discussion below and Christianson et al. 1989 for further detail on rate setting.)

During 1987, Blue Cross/Blue Shield argued that it was being "selected against" by new enrollees because of the relatively large number of mental health providers in its network. Because beneficiaries with severe mental illness were likely to find that their provider participated in the Blue Cross/Blue Shield Plan, they may have been encouraged by their providers to join that plan. In August 1987, Blue Cross/Blue Shield announced that it intended to terminate its participation in the demonstration, citing financial losses resulting from unexpectedly high use of services by all of its enrollees, including the blind/disabled group. Since Blue Cross/Blue Shield enrolled over 50 percent of this group in Hennepin County, state officials were concerned about the mental health effects of transferring beneficiaries to the three remaining plans, as well as the willingness and capacity of these plans to accept all of these enrollees. Therefore, the blind and disabled group of beneficiaries was transferred back to fee-for-service Medicaid effective January 1, 1988.

Research Design

The primary hypotheses addressed in this chapter are that

- chronically mentally ill Medicaid beneficiaries enrolled in prepaid plans will utilize fewer alcohol/drug abuse treatment services (inpatient and outpatient) than will individuals in fee-for-service Medicaid and
- chronically mentally ill Medicaid beneficiaries with dual disorders enrolled in prepaid plans will utilize fewer physical, mental, and alcohol/drug abuse treatment services than will individuals with dual disorders in fee-for-service Medicaid.

A randomized, time series, control group design is used to test these hypotheses. The advantages of this design include the elimination of threats to internal validity, including the effects of unique historical events, maturation of the sample, testing or instrumentation effects, effects due to regression toward the mean, selection, mortality, and any interaction of these effects (Campbell and Stanley 1966). In addition, estimates can be made with more precision and a smaller sample size than is possible with quasi-experimental designs.

Several steps were taken in constructing the sample used in this study. First, Medicaid recipients eighteen to sixty-five years old whose eligibility status was classified as disabled were identified from Medicaid records. For these individuals, an algorithm based on ICD-9 diagnosis codes and the number and frequency of claims for specific mental health diagnoses was applied using Medicaid claims tapes for disabled beneficiaries covering the two years preceding November 1986. (See Moscovice, Finch, and Lurie 1989 for a discussion of this algorithm.) This approach yielded 500 individuals (among the disabled population) who were randomly assigned to the prepaid group and were considered to be suffering from severe chronic mental illness. However, 104 were excluded from the study sample for a variety of reasons (e.g., language, deceased, moved out of the area). About 93 percent of the remaining individuals (369 persons) were interviewed at baseline. Similarly, 510 individuals assigned to fee-for-service Medicaid were identified as chronically mentally ill using the algorithm, with 90 excluded from the study and 370 (about 88 percent) of the remainder interviewed at baseline.

The baseline interviews were conducted before the prepaid group in the study sample actually began to receive services from health plan providers. A follow-up interview was planned for one year after the baseline interview for all study members. However, when the state canceled the demonstration for the disabled group as of January 1988, a revision of the planned interview schedule was necessary. For individuals enrolled in prepaid plans, follow-up data were collected during the period between notification of the state's intent to withdraw clients and two weeks following their disenrollment from the HMO. This resulted in follow-up periods of seven to twelve months, with an average of nine months. Follow-up data for the fee-for-service group were collected according to the same time frame, with individuals randomly selected for interview at seven to twelve months. Follow-up interviews were completed with 354 individuals in the prepaid group and 366 in the fee-for-service group, resulting in complete baseline/follow-up data for about 96 percent of the individuals completing the baseline survey.

In addition to the self-report data, several other data sources were used in the analysis. Medicaid and Medicare claims tapes provided information on the utilization of services by the fee-for-service group, while Medicare and "dummy claims" tapes submitted to the state by the health plans provided similar data for the prepaid group. Medical chart audits were performed for all physician visits for three of the four prepaid plans, with the results compared to data on the dummy claims tapes to determine whether there was underreporting by the prepaid plans in this service category.

Baseline Characteristics of Study Sample

In this section, data on the demographic characteristics and self-reported utilization of services by the study sample at baseline are presented. These data are disaggregated into two groups. The first group consists of sample members who reported an inpatient treatment episode for alcohol/drug abuse in the prior year or an outpatient treatment episode in the previous three months. The second group consists of individuals with no reported use in either of these categories.

The summary of demographic characteristics (table 13.1) indicates that severely mentally ill individuals with recent histories of inpatient or outpatient treatment for alcohol or drug abuse are likely to be male and younger than individuals with no recent history of treatment. They also are likely to score lower in social functioning (as

Table 13.1   Characteristics of Combined Sample at Baseline
(Self-report Data)

Variable	Total	Prior Treatment for Alcohol/Drug Abuse (*N* = 94)	No Prior Treatment for Alcohol/Drug Abuse (*N* = 645)	*p*-value
Demographics				
Age (years)	41.6	38.9	42.0	.02
		(94)[a]	(645)	
Single (%)	94.8	96.8	94.6	.36
		(93)	(643)	
Living alone (%)	62.5	58.7	63.8	.34
		(92)	(639)	
Income ($/month)	399.44	384.50	401.62	.56
		(90)	(618)	
Female (%)	56.0	38.3	58.6	<.01
		(94)	(645)	
Global Assessment Scale	54.9	52.4	55.5	.02
		(92)	(640)	
Utilization				
Probability of inpatient admission in previous year				
Physical health	.23	.31	.22	.05
		(94)	(644)	
Mental	.23	.34	.22	.01
		(93)	(641)	
Probability of outpatient visit in previous 3 months				
Physical health	.69	.68	.69	.94
		(94)	(641)	
Mental health	.76	.73	.77	.43
		(93)	(643)	
Number of outpatient visits in previous 3 months				
Physical health	3.0	3.5	2.9	.29
		(94)	(641)	
Mental health	5.0	7.2	4.7	<.01
		(93)	(643)	

[a]Numbers in parentheses, numbers of observations.

measured by the Global Assessment Scale). This is consistent with
the profile of individuals with dual disorders found in the existing
literature. No significant differences were found with respect to marital status, living arrangement, or income.

The proportion of the sample reporting recent treatment for alcohol or drug abuse is smaller (12.7 percent) than the range typically reported in the literature. This could reflect differences in the ways that samples were selected. It also seems plausible, however, that respondents may have underreported alcohol/drug abuse treatment in responding to interviewers. (Assuming that underreporting is randomly distributed, this has no effect on the prepaid/fee-for-service comparisons reported later in this chapter.)

With respect to the utilization of inpatient care, sample members with prior treatment for alcohol/drug abuse were significantly more likely to have had an inpatient admission for both physical and mental health care during the prior year. There were no significant differences in the probability of having an outpatient visit for physical or mental health care. However, the average number of visits for mental health care among those with prior treatment for alcohol/drug abuse was significantly higher (7.2) than for those with no recent history of treatment (4.7).

Prepaid versus Fee-for-Service Comparisons

Inpatient Utilization

Prepaid versus fee-for-service comparisons of inpatient utilization are presented in table 13.2. When an individual was a Medicare beneficiary, data on inpatient utilization were taken from Medicare claims files. For all others, inpatient data were taken from Medicaid and prepaid plan claims files (as submitted to Medicaid).

For the total sample, only five individuals used hospital inpatient services for the treatment of alcohol or drug abuse; therefore, prepaid versus fee-for-service differences were not examined for this variable. With respect to physical and mental health care, differences in inpatient utilization were found when the sample was disaggregated by whether or not an individual reported a recent history of treatment for alcohol or drug abuse. For those with no recent history, prepaid enrollees in plans had a significantly lower probability of an inpatient admission for physical health care reasons and spent fewer days, on average, in the hospital. This result must be interpreted cautiously, however. At baseline, the only significant utilization difference in the randomized sample was in the area of inpatient treatment for physical health care, with enrollees in prepaid plans less likely to report an admission during the year before enrollment. Therefore, this significant difference probably reflects a continued lower use of physical health care rather than a "prepaid effect." With

Table 13.2   Inpatient Utilization:
Prepaid (PPD) versus Fee-for-Service (FFS) Comparisons
(Annualized Claims Data)

Variable	Prepaid	FFS	Difference (PPD − FFS)	p-value
No baseline history of	(N = 324)	(N = 321)		
AL/DA treatment				
Physical health care				
Probability of admission	.09	.15	−.06	.01
Mean inpatient days	0.64	2.86	−2.22	.03
Mental health care				
Probability of admission	.10	.13	−.03	.25
Mean inpatient days	1.56	3.46	−1.90	.03
Baseline history of AL/DA	(N = 45)	(N = 49)		
treatment				
Physical health care				
Probability of admission	.18	.14	.04	.64
Mean inpatient days	0.99	0.91	0.08	.91
Mental health care				
Probability of admission	.16	.33	−.17	.05
Mean inpatient days	1.57	9.84	−8.27	.01

Note: AL/DA, alcohol/drug abuse.

respect to mental health care, there was no significant difference in the probability of an admission, but the average number of treatment days was less for the prepaid group.

The most intriguing results of the analysis of inpatient use relate to mental health care treatment differences for individuals with dual disorders versus those with no recent history of alcohol or drug abuse treatment. For the dual-disorder group, the probability of admission is significantly lower in the prepaid group, as is the average number of inpatient treatment days. In fact, for the prepaid group, the average number of inpatient treatment days for mental health is almost identical for enrollees with and without dual disorders. In contrast, in the fee-for-service groups, the average number of mental health inpatient treatment days is substantially higher for dual-disorder individuals (9.84 versus 3.46).

In summary, enrollees in prepaid plans with dual disorders are significantly less likely to be admitted to inpatient treatment for mental health care, a finding that does not apply to enrollees without dual disorders. However, the average number of inpatient mental health treatment days per enrollee does not vary across the two groups and is significantly less, in both cases, than use by the fee-for-service group. The magnitude of the difference in treatment days is much greater for the dual-disorder group because of relatively high fee-for-service use in this group. Apparently, with respect to mental health inpatient services, HMOs do not distinguish among enrollees based on past history of alcohol or drug abuse treatment, providing significantly fewer services to all enrollees.

Outpatient Utilization

Prepaid versus fee-for-service comparisons of outpatient utilization are contained in table 13.3. These comparisons are based on interview responses pertaining to visits made to any type of provider during the previous three months. A comparison of medical records to dummy claims data provided by the prepaid plans indicated that the plan data consistently underreported outpatient visits. Therefore,

Table 13.3   Outpatient Utilization:
Prepaid (PPD) versus Fee-for-Service (FFS) Comparisons
(Self-report Data—Previous Three Months)

Variable	Prepaid	FFS	Difference (PPD − FFS)	p-value
Total sample	$(N = 369)$	$(N = 370)$		
Probability of outpatient visit for AL/DA treatment	.04	.10	−.06	<.01
Mean number of visits for AL/DA treatment	1.03	0.79	0.24	0.66
Disaggregated sample				
No baseline history of AL/DA treatment	$(N = 324)$	$(N = 321)$		
Physical health care				
Probability of visit	.59	.68	−.09	.02
Mean number of visits	2.33	3.36	−1.03	0.01
Mental health care				
Probability of visit	.69	.71	−.02	.46
Mean number of visits	4.36	5.60	−1.24	0.06
AL/DA care				
Probability of visit	.02	.04	−.02	.07
Mean number of visits	0.76	0.37	0.39	0.49
Baseline history of AL/DA treatment	$(N = 45)$	$(N = 49)$		
Physical health care				
Probability of visit	.53	.69	−.16	.11
Mean number of visits	1.91	3.41	−1.50	0.04
Mental health care				
Probability of visit	.69	.71	−.02	.79
Mean number of visits	3.77	5.83	−2.06	0.10
AL/DA care				
Probability of visit	.20	.49	−.29	<.01
Mean number of visits	2.98	3.53	−0.55	0.75

Note: AL/DA, alcohol/drug abuse.

any analysis based on these claims data would be biased in favor of finding a prepaid effect. On the other hand, while there may be misreporting of visits in the interviews, there is no reason to believe that it would be systematically concentrated in either the prepaid or the fee-for-service group. Therefore, the estimated treatment/control differences still represent unbiased estimates of true differences in outpatient utilization.

Physical health care visits were defined as visits to any source for physical health care, including hospital emergency rooms, hospital clinics, and community health clinics. Mental health visits were defined as visits to any mental health professional or to a general physician's office for the purpose of mental health care (not including visits to drop-in centers, day treatment programs, or residential treatment facilities). Alcohol/drug abuse visits include visits to any source of care for the treatment of alcohol or drug abuse.

In the total sample, the probability of an outpatient visit for alcohol or drug abuse treatment was significantly less in the prepaid group. In the disaggregated samples, this was also true, although the magnitude and significance of the difference were greater in the dual-disorder group. In no case was the mean number of visits significantly different in the prepaid versus fee-for-service comparisons.

With respect to physical health care, the prepaid group with no recent history of alcohol or drug abuse was significantly less likely to report a visit. The observed difference in this measure for the dual-disorder group was even greater but, because of the smaller sample size, was not significant at conventional levels. The average number of visits annually was significantly less for prepaid group enrollees in both comparisons. A similar pattern emerged with respect to mental health outpatient visits. Interestingly, the mental health results were somewhat sensitive to the definition of a "mental health visit." When visits to drop-in centers, day treatment programs, and residential treatment facilities were included, the p-values for observed differences in mean visits fell to .10 for individuals with no baseline history and .85 for dual-disorder groups, while the number of reported visits approximately doubled in all cases (results not reported in table 13.3).

Adjusted Comparisons

The estimates reported in tables 13.2 and 13.3 are based on comparisons of group means, relying on the randomization process to generate groups with comparable characteristics. In general, the absence of significant differences in baseline characteristics between the groups supports this approach. However, the use of covariates to calculate "regression-adjusted means" has the potential to increase the efficiency of estimated group differences and thereby increase the significance levels for estimated differences. It is also useful in controlling for possible differences existing in the samples after disaggregating for prior history of alcohol or chemical abuse treatment. Therefore, for all binary measures (probability of admission, probability of visit) in tables 13.2 and 13.3, regression-adjusted means were calculated using logit analysis. Variables were entered in the logit specification to control for age, gender, whether the respondent lived alone, general health status, physical functioning, and days in the health plan (for the prepaid group members). The resulting p-values for the different probabilities of inpatient admission were virtually identical to those reported in table 13.2. With respect to the probabilities of an outpatient visit (table 13.3), there were only minor changes in significance levels for prepaid versus fee-for-service differences when comparing regression-adjusted means instead of unadjusted means. In the group with no baseline history of treatment, the p-value for a visit for physical health care rose from .02 to .08, with a similar increase for alcohol and drug abuse treatment (from .07 to .14).

Prepaid versus fee-for-service comparisons of mean number of visits (table 13.3) were also estimated using regression analysis, after redefining the outcome variable to equal the difference in number of visits (during the previous three-month period) reported in the baseline and follow-up surveys. This redefinition avoided the estimation problems associated with a truncated dependent variable, with a relatively large number of respondents reporting no visits. The same covariates utilized in the logistic equation were used in these regressions. Two important changes in p-values were observed. For individuals with and without baseline histories of alcohol or drug abuse treatment, differences between the prepaid and fee-for-service groups were no longer significant for physical and mental health visits.

In summary, comparisons of regression-adjusted means support the findings relating to significant reductions in the probability of inpatient admissions and visits, as reported in tables 13.2 and 13.3. However, based on the findings of the multivariate analysis, there do not seem to be significant differences in the change in visits of any type, from baseline to follow-up period. This is true for subgroups both with and without histories of alcohol or drug abuse treatment.

Summary and Conclusions

In the Hennepin County demonstration, prepaid health plans reduced the likelihood of outpatient visits for alcohol and chemical
dependency treatment for a chronically mentally ill population but
did not reduce the mean number of visits. Of special interest is the
effect of the prepaid plans on the subgroup of enrollees with a recent
history of treatment for alcohol and drug abuse. For this group there
was a large and significant reduction in the probability of an alcohol
or drug abuse treatment visit (20 versus 49 percent), but no significant difference in the average number of visits. The probability of
making a physical or a mental health visit, however, was not significantly different for prepaid plan enrollees than the probability for
similar individuals in fee-for-service Medicaid. With respect to inpatient utilization for this subgroup, there was some evidence of reductions in inpatient mental health treatment but not in inpatient physical health treatment. Inpatient treatment for alcohol or drug abuse
occurred too infrequently to analyze.

The observed reductions in service utilization were not likely to
have been caused by a disruption in provider relationships or treatment regimes due to the transfer of Medicaid beneficiaries to prepaid
plans. At the follow-up interview, only 13 percent of respondents
indicated that they changed their usual source of care as a result of
enrollment in a prepaid plan. Therefore, the observed differences are
more likely to reflect changes in provider or beneficiary behavior in
response to the financial incentives and utilization review mechanisms present in the plans.

There are several limitations to the research results reported in
this chapter that pertain to the setting, data, or research design.
First, providers in the Twin Cities have considerable experience prac-
ticing medicine as part of prepaid organizations in a competitive
environment. Therefore, the observed differences in the study may
not be generalizable to other communities where providers are less
sophisticated in participating in prepaid plans. It is important to
note, however, that three of the four prepaid plans were relatively
new, while the fourth, sponsored by Blue Cross/Blue Shield, was a
newly formed adjunct to a private sector plan. In this respect, the
demonstration may be representative of what might occur in other
communities, where relatively new prepaid plans are likely to provide services to Medicaid beneficiaries.

Second, the relatively short time period that enrollees were in
prepaid plans may have influenced the findings. Although the period
covered by the study was long enough to detect any immediate conse-

quences for utilization that were associated with enrollment in prepaid plans, it may not have been sufficient to detect the longer-term differences in utilization that would pertain as the prepaid plans refined their utilization review activities for this population and enrollees accommodated their care-seeking behavior to the control and monitoring activities adopted by the plans.

Third, there are limitations in using either self-reported or dummy claims data to assess the utilization of services. These limitations were addressed in the analysis by using a mixed strategy for estimating differences in utilization. For self-reported data, used to estimate differences in outpatient utilization, the issue of recall is important for individuals suffering from chronic mental illness or for their proxy respondents. However, there is no reason to believe that inaccurate recall would bias the estimated differences in prepaid versus fee-for-service utilization. For dummy claims data, the issue is whether health plans have an incentive to report utilization accurately and completely. In particular, while the prepaid plans seemed to have reported hospital utilization data accurately, there were valid reasons to suspect underreporting of physician visits and emergency room data. Therefore, dummy claims data were used only in the analysis of differences in inpatient utilization. (With respect to emergency room use, data were collected directly from area hospitals to address this issue and are now being analyzed.)

Fourth, the method adopted for identifying individuals with dual disorders was probably conservative. For example, individuals who sought outpatient treatment for alcohol or drug abuse four months before the follow-up interview but did not seek care subsequently would not be included, based on their interview responses, in the dual-disorder group. Future research might profitably explore the sensitivity of the findings to other categorization methods based on self-reports of the frequency of alcohol or drug use.

Acknowledgments

Dr. Lurie is a Henry J. Kaiser Family Foundation Faculty Scholar in General Internal Medicine. Financial support for this research was provided by Hennepin County, National Institute of Mental Health, the Bush Foundation, and the State of Minnesota. The authors thank Teh-wei Hu and Willard Manning for their helpful comments.

References

"Blue Cross to Pull Out of Trial Health Care Programs for Poor." 1987. *Minneapolis Star and Tribune,* 9 August.

Campbell, D., and J. Stanley. 1966. *Experimental and Quasi Experimental Designs for Research.* Chicago: Rand McNally.

Caton, C., A. Gralnick, S. Bender, and R. Simon. 1989. "Young Chronic Patients and Substance Abuse." *Hospital and Community Psychiatry* 40:1037–40.

Christianson, J., N. Lurie, M. Finch, and I. Moscovice. 1988. "Mandatory Enrollment of Medicaid-eligible Mentally Ill Persons in Prepaid Health Plans: The Minnesota Demonstration Project." *Administration and Policy in Mental Health,* 16, no. 2:51–64.

Drake, R., F. Osher, and M. Wallach. 1989. "Alcohol Use and Abuse in Schizophrenia: A Prospective Community Study." *Journal of Nervous and Mental Disease* 177:408–14.

Drake, R., and M. Wallach. 1989. "Substance Abuse among the Chronic Mentally Ill." *Hospital and Community Psychiatry* 40:1041–46.

Kay, S., M. Kalathara, and A. Meinzer. 1989. "Diagnostic and Behavioral Characteristics of Psychiatric Patients Who Abuse Substances." *Hospital and Community Psychiatry* 40:1062–64.

Kofoed, L., J. Kania, T. Walsh, and R. Atkinson. 1986. "Outpatient Treatment of Patients with Substance Abuse and Coexisting Psychiatric Disorders." *American Journal of Psychiatry* 143:867–72.

Luft, H. 1981. *Health Maintenance Organizations: Dimensions of Performance.* New York: John Wiley.

Miller, F., and J. Tanenbaum. 1989. "Drug Abuse in Schizophrenia." *Hospital and Community Psychiatry* 40:847–49.

Moscovice, I., M. Finch, and N. Lurie. 1989. "Plan Choice by the Mentally Ill in Medicaid Prepaid Health Plans." *Health Economics and Health Services Research* 10:265–78.

Pulver, A., P. Wolyniec, M. Wagner, C. Moorman, and J. McGrath. 1989. "An Epidemiologic Investigation of Alcohol-dependent Schizophrenics." *Acta Psychiatrica Scandinavica* 79:603–12.

Ridgely, M., H. Goldman, and J. Talbott. 1989. "Treatment of Chronic Mentally Ill Young Adults with Substance Abuse Problems: Emerging National Trends." *Adolescent Psychiatry: Developmental and Clinical Studies* 16:288–313.

Schlesinger, M. 1986. "On the Limits of Expanding Health Care Reform: Chronic Care in Prepaid Settings." *Milbank Quarterly* 64, no. 2:189–215.

14

A Mental Health Capitation Experiment: Evaluating the Monroe-Livingston Experience

Haroutun M. Babigian, M.D.,
Olivia S. Mitchell, Ph.D.,
Phyllis E. Marshall, M.S.W.,
and Sylvia K. Reed, Ph.D.

Health care cost inflation has prompted the development of many mechanisms to control and contain such costs. Frequently, these mechanisms incorporate a capitation feature, where a preset premium is paid in exchange for the enrolled patient's full treatment costs (e.g., health maintenance organizations) or for care of a particular condition (e.g., diagnosis-related groups). Such capitation schemes have met with mixed reviews from the general medical community (Sederer and St. Clair 1989; Sapolsky 1986; Weisman 1988). In the mental health care community, capitation systems have also been viewed with some apprehension. Nevertheless, many analysts recognize that the chronically mentally ill have not been served particularly well by the current mental health delivery system and suggest that a capitation system combined with community support services in place of hospitalization would be both cheaper and potentially more effective (Bacharach and Lamb 1989; Keisler and Morton 1988).

The purpose of this chapter is to describe costs and benefits from the application of a capitation method to a population of seriously and persistently mentally ill patients under treatment in Rochester, New York. The overall project, described in detail in earlier articles, is part of a larger demonstration that integrates and coordinates the services provided to mentally ill patients in a two-county area, Monroe and Livingston counties (Marshall 1986; Babigian and Reed 1987b; Babigian and Marshall 1989; Plum 1989). This chapter reports preliminary results from the first follow-up year using a cost-benefit framework. We found that the cost of maintaining seriously mentally ill patients is quite high, while monetizeable benefits are negligible. The first-year data also indicate that reduced costs of experimental continuous patients ($72,843) relative to control group patients ($83,746) resulted almost entirely from reductions in hospitalization. Finally, for patients enrolled in the capitation payments system (CPS), costs of care were much lower than those for control patients, and many psychological benefits could be quantified. Experimental patients not enrolled in the CPS treatment program were more expensive and benefited less than their control group counterparts.

Previous Studies

In the mental health area, two principal problems have been identified as particularly relevant to those designing capitation delivery systems (Babigian and Reed 1987a). First, there is a perception that mentally ill patients often suffer from discontinuous care, in that they are often seen in more than one facility, and may receive much of their care from state psychiatric facilities. As patients move from one facility to the next, there may be inadequate sharing of information regarding effective treatments and illness dynamics. Patients are often not able to assist treatment personnel in maintaining consistency of care. Treatment plans can change from one somatic therapy to another and may or may not include additional supports for the patient. Patients also drop out of treatment programs, often as their illness is intensifying. The disruptive effects of treatment discontinuity can be devastating for these patients, preventing effective adaptation to their illness.

Many of these problems may be alleviated by a capitation-based treatment program, since the responsible agency can use precommitted premiums to provide whatever services are needed to manage each patient's illness most effectively. A system with adequate capitation fees can naturally lead to the development of needed programs, especially if local coordination is available among caregiving agencies. In other words, a capitation mechanism can meet the need identified by Lehman (1989), who argued that policy should be directed at improving care through service coordination and integration.

A second issue often raised in the mental health context is that capitation may provide incentives to substitute less expensive support services for more expensive hospitalization (Hadley et al. 1989). This is because the enrolling agency assumes responsibility for enrolled patients and has fiscal incentives to avoid serious illness or problems. This can be beneficial to patients. For instance, when patients drop out of a treatment program, it is usually in the enrolling agency's best interest actively to seek them out; this is also usually in the patients' best interest. In addition, the capitation approach tends to encourage the enrolling agency to maintain mentally ill patients in the least restrictive setting possible, a goal generally endorsed by the mental health treatment community (Department of Health and Human Services 1980).

Perhaps because it is still fairly new, the capitation approach in the mental health area has met with various problems. Long-term deinstitutionalization trends dramatically reduced censuses in state psychiatric hospitals, yet many locales were unprepared to fund and target community services to this difficult patient group (Deiker 1986; Mechanic and Aiken 1989). It also appears that effective mental health treatments are often predominantly social in nature (Stein and Test 1978), but as such tend not to be covered by health payers. For example, case management services often play a key role in maintaining mentally ill patients in the community but are still not covered by most insurance plans and have only been covered by Medicaid since 1989.

Capitation-like models in the mental health field are being tested in several places and have yielded only preliminary and very mixed results. In Arizona, Santiago (1989) was impeded by an inadequate capitation rate set for his demonstration by the state Division of Behavioral Health. This problem, along with "dissension and antagonism among providers," which prompted legal action, reflects an often-difficult political climate for capitation programs in the mental health area (Santiago et al. 1986). Change in administrators caused delays in startup for a Philadelphia capitation project, and the concurrent closing of the local state hospital redirected planners who would have otherwise been concentrating on the demonstration (Hadley and Glover 1989; Hadley et al. 1989). A federal Civilian Health and Medical Program of the Uniformed Services (CHAMPUS) project experienced complications with changes in contracts as well as startup, personnel, and data management, making implementation difficult (Burns et al. 1989). This project, like those in Arizona and Philadelphia, is still collecting data, and findings are just emerging. In Rhode Island, a capitation program was utilized to deinstitutionalize over two hundred seriously ill state hospital patients to community settings (Mauch 1989; Christianson and Linehan 1989). In California, a four-city model program is under way, with an evaluation format adapted from that devised for the Rochester study.

The Monroe-Livingston Capitation System

In 1987, five community mental health centers with responsibility for catchment areas in the Rochester, New York, area formed a locally controlled not-for-profit management corporation under the rubric of Integrated Mental Health, Inc. (IMH). IMH was then contractually delegated state and county responsibility for planning and managing the mental health delivery system in Monroe and Livingston counties and developed capitation agreements as part of a larger demonstration coordination project (Marshall 1986). Designated "lead agencies," these five community mental health centers developed their programs independently, and some features of programs were quite different between agencies, although information and ideas were shared extensively.

The CPS was structured to deliver mental health care to patients being released from the local state psychiatric hospital, Rochester Psychiatric Center (RPC). Features of the capitation program are shown in table 14.1.

A total of 1,587 patients met criteria for continuous or intermittent assignment levels during the 1987–88 base-year period, of whom 40 percent were prerandomized to a control group to facilitate evaluation, as shown in figure 14.1. Patients prerandomized to the experimental condition were placed on a CPS roster, from which all CPS enrollments were to occur.

An evaluation study of CPS was funded by the National Institute of Mental Health (NIMH) to review the first two years of operation of this capitation system for mental health delivery. At present, preliminary evidence is available for the first year of follow-up only (second-year data collection was completed in December 1990). The NIMH evaluation focuses on the capitation financing method rather than on specific mental health treatments or programs. Only continuous (long-stay) and intermittent (revolving-door) patients are examined in the research project, and this chapter describes outcomes only for patients in the continuous grouping. This focus is prompted by our particular interest in capitation delivery systems for this most chronically and seriously ill group. Also, the prepayment capitation amounts and associated care requirements differ markedly across continuous and intermittent patients, generating very different incentives for the lead agencies. For continuous patients, all care must be covered by the preset fee.[1] In contrast, hospitalization costs for intermittent patients were not the lead agencies' responsibility, generating reduced incentive to avoid hospitalization in this population. Thus, the clearest picture of the effects of the capitation system must necessarily be drawn from the continuous population's experiences.

Experimental Design and Data Sources

The study design for the evaluation was derived from cancer research to allow the flexibility allowed for patient and lead agency choice. A schematic of this design is shown in figure 14.2. Individuals were contacted for participation in the study if they met eligibility criteria and were (1) designated for discharge from RPC, (2) enrolled in RPC outpatient programs, or (3) enrolled in community mental health center outpatient programs. Comparisons were made on available data to determine whether equivalence of control and experimental groups was maintained in study sample selection, and no difference was found. Individuals who were contacted for study enrollment generally had more hospitalization and outpatient care than patients who were not contacted for participation. Of those contacted for study participation, those who chose to participate in the study did not differ on available measures from those who refused or were unable to participate.

It was anticipated that control group patients would continue to be treated with the normally available care. Experimental group patients who did not enroll in the CPS were hypothesized to receive treatment akin to that received by control group members. This study's central hypotheses is that experimental group treatment will yield greater social benefits as compared to control group treatment, without incurring additional social costs or imposing greater burdens on health care payers, families, or the community. It is important, when discussing costs and benefits, to emphasize that we seek to measure *social* benefits and costs. *Social costs* differ from private or government-sector costs in an important way: social cost-accounting strives to recognize the full economic value of resources used in a given production project. For this reason, in assessing costs of caring for the patient population in this study, we focus not just on actual bills issued and paid, but also on whether resources are used efficiently in the course of generating output. In addition, it is necessary to go beyond monetizeable costs and try to measure the nonmonetary costs incurred by both treatment modes. Assessing *social benefits* also

Table 14.1   Features of Capitation

Who pays capitation?	The state of New York contracts with IMH based on proposed enrollment plans submitted by the lead agencies. Adjustments are made for actual variance from the plan. All possible accounts receivable are collected for services provided, with revenues returned to the state and IMH.
Who is at risk?	The lead agencies who enroll patients in CPS are at risk if expenses exceed the capitation revenues. To date, in combined rate groups, capitation revenues have been sufficient to cover expenses.
Who is eligible? What are the capitation rates?	Eligibility is based on utilization of state psychiatric center care during the past 3 years, with 3 different capitation rates (adjusted annually for inflation) based on levels of utilization: • *Continuous* ($41,184): >270 inpatient days/3 years • *Intermittent* ($13,728): 45–270 inpatient days/3 years • *Outpatient* ($5,280): >25 visits & on RPC outpatient rolls Rates were restructured in 1990 to approximate capitation costs more closely, yielding continuous = $28,004, intermittent = $15,653, and outpatient = $11,682.
What is the care responsibility?	The responsibility of the lead agency is at one of two levels: • *Continuous*: coordination and provision of all care, including all inpatient and ambulatory mental health and health care, medications, residential care, and transportation. • *Intermittent and Outpatient*: coordination of all care, provision of all ambulatory mental health care and medications.
What are rates based on?	Lacking solid information, rates were based on average projected treatment plans, negotiated between the state OMH and IMH. A major purpose of the demonstration was to determine what the expenses would be if this population were adequately served.
Enrollment/Disenrollment	Patients contacted for enrollment in CPS were involved in developing a treatment plan and could choose to enroll or not. The patient could choose to change lead agency

(continued)

Table 14.1   (*Continued*)

	or to drop out of CPS at any time. Lead agencies could disenroll patients for return to long-term psychiatric hospitalization, if there was persistent abridgement of their treatment plans. Loss of contact, leaving the area, and death also resulted in disenrollment. Approximately 10% of ever-enrolled CPS patients were disenrolled, with the most common reason being return to long-term hospitalization. Most disenrolled patients were eventually reenrolled in CPS.
Reinsurance	Initially, there was a plan to commit a percentage of CPS revenues into a fund to be used for exceptionally high-cost patients. With the provisions for disenrollment and the adequate capitation funding, this fund became less critical and was dropped.

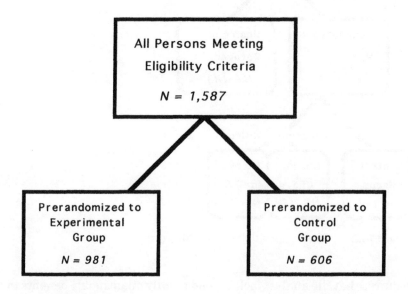

34.8% RPC Inpatient	35.8% RPC Inpatient
19.5% RPC Outpatient	19.3% RPC Outpatient
359.9 Avg 3-Yr Inpatient Days	350.7 Avg 3-Yr Inpatient Days
59.6% Male	57.6% Male
29.1% Minority	31.5% Minority

Figure 14.1   Prerandomization to experimental and control conditions

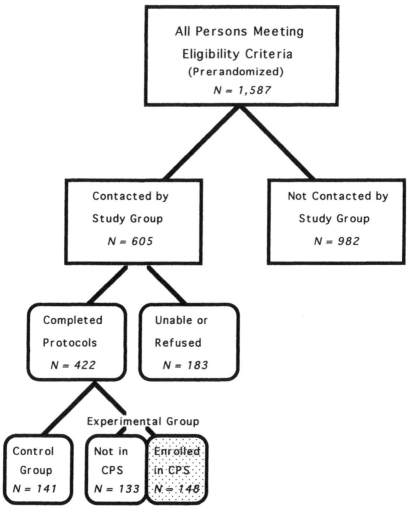

Figure 14.2   The composition of the study group

requires that the analyst look beyond readily quantifiable benefits to
include measures of all outputs generated. This demands analysis of
qualitative outcomes as well as monetary ones, going beyond revenues to include less easily monetizeable changes. In addition, a full
social evaluation analysis must incorporate not only benefits from
the program accruing to government units, but also individual patients, communities and families, and health care providers.

The NIMH evaluation study covers a sample of 422 patients for whom first-year follow-up data were obtained on 77 percent. No significant differences in baseline measures were found between those who were followed at year 1 and those who did not complete protocols at that time. Of the overall group, 226 (54 percent) were continuous patients at first follow-up and constitute the group analyzed in the present cost-benefit study. Most of these continuous patients were selected into the evaluation study as they were identified for discharge from the Rochester Psychiatric Center (81 percent) and at baseline had spent an average of two of the prior three years hospitalized. Three-fourths of the group carried diagnoses of schizophrenia, with the remainder split between major affective disorders and other conditions. Average ratings of functioning reflected major dysfunction in several areas (Global Assessment Scale [GAS] score average = 38) and were consistent with hospitalization.

The study protocol included measures of clinical symptoms, level of functioning, quality of life, family burden, addiction, and resource utilization. Patient interviews were conducted at baseline and again at one- and two-year follow-up anniversaries of baseline. As part of the first-year follow-up process, patients were interviewed regarding their use of services during the past month using a resource index (RI) questionnaire that summarizes subjects' utilization of services and other relevant financial information. For purposes of the present analysis, patient self-reported services (both mental health and other resources) were obtained from the RI and annualized to obtain group average counts. The exception is mental health services provided by IMH agencies, for which actual counts were obtained from the system data file for this analysis.[2] In addition, interviews were also conducted for a "significant other" as identified by each patient in approximately 50 percent of study cases. This interview aided in ascertaining what burdens or benefits, if any, were imposed by patients in the experimental and control groups. Such interviews were completed for approximately 50 percent of the enrolled patients at baseline, with approximately the same proportion of completed study patient interviews at follow-up.

Baseline Comparisons

Analysis of baseline data reveals no important significant differences between study experimental and control group patients in terms of psychological or demographic descriptors. This provides reassurance that patients were classified randomly for study purposes and indicates that clear-cut comparisons can be drawn between experimental and control group patients. Hence, in results reported below, we always focus first on experimental versus control group costs and benefits.

There is also some question as to whether experimental group patients who enrolled in the CPS treatment mode differ significantly from those experimental group patients who did not enroll. Non-enrollment in CPS could occur for two reasons: first, the CPS lead agencies were allowed to select from the pool of eligible experimental prospects and, second, patients were permitted to enroll or not as they chose.[3] We analyzed the extent to which systematic selection took place for enrollment into CPS by identifying several possible selection variables based on interviews with CPS agency personnel and review of patient screening forms required by IMH. Variables available for study included age, sex, diagnosis (schizophrenia/psychosis versus other), GAS score, overall number of symptoms (number of items rated moderate or worse on the Brief Psychiatric Rating Scale), global alogia (includes poverty of content, poverty of speech, and other communication deficits), hostility, suspiciousness, uncooperativeness, interviewer rating of substance abuse problems, completion of a significant other interview, rating of intelligence, ethnicity (white versus minority), full versus brief protocol, and days of hospitalization over the past three years. In addition, two composite variables were created by summing features recorded from the patient records at baseline. A "care" variable described ability to perform basic activities of daily living, incontinence, careless smoking, medical care needs, firesetting, and other unusual care needs. A "behavior" variable described aggressive behavior, violence, self-harm, inappropriate acting out, and other behavior problems. All of these variables in combination accounted for only 19.5 percent of the variance in enrollment status of experimental group continuous patients.[4] The fact that the included variables do not account for much of enrollment status variance suggests that selection bias, while present, is not highly correlated with readily observable variables. Future analyses will focus in detail on factors related to selection into CPS and their relationship to outcome measures.

First-Year Follow-up

At first-year follow-up, 95 percent of the 422 total study patients were located and more than 77 percent (325) were interviewed. An abbreviated study protocol was used for patients who were unable to tolerate a full interview, and partial protocols or better were obtained for

179 continuous patients and 146 intermittent patients at the one-year point. Completed protocols for continuous patients included 57 control group patients, 58 CPS-enrolled experimental group patients, and 64 nonenrolled experimental group patients.

Cost-Benefit Method

Our approach to social cost-benefit analysis was modeled after that developed by Burton Weisbrod and associates (1980, 1981, 1983). Table 14.2 organizes the key issues into costs versus benefits and further recognizes both monetizeable and nonmonetary factors. Costs are categorized according to whether they are associated with mental health treatment (inpatient and outpatient), substance abuse, medical and dental treatment, maintenance, social services, community burdens (including family), and negative patient outcomes. Benefits include employment-related outcomes, contributions to community and family resources, and positive patient outcomes. All information is presented for both the overall control and the experimental groups, as well as the CPS-enrolled and nonenrolled patients within the experimental group. Monetary figures are presented in 1988 dollars; figures obtained for other years were indexed using either the overall Consumer Price Index or the health price subindex, as appropriate.

Per-Unit Cost Estimates

The most critical single number in the cost analysis turns out, not surprisingly, to be the per diem rate at the state psychiatric center (RPC). For various reasons, the state budgeting process does not generate a true economic cost of care at this institution (as is probably the case in most states). Specifically, operating costs are not fully reflected in the hospital's budget, costs of capital in the form of building and equipment are not carried on the books, and rates of return on labor and hospital plant are not recognized. Hence, the per diem cost had to be estimated from other sources to obtain a more accurate assessment of the true economic cost of hospitalizing a patient in that institution. This chapter uses a community psychiatric hospital per diem rate of $309 as the best estimate of true RPC costs in 1988. Although the state facility is generally less fully staffed than are community psychiatric hospitals, salaries at the state hospital are much higher, administration is more substantial, and there are many hidden costs not taken into account (extensive prime land holdings, computer processing, patient nutrition, and physical plant, among others).

Table 14.2 Benefits and Costs for Continuous Patients—1988 Adjusted Costs per Service Unit Based on the First Follow-up Year (N = 211)

Category (units)	Cost/ Unit	Category Units (Person/Year) Based on RI				Cost/Group			
		Control (67)	Experi- mental (144)	Enrolled (70)	Not Enrolled (74)	Control (67)	Experi- mental (144)	Enrolled (70)	Not Enrolled (74)
Costs									
Outpatient mental health									
Clinic (full visit, assessment, in crisis)	$88	4.43	6.50	10.41	2.79	$390	$572	$916	$246
Clinic (brief & med visits)	$44	10.06	14.78	21.26	8.66	$443	$650	$935	$381
Outpatient visit (non-IMH)	$55	1.68	0.00	0.00	0.00	$92	$0	$0	$0
Case management (hour)	$49	9.73	19.90	34.20	6.37	$477	$975	$1,676	$312
Case management (non-IMH)	$49	1.26	6.74	13.09	0.81	$62	$330	$641	$40
Group & family (visit)	$35	0.00	0.07	0.10	0.04	$0	$2	$4	$1
Day treatment (visit)	$77	1.87	0.01	0.01	0.00	$144	$1	$1	$0
Continuing treatment (visit)	$46	11.18	16.83	26.86	7.35	$514	$774	$1,236	$338
Crisis (visit)	$150	0.60	0.81	0.99	0.64	$90	$122	$149	$96
Psychosocial club (visit)	$48	3.00	8.35	16.56	0.58	$144	$401	$795	$28
Sheltered workshop (visit) (tx only)	$29	7.90	17.09	23.63	10.91	$229	$496	$685	$316
Day training (visit)	$46	0.00	2.00	1.11	2.84	$0	$92	$51	$131
Rehabilitation (visit)	$46	8.06	6.45	12.40	0.82	$371	$297	$570	$38
On-site rehab (visit)	$5	7.87	3.89	5.66	2.22	$39	$19	$28	$11
Transportation	$7	1.27	7.09	14.49	0.09	$9	$50	$101	$1
Volunteer friend (hour)	$8	3.74	3.11	2.78	3.43	$30	$25	$22	$27
TOTAL—outpatient mental health						$3,034	$4,806	$7,811	$1,966
Medication costs						$1,767	$1,848	$1,614	$2,145
TOTAL—outpatient MH and medication						$4,801	$6,654	$9,425	$4,111
Residential mental health care									
IMH inpatient (day)	$309	1.06	4.15	7.53	0.96	$328	$1,282	$2,327	$297

	Unit cost								
RPC inpatient (day)	$309	228.90	180.23	98.11	257.91	$70,730	$55,691	$30,316	$79,694
Community residence (day)	$57	32.97	34.20	52.67	16.73	$1,879	$1,949	$3,002	$954
Family care (day)	$25	0.25	0.42	0.86	0.00	$6	$11	$22	$0
Crisis residence (day)	$50	0.51	0.57	1.03	0.14	$26	$29	$52	$7
TOTAL—residential MH care						$72,969	$58,962	$35,718	$80,951
Substance abuse									
Inpatient (day)	$101	0.00	0.00	0.00	0.00	$0	$0	$0	$0
Outpatient substance abuse (visit)	$60	2.74	4.95	4.36	5.49	$164	$297	$261	$329
Alc/narc anonymous	$8	6.53	3.05	3.49	2.64	$52	$24	$28	$21
TOTAL—substance abuse						$216	$321	$289	$350
Dental (visit)	$65	5.89	4.74	3.49	5.90	$383	$308	$227	$384
Medical									
Outpatient clinic (visit)	$91	7.37	5.16	6.60	5.01	$671	$470	$601	$456
Inpatient hospital (day)	$360	2.11	2.74	0.44	4.88	$760	$986	$158	$1,757
Emergency room (visit)	$144	0.63	0.53	0.65	0.41	$91	$76	$94	$59
TOTAL—medical						$1,521	$1,532	$853	$2,272
Religious counseling (visit)	$25	1.26	0.74	1.09	0.41	$32	$19	$27	$10
Social services									
DSS case management (visit)	$23	1.47	0.84	0.65	1.02	$34	$19	$15	$23
Jail (night)	$80	6.32	0.00	0.00	0.00	$506	$0	$0	$0
Legal contacts (hour)	$92	0.42	1.16	0.87	1.42	$39	$107	$80	$131
Probation (hour)	$21	0.42	0.84	0.87	0.81	$9	$18	$18	$17
Court contacts (case)	$916	0.22	0.84	0.22	1.42	$202	$769	$202	$1,301
Police contacts (hour)	$35	0.22	0.95	1.09	0.81	$8	$33	$38	$28
Arrests (contact)	$100	0.00	0.32	0.22	0.41	$0	$32	$22	$41
Other services (hour)	$35	0.84	0.95	1.31	0.61	$29	$33	$46	$21
TOTAL—social services						$825	$1,012	$421	$1,563
Non-mental health residential maintenance costs									
Single apt/rental (year)	$8,630	0.05	0.09	0.13	0.05	$432	$777	$1,122	$432
W/other(s)/rental (year)	$6,700	0.03	0.02	0.14	0.02	$201	$134	$938	$134

(*continued*)

Table 14.2 *(Continued)*

Category (units)	Cost/Unit	Category Units (Person/Year) Based on RI				Cost/Group			
		Control (67)	Experimental (144)	Enrolled (70)	Not Enrolled (74)	Control (67)	Experimental (144)	Enrolled (70)	Not Enrolled (74)
W/family or relatives (year)	$5,400	0.02	0.04	0.08	0.01	$108	$216	$432	$54
Boarding house (year)	$7,950	0.00	0.02	0.03	0.02	$0	$159	$239	$159
Other cost (year)	$6,815	0.20	0.24	0.33	0.18	$1,363	$1,636	$2,249	$1,227
Shelter w/meals (night)	$14	0.42	0.31	0.44	0.20	$6	$4	$6	$3
Soup kitchen (meal)	$2	0.00	6.11	12.65	0.00	$0	$12	$25	$0
TOTAL—maintenance costs						$2,109	$2,938	$5,011	$2,008
Community burden costs[a]									
% w/interviewed SO		49.1%	57.4%	59.6%	55.6%				
Annual spending by SO						$818	$1,004	$1,015	$993
Annual overnights w/SO		28.3	13.8	23.5	3.8				
Annual meals from SO	$2	36.2	47.0	65.6	30.4	$72	$94	$131	$61
% reporting burden		66.7%	80.3%	77.4%	82.9%				
% reporting lost work time		3.7%	6.0%	0.0%	11.4%				
% reporting emotional problems		37.0%	47.0%	38.7%	54.3%				
% disrupting neighborhood		0.0%	1.5%	0.0%	2.9%				

Patient outcomes									
% w/negative outcomes		9.6%	6.4%	0.0%	11.9%				
% in supervised residential settings at follow-up		81.1%	77.3%	64.7%	86.8%				
Mean number of moderate to severe symptoms (range = 0 to 24)		3.00	3.37	2.45	4.08				
% dissatisfied w/life		20.8%	21.8%	13.3%	28.6%				
% reporting victimization		21.8%	37.4%	25.0%	47.6%				
Total costs						$83,746	$72,843	$53,116	$92,702
Benefits									
Employment (hours)									
% working competitively	$3.35	1.5%	2.8%	4.3%	1.4%				
Volunteer work	$3.10	0.00	0.00	1.03	1.30	$0	$0	$3	$4
Job training	$3.10	0.00	0.33	0.00	0.00	$0	$1	$0	$0
Workshop/rehabilitation		157.25	130.17	124.80	135.24	$487	$404	$387	$419
Competitive work	$3.35	53.73	14.67	40.63	8.76	$180	$49	$136	$29
TOTAL—earnings						$667	$454	$526	$453
% contributing to community resources		18.5%	15.2%	19.4%	11.4%				
% contributing to home production		44.4%	39.4%	45.2%	34.3%				
Patient outcomes									
% in unsupervised settings		22.7%	22.7%	35.3%	13.2%				
% satisfied w/life		62.5%	59.4%	60.0%	58.9%				
% w/GAS score of 41 or more		50.9%	37.8%	52.6%	24.2%				

[a]Costs are per patient with reporting significant other (SO).

Mental health per unit costs were derived from lead agency–reported service units divided into reported expenses by service type in 1988 (from state-mandated agency year-end expenditure reports). Substance abuse unit service costs were obtained by dividing service units into total expenses for appropriate programs, using reports similar to those used for mental health treatment costs. Social services and law enforcement cost estimates were obtained through contacts with local departments of social services and public safety. Medical costs were determined by comparing Medicaid reimbursement rates, charges levied by private providers, computations from a major hospital's budget stepdown procedure, and community average costs obtained from the Rochester Area Hospitals Corporation. Patient maintenance costs were based on estimates provided by case managers who work with mentally ill clients, combined with federal food consumption charts. All costs of residence, clothing, food, and other living expenses are included in the maintenance estimates by type of residential setting.

Per Unit Benefit Estimates

This study focuses on a seriously ill patient population that had experienced substantial hospitalization periods before the initiation of the experiment. By design, then, the experiment was structured so that the patients' poor condition makes it somewhat unlikely that significant monetary benefits will be detected after a year in the experiment. Nonetheless, one benefit that might be anticipated and can be quantified is patient gainful employment. Although patients are often unable to specify how much they actually earned, they can usually indicate whether they worked, whether it was in competitive or sheltered employment, and how many hours they worked in a given time period. These employment estimates are evaluated at the minimum wage for volunteer and competitive employment at the time ($3.35 per hour), consistent with the approach taken in Weisbrod and Stein (1980); in the case of sheltered and rehabilitation workplaces we applied a somewhat lower wage rate ($3.10 per hour), recognizing that productivity was somewhat lower here. To date, the employment outcomes are the only benefits monetized for the purposes of the study.

Utilization Estimates

Mental health service counts were derived from the Integrated Mental Health system data file. Other self-reported usage rates were obtained from patient resource index surveys and averaged to obtain counts for non-IMH mental health and all other service utilization. These counts were then combined with the per unit costs discussed above to yield annualized cost and benefit figures. We also present several costs and benefits that are not monetized but nevertheless indicate the quality of patient and family life, as well as other outcomes. Some of these outcomes are patient scores on psychological/functioning tests, whereas others are indicators of positive outcomes (e.g., percentage living in unsupervised settings, percentage contributing to home or community resources) or of negative outcomes (e.g., percentage reporting victimization).

Community costs and benefits are reported by only about one-half of the subjects' "significant others" (SOs), sometimes because a patient lacked a SO but other times because family members refused to talk about the patient. No single assumption or set of assumptions seems to be descriptive of the patient group lacking a SO. Table 14.2 simply averages SO costs and benefits across the subsample responding to the protocol, making no attempt to spread the results across the full group. This probably inflates reported costs to the extent that significant others are not involved with some patients but may understate family/community benefits.

Findings and Discussion

Costs and Benefits: Experimental versus Control Groups

As table 14.2 shows clearly, total costs for continuous patients in this sample are very high, averaging (in 1988 dollars) $72,843 per year for experimental patients and $83,746 per year for control patients. Over three-fourths of this cost is accounted for by inpatient mental health care. When outpatient mental health care is included, over 85 percent of the measured costs are directly attributable to mental health treatment costs (see fig. 14.3). This average level of costs and the fraction of costs attributable to mental health costs are higher than those reported by Weisbrod and Stein (1980), primarily because their study sample consisted of patients who were not chronically institutionalized. In contrast, the Rochester patients included in the present study were much more severely impaired than those analyzed in Wisconsin, having spent two of the previous three years in a mental hospital.

Table 14.2 also shows that the experimental group experienced a significant total cost advantage as compared to the control group.

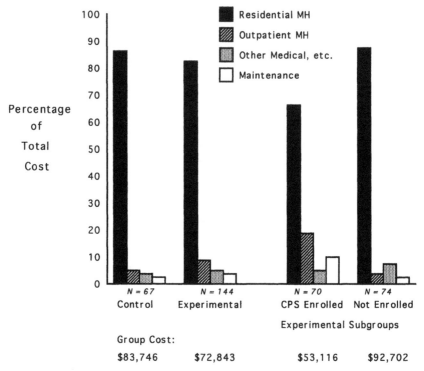

Figure 14.3   The percentage of the group cost by category (continuous patients, 1988 dollars). *MH,* mental health.

This is because of lower mental health hospitalization rates, as the experimental group spent an average of only 184 days hospitalized during their first year, in contrast to 230 days for the control group. Control and experimental group costs and utilization and cost patterns are also fairly similar along other cost dimensions translated into monetary terms.

Focusing next on monetized measures of benefits, table 14.2 shows that beneficial employment outcomes are minimal for both groups. Patients in both experimental and control groups earned an annual average of $450–670, less than 1 percent of total costs as assessed. These earnings rates are far below the rates reported by Weisbrod and Stein (1980), again attesting to the much less favorable mental health status of the Rochester patient group.

Turning attention to nonmonetary benefit and cost measures, there is slight evidence favoring the experimental group: fewer experimental group patients experienced negative outcomes than did control group members (e.g., mortality), more experimental group members worked in competitive employment, and fewer experimental group members required supervised residential living. However, the evidence does not clearly favor the experimental group, inasmuch as experimental group patients reported being slightly less satisfied with life (59 versus 63 percent), were victimized more often (37 versus 22 percent), and contributed less to home and community and patients' SOs reported more problems for experimental group members than for control group patients for all four community burden measures. These differences in outcomes are fairly small, however, and in fact are not statistically significant; hence, the evidence on nonpecuniary outcomes does not clearly favor one group over the other.

A finding not reported in table 14.2 but evident from an earlier screening of the data suggests a confounding finding regarding nonpecuniary benefits and costs worth reporting here: both patient groups apparently showed significant improvement in psychiatric rating comparing their baseline assessment to that at first year follow-up. This may be due to the fact that most patients were interviewed at baseline when they were in the hospital, and many fewer were hospitalized a year later. Alternatively, it may be that changes occurred in the community during the CPS implementation period, which could have resulted in improved prospects for all patients. For example, case management services have expanded greatly over time, not just for CPS patients but for other patients as well. Some benefits available to CPS patients, such as the ability to purchase needed resources, have been applied variably to other patients with obvious need so that clinical ethical dilemmas could be avoided. All CPS programs were combined with existing and expanded long-term care programs to create off-site centers for continuing care under the direction of the CPS coordinators. This level of improvement in overall care for control group patients was not anticipated and to some extent confounds the study's conclusions.

Costs and Benefits: Enrolled versus Nonenrolled Experimental Patients

Superficial similarities between experimental and control group costs and benefits obscure some striking differences in behavior between the two subgroups within the experimental category. A perusal of the last two columns of table 14.2 shows that the CPS-enrolled experimental group members consistently cost much less than the CPS-nonenrolled subsample. The overall differences are pronounced:

enrolled experimental group patient total costs averaged only 58.6 percent of nonenrolled experimental group patient costs ($53,116 versus on an annual basis $92,702). This cost gap is mainly attributable to significant differences in psychiatric hospitalization days, inasmuch as CPS-enrolled patients were hospitalized only one-sixth as much as nonenrollees. At first-year follow-up, almost two-thirds of the nonenrolled experimental group was in the hospital versus only a handful of enrolled experimental group patients (for study purposes they were counted in the CPS-enrolled group, although they became disenrolled from CPS formally because of long-term rehospitalization needs).

The thesis that outpatient care might be substituted for inpatient care at a considerable reduction in cost is given some support in this analysis, since outpatient mental health costs are higher for the enrolled experimental group subset. Outpatient care expenditures for CPS-enrolled experimental group members more than doubled those for the control group. The only area in which costs were notably higher for the CPS-enrolled experimental group is in the maintenance area, and these costs are partially offset in the other cost categories by virtue of the fact that maintenance costs for those hospitalized are included in the per diem hospital rate.

Also of interest is the fact that a higher proportion of CPS-enrolled experimental group patients were living in nonsupervised residential settings than were other groups ($\chi^2 = 8.7$, $p < .05$). For many years, it has been a national policy that patients should be maintained in the least restrictive setting possible (Department of Health and Human Services 1980). Indeed, there is reason to believe that patients are made less functional by extended hospitalization. Patients frequently prefer the privacy of their own house or apartment, but in the past such placements were ill advised because the patients would become isolated or tend to drop out of services and their illness would become exacerbated. With the incentives for capitation system teams to maintain an active support relationship with community patients, the benefit of allowing patients to maintain their preferred residential settings is enhanced.

A final point to note is the relative failure of the CPS-nonenrolled experimental group patients to show improvement during the first-year follow-up. These patients were significantly more likely to be rated as impaired in function (GAS scores below 41) as compared to either other group ($\chi^2 = 12.5$, $p < .01$) and reported higher levels of victimization ($\chi^2 = 25.2$, $p < .0001$). Inpatient medical costs for the nonenrolled experimental group are almost five times as high as for CPS-enrolled patients and are double those for the control group patients. This group also was a much heavier user of social services, including the jails and the court system, and imposed apparently heavier costs on their families and neighborhoods.

Summary and Conclusions

In summary, our preliminary conclusions from first-year data are the following:

1. *The net cost of maintaining seriously mentally ill patients is very high: $72,843 for the experimental group and $83,746 for the control group* (in 1988 dollars). More than three-fourths of this cost is accounted for directly by inpatient mental health care and, when outpatient mental health care is also included, more than four-fifths of all measured costs are directly attributable to mental health treatment and hospitalization. This is consistent with findings of a variety of aggressive community-based treatment programs that have been able to reduce hospitalization significantly in seriously mentally ill populations (Stein and Test 1978; Bond and Boyer 1988). Patient earnings in both experimental and control groups amounted to less than 1 percent of total costs as assessed.

2. *The first-year Monroe-Livingston capitation data indicate that benefits are very similar for experimental and control group patients.* Without appreciable changes in patient outcomes, there is some evidence that outpatient care can be substituted for inpatient care at a considerable reduction in cost, based on the considerably lower hospital utilization of the CPS group.

3. *For patients enrolled in CPS treatment, costs of care were much lower than those for control patients, and many psychological benefits could be quantified.*

4. *Patients who were not enrolled in the CPS treatment program were far more expensive and benefited less than their CPS-enrolled counterparts.* Annual per capita costs for CPS-enrolled patients were only 63 percent of control group expenses but were 110 percent of control group expenses among CPS nonenrolled patients.

Second-year data for further study of a number of issues will be available shortly. There is reason to believe that the startup process made first-year costs higher than long-run average costs, so that the full effect of the financing mechanism was not adequately captured during the program's first year. In ongoing research, we are examining second-year data to determine whether per unit costs have fallen. Work in progress will also compare utilization rates extracted from the IMH system data files with those derived from patient self-reports, and a new version of the cost-benefit table will be derived. Another research project in progress is a distributional analysis examining who pays for experimental and control patient care. We will track payment shifts among federal, state, local, and voluntary sources and will discover new information about who bears the cost burden of capitation.

One of the unusual features of this evaluation analysis is that data are being collected for a second follow-up year. We hypothesize that in the second year the CPS-enrolled group will continue to improve in functioning and require minimal rehospitalization, whereas control patients will begin to show an increased incidence of deterioration. Meanwhile it is to be expected that the nonenrolled experimental group may show improvement as some are discharged from the hospital during the project's second year. As noted above, many community programs have been enhanced because of the advent of the IMH delivery system and the capitation experiment itself. Evidently the community has benefited from the resource enhancement and the new emphasis on care for seriously and persistently mentally ill persons. However, this gain works against the evaluation study by improving the outcomes of the control group. This overall community gain in care may be one of the more important outcomes of this limited demonstration of the Monroe-Livingston capitation system, although it would probably not have occurred in an underfunded capitation system.

An important remaining question is whether experimental group patients who did not enroll in the CPS project could be maintained in the community at comparable costs and benefits. If so, total costs would almost surely be much less than reflected in the present analysis. Our initial analysis failed to reveal any selection factors that importantly predicted enrollment status, suggesting that supply-side constraints (lack of available CPS slots) may have been a major reason for nonenrollment. Further work on this front is proceeding, but the evidence thus far suggests that treatment costs for all experimental group patients taken together would have actually fallen substantially if it had been possible to enroll more patients in the program. It also remains to be seen whether patients who will be deinstitutionalized in the near future could be cared for under standard CPS procedures. As the census at the state hospital continues to drop, remaining patients become extremely difficult to work with and place.[5] It is our conclusion that, if these patients can be maintained in community settings, costs will be substantially lower than in the hospital and patient outcomes will improve.

Acknowledgments

This research is supported through National Institute of Health grant 1 RO1 MH 40053 to the University of Rochester. The authors acknowledge and express gratitude for the capable assistance of project coordinator Suzanne W. Brown, coinvestigator Robert S. Cole, systems programmer Graciela P. Viturro, and graduate assistant Kevin Hennessy.

Notes

1. Not included would be a few incidental support services provided by family members, clergy, and other nontreatment personnel and maintenance costs covered by SSI.

2. The system data file contains records of all services provided to all patients registered with participating specialty mental health programs. In an earlier analysis, patient reports of service utilization were compared to the system data file counts to determine the reliability of self-reports from this patient population. In general, these counts proved surprisingly close as long as services were grouped into rather aggregate clusters (e.g., case management was combined with clinic visits, and most types of day treatment services were grouped). The primary area in which patients consistently reported more services than were obtained from the system files was hours of sheltered workshop. Upon reviewing this difference, it was learned that several programs were providing "informal" sheltered work through subsidized employment of their patients within their programs. Patients reported these earnings as sheltered work, but there were no matching records in the system files.

3. Subjects were defined as enrolled if they had spent more than thirty days enrolled in CPS during their first follow-up year.

4. By descending order of contribution, variables contributing the most among the continuous group were rating of intelligence, three-year hospital days, number of different symptoms, and the care composite variable.

5. In late 1987, the RPC adult census was near 750; by the end of 1990, it had been reduced below 450.

References

Babigian, H. M., and P. E. Marshall. 1989. "Rochester: A Comprehensive Capitation Experiment." In D. Mechanic and L. H. Aiken (eds.): *Paying for Services: Promises and Pitfalls of Capitation*, pp. 43–54. New Directions for Mental Health Services, no. 43. San Francisco: Jossey-Bass.

Babigian, H. M., and S. K. Reed. 1987a. "Capitation Payment Systems for the Chronically Mentally Ill." *Psychiatric Annals* 17, no. 9:599–602.

———. 1987b. "An Experimental Model: Capitation Payment System for the Chronically Mentally Ill." *Psychiatric Annals* 17, no. 9:604–9.

Bacharach, L. L., and H. R. Lamb. 1989. "Public Psychiatry in an Era of Deinstitutionalization." In C. Beels and L. L. Bacharach (eds.): *Survival Strategies for Public Psychiatry*, pp. 9–25. New Directions for Mental Health Services, no. 42. San Francisco: Jossey-Bass.

Bond, G. R., and S. L. Boyer. 1988. "Rehabilitation Programs and Outcomes." In J. A. Ciardiello and M. D. Bell (eds.): *Vocational Rehabilitation of Persons with Prolonged Mental Illness*, pp. 231–63. Baltimore: Johns Hopkins University Press.

Burns, B. J., J. Smith, H. H. Goldman, L. E. Barth, and R. F. Coulam. 1989. "The Champus/Tidewater Demonstration Project." In D. Mechanic and L. H. Aiken (eds.): *Paying for Services: Promises and Pitfalls of Capitation*, pp. 77–86. New Directions for Mental Health Services, no. 43. San Francisco: Jossey-Bass.

Christianson, J. B., and M. S. Linehan. 1989. "Capitated Payments for Mental Health Care: The Rhode Island Programs." *Community Mental Health Journal* 25, no. 2:121–31.

Deiker, T. 1986. "How to Insure That the Money Follows the Patient: A Strategy for Funding Community Services." *Hospital and Community Psychiatry* 37:256–60.

Department of Health and Human Services. 1980. "Toward a National Plan for the Chronically Mentally Ill." Washington, D.C.: Steering Committee on the Chronically Mentally Ill.

Hadley, T. R., and R. Glover. 1989. "Philadelphia: Using Medicaid as a Basis of Capitation." In D. Mechanic and L. H. Aiken (eds.): *Paying for Services: Promises and Pitfalls of Capitation*, pp. 65–76. New Directions for Mental Health Services, no. 43. San Francisco: Jossey-Bass.

Hadley, T. R., A. P. Schinnar, A. B. Rothbard, and M. S. Kinosian. 1989. "Capitation Financing of Public Mental Health Services for the Chronically Mentally Ill." *Administration and Policy in Mental Health* 16, no. 4:201–13.

Keisler, C. A., and T. L. Morton. 1988. "Prospective Payment System for Inpatient Psychiatry." *American Psychologist* 43:141–50.

Lehman, A. F. 1989. "Strategies for Improving Services for the Chronic Mentally Ill." *Hospital and Community Psychiatry* 40:916–20.

Marshall, P. E. 1986. "Integrated Mental Health: A Creative Model for Community Mental Health in the 1980's." *Journal of Mental Health Administration* 13, no. 2:23–29.

Mauch, D. 1989. "Rhode Island: An Early Effort at Managed Care." In D. Mechanic and L. H. Aiken (eds.): *Paying for Services: Promises and Pitfalls of Capitation*, pp. 55–64. New Directions for Mental Health Services, no. 43. San Francisco: Jossey-Bass.

Mechanic, D., and L. H. Aiken. 1989. "Capitation in Mental Health: Potentials and Cautions." In D. Mechanic and L. H. Aiken (eds.): *Paying for Services: Promises and Pitfalls of Capitation*, pp. 5–18. New Directions for Mental Health Services, no. 43. San Francisco: Jossey-Bass.

Plum, K. C. 1989. "Analysis of a Capitation Plan for the Chronically Mentally Ill." *Nursing Economics* 7, no. 5:250–65.

Santiago, J. M. 1989. "Arizona: Struggles and Resistance in Implementing Capitation." In D. Mechanic and L. H. Aiken (eds.): *Paying for Services: Promises and Pitfalls of Capitation*, pp. 87–96. New Directions for Mental Health Services, no. 43. San Francisco: Jossey-Bass.

Santiago, J. M., A. Gittler, A. Beigel, L. Stein, and P. J. Brown. 1986. "Changing a State Mental Health System through Litigation: The Arizona Experiment." *American Journal of Psychiatry* 143:1575–79.

Sapolsky, H. M. 1986. "Prospective Payment in Perspective." *Journal of Health Politics, Policy and Law* 11:633–45.

Sederer, L. I., and R. L. St. Clair. 1989. "Managed Care and the Massachusetts Experience." *American Journal of Psychiatry* 146:1142–48.

Stein, L. I., and M. A. Test (eds.). 1978. *Alternatives to Mental Hospital Treatment*. New York: Plenum Press.

Weisbrod, B. 1981. "Benefit-Cost Analysis of a Controlled Experiment Treating the Mentally Ill." *Journal of Human Resources* 16:523–48.

———. 1983. "A Guide to Benefit-Cost Analysis, as Seen through a Controlled Experiment in Treating the Mentally Ill." In A. Razin, E. Helpman, and E. Sadka (eds.): *Social Policy Evaluation*, pp. 5–42. New York: Academic Press.

Weisbrod, B., M. A. Test, and L. I. Stein. 1980. "Alternatives to Mental Hospital Treatment II: Economic Benefit-Cost Analysis." *Archives of General Psychiatry* 37:400–405.

Weisman, E. 1988. "Managed Care: Delivering Quality and Value." *Quality Review Bulletin* 14, no. 12:372–74.

15

The Short-Run Effects of a Contracted Provider Arrangement for Mental Health Care

Robert J. Schmitz, Ph.D.

A s a result of the rapid growth in outlays for health care during the 1980s, government payers have devoted increasing effort to changing the locus of risk bearing. Notable examples include the introduction of risk HMOs for Medicare beneficiaries, permitted under TEFRA, and the implementation of prospective payment for Medicare hospice and hospital inpatient care. Underlying these innovations is the belief that placing providers or third-party contractors at risk for the cost of care can generate incentives to increase efficiency without reducing the quality of care.

The effect of the two innovations in Medicare payment noted above on utilization and outlays has been difficult to assess. Enrollment in Medicare HMOs is voluntary, so that the effects of self-selection could not easily be disentangled from the effects of risk contracting itself. The Medicare prospective payment system for hospital care was implemented in nearly all hospitals on their fiscal year start dates after October 1983. As a result, separation of PPS effects from changes that would have occurred even in its absence has been difficult. In the absence of an appropriate comparison group, temporal changes in behavior are relied on much more heavily as indicators; the rapid expansion of Medicare part B physician and outpatient care subsequent to the implementation of the PPS has prompted many to conclude that the PPS has induced a substitution of outpatient care (which continues to be reimbursed under "reasonable and customary" rules) for inpatient care (now covered by the PPS). However, the true effect of the PPS, net of other influences on Medicare utilization and outlays, has remained a matter of guesswork.

An opportunity to assess better the consequences of third-party risk bearing arose in 1986, when the Civilian Health and Medical

Program of the Uniformed Services established a contracted provider arrangement (CPA) for all mental health care rendered to CHAMPUS beneficiaries residing within a designated catchment area in the Norfolk, Virginia, metropolitan area. CHAMPUS entered into a contract with Sentara First Step, Inc., which required First Step to establish a provider network, institute a system of case management for mental health care, negotiate payment rates, and reimburse all claims for mental health care by network and nonnetwork providers. The contract placed First Step at risk for nearly all outlays for mental health care to CHAMPUS beneficiaries in the Norfolk area. The CPA was implemented only in Norfolk, giving rise to a quasi experiment that permits attribution of outcomes to the arrangement. First Step reduced substantially the level of payment for inpatient professional psychiatric care; it also reduced slightly the rate of payment for outpatient mental health visits. The cost effectiveness of the CPA was evaluated by Coulam and Smith (1990), who concluded that mental health outlays by CHAMPUS were reduced by 31 percent.

This chapter reports the effects of the CPA on measures of inpatient and outpatient care provided to CHAMPUS beneficiaries in Norfolk. With claims data covering CHAMPUS-eligible individuals who used mental health care during the period 1985–88 and who resided in Norfolk or in San Diego, outcomes of the intervention were assessed using a so-called "double-difference" model, also termed a "non-equivalent control group" design by Judd and Kenny (1981). Although the CPA does not seem to have altered greatly the probability of hospitalization in this group, it did reduce markedly the average length of inpatient stays for mental health care among dependents of active-duty personnel; it may also have reduced lengths of stay for retired military personnel and their eligible dependents. Outpatient mental health visits per user seem to have been largely unaffected by the intervention, at least for the overall CHAMPUS population. Outpatient visits by CHAMPUS beneficiaries who experienced at least one inpatient stay for mental health care increased, however, suggesting that the CPA did induce some substitution of outpatient care for the inpatient care whose relative price, to providers, declined as a result of the CPA.

A Description of CHAMPUS and the Contracted Provider Arrangement

All active-duty and retired military personnel are considered to be *sponsors* under CHAMPUS. Spouses and children under the age of twenty-one (twenty-three if a full-time student) of sponsors are eligible for coverage under CHAMPUS.[1] Under certain circumstances, the former spouse or survivor of a sponsor may also be eligible for CHAMPUS coverage. CHAMPUS is secondary payer to all government and private health care coverage except Medicaid. All health care (mental and nonmental health) is subject to 25 percent coinsurance for beneficiaries of retired sponsors; beneficiaries of active duty sponsors pay 20 percent coinsurance for outpatient care and about ten dollars per day for inpatient care. The deductible for both active-duty and retired sponsors is fifty dollars per person or one hundred dollars per family. In this chapter we abuse proper terminology somewhat by referring to individuals who are eligible for CHAMPUS by virtue of their relationship to an active-duty sponsor as *active-duty beneficiaries. Retired beneficiaries* are defined in an analogous manner.

Because the CHAMPUS mental health benefit is much more generous than coverage under most private insurance plans and HMOs, CHAMPUS pays a far higher proportion (92.5 percent) of mental health costs for its beneficiaries than it does for the remaining elements of care (35 percent). As a means of containing cost and of implementing a congressionally mandated partial hospitalization benefit, the Office of the Civilian Health and Medical Program of the Uniformed Services (OCHAMPUS) designed a demonstration for a preferred provider organization to manage all mental health services in the vicinity of Norfolk, Virginia.

As part of the design, OCHAMPUS would procure a fixed-price contract with one entity to finance all mental health benefits for CHAMPUS beneficiaries in the designated area. Adjustments to the fixed price were permitted only if the number of eligible beneficiaries in the area proved to be much larger or smaller than specified in the contract. The contractor would be required to implement a system of case management for all users of mental health services and to establish a network of contract providers willing to accept specified rates of payment (which would also apply to nonnetwork providers). Normal CHAMPUS coverage for medical use remained in place.

The contract was awarded in April 1986 to the Sentara Alternative Delivery System Corporation, which operated as a CPA contractor under the name First Step. CPA operations began in October 1986. First Step negotiated a discount of about 40 percent from the inpatient fees of contract providers; outpatient fees remained unchanged for the most part.[2] These discounts were evidently offered in the expectation that case management workers would channel patients to network providers. First Step also promised a bonus to providers if the network succeeded. Beneficiaries retained their freedom of choice and were permitted to use network or nonnetwork providers. Coinsurance payments were waived for beneficiaries who used contract providers. Providers outside the network were reimbursed at the same rate as network providers but received no bonuses.

In practice, the case management function did not work as envisioned. First Step had assumed that intake workers would be the first to see a patient and would therefore be able to channel him or her to an appropriate provider (to a network provider wherever possible). Most patients, however, had already seen a provider before meeting with an intake worker. In many cases, a proposed plan of treatment had already been developed. Hence, the case management system generally did not channel patients to network providers. As a result, the major intervention associated with the CPA was a significant reduction in the inpatient fees paid to mental health providers in Norfolk for care rendered to CHAMPUS beneficiaries.

Hypotheses and Methods

The reduction in payment to providers in Norfolk that accompanied implementation of the CPA would be expected to generate both income and substitution effects on several dimensions of provider behavior. The decline in the relative price received for inpatient care ought to have produced a reduction in the level of inpatient relative to outpatient care offered by providers. This reduction could take the form of a decline in the rate of inpatient psychiatric admission, a fall in the typical length of an inpatient psychiatric stay, or both. At the same time, the reduction in average payment for mental health relative to non–mental health care may induce some substitution of medical care for mental health care. Some of this substitution could be purely artificial (i.e., changes in the manner in which some procedures or visits are coded on claims to CHAMPUS); in addition, beneficiaries themselves may seek substitutes for mental health services if they now find them more difficult to obtain.[3] Finally, providers may attempt to substitute non-CHAMPUS for CHAMPUS patients, at least to some degree, since the typical payment for treating CHAMPUS patients declined relative to that for treating others. Some (nonnetwork) providers may have responded to the reduction in fees by refusing to accept CHAMPUS beneficiaries as new patients or by balance billing CHAMPUS patients.[4] The number of providers serving CHAMPUS beneficiaries may, therefore, have declined, and the composition and patterns of practice of those who remained are likely to differ from the pre-CPA pattern, altering the nature of care in ways difficult to predict.[5]

If we assume that the income effect is small relative to the various forms of substitution effects cited above, then several hypotheses concerning the expected effect of the CPA may be generated. In all cases, the hypotheses involve comparisons of some observable quantity (say, hospital admissions) to the level that would be expected to prevail had the contracted provider arrangement not been implemented. This chapter addresses the first two of the hypotheses presented below. The third is left as a subject for future work.

1. CHAMPUS mental health hospital admissions and inpatient days are predicted to decline. As noted above, the decrease in inpatient fees is expected to reduce the willingness of mental health providers to furnish care in inpatient settings.

2. The ratio of CHAMPUS outpatient mental health visits to inpatient mental health days is predicted to increase. Because providers may optimize across several margins (inpatient/outpatient, CHAMPUS beneficiaries/private pay or other insurance, and, in some cases, medical/mental health care), it is impossible to predict whether the absolute level of outpatient visits per patient or per beneficiary will rise or fall. The rise in the relative payment for outpatient versus inpatient care, however, should increase the ratio of outpatient to inpatient care.

3. The ratio of inpatient non–mental health days to inpatient mental health days is similarly predicted to increase. The predicted decline in inpatient mental health days and the possible substitution of some non–mental health medical care for inpatient mental health services should increase this ratio.

Attribution of changes in outcomes to a particular observed intervention is always a tricky matter. In the absence of random assignment of CHAMPUS beneficiaries to CPA and fee-for-service (i.e., treatment and comparison) groups, a true experimental estimator of the effects of the CPA is not available. Estimates of the effect of the CPA must therefore rely on the use of appropriately chosen proxies for the two groups. The most obvious way of proceeding is to compare outcome measures in Norfolk for periods of time before and after the implementation of the CPA. If Y is an outcome measure, say, mean outpatient mental health visits per beneficiary (assumed to be an unbiased estimate of its population mean μ), then this "single difference" estimator may be represented as

$$D = Y(\text{post}) - Y(\text{pre}); E(D) = \mu_{\text{post}} - \mu_{\text{pre}} \qquad (15.1)$$

Since D is an unbiased estimator of $\mu_{\text{post}} - \mu_{\text{pre}}$, it is also an unbiased estimator of the effect of the CPA on Y if the CPA is the only nonrandom influence on μ in the period after imposition of the CPA that is not present in the period before imposition. Equation (15.1) may be recast as a regression equation to allow for effects of observable influences on μ. If the expected value of Y for individual i in period t is given by $\mu_{it} = X\beta + \delta POST$, where POST is an indicator variable set equal to one after October 1, 1986, and zero otherwise and X_i represents other observable influences on Y, then the value of Y for individual i may be written as its expected value plus a random deviation from that expected value given by u_{it}.[6]

$$Y_{it} = X_i\beta + \delta POST + u_{it} \qquad (15.2)$$

The linear regression estimate $\hat{\delta}$ is a measure of the effect of the CPA analogous to D.

The principal difficulty with estimates of this type is that all temporal changes in Y are ascribed to the CPA. It seems dangerous to assume that there are no unobservable factors that may cause Y to change over time. Bias arising from such extraneous influences on utilization cannot be ruled out. To see this, think of δ as composed of two distinct effects: a change in Y that would have occurred in Norfolk after October 1986 even if the CPA had not been implemented (denoted by δ_N) and a change brought about by the CPA itself (denoted by δ_{CPA}). For the sake of simplicity, we may conjecture that δ is the simple sum of the two effects: $\delta = \delta_N + \delta_{CPA}$. If equation (15.2) is estimated by least squares using data from the Norfolk area only, then δ can be estimated but not δ_{CPA}, the parameter we seek. Using δ as an estimator of δ_{CPA} introduces a bias equal to δ_N. As a practical matter, the potential bias should not lead us to reject the pre-post estimator out of hand, since unbiased estimators cannot be guaranteed in any event. If δ_N is believed to be small relative to δ_{CPA}, then the small resulting bias might be considered acceptable in a nonexperimental situation such as this one.

An alternative and perhaps superior measure of the effect of a CPA can be constructed since outcome data for a sample of CHAMPUS beneficiaries residing in San Diego are also available. Consider the following analogue to equation (15.1):

$$D' = [Y(\text{post}) - Y(\text{pre})]_{\text{Norfolk}} - [Y(\text{post}) - Y(\text{pre})]_{\text{SanDiego}}, \qquad (15.3)$$

which may be rendered in regression form as

$$Y_{it} = X_{it}\gamma + \delta_1 POST + \delta_2 NORFOLK + \delta_3 POST \cdot NORFOLK + u_{it} \qquad (15.4)$$

where the dummy variable NORFOLK is set to one for beneficiaries residing in the Norfolk demonstration catchment area and to zero otherwise. The measures D' and δ_3 constitute candidate estimators of the effect of CPA that appear, at least, to impose less stringent assumptions than do D and δ. That is, D' and δ_3 do not force us to assume that no changes would have occurred in Norfolk had the CPA not been implemented; they require instead the weaker assumption that whatever changes occurred in Norfolk that were unrelated to the implementation of the CPA also occurred in San Diego at about the same time. On an intuitive level, specifications (15.3) and (15.4) may be regarded as "differencing out" all influences on outcomes other than the CPA (and random sampling error). The underlying assertion is that pre-post differences in outcomes for San Diego beneficiaries are a better control for pre-post differences in outcomes for Norfolk beneficiaries than pre-CPA levels of outcomes for Norfolk beneficiaries are for post-CPA levels for Norfolk beneficiaries.

It is worth pointing out here (especially in light of results to be presented later) that the superiority of D' and δ_3 relative to D and δ cannot be guaranteed. Unobserved influences impinging on utilization in San Diego after implementation of the CPA could induce bias in δ_3 that is more severe than that in δ as an estimator of CPA effects.[7]

Two related empirical models are used here to gauge the response of mental health utilization in Norfolk to the imposition of a CPA: a multiple regression model based on equation (15.4) and a Poisson model that gives rise to a different and more precise estimator of CPA effects. Both models rely on the logic of "pre-post with comparison group" estimators to identify treatment effects. Because the Poisson model has a slightly different structure, it will be described here briefly before proceeding to the results.

Suppose that mental health utilization, measured, say, by visits, follows a Poisson distribution over some span of time T. Under the null hypothesis of no change in the distribution of visits, the number of visits occurring during the first half of the period is a binomial random variable whose expected value is equal to one-half the total number of visits occurring over the whole period. If the expected value, λ, of the Poisson distribution of visits increases or decreases from the first half to the second half of the period, then the share of visits occurring in the second half is expected to increase or decrease. For any particular individual i, then, the expected number of outpatient visits is given by $p_{it}T_i$ where p_{it} is the binomial proportion of visits occurring in period t for the individual and T_i is the total number of visits for the individual over the entire four-year period. The actual number can be written as

$$n_{it} = p_{it}T_i + \epsilon_{it} \tag{15.5}$$

where $\epsilon_{it} \equiv (n_{it} - p_{it}T_i)$ is asymptotically normally distributed with mean zero and variance $p_{it}(1 - p_{it})T_i$. If we now specify the expected proportion of individual i's total visits T_i occurring in period t as a linear relation similar to equation (15.4), we have

$$p_{it} = X_{it}\gamma' + \delta_1'\text{POST} + \delta_2'\text{NORFOLK} + \delta_3'\text{POST·NORFOLK} \qquad (15.6)$$

Substitution of (15.6) into (15.5) yields a regression equation for visits in period t:

$$n_{it} = T_i(X_{it}\gamma' + \delta_1'\text{POST} + \delta_2'\text{NORFOLK} + \delta_3'\text{POST·NORFOLK}) + \epsilon_{it}. \quad (15.7)$$

Equation (15.7), in contrast to (15.4), is scaled to the total utilization (visits) of each individual. Since T_i is itself determined largely by unobserved person-specific characteristics, the least squares estimate of δ_3' can be shown to be more efficient as an estimator of CPA effects than the OLS estimate of δ_3 from equation (15.4).

The Data

The primary research sample consisted of all CHAMPUS beneficiaries residing in either the Norfolk CPA catchment area or the San Diego metropolitan statistical area who filed at least one CHAMPUS claim for mental health care during the period from October 1, 1984, through September 30, 1988. Counts of selected measures of medical and mental health care use (including outpatient mental health visits, hospital admissions for mental health care, and inpatient days of mental health care) were aggregated by year for each beneficiary in the sample. All such counts were compiled from claims appearing in the CHAMPUS quick response data file. Three groups of beneficiaries were deleted from the sample:

- beneficiaries who did not continuously reside in either Norfolk or San Diego as indicated by the residence field appearing on the claim form. Because residence is recorded in the quick response data file only when a claim is filed, beneficiaries who move but file no claims are not deleted from the file by this practice.
- beneficiaries whose sponsor retired from the military or (much more rarely) returned to active-duty service after an earlier retirement during the four-year period. Beneficiaries of active-duty sponsors receive a slightly richer mix of benefits than do beneficiaries of retired sponsors; deleting these individuals from the sample eliminates complications due to changes in coverage.
- beneficiaries who were under age twelve in 1988.

All CHAMPUS claims for San Diego are missing for August and September of 1988. These missing claims will, of course, tend to bias downward all measures of utilization for San Diego for that year. For this reason, positive coefficients of NORFOLK·POST do not necessarily indicate an increase in the relative outcome variable as a result of the CPA; negative coefficients of NORFOLK·POST may well *understate* the true effects of the CPA.

Results

Tables 15.1 and 15.2 display the mental health utilization of CHAMPUS beneficiaries in Norfolk and San Diego from 1985 through 1988.

Table 15.1   Inpatient Mental Health Use by CHAMPUS Beneficiaries in Norfolk and San Diego

	MH Inpatient Admissions		MH Inpatient	Mean Length of Stay
Location and Year	Users	Admissions	Days	(Days)
Active Duty Sponsors				
Norfolk FY 1985	40	66	1,646	24.9
Norfolk FY 1986	34	47	1,156	24.6
Norfolk FY 1987	59	70	1,208	17.3
Norfolk FY 1988	76	103	1,375	13.3
Number of distinct users	180		186	
San Diego FY 1985	23	28	587	21.0
San Diego FY 1986	43	54	1,656	30.7
San Diego FY 1987	48	60	1,663	27.7
San Diego FY 1988	58	80	1,891	23.6
Number of distinct users	151		157	
Retired Sponsors				
Norfolk FY 1985	54	75	1,664	22.2
Norfolk FY 1986	42	52	1,287	24.8
Norfolk FY 1987	62	78	1,435	18.4
Norfolk FY 1988	44	57	943	16.5
Number of distinct users	173		178	
San Diego FY 1985	57	75	1,612	21.5
San Diego FY 1986	39	52	1,339	25.8
San Diego FY 1987	44	58	1,330	22.9
San Diego FY 1988	29	37	603	16.3
Number of distinct users	142		146	

Notes: Inpatient days are assigned to the year in which they occurred regardless of the year of admission. Because some individuals were hospitalized at the beginning of FY 1985, the number of beneficiaries with inpatient days exceeds the number with a hospital admission. MH, mental health; FY, fiscal year.

Table 15.2   Outpatient Mental Health Use
by CHAMPUS Beneficiaries in Norfolk and San Diego

		Mental Health Outpatient Visits		
Location and Year	Number of Users	Total	Ever Inpatient	Never Inpatient
Active Duty Sponsors				
Norfolk FY 1985	305	3,520	493	3,027
Norfolk FY 1986	323	4,286	973	3,313
Norfolk FY 1987	359	4,629	1,168	3,461
Norfolk FY 1988	497	6,560	1,255	5,305
Number of distinct users	1,042			
San Diego FY 1985	445	7,350	578	6,772
San Diego FY 1986	482	8,370	1,089	7,281
San Diego FY 1987	585	10,248	1,144	9,104
San Diego FY 1988	559	9,639	1,298	8,341
Number of distinct users	1,297			
Retired Sponsors				
Norfolk FY 1985	288	3,335	2,545	790
Norfolk FY 1986	275	3,327	2,623	704
Norfolk FY 1987	262	3,532	2,575	957
Norfolk FY 1988	252	3,364	2,595	769
Number of distinct users	627			
San Diego FY 1985	410	5,604	5,116	488
San Diego FY 1986	413	6,167	5,245	922
San Diego FY 1987	415	7,192	6,157	1,035
San Diego FY 1988	384	5,776	5,190	586
Number of distinct users	919			

Note: Inpatient days are assigned to the year in which they occurred regardless of the year of admission. Because some individuals were hospitalized at the beginning of FY 1985, the number of beneficiaries with inpatient days exceeds the number with a hospital admission.

Inpatient mental health treatment is infrequent in this group, as it is generally in the population. Although the two locations each contain about 230,000 CHAMPUS eligibles, fewer than 125 were hospitalized during any year in either location. The information presented in table 15.1 provides no evidence that the CPA reduced admission rates; indeed, one might argue that the program stimulated mental health admissions. Between FY 1986 (the last year of cost reimbursement in Norfolk) and FY 1988, the number of admissions increased faster in Norfolk than in San Diego for dependents of active-duty sponsors. Among retired sponsors, admissions over the period increased slightly in Norfolk and declined in San Diego. The differences are not statistically significant, however, and should not be overemphasized.

Even though mental health admissions among beneficiaries of active-duty sponsors increased by 80 percent between 1985–86 and 1987–88, mental health inpatient days actually declined slightly over the period. This was the result of a striking fall in mean length of stay among this group, as seen in the last column. Among both active-duty and retired beneficiaries in Norfolk the average length of stay dropped sharply in 1987, the first year of the CPA, and declined again slightly in the following year. In San Diego, no such abrupt change is evident, although inpatient stays of retirees and their dependents in San Diego fell substantially in 1988.

Outpatient mental health use by CHAMPUS beneficiaries is shown in table 15.2. The intensity of outpatient use is clearly greater in San Diego; while the number of outpatient users in San Diego is about one-third greater than in Norfolk (retired and active duty combined), the total number of outpatient visits in San Diego over the four-year period is nearly double the number in Norfolk. Outpatient mental health visits during the CPA period were 43 percent higher than during the preceding two-year period among active-duty beneficiaries in Norfolk; among the same population, the rate of increase in San Diego over the same time period was much lower—about 27 percent. In both Norfolk and San Diego, the increase in outpatient visits was particularly great among beneficiaries who had received mental health inpatient care at some time during the period, although the increase was still much greater for Norfolk—65 percent compared to 46 percent. The situation among retirees was quite different. Rates of increase were much lower over the period in both Norfolk and San Diego than among the active-duty beneficiaries and were lower for Norfolk than for San Diego beneficiaries. Indeed, among retirees who were ever mental health inpatients during 1985–88, outpatient visits increased by 10 percent from 1985–86 in San Diego and not at all in Norfolk.

Estimates of the regression of inpatient length of stay and outpatient visits on local covariates are shown in table 15.3. With the exception of age, all covariates included in the models are dummy variables and all were drawn from CHAMPUS claims files. The variables are defined below:

FY86, FY87, FY88   Dummy variables for the last three federal fiscal years covered by the data

POST   Dummy variable for fiscal year 1987 or 1988; used only in interactions

NORFOLK   Dummy variable for residence in the Norfolk area covered by the CPA

NAVY	Dummy variable for navy sponsor
AGE	Age in years
ACTIVE	Dummy variable for active-duty sponsor
EVER INPAT	Dummy variable =1 if beneficiary was hospitalized with mental health diagnosis at any time during 1985–88; 0 otherwise.

The CPA effect represented by δ_3 in equation (15.4) is given by the coefficient of NORFOLK·POST in the table. By this measure, the CPA led to a reduction of over eleven days in the length of inpatient mental health stays among active duty beneficiaries.[8] Among retired beneficiaries, the estimated 1.6-day reduction is insignificantly different from zero and provides no evidence on the effect of the CPA.[9]

Table 15.3   OLS Regression Results for CHAMPUS Mental Health Inpatient Length of Stay and Number of Outpatient Visits

Independent Variable	Active-Duty Military			Retired Military		
	Inpatient LOS	Outpatient Visits		Inpatient LOS	Outpatient Visits	
Constant	47.53	6.10	5.34	43.63	2.82	2.16
	(7.56)	(6.76)	(5.88)	(8.49)	(3.20)	(2.42)
FY 1986	3.94	0.70	0.69	2.91	0.37	0.37
	(2.80)	(1.96)	(1.93)	(1.22)	(0.89)	(0.88)
FY 1987	5.31	1.58	1.55	−2.67	1.39	1.39
	(1.57)	(3.69)	(3.65)	(−0.91)	(2.86)	(2.85)
FY 1988	2.39	2.07	2.03	−5.26	0.40	0.39
	(0.71)	(4.83)	(4.76)	(−1.67)	(0.81)	(0.80)
NORFOLK	1.19	−2.35	−2.37	−1.62	−1.07	−1.20
	(0.43)	(−6.47)	(−6.24)	(−0.68)	(−2.48)	(−2.60)
NAVY	1.15	0.27	0.24	2.32	0.13	0.11
	(0.55)	(0.91)	(0.82)	(1.29)	(0.40)	(0.36)
AGE	−1.68	−0.14	−0.10	−1.17	0.24	0.27
	(−3.78)	(−2.10)	(−1.56)	(−3.82)	(4.72)	(5.22)
AGE^2	0.02	0.004	0.003	0.01	−0.003	−0.003
	(2.53)	(3.37)	(2.98)	(3.08)	(−4.85)	(−5.29)
NORFOLK·POST	−11.52	0.02	−0.27	−1.60	−0.51	−0.68
	(−3.30)	(0.04)	(−0.51)	(−0.46)	(−0.84)	(−1.06)
EVER INPAT		2.80			1.75	
		(4.56)			(2.72)	
EVER INPAT· NORFOLK		−0.75			0.03	
		(−0.75)			(0.03)	
EVER INPAT· NORFOLK·POST		2.17			0.93	
		(1.94)			(0.77)	
R^2	0.26	0.02	0.02	0.19	0.01	0.01
N	298	9,356	9,356	256	6,184	6,184

Note: The t-statistics appear in parentheses.

If the CPA did induce a reduction in length of stay, it is reasonable to ask whether outpatient visits were increased as a result. That is, did providers attempt to substitute outpatient for inpatient care? A suggestive answer is provided by the regression estimates for outpatient visits based on equation (15.4), also shown in table 15.3. The overall CPA effect, measured again by the coefficient of NOR-FOLK·POST, is insignificantly different from zero. An intuitive measure of substitution-induced increases in outpatient visits is the OLS coefficient of the interaction of the CPA indicator with a dummy variable set equal to one for beneficiaries who were mental health inpatients at any time during the four-year period. Among active-duty beneficiaries, 2.2 additional visits are estimated to have been provided to these individuals as a result of the CPA. Among retired

Table 15.4   OLS Regression Results for CHAMPUS Mental Health Outpatient Visit Shares

Independent Variable	Active-Duty Military		Retired Military	
	(a)	(b)	(c)	(d)
Constant	0.21	0.22	0.27	0.27
	(8.34)	(8.25)	(10.85)	(10.72)
FY 1986	−0.006	−0.006	−0.03	−0.03
	(−0.58)	(−0.58)	(−2.17)	(−2.17)
FY 1987	0.02	0.02	−0.004	−0.004
	(1.93)	(1.93)	(−0.27)	(−0.27)
FY 1988	0.08	0.08	−0.02	−0.02
	(6.74)	(6.74)	(−1.67)	(−1.68)
NORFOLK	−0.02	−0.01	0.004	0.01
	(−1.57)	(−1.08)	(0.30)	(0.97)
NAVY	0.0005	0.0004	0.00004	0.00004
	(0.05)	(0.051)	(0.004)	(0.005)
AGE	0.001	0.001	−0.003	−0.0003
	(0.61)	(0.58)	(−0.21)	(−0.24)
AGE^2	−0.00002	−0.00002	0.000004	0.000005
	(−0.62)	(−0.59)	(0.21)	(0.25)
NORFOLK·POST	0.03	0.02	−0.007	−0.03
	(2.24)	(1.57)	(−0.43)	(−1.38)
EVER INPAT		0.0008		−0.0001
		(0.05)		(−0.01)
EVER INPAT·NORFOLK		−0.03		−0.04
		(−1.02)		(−1.51)
EVER INPAT·NORFOLK·POST		0.05		0.09
		(1.69)		(2.62)
R^2	0.01	0.01	0.001	0.002
N	9,356	9,356	6,184	6,184

Notes: The t-statistics appear in parentheses. Specifications (b) and (d) include as regressors EVER INPAT and its interaction with both NORFOLK and the CPA indicator NORFOLK·POST. Specifications (a) and (c) omit these terms.

beneficiaries, no increase in outpatient visits of those ever hospitalized can be attributed to the CPA.

Table 15.4 presents estimates of the effect of the CPA on the
share of outpatient visits occurring in 1987–88. They represent OLS
estimates of equation (15.7).[10] Specifications (b) and (d) include as
regressors the terms EVERINPAT and its interaction with both Norfolk
and the CPA indicator NORFOLK·POST. Specifications (a) and (c) omit
these terms. Among active-duty beneficiaries, the CPA seems to have
increased the proportion of outpatient visits occurring during 1987–
88 by 0.03. The increase was especially pronounced among beneficiaries who had been mental health inpatients at some point; the proportion of visits occurring during the CPA period for these individuals
was higher by 0.05 than would have been otherwise expected. This
result is statistically significant only at the .10 level.

Among retired beneficiaries, the results are more difficult to
interpret. There seems to be no overall effect of the CPA as indicated
by the NORFOLK·POST interaction in specification (c). However, among
those who were ever inpatients, the effect of the CPA is estimated to
be nearly double that for active-duty beneficiaries.

Summary and Conclusions

The principal change in incentives facing mental health providers as
a result of implementation of the CPA in Norfolk was a sharp reduction in payment for care provided in inpatient settings relative to
care provided to outpatients. After implementation, inpatient lengths
of stay for mental health care in Norfolk fell substantially. Among
retirees we nevertheless cannot reject the hypothesis that the CPA had
no effect on the length of inpatient mental health stays—a result
largely due to a concurrent fall in length of inpatient stays among
retirees in San Diego.

To the extent that providers may have been led to substitute
outpatient care for these reduced levels of inpatient care we might
therefore expect to find increased levels of outpatient care provided to
those who had been inpatients, especially to active-duty inpatients.
In the simple visit regressions of table 15.3, this outcome is indeed
observed. Surprisingly, much more efficient estimates of CPA effects
result when the four-year total of outpatient visits is explicitly controlled for, and these estimates reverse this finding. The increase in
the share of outpatient visits provided during the CPA period for
those who had ever been inpatients was greater for retirees than for
active-duty beneficiaries. One possible explanation for this result is

that providers may, in some cases, have attempted to avert hospitalizations altogether by increasing the level of outpatient care to patients deemed to be at especially high risk of hospitalization.[11] The average number of outpatient visits per retired beneficiary who was at some time an inpatient is far greater than for similar active-duty beneficiaries. This may be due to the greater average age of retired beneficiaries in this category. Whatever the reason, greater familiarity between mental health provider and patient may have allowed greater scope for avoidance of hospitalization for retirees by greater provision of outpatient care.

The at-risk contractor for the CPA demonstration seems to have been capable of reducing inpatient utilization by reducing the level of payment to mental health providers for care furnished in this setting. As a consequence, levels of outpatient care seem to have increased, particularly for those who had used some inpatient care. The consequences of this change for the level of beneficiary well-being and for the consumption of medical care cannot be evaluated here. Given the potential for significant cost reduction, such issues warrant investigation.

Notes

1. Active-duty military personnel are not covered by CHAMPUS but receive care under the military direct care system.

2. In April 1987, inpatient and outpatient fees were increased by 3 percent.

3. It is also possible that physical (psychosomatic) symptoms may have appeared or been exacerbated in some people if mental health services were reduced.

4. Whether such practices were widespread is uncertain. Coulam and Smith (1990, 17) reported that "non-contract providers, especially institutional providers, responded to the CPA network price competition by informing the public that they too would accept the First Step reimbursement rates and would not bill the balance to the user."

5. The income effect of the reduction in average payment would tend to increase the total volume of (inpatient and outpatient) services provided. This latter effect is likely to be weak for most providers, unless inpatient care furnished to CHAMPUS beneficiaries represents a high proportion of their receipts. This tendency to increase services affects the level of mental health care offered generally to the community, not just to CHAMPUS beneficiaries. A similar prediction arises from the so-called target income hypothesis, which asserts that providers will attempt to "make up" for the reduction in fees by increasing services to achieve a specified level of income.

6. The vector of observable influences X_i might also be written with a

time subscript, X_{it}. The subscript is suppressed here because no time-varying covariates are used in subsequent analyses.

7. Suppose that outcomes for San Diego beneficiaries follow the relationship $E(Y) = X\beta + \alpha\text{POST}$ and that Norfolk beneficiaries follow $E(Y) = X\beta + \delta\text{POST}$ with $\delta = \delta_N + \delta_{\text{CPA}}$ as before. The term δ_3 in equation (15.4) can be shown to estimate the quantity $(\delta_N - \alpha) + \delta_{\text{CPA}}$, whose individual terms cannot be estimated. If non-CPA influences on outcomes after October 1986 affect Norfolk and San Diego beneficiaries similarly, then $\delta_N \approx \alpha$; in this case the bias in δ_3 as an estimator of δ_{CPA} will be small. If, however, α is large relative to δ_N, then the simple pre-post estimators, D or δ, will be superior to (have smaller bias than) those that attempt to exploit information from the external comparison group.

8. As estimated in a logarithmic specification (which exhibited poorer fit than the arithmetic model shown in table 15.3), the CPA decline in LOS was 28 percent.

9. The standard errors of the estimates of δ_3 were virtually identical at about 3.47 days. The much smaller absolute size of the parameter estimate among the retired, therefore, prevented rejection of the null hypothesis of no effect.

10. Both sides of (15.7) were divided by T_i before estimation. All observations were weighted by $T_i^{1/2}$ to reduce heteroscedasticity arising from variations in T_i across individuals.

11. Patients who had been hospitalized previously or who would be hospitalized at some point during the four-year period are likely to be heavily represented in this high-risk group.

References

Coulam, Robert, and Joseph Smith. 1990. "Evaluation of the CPA-Norfolk Demonstration: Final Report." U.S. Department of Defense contract MDA907-87-C-0003. Cambridge, Mass.: Abt Associates, June 26.

Judd, Charles, and David Kenny. 1981. *Estimating the Effects of Social Interventions*. Cambridge: Cambridge University Press.

Index

Designed by Joanna Hill
Composed by The Composing Room of Michigan, Inc.
in Century text and Frutiger display
Printed by The Maple Press on
60-lb. Glatfelter Offset, A-50, and bound in
Holliston Roxite B grade cloth